THE
HIDDEN

of
EAST ANGLIA

NORFOLK, SUFFOLK, CAMBRIDGESHIRE & ESSEX

Edited by

CHRIS TAYLOR

Front Cover: Thaxted, Essex
By Eleanor Tanner
One of a limited edition series available from
Crown Pictures, Lindsell. See page 430

ACKNOWLEDGEMENTS

This book would not have been compiled without the dedicated help of the following:
Elaine, Hong - Administration. Les & Graham - Artists. Bob, Gareth, Les - Research.
Chris, Jenny, Alice, Les - Editing & DTP.

Map origination by Paul and Simon at Legend DTP, Stockport, 061 419-9748

All have contributed to what we hope is an interesting, useful and enjoyable publication.

OTHER TITLES IN THIS SERIES

The Hidden Places of Devon and Cornwall
The Hidden Places of East Anglia
The Hidden Places of The Cotswolds
The Hidden Places of Dorset, Hampshire and Isle of Wight
The Hidden Places of the Lake District and Cumbria
The Hidden Places of Lancashire and Cheshire
The Hidden Places of Northumberland and Durham
The Hidden Places of North Wales
The Hidden Places of the Heart of England
The Hidden Places of the South East
The Hidden Places of South Wales
The Hidden Places of Scotland
The Hidden Places of Thames and Chilterns
The Hidden Places of Yorkshire and Humberside

Introduction

THE HIDDEN PLACES is designed to be an easily used book, taking you, in this instance, on a gentle meander through the beautiful countryside of Cambridgeshire, Norfolk, Suffolk and Essex. However, our books cover many counties and now encompass most of the United Kingdom. We have combined descriptions of the well-known and enduring tourist attractions with those more secluded and as yet little known venues, easy to miss unless you know exactly where you are going.

We include hotels, inns, restaurants, various types of accommodation, historic houses, museums, gardens and general attractions throughout this fascinating area, together with our research on the local history. For each attraction there is a line drawing and a brief description of the services offered. A map at the beginning of each chapter shows you each area, with many charming line drawings of the places we found on our journey.

We do not include firm prices or award merits. We merely wish to point out *The Hidden Places* that hopefully will improve your holiday or business trip and tempt you to return. The places featured in this book will we are sure, be pleased if you mention that it was The Hidden Places which prompted you to visit.

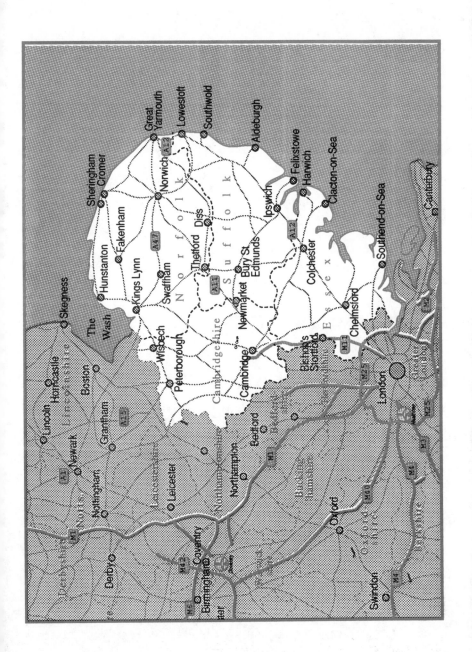

THE HIDDEN PLACES OF
EAST ANGLIA

CONTENTS

CHAPTER ONE

Cambridge and South Cambridgeshire.

Kings College Chapel, Cambridge

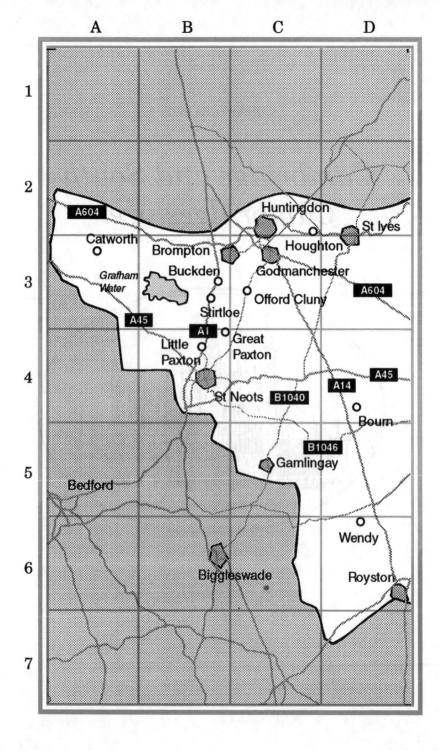

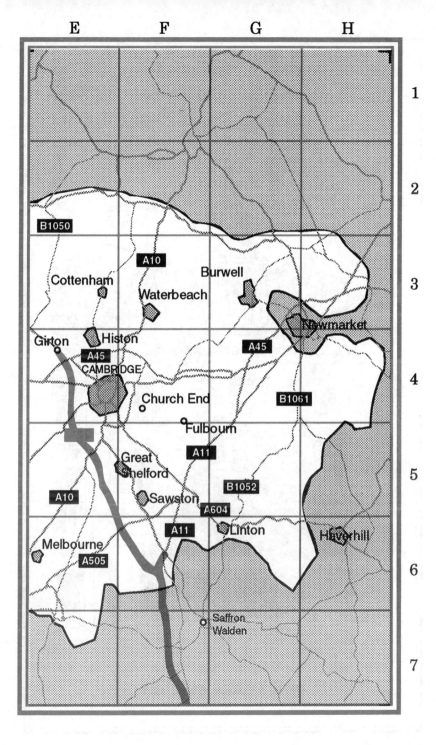

Christ's College, Cambridge

Cambridge and South Cambridgeshire.

The City of **Cambridge** really needs no introduction as it is without doubt one of the great centres of learning with a unique history and reputation known throughout the world. With the building of the M11 Motorway, and frequent rail services to London, the city is very accessible even boasting its own airport to the east of the centre. If you are travelling from outside the U.K the nearest International Airport is at Stansted which is well connected by road and rail. Popularity does, however, have its price, and at certain times of the year you will definitely have the feeling that you are not alone!

Like Edinburgh during the Festival you will nearly always find somewhere to stay even when it's busy, but do book in advance in the Summer and / or make use of the Tourist Information Centre's wealth of local knowledge and use their booking service. They are right in the thick of the action on Wheeler Street and it is by far the best bet to park and walk there. There are lots of helpful signposts dotted about and their phone number like all the other Tourist Information Centres (T.I.C.s) is at the back of the book, but if you are feeling lazy it's (0223) 322640.

The aim of this book however, while not to ignore the obvious, is to try to introduce you to some of the smaller towns and villages, which are no less worthy of your attention whether you are a tourist or a 'local' looking for somewhere different .

This part of the world is a classic example where a visit to the city is a must, but on our journey around the area we discovered a wealth of interesting places to stay and visit and it would be a shame not to balance your time here with a foray into the surrounding countryside.

If Cambridge is your first port of call then you might like to find your way round by joining a tour of the City which leaves from the T.I.C. on foot and is the ideal way to find your bearings as well as giving a fascinating insight into this beautiful City. Alternatively there are bus tours which leave from the railway station.

With or without this introduction it is soon apparent that life revolves around the colleges, a collection of buildings, each with a different character, representing continuous academic growth for over 700 years.

The growth of the city as a place of learning began in 1284 when the oldest college, Peterhouse was founded by the Bishop of Ely. The 14th and 15th centuries saw rapid expansion with a cluster of buildings springing up along the river Cam. As much of the early learning was based on theological work, the churches and chapels formed an integral part of the colleges, and the jewel in this architectural crown is **Kings College Chapel**. Best viewed from the river this is a simply stunning building started in 1446 by Henry VI with an interior to match the spectacle of the exterior. Of particular note is the fan vaulted ceiling, built between 1512 and 1515 and the stained glass windows added just after. More recently the Rubens masterpiece 'The Adoration of the Magi' was donated and although well used by the world famous choir, the chapel is open to the public from 0900 to 1545 during term time and until 1700 in the vacations on Mondays to Saturdays. The times vary a little more on Sundays, but it is a must on your tour.

The colleges themselves are also surprisingly visitor friendly and you can at least walk into most of the central courtyards and chapels . Please remember however that the colleges are closed to visitors during the exam period from May to Mid June and that being private property there is no automatic right of way.

"All work and no play " etc. is as true today as it has always been, and there are numerous opportunities for recreation and entertainment here which are not solely the preserve of the college community. The ubiquitous flat bottomed boats or punts can be hired, while another way of avoiding the traffic congestion is to hire a bicycle, and there are several firms in Cambridge offering this service.

Both body and soul can be well fed here and a visit to the **Fitzwilliam Museum** on Trumpington Street conveniently placed in the centre near Peterhouse college is well worthwhile. The fine art treasures are particularly impressive with works from van Dyke to Monet to Matisse. Phone (0223) 332900.

Still in this area, it will be of particular interest to American readers that the chapel to Peterhouse was originally called St Peter's and dates back to the 12th century. It has a memorial tablet to Godfrey Washington showing the family crest of stars and stripes. Near to the bulk of the colleges but an antidote to the academic is an interesting place to visit in the form of the Cambridge Folk Museum which is full of artifacts showing how domestic life and local trades have developed over the centuries. There is also on Lensfield Road the **Scott Polar Research Institute** which displays memorabilia from Polar expeditions.

If you are trying to escape from the madding crowd, Cambridge is blessed with a large number of open spaces, most notably The Backs which stretch along the banks of the Cam. Still very central and a short

King's College, Cambridge

Punting on the Cam

walk from the railway station is the **University Botanic Garden**. The gardens contain many rare species and are open to the public from 8.30 am to 6.30 pm with reduced hours on Sundays opening at 2.30 pm.

Heading back into the centre and bounded by Parkside and Gonville Place is a large expanse of grass called Parkers Piece where you will find a super place to eat in the form of **Hobbs Pavilion Restaurant** . This wonderful example of an eccentric eatery is housed in a cricket pavilion which is dedicated to the man who was for many the greatest batsman the world has seen. Hobbs Pavilion stands in the centre of the city just behind the University Arms Hotel and overlooking a plot of land known as Parkers Piece.

Run by Stephen and Susan Hill, this is a sheer delight and has been catering for both cricketers who play on the field outside and for the public since 1978 when it was run as a self service restaurant.

Nowadays there is a varied menu available lunchtime and evenings with pancakes of all kinds, both sweet and savoury, being a firm favourite. There are also fixed price menus which are excellent value for money. Salads are another popular choice here and vegetarians and vegans are both catered for. On the side of temptation however there are ice creams and desserts here which are pure indulgence. Whatever you fancy one thing is certain, and that is that the food will be first rate. Well behaved children are welcome, but leave your plastic as credit cards are not. There will be much to occupy you on a visit to Cambridge, but this is such a one-off that it would be a great shame if you were to miss it during your stay. In short - a must.

Hobbs Pavilion Restaurant, Parkers Piece, Cambridge

Wherever you eat, and there are hundreds of pubs and **restaurants** here, it is advisable to book a table to avoid disappointment especially at weekends and during the summer when restaurants can fill up very quickly from 7.00pm onwards and you may be faced with a long wait!

Entertainment is varied and ranges from street entertainers and musicians to mainstream theatre and concerts. The local press publish details as do the TIC, in fact there is an excellent theatre right by the tourist office on Wheeler Street in the **Corn Exchange**. Box Office number is 463204 if dialling locally.

There are many people who visit Cambridge who never set foot outside the City and while there is enough here to satisfy the most avid tourist there is so much to see and do within a relatively short distance of the city.

The oddly named Gog Magog Hills are approximately 3 miles south east of the city, and offer a good vantage point from which to observe the many towers and spires of the Cambridge colleges and chapels. There are footpaths to Wandlebury Camp which is the site of an Iron Age fort. Still on foot and even closer to town it is well worth taking a pleasant stroll across the riverside meadows to Grantchester a delightful area full of interesting thatched buildings, which is often overlooked by the visitor. This was home to Rupert Brook the poet who wrote so eloquently about the futility of war, and it is rather interesting to note that four miles to the west of Cambridge is the **American Military Cemetery** at **Madingley**. Many people intent on reaching their destination must miss the sign on the A45 which is a pity because, American or not, you cannot fail to be moved by the experience of a short visit here. Madingley has become a place of pilgrimage for the families of those American Servicemen who operated from the many bases in the area during the Second World War. On a lighter note the village pub, The Three Horseshoes is very popular and a good choice if you are heading in or out of Cambridge. There is a good range of food in a welcoming atmosphere and if the weather is kind there is a charming patio room where you may enjoy your food. Phone (0954) 210221.

Further West just South of the spot where the A1198 crosses the A45 is Britain's oldest surviving postmill at **Bourn**, the base and outer structure dating from 1636.

South on the A1198 is another place worth a visit in the shape of **Wimpole Hall**. This National Trust property can also be easily reached from Junction 12 off the M11 taking the A603 westbound. The Hall dates back over 300 years and has an imposing main house with a with a fine library and magnificent state rooms. If you feel that the younger members of your group may not share your love of old buildings then do not fear as the estate has a well organised farm where they can meet the animals and see the workings of a farm first hand. The park is well landscaped and there are many different walks for you to enjoy. Open Tuesday,

Wednesday, Thursday, Saturday, and Sunday. Also Bank Holiday Mondays. Admission charge payable. Family tickets and group discounts available. Phone (0223) 207257.

The A1198 will eventually take you to Royston over the border in Hertfordshire, but before the road intersects the A505 in the village of **Kneesworth** good quality accommodation can be found at **Kneesworth Grange**, a lovely old house with a conservatory where breakfast is served. 3 rooms all very pretty and en suite. Phone (0763) 248674.

To the west just over the border into Hertfordshire is the small village of **Ashwell** On Hill Street, just down from the Market is **Day's Bakery and Cafe**. It is the ideal place to stop for a bite to eat or just a cuppa, and to be tempted into buying a 'something' for later. As well as salads, pasties and sandwiches there is always a variety of hot and cold meals available from 10.30am to 3.00pm. As you would expect there is a wonderful selection of fresh cream cakes and you can choose from the many fancy cakes from the counter.

Day's Bakers opened in Ashwell in the 1840's and has always been a family bakery with all the products being made from scratch and with only the finest ingredients.

In 1988 they won the title of 'Family Baker of the Year' as a result of a recommendation of a customer and this reflects the emphasis they place on quality. Day's is particularly famous for its Pork pies, the large sizes of which are still hand raised in the traditional manner. Another speciality are the fruit cakes for weddings and birthdays. They have a reputation for their model cakes, and Clive the resident cake decorator regularly produces unusual celebration cakes. Whether you are weary and looking for refreshment or just after indulging a sweet tooth Day's are well worth finding.

Did You Know...

There is a full list of

Tourist Information Centres

at the back of the book?

Days Bakery and Cafe, 61 High Street, Ashwell, Nr Baldock, Herts

11

Anglesey Abbey

From here if you head eastward it is worth a detour to the village of **Melbourn** and no we haven't missed the 'e' off the end. Somewhat smaller than its Australian namesake it does nevertheless boast some excellent places to eat and the delightfully named **Pink Geranium** on Station Road is a restaurant which has an enviable reputation throughout the region. The proprietor is a local celebrity and the food is all freshly prepared and home made. Sophisticated eating at its best. Bookings on (0763) 260215.

Alternatively, **The Sheen Mill Hotel** and Restaurant is right on the river and there is also the added bonus of accommodation in a charming 17th century mill. Bookings for rooms or restaurant on (0763) 261393. In short, two superb establishments in a small village tucked away off the A10. Neither is cheap but you certainly get what you pay for. Tearing yourself away from the gastronomic delights of Melbourn, and just before you reach the M11 again, why not nip across to the A505 where there is a fascinating place to visit at **Duxford**, home of the grandly titled **Imperial War Museum**.

The name is a bit of a misnomer as the airfield has the finest collection of both civil and military aircraft in the country. There is a Concorde for example, a number of military vehicles, and special exhibitions. There is also an adventure playground, and a restaurant as well as shops all on a large but accessible site. Very easy to spend a few hours here. Open daily except Christmas and New Years Day. Phone (0223) 835000.

Crossing the M11 at Junction 10 the road joins the A11 for a short while before the signs to Linton appear. This is where you will find **Linton Zoo and Gardens**, a short distance from the centre of the village on the B1052. This is very much a place where conservation is the keyword and there is always something new to discover as they take on board another endangered species. There are large landscaped gardens to enjoy and it is an ideal spot for a picnic. A childrens play area and souvenir shop are also on site and the zoo is open every day except Christmas day. Phone (0223) 891308. Please note that dogs are not allowed in the park.

The **Old Red Lion** is a beautiful 17th century country pub situated on the A604 at Horseheath, to the east of Linton, offering a superb menu for lunchtime snacks and afternoon cream teas or dinner.

The house has been totally refurbished with flagstone floors, open fires and a wealth of timber beams. A fine selection of real ales, open all day and everyday. It also offers fourteen letting bedrooms furnished to a very high standard with en-suite, TV's and tea/coffee making facilities at very competitive rates.

Close by is Chilford Hall with its vineyard and Cambridge is just fifteen minutes drive away

The Old Red Lion Inn and Accommodation, Linton Road,
Horseheath 0223 892909

North of here and a pleasant saunter up the B1052 is **Newmarket** which is actually in Suffolk, but as you will see from a map practically surrounded by Cambridgeshire on all sides. 'Home' of British horseracing we make no apology for mentioning the town here as it is very accessible from Cambridge and the racecourse itself is right on the border. The racecourse owners really have tried to make this a place to go for a great day out and apart from the classic races held here such as the 1000 and 2000 guineas there are many other meeting held here with the evening races in the Summer being supported by live entertainment, and with lots for the children to do as well. The local press will publish details of the meetings or phone (0638) 663482. On days when there is no racing there is a fascinating Museum in the centre of Newmarket full of memorabilia and well worth a visit. Admission charge payable Phone (0638) 667333.

Back in the county proper and north of the A45 are three places worth visiting which form a triangle to the north east of Cambridge itself.

Anglesey Abbey off the B1102 is an outstanding building which started as an Augustinian Abbey in 1135 and the monks remained here for almost four centuries before the property underwent conversion to a Tudor manor house. Inside however there is a superb vaulted ceiling which is one of the clues to its earlier origins. Outside are large gardens in formal 18th century style with statues lining a walkway or providing a focal point for the wide variety of floral displays. There is much to see here and as a bonus do make a point of looking out for the **Lode Mill**. A mill has stood on the site since the time of the Domesday Book and once a month the mill grinds corn for sale to the public. The facilities at the mill and Abbey include a shop and a licensed restaurant serving teas lunches and snacks. Free parking for cars and coaches. Admission charge and with the exception of guide dogs no dogs are allowed in the gardens. Phone (0223) 811200.

A few miles north as the crow flies will bring you to one of the most important wetland reserves in Europe at **Wicken Fen.**

The reserve is host to thousands of birds and insects who thrive in this unspoilt habitat. Nowadays the water level is kept up whereas at one time vast areas of the fens were drained to provide farmland. Owned by the National Trust there is a visitor centre which has lots of information, and there are raised walkways across the water which makes access to the centre of the fen quite easy.

Back on the A10 heading South and just past the village of **Chittering** is a small site worth a visit in the form of **Denny Abbey** which was founded in the 12th century as a dependent priory of the large monastery at Ely. The remains include the church and the refectory. Admission charge payable. Free to English Heritage members.

Situated three miles north of Cambridge just off the A10, you will find a real gem of a place in the village of **Waterbeach** called **Berry House.** This Grade II listed house dates from around 1820, although there is evidence of much earlier building, and is today the home of Sally Peck who offers super accommodation in a village setting, yet so near to the many attractions of Cambridge. Ely too is close at hand and a short drive will bring you to Anglesey Abbey, Wimpole Hall, and Audley End House. For horse racing enthusiasts Newmarket is only about 25 minutes drive.

Berry House, High St. Waterbeach Nr. Cambridge 01223 860702

The accommodation at Berry House is in a converted beamed coach house with a large reception room and 2 quite delightful bedrooms, both en-suite , which are furnished with Georgian and Edwardian antiques, and the larger double room can also be used as a twin or family room.

Dinner can be arranged in advance, and as the house is not licensed, guests are welcome to bring their own drinks. There is even a fridge in the guest lounge stocked with complimentary mineral water, mixers and ice.

In all, a perfect choice for anyone wanting the best of both worlds, with first class accommodation and food in a delightful rural location yet a few minutes away from Cambridge and many other places of interest. Well recommended.

From Waterbeach heading towards Cambridge again you will find the road crosses the A45 North of the city. Passing across the top of the M11 at junction 14 the choice is either to go to St Neots due West on the A45 or to veer off towards Huntingdon. Staying on the A45 past the American Cemetery at Madingley the town of **St Neots** is a pleasant drive and also a convenient stopping off point if you find yourself on the A1 which passes by the town. Well worth a little amble around on foot as there are some old pubs tucked away and some interesting buildings all too easy to miss if you simply drive in and out.

The A45 takes a dog leg here and re-emerges a mile or two north. This is an interesting diversion as it leads to Grafham Water which is a huge reservoir, but don't let that put you off as it has good leisure facilities and the water company has done a good job in providing well signed walks as well as a host of water based activities. An excellent spot for a picnic by the way.

Just before the border with Northampton is **Kimbolton**. Kimbolton is an Anglo-Saxon name, meaning Cenebald's Tun or small estate. By 1200 the Lord of the Manor was Geoffrey Fitz-Piers, Chief Justicular to King John, who granted Geoffrey the right to hold a fair and a market.

Henry VIII's first wife Catherine of Aragon, lived the last eighteen months of her life exiled at the castle. From the 17th to the twentieth century the castle and the estate was in the hands of the Montague family, subsequently the Dukes of Manchester. In 1950 the castle was sold to the grammar school.

Situated on East Street, at the rear of the main street, and very close to the Castle is a delightful whitewashed medieval townhouse, its frontage featuring beams weathered by the passing centuries. Here Barbara Johnson and her daughter Kathleen run a lovely **Tea Room**. Everything on the menu is home-made. The choice of delights includes Chocolate Fudge Cake, Passion Cake, and Coffee Chiffon, and a selection of cheese cakes. As if that wasn't enough they even make their own ice-cream, which includes Chocolate Nut Sundae and Peach Melba. The sandwich selection includes Turkey Waldorf and the more traditional Beef with horse radish, and it can all be washed down with a choice of teas. No wonder that the Tea Room is Egon Roney recommended.

The Tea Room, 9 East Street, Kimbolton, Nr Huntingdon
01480-860415

A short distance to the north is **Catworth**. On the High St in Catworth, which is conveniently placed for Graffham Water, and a short distance from the A14 link road, you will notice **The Racehorse** pub where the road bends round into the village. Run by Anthea and Roy Wilkes who incidentally hail from Worcestershire, the Racehorse looks quite small from the front , but this is a bit of a dark horse if you will forgive the pun as there is a large car park and outside seating, while inside there is a restaurant and 2 bars.

The Racehorse Pub Hugh St. Catworth. 01832 710262

On the subject of food, it is for this reason that the pub is very popular and therefore well worth visiting if you are in the area, or are one of the

The Cromwell Museum, Huntingdon

increasing number of locals to discover the place as the Wilkes have only been here since 1993.

Anthea provides a varied menu which is all tremendous value for money and very well cooked. Keeping to the racing theme you might try Horseshoe pie which has the tips of a pastry horseshoe pointing out of the crust. There are plenty of beers and wines to complement your meal, and children are welcome. If it's good pub food you are looking for this is hard to beat.

Back on the A14 and before you once again come across the A1 is **Ellington** where, on the main street, you will find the 18th century **Mermaid Inn**, run by Maureen Brown who took over the business 5 years ago. The Inn is conveniently located for the attractions of Grafham Water nearby, while in the village itself, the local church which is adjacent to the Mermaid, has an interesting Tudor one hand clock. Lunches and Bar Snacks are available, and there is one double room if you need somewhere to stay. There are beams inside which add to the atmosphere while out of doors there is a rear patio and facilities for a game of French Boules. A handy place to stop near to the A1 and A604 turnoff.

The Mermaid Inn, Ellington. 01480 891450.

The village of **Brampton** has the one time home of the famous diarist Samuel Pepys who so vividly described the major events of the 17th century, including The Great Fire of London.

Just up the road is the market town of **Huntingdon** whose local M.P is John Major the Prime Minister. Apart from the above mentioned politician the town was the birthplace of both Samuel Pepys and Oliver Cromwell, and relics from this era can be seen at the museum which was the former grammar school attended by both Cromwell and Pepys.

There is a large market square in the centre and a short distance away

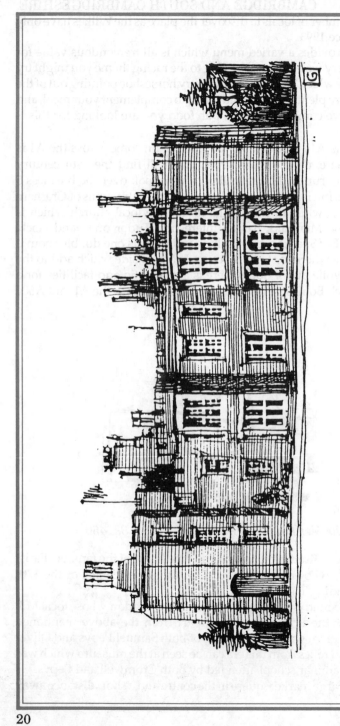

Hitchingbrooke, Huntingdon

CAMBRIDGE AND SOUTH CAMBRIDGESHIRE.

is **Hinchingbrooke House** which today serves also as a school but which was a home for both the Cromwells and the Earls of Sandwich. Just across the Ouse and worthy of your attention is Godmanchester which has a varied collection of buildings from many different periods, and one or two good pubs.

Between Huntingdon and St Ives on the A1123 is **Wyton** and **Tacchi's Garden Scene** which locals may remember opened in 1992. The site had however been in the family for many years, and the business on this site was that of nurserymen who provided high quality shrubs and trees for local authority projects and to landscaping contractors.

One of the places which has plants from Tacchi nurseries is Euro Disney outside Paris. As their other sites were developed Wyton was turned into a garden centre which now specialises in landscaping materials and outdoor plants and provides anyone interested in transforming their garden into something really special with all the advice and materials they need.

As you wander round the displays it is worth noting that they are all made out of materials and products which are available on site, and this is the place to go for plants, sheds, paving, statues, fencing etc.. Ponds are becoming increasingly popular and there is an aquatic centre here too fully stocked with both pond and tropical fish as well as all the equipment you will need . Stephen Woods the manager and his staff will be there to assist you . A reputable family firm which is now making itself available to a wider audience. One for the more serious gardener.

Tacchi's Garden Scene, Wyton. 01480 433349.

Finally our tour brings us to **St Ives** but do find the time for a brief stop at Hemingford Grey, where there are wonderful views of the river and a superb moated manor house dating back to the 12th century. The church which dates from the same period is very photogenic and is right

21

on a bend in the river. A charming place to stop off if you are in the area. St Ives itself is an ancient town which once held a huge local fair. A particularly interesting local landmark is the bridge which has stood since the 15th century and has a very rare medieval chapel built on one side. It is here we finish this chapter before pressing on north towards Peterborough and the Cambridgeshire Fens.

CHAPTER TWO

North Cambridgeshire and the Fens

Ely Cathedral

23

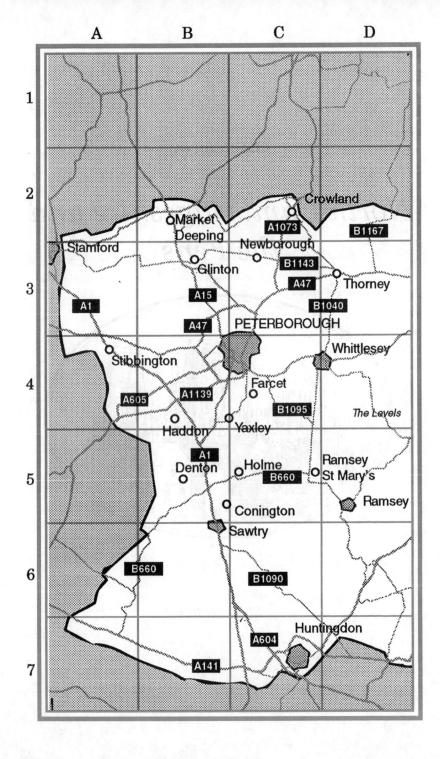

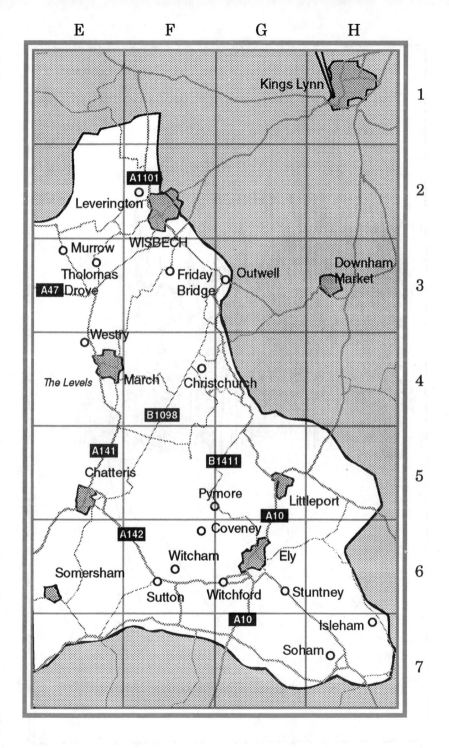

Peterborough Cathedral

CHAPTER TWO

North Cambridgeshire and the Fens

Far removed from the hustle and bustle of modern life, the Fens are like a breath of fresh air. Travelling on the open road you can experience the pleasure of touring through peaceful countryside at your own pace.

Before the Fens were drained this was a world of mists, marshes and bogs. Of small islands, inhabited by independent folk, their livelihood the fish and waterfowl of this eerie watery place. The region is full of legends of web-footed people, ghosts and witchcraft.

Today the landscape is a result of the ingenuity of man, his constant desire to tame the wilderness and create farmland. This fascinating story spans the centuries, from the earliest Roman and Anglo-Saxon times, when the first embankments and drains were constructed to lessen the frequent flooding.

Throughout the middle ages large areas of marsh and fen were reclaimed, with much of the work undertaken by the monasteries. By the early 17th century the attention turned to the remaining undrained fens. In 1630, the Dutch engineer Cornelius Vermuyden was commissioned by the Earl of Bedford to drain the remaining wetlands of Cambridgeshire. The significant influence of the Dutch lives on in the architecture and place names of the fens.

Local opposition was considerable as the systematic drainage of the land threatened the traditional fishing and wildfowling rights of the Fen dwellers, and their fierce resistance and destruction of the drainage works earned them the name "Fen Tigers".

Today the Fens have a sophisticated network of drains, embankments and electric pumps, capable of raising thousands of gallons of water a second, to protect the land from the ever present threat of rain and tide.

History of the drainage can be seen at **Stretham Beam Engine** and the **Prickwillow Land Drainage museum**, both near Ely, or at one of the many other small museums that seem to appear in each fenland town.

Peterborough, Cambridgeshire's second city, just 20 miles to the north of St. Ives, dominates this part of the county. At the heart stands the great Norman Cathedral of St. Peter which gave the city its name. An important site of Christian worship since 655 AD, it retains two early

Saxon sculptures. The present church, built from 1118 to 1238 as a Benedictine Abbey, was made a Cathedral by Henry VIII. His first Queen, Katharine of Aragon, is buried here, as was Mary Queen of Scots for a while after her execution at Fotheringhay.

Located in the centre, the **City Museum and Art Gallery** shows all aspects of the story of Peterborough with the first floor displays dealing with the natural environment and how human beings have used it. There are skeletons of the sea creatures which lived in Peterborough when dinosaurs roamed the earth and also displays of local archaeology. The second floor tells the more recent social history of the city and includes important displays of bone and straw work made by Napoleonic prisoners at nearby Norman Cross.

The Queensgate Centre at the heart of Peterborough provides everything you could possibly want from a shopping trip. With spacious marble halls, decorative fountains and high levels of natural lighting, the centre has maintained the standards of excellence that once earned it the title of Europe's best new covered shopping centre.

On the south side of the city, in an area called Orton Longueville is **Orton Hall Hotel**. The building is a fantastically ornate, former 17th century manor house, and is set in 22 acres in a conservation village close to Nene Park. In addition to the formal restaurant, the hotel incorporates the Old Ramblewood Inn, a country pub serving real ales and hearty meals.

2 miles east of the city centre, at Fourth Drove, Fengate, is **Flag Fen**. Described as one of the most exciting finds of the century, Flag Fen is one of the few ongoing excavations that are open to the public. From Easter to the end of October, guided tours of the excavation offer visitors the opportunity to watch archaeologists gradually uncovering a Bronze Age timber platform, and 1,000 year old swords and spearheads.

Running from the centre of Peterborough, for 7 1/2 miles through Nene Park to Wansford, is the preserved **Nene Valley Steam Railway**. Services operate at weekends, from March to October and some mid-week days in the summer months. With the added highlight of occasional special events, like Thomas the Tank Engine days and Vintage weekends, this is an ideal outing for those who love steam and for younger members of the family. To find out more, ring 01780 782854.

As though forgotten by time, the town of **Stamford** stands in the southern part of Kesteven, Lincolnshire and just on the edge of the county of Cambridgeshire. This is a wonderful town, made up of a series of winding roads, lined with buildings of local stone, mainly of the medieval and Georgian periods. Declared a conservation area in 1967, and proclaimed as 'the finest stone town in England', Stamford provides a present day view of its glorious past. The town was once held as an important religious centre which is apparent from the number of towers and spires that seem to appear round every corner.

Look out for the **Stamford Steam Brewery Museum**, a fascinating stop for all those interested in drinking beer! It was established in 1825 as a malt house and brewery, and was the longest surviving brewery in the town, eventually shutting down in 1974. It has since been open to the public, displaying original 19th century brewing equipment.

The facades of shops remain ornate and decorative while offering modern services and facilities with good old fashioned hospitality. There is a pleasant walk along the River Welland which winds its way through the town and provides scenic views across the meadows and of the town centre itself, before flowing past the estate of Burghley House.

Burghley House is one of the largest and grandest houses of the Elizabethan age. The house was built by the 1st Lord Burghley, Lord High Treasurer to Queen Elizabeth I, and has been home to the Cecil family ever since. Situated on the edge of the town of Stamford, the house is set in a picturesque deer park designed by "Capability' Brown which is famous for hosting the Burghley Horse Trials each September. Guided tours take visitors through 18 magnificent rooms culminating with the state apartments with ceilings painted by Verrio. The rooms are also treasure troves of fine porcelain, paintings and furniture which will appeal to lovers of fine art.

Ideally situated for Burghley House and the Nene Valley railway is Midstone Farm House at Southorpe. This 18th century farmhouse offers bed and breakfast and guests are welcome to explore the garden and paddocks where you could meet cattle, ponies and a pot-bellied pig. For details ring Anne Harrison-Smith on 01780 740136.

Travelling to the east again, and located 7 miles north of Peterborough, are the **Peakirk Waterfowl Gardens**. These were opened in 1957 by the H.R.H. The Duke of Gloucester and are now home to 700 waterfowl of 108 different kinds, including geese, swans and flamingos. The large ponds and gardens make this an interesting and informative place to visit for people of all ages. The beautiful setting and serenity of the park make it a mecca for artists and photographers too.

The pleasure of cruising in the Fens lies in the open, uncrowded waterways, recognised by seasoned boaters as probably the most atmospheric in England. The most popular waterways are the River Great Ouse which wends its way from Huntingdon, through Ely and northwards to King's Lynn, and the Nene-Ouse navigation link, connecting Peterborough with the Great Ouse near Downham Market, passing through March and on to Outwell and Upwell, often likened to Dutch Canal villages. For boat hire, contact Fox Boat Yard in March, tel: 01354 52770.

Many of the towns and villages of the Fens are still unspoilt with riverside locations and are home to traditional markets which reflect the importance of local agriculture. The small villages near Peterborough are no exception.

To the east is the village of **Thorney**. **The Heritage Centre** here tells the story of this unusual village using objects, models, plans and photographs. The Abbey dominates the medieval history of the area and its significance is explained. The village was developed by the Dukes of Bedford as part of their estate, and is a classic example of a 19th century model village with its own style of estate architecture.

To the south of Peterborough is an area that is dominated by the busy A1, but take the time to explore beyond the hard shoulder. Hidden away are numerous small, quaint and often historic villages.

Not so much an Inn more of a national landmark is the **Bell Inn** at **Stilton**. The traffic thunders along towards Peterborough while the Bell stands proudly a short distance off the A1 on the Great North Road at Stilton.

As you approach the village, you will see one of the most impressive hotel signs in the country. The huge sign is a replica of the 16th century original made of copper plate suspended on elaborate wrought iron brackets, and weighs in at two and three-quarters tonnes.

Stilton's position made it a favourite stopping off point during the heyday of coaching when weary travellers could obtain refreshment and break their arduous and frequently dangerous journey, for this too was the age of the highwayman and the most notorious of them all, Dick Turpin, is said to have hidden at The Bell .

Today, it is the most marvellous place to find peace and tranquillity, whether you are just tired of driving and feel you have earned a relaxing lunch or dinner or perhaps want to spend a few days exploring the surrounding area.

Whatever your reason for stepping through the door you will find a welcoming feel to the place and a particularly fine restaurant situated in a beamed room with a log fire and a split level dining area with exposed woodwork and mellow stone creating the right atmosphere for business or pleasure.

In the late 1980s extensive restoration was carried out, and there are now 19 beautiful bedrooms, all en-suite and built around a central courtyard.

We cannot mention The Bell without explaining its connection with the world famous Stilton cheese, for it was a relative of an 18th century landlord called Cooper Thornhill who first supplied the cheese to him, and it was the entrepreneurial Thornhill who made the cheese famous even though the cheese was made elsewhere! That's marketing for you!

Modern day Thornhills can be found using the conference facilities which make this an ideal place for a business meeting or for a short break with exceptional food in an historic setting. Well recommended.

The Bell Inn at Stilton Nr Peterborough. 01733 241066 Fax 01733 245173

To the south of Stilton are the villages of Great and Little Gidding. **Little Gidding** is a place of peace and contemplation in a fast and noisy world. A place of community and of prayer. The first community was founded here by Nicholas Ferrer. It comprised his own extended family and a number of single men and women. In addition to praying three time a day they made and dispensed herbal medicines, they ran a school for their own and local children and practised various crafts. Before his death in 1637 Nicholas Ferrer handed over the leadership of the first community to his brother, with the words 'It is the right, good, old way you are in; keep in it.' That remains the aspiration of the present community, which was formed in the 1970's and which has adopted the name **'The Society of Christ the Sower'** and comprises of married couples and single people from various Christian traditions, following a simple rule.

The centre piece of the community is, as in Nicholas Ferrer's day, the church. Restored by the Ferrers in the 1620's as the centre of this unique experiment in community life, the tiny church has some of the finest furnishings and brasswork of its period. Its powerful spiritual atmosphere has attracted countless pilgrims over the centuries. The original communion silver and brass font - the only one in England - are displayed in the Parlour.

The present community welcomes visitors to its Parlour in the nearby farmhouse, open every day from 11am to 5pm. As well as an interesting exhibition on the community, there are excellent home-made refreshments and lunches. Cake and biscuits, as well as jam made with home-grown fruit, are also for sale, along with books, cards and plants produced by members of the society. In the beds around the community a variety of herbs are grown and similar herbs can be bought from tables near the Parlour. Visitors may also walk around the small farm, where traditional breeds of livestock and poultry are kept, most of the work is done by hand though there is a venerable 1954 Ferguson tractor. In one of the workshops furniture is made to order, including bookcases, cupboards, chairs, tables, and dressers. The Society also run a building company that specialises in restoration of churches and older buildings, though they are happy to tackle any work, charging very fair rates.

Guided tours including a talk about Little Gidding, past and present can be arranged. The chapel in the farmhouse is ideal for quiet days and, if groups wish, a member of the Society can conduct the day. Guest accommodation for both retreats and holidays is available, including a flat ideal for families.

Society of Christ the Sower, Manor Farm, Little Gidding, Nr Huntingdon 01832-293383

This small part of Cambridgeshire that lies to the west of the A1 is all too easy to bypass as you hurtle up or down the Great North Road. This small pocket of land holds many delights such as Grafham Water and the **Hamerton Wildlife Centre.**

The Centre which is run by Sally and Andrew Swales, recognised experts on rare and endangered species, has been open for 3 or 4 years and is a breeding centre for many types of animals whose very existence is threatened. They specialise in rearing marmosets, lemurs, and other small mammals, and have the only breeding group of sloths in the U.K.

They also breed birds and all the animals can be viewed at close range with safety, making this an ideal place to bring children to learn more about the various animals and birds which are bred here. All this in a tranquil rural setting make the centre a must to visit whether you are a local or passing tourist. The centre is well laid out and accessible for the disabled . It is also signposted from the A1 and the A1 M1 link road.

Hamerton Wildlife Centre, Hamerton Nr. Huntingdon .
01832 293362

Returning northwards the Fenland market town on **Whittlesey** lies on the A605 close to the western edge of the Fens and just outside Peterborough. The town dates back to medieval times although there are few reminders left. More recent history has left its mark with a variety of well preserved architecture spanning several centuries. There are examples of timber framed dwellings with thatched roofs, occasional stone buildings and preponderance of mellow buff brick. Whittlesey is also noted for its thatched mud walls - now a rarity.

A local agricultural tradition of The Straw Bear is still celebrated in Whittlesey each year in early January. The Bear is a man dressed in straw who dances through the town on the Saturday before Plough Sunday (the first Sunday after 12th night). The original meaning of the tradition is obscure. It probably stems from pagan times when Corn Gods or other mythical symbols were to be placated or invoked in order to secure soil fertility for the coming season. This annual festival commences on the Friday evening, dancing through the streets on Saturday lasts from 10.45 to 3.30pm and an evening barn dance follows. On the Sunday, the Straw Bear is burnt.

Wisbech, one of the larger Fenland towns lies in the northernmost corner of Cambridgeshire and it was not far from here that the luckless King John lost his baggage train together with a king's fortune in The Wash in 1216. Rest assured, there is little chance of the same thing happening again!

North Brink, Wisbech

There was once a Norman castle in the town, built in 1086, complete with moat and drawbridge. The castle is long gone, but its impact is felt today. The site of the castle is now where you will find The Castle, a Regency villa, and the whole of the centre of town has a 'circular' layout. Two crescents of fine Georgian houses run to the north and south of the Castle grounds. Other signs are evident in those houses built where the castle moat once was, many are suffering from severe subsidence.

Wisbech has had a museum for over 150 years, and the present building was opened in 1847. There is a large collection of Continental and British pottery and porcelain, including a Sevres breakfast service once owned by Napoleon - and a Burmese Buddha. The anti-slavery campaigner, Thomas Clarkson, came from Wisbech, and the museum included material gathered by him as evidence against the trade, as well as objects collected by a local man on the first European expedition up the Niger. Keep an eye out for the Clarkson memorial beside the old bridge.

The Georgian theatre in Alexandra Road was built in 1793 and remained in use as a theatre for just over one hundred years. Since then it has had a chequered career as a school, a tent maker's and a church, but the good news is that in recent years, live theatre has been re-introduced.

On the other side of the river is the Old Market, now a neat garden laid out on the site of former shops which were demolished after the disastrous flood of 1978. The Old Market describes this triangular space surrounded by fine Georgian buildings which testify to the golden days of the river trade.

Leaving Old Market behind continue along the river in the direction of **North Brink**, considered by many to be Wisbech's most outstanding feature and described by Pevsner as one of the finest Georgian brick streets in England. The buildings form a beautiful composition of Georgian designs which tend to be less grand as one gets further from the town. Among these buildings is the North Brink Brewery. Built in 1790, the frontage of this classical Georgian brewery has remained almost unchanged to the present day. The Brewery was purchased by its present owners, Elgoods, in 1878 and still supplies fifty public houses in the Wisbech area.

Further along the river bank, a little further away from the town centre is **Peckover House**. This National Trust property, open to the public from April to October, has well furnished rooms, a fine staircase and an ornate garden, containing an orangery and many rare specimens, for which it is justly famous. The house contains an excellent collection of Cornwallis family portraits and an exhibition on the life and work of Wisbech-born Octavia Hill, a co-founder of the National Trust. Built in 1722, Peckover House is a Grade 1 listed building which makes it of

35

outstanding national importance. Note its stone Doric style doorcase with the segmental pediment above.

If you are seeking accommodation in the area to the north of the town is the village of **Newton** and nearby **Four Winds Country Guesthouse**, which stands in a lovely rural location, surrounded by fens which team with lots of wild life, and benefiting from the regular beautiful sunsets.

Your hostess is Jayne Best, who offers a warm welcome to her charming country house, with its homely atmosphere. There are four rooms available, two doubles and two singles and the doubles are en-suite, with all featuring colour TV and Tea/coffee making facilities. There is a spacious lounge for guests, very friendly and informal with smokers welcome. Should guests wish evening meals are available on request. The quality of Jayne's accommodation and the food have attracted many complementary letters, and surely there can be no better recommendation.

Four Winds Country Guesthouse, Mill Lane, Newton, Nr Wisbech
01945-870479

Like many Fenland towns and villages, **March** was once an island surrounded by marshes. As the land was drained and made more fertile so the town grew and prospered, as a trading and religious centre, a minor port, and in more recent times as a market town, administrative and railway centre.

If you need somewhere to stay here, then try The Olde Griffin Hotel on the High Street. This former Coaching Inn offers reasonably priced accommodation in well-equipped rooms. Run by Mr and Mrs Reeve, it caters well for families. Ring them on tel: 01354 52517.

The railway has been a great influence on the development of the town, encouraging growth away from the older centre around the church. This led to a large expansion north of the river where a huge

Peckover House, Wisbech

marshalling yard was built in the 1930s. The church, St. Wendreda's, named after the town's own Saint, is famous for its spectacular double hammer-beam roof, which reflects the medieval prosperity of the town, with many of the beams decorated with some of the 120 carved angels. The roof represents the zenith of the carpenter's and carver's skill and is not merely decorative - it is a highly sophisticated piece of engineering. The roof was even mentioned by Dorothy Sayers in her novel "The Nine Tailors". The church was also described by Poet Laureate Sir John Betjeman described as "worth cycling 40 miles in headwind to see". Make sure you don't miss it.

In addition to visiting St. Wendreda's you will enjoy a meander along West End. This attractive path is flanked on one side by cottages and on the other by the river and town park. In this area you will also find several interesting pubs. The White Horse is a thatched pub with riverside garden; The Acre is by the park; and The Ship Inn, east of the bridge, has wonderful carved beams.

On the outskirts of March, and well signposted from the A141, is the **Stags Holt Farm Park and Stud**. Stags Holt offers a unique insight into an area not generally associated with tourism. The ancient parkland and Victorian farm buildings certainly provide an ideal backdrop for a day in the country. Among the many horses here, you will find Suffolk Punches, a rare breed with a unique history spanning almost 300 years back to an ancestor known as Crisps Horse of Ufford, thought by some to be a Lincolnshire Trotting Stallion. Horses, however, only make up part of the story at Stags Holt, the collections of harness, carts, wagons, implements and hand tools are fascinating too.

Between March and Ely is the friendly little market town of **Chatteris**. It marks the centre of a nationally famous area of intensive arable farming based on the immensely fertile black fen soil, brought progressively under cultivation over the centuries by drainage schemes, of which the most notable are the Old and New Hundred Foot Rivers to the south and east of the town.

On the High Street is the Chatteris Museum, which has displays of locally found flint instruments through to Roman jewellery and medieval pottery. A splendid set of mobile stocks, used for holding petty criminals are preserved, together with a wide range of material illustrating the town's past. There are many old photographs, posters and handbills exhibited, which help to show how Fenland has changed over the last hundred years.

While you're in Chatteris a great place to stay, or stop for a drink and a bite to eat, is the Cross Keys on Market Hill. This delightful 16th century coaching inn offers the old world charm of yesteryear with traditional hospitality and friendly service. The lounge bar features an oak beamed ceiling and an inglenook fireplace. There is also a restaurant and bar meals are available too.

The city of Ely lies to the east of Chatteris and is the jewel in the Fen's crown. An ideal place to start your visit is the Tourist Information Centre. It is not only a great place to pick loads of information on what to see and where to go in this part of Cambridgeshire, but is a tourist attraction in its own right. The pretty black and white timbered building is the only remaining house, other than Hampton Court, where Oliver Cromwell and his family are known to have lived. The present east wing represents what is left of the original 13th century building. The house is some 750 years old and it has a varied history. In the 1840s it was a public house aptly called "The Cromwell Arms" and from 1905 to 1986 it was the vicarage for the adjoining St. Mary's Church. Inside, several rooms have been refurbished in Cromwellian style and an audio-visual presentation gives an insight into the domestic, military and political aspects of his life. The Tourist Information Centre is located downstairs and is unique in its period style and atmosphere.

Walking towards the Cathedral from here, you will pass on your left the Old Fire Engine House, a restaurant specialising in traditional English food and with an interesting art gallery. The building once housed the local fire engine.

Both the Cathedral and the surrounding fens have played a major role in the history of Ely through the centuries. The fens influence is even reflected in the city's name; Ely was once known as "Elge" or "Elig" because of the large number of eels which could be caught in the surrounding fenland, Elig meaning eel island.

The city owes its existence, however, to St. Etheldreda who founded a religious community on the hill-top site in the 7th century but it was not until 1081 that building of the present Cathedral was begun by the Normans and which now stands as a remarkable example of Romanesque architecture. Undoubtedly, the most outstanding feature of the Cathedral is the Octagon and Lantern, built to replace the Norman tower which collapsed in 1322. They took 30 years and 8 huge oaks to build! Its framework is unique in the world, estimated to weigh 400 tons, and once included a set of bells. It is a medieval engineering feat still much admired by modern architects and builders. Also in the Cathedral are the Brass Rubbing Centre and Stained Glass Museum.

The Cathedral is set within the walls of the Benedictine Monastery, and a walk round the College will reveal that Ely has the largest collection of medieval architecture in England.

If you find yourself near the river, look out for The Maltings. The building dates back to 1868 when it was constructed for malting barley, using high temperatures to cause the barley to sprout, before it could be

Oliver Cromwell's House, Ely

taken to the brewery. In 1971 it was converted into the delightfully attractive building you see today, and is used as a public exhibition and conference centre, cinema and serves drinks, meals and snacks. The riverside walk in front of The Maltings is known as Quai D'Orsay, and was named shortly after the twinning of East Cambridgeshire District with the town of Orsay in France in 1980/1.

Just outside Ely, off the A142 and in the village of **Witchford**, is the **Needham Farm Restaurant**. Chef proprietor Barry Smith has brought his culinary talents from The Savoy, Buckingham Palace, and more recently 'Ferraris' in Ely. Here in a 400 year old timber and flint barn he offers fantastic menus that change regularly. Here you will never be rushed either; the philosophy of the house is that a meal is best enjoyed at leisure. There is even a double room available for overnight accommodation, so go on - treat yourself. Ring for details, tel: 01353 661405.

On Main Street in the unspoilt Fenland village of **Coveney** is **Hill House Farm**, a 240 acre arable farm that offers comfortable bed and breakfast. Run by Hilary Nix the Victorian farmhouse has been tastefully modernised and has full central heating, with open views of the surrounding countryside. The two rooms available are both en-suite, have colour TVs and tea/coffee making facilities. There is, as you might expect, a first class cooked breakfast on offer every morning, and please note that there is no smoking and no pets. The farm also has self catering accommodation for six available.

Coveney is ideally placed for touring the counties of Cambridgeshire, Norfolk and Suffolk, situated, as it is, just three miles west of the historic cathedral City of Ely. The University city of Cambridge is just 17 mile away. Newmarket, Peterborough, Welney Wildfowl Refuge and Wicken Fen are all nearby.

Hill House Farm B&B, 9 Main Street, Coveney, Ely 01353-778369

Ely Cathedral and Market Square

From here, we leave the Cambridgeshire Fens, and cross into Norfolk and our next chapter.

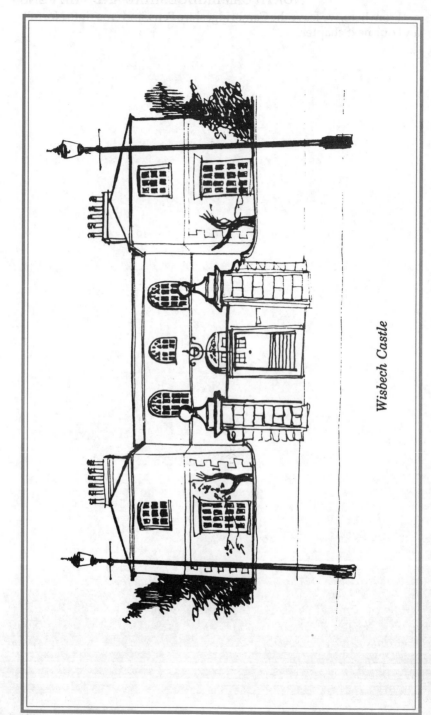

Wisbech Castle

44

CHAPTER THREE

King's Lynn & West Norfolk

Custom House, King's Lynn

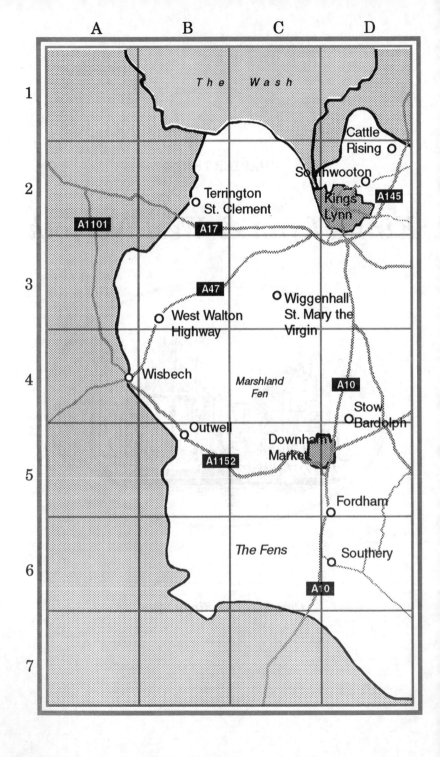

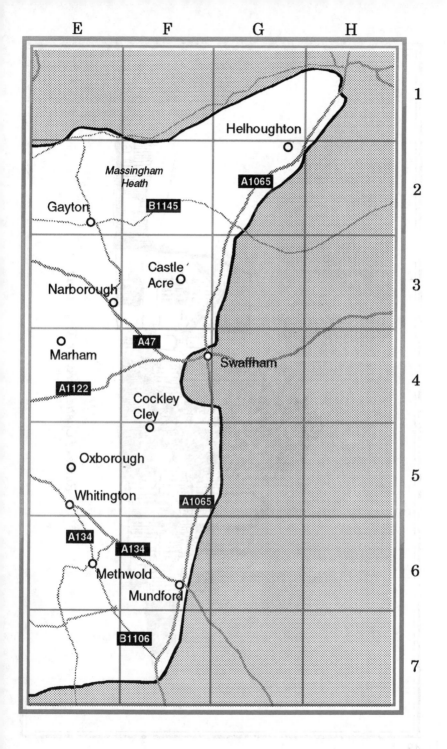

Ruins of Castle Acre, Nr Kings Lynn

King's Lynn & West Norfolk

For many people, a visit to Norfolk is limited to spending a week or two on the 'Broads', and like many others our first trip to the county was to experience a river-boat holiday, memories of the event recalled crowded waterways, cramped boats, muddy riverbanks and the incessant buzz of 'mosquitoes'. Therefore, we planned our next visit to Norfolk, determined to discover the true character of the county and to come away this time with a more comprehensive idea of the attractions it has to offer.

Thankfully, this return visit was to prove a far more rewarding experience, and we were delighted to find a place of surprising variety. There are gentle hills and expansive horizons - a far cry from the uniformly flat land we had been expecting to see - delightful pastoral scenes, a marvellous coastline rich in birdlife and with many solitary places where one can easily escape the crowds. Above, the great expanse of sky offers an unlimited vista - a blessed relief for those of us who are used to the cramped horizons of cities. Once you have experienced a perfect holiday under the deep blue Norfolk skies and have explored its many hidden villages and met the friendly folk who live there, you are sure to remember this part of England with a particular fondness.

We chose to begin our tour of Norfolk in **King's Lynn.** It is situated on the eastern bank of the River Great Ouse at the southernmost end of The Wash, and as the county's third largest town it naturally attracts many visitors. The approach roads from the south do not do the town any favours with their inevitable clutter of industrial estates, but once in the heart of King's Lynn you will find it to be a fascinating place, full of character and historical interest.

For centuries this ancient sea-port was the gateway to the Midlands and an important trade-link with the Continent. First mentioned in the Domesday Book as the harbour of Lena (from the Celtic word 'lindo', meaning lake), it became known as Lynn Episcopi or 'Bishop's Lynn' during the Middle Ages when the town was officially founded by Herbert de Losinga, the first bishop of Norwich. In 1537, after the Dissolution of the Monasteries, Henry VIII firmly quashed this ecclesiastical association by granting it a charter, and it took on its present name of Lynn Regis, or King's Lynn.

A previous charter had been granted by King John who visited the town in 1205, and it was on the occasion of his later visit in 1216 - prior to his final trip to Newark - that he 'lost his jewels in the Wash'. When travelling between his estates King John tended to take many of his personal treasures with him, and after enjoying the local hospitality of the people of King's Lynn in September of 1216, he decided to carry on to Swineshead. As his convoy traversed the estuary between Cross Keys and Long Sutton, the tide swept in unexpectedly fast and the royal wagons became embroiled in the treacherous quicksands. A historical event that has caused much merriment in history lessons at school, sounding as it does like an unfortunate mishap in the launderette.

Over on the Lincolnshire border, the King must have lost much of his spirit as he witnessed his beloved treasure sinking below the waters. The Crown Jewels, his formal regalia, goblets and candelabra, his coronation robe and the Sword of Tristram given to him by his grandmother all disappeared within a matter of minutes. Presumably, these treasures still lie out at sea waiting for some lucky diver to recover them, and to add insult to injury poor John contracted dysentery whilst in the town and later died at Newark. An alternative story claims that he fell ill at Swineshead after being given a dish of peaches and new ale, and some believe he was poisoned by a monk who had heard that the King intended to raise the price of bread.

The heart of King's Lynn encapsulates the Georgian era with many charming houses from that period, but the feeling you get as you stroll around is of a much older harbour town. Architectural treasures such as the National Trust-owned St George's Guildhall can be seen in King Street; it is distinctively built of flint in a chequer-board design and is reputedly the oldest hall in England, built around 1406. Shakespeare is said to have performed here, and it is gratifying to find that this splendid building is still used for civic functions and continues to enjoy an important role today.

The parish church of St Margaret's dates back to around 1100 and was founded by Bishop Herbert de Losinga. Particularly eye catching are the watermarks on the western towers. In 1953, a tremendous storm combined with an unusually high tide and succeeded in rising the North Sea way beyond its normal level. Vast tracts of land from Yorkshire down to the Thames area and even further down into Kent were affected, and the entire east coast was flooded. King's Lynn itself was engulfed, and the flood certainly left its mark on St Margaret's.

Other architectural highlights to look out for include the handsome Custom House, built in 1683 on the banks of the Purfleet, and the magnificent 15th century South Gates which stand proud at the entrance to the town. Buildings such as these, together with its many fascinating warehouses and narrow streets all add to the charm of King's Lynn.

Though it is by no means a pretty town thanks to the efforts of the King's Lynn Preservation Trust that many of the town's more interesting buildings have been saved.

With our love of the sea, it was a real treat for us to visit **True's Yard** in North Street. The cottages with their lobster pots and fishing nets strewn about outside really evoke the traditional feel of an old fishing village. Taking its name from Sir William True who owned the properties in 1789, this is the last remaining fisherman's yard in the town, and the North End Trust was specifically set up in 1987 to save it. Much restoration work was carried out, and today the Yard is often visited by school children and students as part of special educational projects, giving them a fascinating insight into the fishing trade of King's Lynn.

Among the attractions here are a 19th century fishing smack, a museum, a giftshop and a tea-room, and you can also enjoy guided tours of the fishing fleet. This would also be a wonderful place to spend an hour or two if you would like to trace your ancestry in the area, and plenty of help is at hand to assist you in this. Nearby stands the lovely medieval chapel of St Nicholas, the patron saint of all fishermen, watching over the yard and its people. Here, chandlers, boat builders, rope and sail makers plied their trade at the turn of the century, before the decline of the fishing industry closed that particular chapter in the history of the town. It is good to know that there are still people out there who care enough about the past to dedicate their time and efforts to keeping this important part of it alive.

True's Yard, North Street, King's Lynn 01553 770479

As you explore the town, look out for a curious brick, shaped like a diamond with a heart carved in the centre, in one of the walls of a house on the north-west corner of the Tuesday Market. Legend has it that an unfortunate woman named Margaret Read was pronounced a witch and condemned to be burnt at the stake in the market place. As the fires consumed her, they say that her heart erupted from her body and hit the wall in this same spot, and was later seen heading off down the street before bounding into the Great Ouse!

If you enjoy discovering what the local art scene has to offer then a visit to the **King's Lynn Arts Centre** will be most rewarding. The events and exhibitions change so regularly that it is impossible to single out any specific attraction, but it is certainly worth turning up to see what musical or artistic show is being staged here that particular week. Workshops and courses on landscape painting are available throughout the year, so if you are interested do write to the King's Lynn Arts Centre, 27-29 King Street, King's Lynn, Norfolk PE30 1HA for details prior to your visit.

There are plenty of excellent places to stay and eat in the town and we are sure that the following, all in easy reach of the town centre, will be of interest to our readers.

Gifford's Wine Bar is tucked away in a side street, a stones throw from the Custom House, the most famous of Lynn's wealth of historic buildings. The walk from the Saturday Market Place, taking in Nelson Street, to the Tuesday Market Place, which is probably one of the finest market squares in England, is full of splendid buildings that are testimony to the great wealth Lynn generated as a premier port from the 12th century. In 1722 Daniel Defoe noted that, excepting London and Bristol, Lynn imported more wine than any other port in the country. Several wine vaults remain under the town.

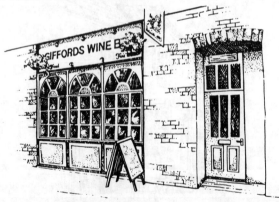

Gifford's Wine Bar, Purfleet Street, King's Lynn 01553 769177

What could be more appropriate, therefore, than to break your explorations at Giffords, owned and run by Alison Gifford. Purfleet Street is the link between the historic riverside and the new shopping precinct. This is not 'just' a wine bar. The range of coffees served is unusual, and there are scones, teacakes and home-made cakes in the mornings and afternoons. The lunches are good value with several vegetarian choices and Woodforde's Norfolk beer comes straight from the barrel.

Supper is served from 6pm. The food is unpretentious, the mood relaxed and friendly staff will ensure you enjoy your visit.

If you would like to sample Peking and Cantonese cuisine at its very best, we are pleased to recommend **Silk Road Restaurant** at 1A Railway Road. The menu here has been carefully planned to offer the true flavour and passion of the East, which you can enjoy in very pleasant and friendly surroundings. In addition to the Take Away service, Chinese Banquets for private functions are also available, with many dishes not listed in the menu. We were particularly impressed by the wide range of herbs and vegetables used to accompany all the main meals.

Did You Know...

The Hidden Places Series

Covers most of Britain?

For our full list see back of book

Silk Road Restaurant, 1A Railway Road, King's Lynn
01553 770942

If you are looking for accommodation close to the centre of town but far enough away to enjoy a bit of peace and quiet, we can wholeheartedly recommend **Stuart House Hotel** in Goodwins Road. Proprietors Irene and Norman Squires have created a genuinely friendly and relaxing atmosphere here, and the hotel is very comfortably furnished and spotlessly clean throughout. The accommodation consists of 21 well appointed bedrooms ranging from single to family rooms, most offering en-suite bath or shower room and all with colour television, radio, direct dial telephone and tea and coffee making facilities. There is a pleasant resident's lounge with cocktail bar where you can relax after a tiring day visiting some of the many local attractions, but we have no doubt that one of your fondest memories of the hotel will be of the time spent in the delightful restaurant. Here you can enjoy a superb Full English Breakfast and evening meal, making your selection from the wide variety of dishes on the a la carte and table d'hote menus. The food is very reasonably priced and a good range of wines is available to accompany your meal.

Stuart House Hotel, 35 Goodwins Road, King's Lynn   01553 772169

Two miles northeast of King's Lynn town centre, we came to the peaceful residential area of **South Wootton**. Those looking for traditional-style accommodation in this delightful part of West Norfolk should look here for the **Grange Hotel** in Willow Park. This handsome Edwardian building stands in 2 acres of landscaped gardens and was formerly the centre of a 27-acre estate founded in 1910 by a prominent local gate maker. Much of the internal woodwork and decorative features are original giving the hotel a wonderful period feel. Owners Jeanne and Roy Spicer provide their guests with first-class hospitality and service. Excellent meals are served in the dining room, and the spacious en suite bedrooms are all appointed to a high standard.

The Grange Hotel, Willow Bank, South Wootton Lane, King's Lynn
01553 673777

Caithness Crystal is based on the outskirts of the town at Oldmellow Road on the Hardwick Industrial Estate and is well worth a visit if you wish to purchase the beautiful crystal ware on offer there. A conducted tour will take you on a fascinating trip around the factory, allowing you a closer look at the intricate art of glass blowing, hand cutting and the skill of the polisher. After your tour and an opportunity to purchase some of the fine work on display (which you can have engraved while you wait) you may like to relax over a cream tea. The centre is open from March to December and no booking is required.

Leaving King's Lynn on the A1078 and heading northwards through South and North Wootton respectively, we decided to stop and explore

54

the romantically named **Castle Rising**. The impressive castle with its huge earthworks is very popular with visitors to this part of Norfolk, and to get to the keep you must first cross a brick bridge spanning a surprisingly high 'ditch'. Strikingly rectangular and remarkably well preserved, you do not need to use your imagination very vividly to conjure up a picture of what the building would have looked like in its heyday. The sheer substance of it, the steep flights of stairs leading up to the interior of the keep, and its splendid position on a lofty mound to the south of Castle Rising village - all this gives the impression of a virtually unassailable stronghold.

The castle was built in the 12th century and has enjoyed a distinguished history with many kings and queens having stayed there. The castle is open daily except Mondays in winter, and those who enjoy the spectacle of knights on horseback will be pleased to know that medieval tournaments are held here during the summer months.

Before the sea receded during the Middle Ages, it was possible to navigate the River Babingley from the Wash to Castle Rising, and indeed the village was a busy port at that time. It remained an important town and borough right up until the 17th century, and one of the best buildings in the village, Trinity Hospital, dates from that era. This is a group of low, red brick almshouses, founded in 1614 by Henry Howard, the Earl of Northampton, to provide accommodation for poor spinsters, and it continues to operate as such today.

The Post Office, Castle Rising 01553 631211

You don't really need an excuse to pop into a post office, as you always need to buy stamps and postcards when you are away on holiday. However, in **The Post Office** at Castle Rising, you can also sit down to write your postcards and enjoy a pot of tea and a plate of cakes during the summer. Main post offices in big towns, please take heed! This is one of those wonderful little places where everyone knows each other and stops to pass the time of day, much to the delight of inquisitive visitors like us who get to hear some interesting snippets of conversation! You can also stock up here with fresh vegetables, local books of interest and gifts to take home with you. If you fancy something stronger than tea, you can always pop into the pub next door! Run by Dennis and Frances Fretwell, The Post Office was converted from three 400-year-old cottages, and as you would imagine it is quite the hub of life in the village. We couldn't help thinking that it must be great fun to work there!

If you head west from King's Lynn on the A17, you will shortly come to the village of **Terrington St Clement,** which is set right in the heart of the Terrington Marsh, a lush area of farmland. A sure sign of the village's prosperity is the splendid church of St Clement's - as sturdy and ornate a place of worship as one could wish to find. Inside, the fittings are superb, with a Georgian screen, various features from the Jacobean period and an impressive 17th century font cover with beautiful illustrations from both the Old and New Testaments. Small wonder that the church is often referred to as the 'Cathedral of the Fens'! However, opportunities to view this fine interior would appear to be somewhat governed by chance, as the church has become neglected over the years and is often found to be locked up.

As one would perhaps expect in such a fertile area, there are two places of interest in Terrington St Clement which are sure to appeal to all those who enjoy working in their gardens.

Most people will not need an introduction to the conifer as many of us probably have one or two varieties in our gardens. However, a visit to the **Ornamental Conifers & Heathers Centre** in Terrington St Clement will give you an insight into the enormous range of sizes, shapes and colours that these plants come in, with over 200 varieties to choose from. The centre offers visitors a chance to discuss any problems they might have, and provides help with designing your own garden, using appropriate plants. In addition to conifers, they stock heathers, carpet juniper and many other ground cover plants. We thought it made a nice change to see a landscaped area which really gives you an idea of what they will look like in situ!

To find the centre, turn off the A17 following signs to the African Violet Centre, then turn right at the end of the road. Take the first left, go past the village sign and turn left again at the BP garage. Bear right at the chip shop and you will find the centre at the first bungalow on the right down Chapel Road.

Ornamental Conifers & Heathers, Chapel Road, Terrington St Clement 01533 828874

The African Violet Centre is a nursery unique in Britain, specialising solely in the production of African violets. Founded in 1970 by author and broadcaster, the Reverend Tony Clements, some quarter of a million African violets are grown here annually, in a wide range of colour and type. The plant breeding programme ensures a constant stream of new varieties, and these may be seen and purchased both at the Centre itself and at the principal flower shows held throughout Britain each year.

For many one of the great delights of exploring this part of the county is discovering the wonderful churches scattered throughout the local villages. The church at Walpole St Peter is thought by many to be the most beautiful of all the churches in England, and indeed its glorious interior makes it more deserving than most of the name 'Cathedral of the Fens'. Walpole St Andrew's church has an intriguing little chamber - most probably an anchorite's cell - set in the west wall, and like so many places of worship in the region, the pure light from the Marsh streams through the windows and lights up the interior to great effect. We always think it is the little things that capture the imagination, and at St Peter's you should look out for the vicar's 'all-weather' shelter which is used when conducting a particularly wet funeral!

St Peter's also has a rather poor effigy of a local character known as 'Tom Hickathrift'. Said to have been a giant, the grave at Tilney where he is purported to be buried would put him at around 7ft tall. When still a young lad of 10 years of age, he had apparently already reached a height of 6ft, and yet it seems that he was more renowned for his stupidity than any other distinguishing feature. He was born during the reign of William the Conqueror, and there are various accounts of his great strength. One of his tasks was to deliver beer kegs to Wisbech from King's Lynn, and he decided to take a short-cut across land belonging to a fearsome giant. Predictably enough, the giant emerged from his lair to challenge the intruder, and after a fight of epic proportions, Tom eventually defeated the creature. Discovering a hoard of treasure in the giant's cave, Tom came out of his adventure both victorious and rich and from that day on, locals always referred to this 'great' hero as Mr Thomas Hickathrift!

If, like many, you enjoy a prime beef steak but are unhappy with the additives and chemicals that seem to be encroaching into our meat these days, then you will certainly appreciate the meals at **Stratton Farm**. Derek and Sue King run a working beef farm here at Walton Highway, and the many prizes that their cattle have won are testimony to how successful they have been. The farm is situated in 22 acres of land and supports a small herd of Shorthorn cattle. Derek and Sue are more than happy for their guests to wander around and look at the way the farm is operated. Here too, you can stock up for your freezer, with sides of pork with no anti-biotics and no added copper. Sausages, beefburgers and

57

steaks are all available, and all joints can be cut to your requirement. Derek believes in hanging the beef for at least a fortnight to give it a chance to mature, so it is really tender when you come to cook it.

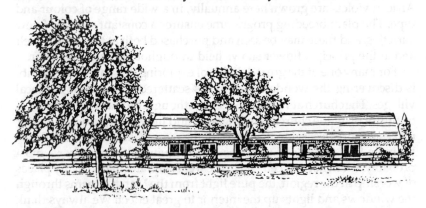

Stratton Farm, West Drove North, Walton Highway 01945 880162

Accommodation is in three en-suite rooms, all with colour television, full central heating and tea and coffee making facilities, and one of the rooms has been designed especially for wheelchair users. Guests can enjoy a dip in the covered heated swimming pool in summer, and there is also a small carp lake in the landscaped garden. It should also be noted that this is strictly a non-smoking establishment. To find Stratton Farm from King's Lynn, take the A47 to Wisbech, then turn right at the Little Chef roundabout, following signs to **Walton Highway.** Turn right again in quarter of a mile, go through the village past two pubs, then turn left into West Drove North after the Robin Hood. A private drive to the farm is half a mile further on to your left.

Admirers of church architecture will find plenty to marvel at in the surrounding villages, many of which seem to favour a position in the latter pages of the telephone directory. After the Walpoles and Walton Highway, we pass through **West Walton** and **Walsoken,** and definitely began to suspect a conspiracy when we came to **Wiggenhall St Germans, Wiggenhall St Mary Magdalene, Wiggenhall St Mary the Virgin** (watch out for the superb bench-ends here) and **Wiggenhall St Peter** (with its ruined but romantic church).

South of the Wiggenhalls are the two charming villages of **South Runcton** and **Runcton Holme,** both quiet backwaters, and just beyond **Thorpland** we came across the handsome **Wallington Hall.** The Bell family built this imposing Elizabethan house in 1525, and above the gateway you can make out a carving of bells as a rather neat architectural pun.

Further south on the A10 is **Stow Bardolph** with its splendid park, fine dwellings and restored Hall, and inside the Holy Trinity Church is a most amusing and unusual effigy made of wax. Open up the large mahogany cupboard and the life-sized figure of Sarah Hare is revealed. A beauty she most certainly was not: she appears to be covered with boils. The daughter of Sir Thomas Hare, Sarah died in 1744 as a result (so it is said) of pricking her finger while sewing on a Sunday. Divine retribution or tetanus, we wondered? Apparently the figure is remarkably like its original, and the gown she wears was chosen by her sometime before her death - which made us suspect that she may have had a premonition of her unfortunate demise.

Nearby **Wimbotsham** is worth a detour if only to admire the carved bench-ends depicting various animals at St Mary's church, and from here we made our way to **Downham Market**. Once the site for the great horse fairs, this striking market town stands on the very edge of the Fen and is built of the distinctive brick and Carr- (or iron-) stone. One of the finest examples of this can be seen at Dial House in Railway Road (now a guest house), which was built in the late 1600s, and it is encouraging to note that even with some of the modern housing, this same material is being used.

High as the town is, the parish church is situated on even higher ground and is well worth a visit to admire the splendid glass chandelier which dates back to around 1730. Another feature of the town much loved by postcard manufacturers is the elegant if overly embellished cast-iron clock tower in the market place. This was built by William Cunliffe in 1878 and its backdrop of attractive cottages makes the perfect setting for a holiday snap.

Viscount Horatio Nelson was born in the Norfolk village of Burnham Thorpe and came to Downham Market to be educated, while one of his school friends, Captain George William Manby, lived both in the town and at Denver Sluice. We have Manby to thank for his invention of the life saving shore-to-ship rocket line. He served for some years as Barrackmaster at the naval yards in Yarmouth, and wrote extensively on methods of life saving, criminal law and other diverse subjects.

The Castle Hotel in Downham Market is a striking building with a rich mixture of architectural styles. Its traditional tile roof, castle-like facade and classical portico command your attention immediately, and these are offset by a lovely splash of colour from the hanging baskets and flower troughs which adorn the walls. The stylish interior of the hotel really appealed to us with its warm colours and attractive furnishings. The accommodation comprises 15 well appointed bedrooms, most of which offer private bath and/or shower together with full central heating, colour television, direct dial telephone, electric shaver points and complimentary beverage trays. The choice also includes four-poster suites and one room with its own jacuzzi bath.

Guests can enjoy superb home-made food in the elegant yet relaxed atmosphere of the restaurant, which is also open to non-residents. An a la carte and table d'hote menu are available together with a good range of wines, or you can simply pop in for a traditional cream tea. The Castle began its life as a coaching inn 300 years ago, and although it can now offer banqueting facilities for up to 100 people, it still retains an intimate, welcoming atmosphere where guests receive plenty of individual attention.

The Castle Hotel, Downham Market 01366 384311

Heading south out of Downham Market on the B1507, we went in search of the **Daymond Services** boat hire company.

Boats for hire from Daymond Services, 4 Spruce Road, Clackclose Park, Downham Market 01366 384404

At **Denver** village, we drove west for two miles towards the River

Great Ouse and found them in a lovely situation at Denver Sluice, next to the Jenyns Arms pub and just upstream from the river's tidal limit. From here you can look out at the swans, and if you are very lucky, the occasional seal. From this point, it's possible to reach over 200 miles of inland waterways from Cambridge in the south, to Bedford in the west. Frank and Heather Daymond have greatly expanded their fleet since they established their boat hire operation in 1986. They are now able to cater for everything from an hour's trip in a rowing boat to a full week's hire of a four berth Beaver canal boat. As a small family firm, they pride themselves on the standard of their craft and the quality of their personal service.

In the past, the inhabitants of these low lying lands must have constantly kept an eye out for heavy rains, for the fens could so easily become awash - meaning certain death for cattle and great destruction of crops. Since the Roman occupation engineers had turned their attention to the problem of drainage, but it was not until the 17th century that the Dutch engineer, Cornelius Vermuyden, had any degree of success. As part of a scheme to drain around 20,000 acres of land owned by the Duke of Bedford, he built the first sluice at Denver in 1651. Various modifications were made to the system over the years but the basic principle remains the same, and the oldest surviving sluice - built in 1834 - is still in use today. Opened in 1964, the new Great Denver Sluice runs parallel with this, and together they control the flow of a large complex of rivers and drainage channels and are able to divert floodwaters into the Flood Relief Channel that runs alongside the Great Ouse.

The two great drainage cuts constructed by Vermuyden are known as the Old and New Bedford Rivers, and the strip of land between them - no more than one kilometre wide at any one point - is called the Ouse Washes. This is deliberately allowed to flood during the winter months so that the fields on either side remain dry. The drains run side by side for 22 kilometres, from Denver to Earith in Cambridgeshire, and this has become a favourite route for walkers, with a rich variety of bird, animal and insect life for naturalists to enjoy. Keen birdwatchers may like to stop off at the village of Welney, where there is a visitor centre run by the Wildfowl Trust, and hides are available.

A couple of miles south of Denver, just off the A10, lies the attractive village of **Hilgay** with its charming market square. A beautiful avenue of lime trees sweeps up to All Saint's Church, and here we found the tombstone of Captain Manby (suitably embellished with a carving of a ship and anchor), who was church warden at one time.

On the banks of the River Wissey in the village, we discovered the delightful **Crosskeys Riverside Hotel**. These fine old buildings started life as a coaching inn in the 17th century and now form a superb hotel

61

offering comfortable accommodation in a peaceful setting at the gateway to West Norfolk. There are five tastefully decorated en-suite bedrooms, three of them offering the additional luxury of a four poster bed. The hotel has retained much of its original character, particularly in the dining room with its old oak beams and inglenook fireplace, and here you can make your selection from the wide choice of dishes featured in the a la carte and table d'hote menus. Boating on the river is available and owners Alan and Christine Bulmer also have a coarse fishing license for the use of their guests. We thought this would be the perfect setting for a country break and the ideal base for walking and touring in Norfolk.

Crosskeys Riverside Hotel, Hilgay 01366 387777

Between Hilgay and the neighbouring village of **Fordham** lies the 17th century Snowre Hall, which can be admired from the outside. Its sleepy atmosphere belies the fact that it has also played its part in English history: Charles Stuart having hidden here in a secret room before his final trip to Newark.

A short distance to the south-west of Hilgay, on the other side of the Great Ouse, is a little village called **Ten Mile Bank**. Here, **The Windmill** is a must for those who enjoy the sport of angling, for enthusiasts gather here from all over the region to take part in competitions. You can purchase tickets for a day's fishing and enjoy the lively river scene, with plenty of wildlife and small craft jostling for mooring space. This 160-year-old pub stands next to a bridge which used to be a toll bridge, although there is no longer any sign of the windmill from which the pub takes its name. After a few hour's fishing or a pleasant walk along the riverbank, you can stop off at The Windmill for a snack at the bar or a good steak in the restaurant. Jan and Lee Pack run a delightful riverside pub which is well worth a visit when you are in the area.

The Windmill, Ten Mile Bank, Downham Market 01366 6445

Heading south-east from here on the B1386 across the Southery and Methwold Fens, we came to the sprawling village of **Feltwell** with its two fine churches, then took the road south to the particularly pretty village of **Hockwold cum Wilton**. The handsome red-brick Hockwold Hall was built by the Heveningham Family following the familiar E-plan and is a fine example of its kind.

We were now approaching that part of East Anglia known as Breckland, some 300 square miles of sandy heathland which have been liberally planted with Scots and Corsican pine by the Forestry Commission, mainly to stabilise the thin soil. One of the strangest natural features of Breckland are the many meres or pools that appear regularly throughout the region. No matter what the mean rainfall has been, a mere will well up seemingly overnight and then later disappear, all subject to the level of the water table in the chalk below the heath. William the Conqueror set up camp in this wild country while ferreting out the native Saxons under the leadership of Hereward the Wake.

Although **Weeting** village is undistinguished (apart from its 12th century moated castle which is maintained by English Heritage), the surrounding area is rich in archaeological sites - this is, after all, the earliest inhabited part of Norfolk. Weeting Heath is also a marvellous spot for birdwatchers, although you need to be a true enthusiast as you may only observe the birds from the hides dotted around this lovely part of Breckland. The area is well known for its plant and animal life as well as its great variety of birds, and permits may be obtained from the warden from April to August. To find the site, take the Weeting road heading towards Thetford.

Some three miles to the east of Weeting off the A134 you will come to **Grimes Graves**; not graves at all, in fact, but a series of Neolithic flint mines which are now managed by English Heritage. This is a fascinating area and we had certainly never seen anything quite like it; the massive site covers around 30 acres and contains over 300 pits and shafts dug by early man using deer antlers as picks some 4,000 years ago. It is probable that Breckland was at that time covered by an immense oak forest, and flint tools would have been in great demand by Stone Age farmers for clearing the land. The region, in fact, takes its name from these small areas of cultivated land called 'brecks' or 'brakes'. Some of the shafts at Grimes Graves have been excavated and you can descend one of these to see the galleries 30ft below. There is also a museum which houses artifacts that have come to light during the excavations, and the surrounding area has been designated a Site of Special Scientific Interest due to the great variety of bird life to be found there.

Heading northwards on the A134, the village of **Northwold** caught our eye with its distinctive cottages, many of them built from local chalk

63

and several painted with delightful pastel washes. We can recommend a visit to the parish church of St Andrew's, which boasts one of the few surviving Easter Sepulchres in the country; dilapidated but beautiful, it dates back to the latter part of the 14th century.

A little bit tricky to find, but well worth the effort, is **Oxburgh Hall**, a National Trust property lying midway between Thetford and King's Lynn. To reach it, turn off the A134 at Stoke Ferry and drive a couple of miles north-east in the direction of Swaffham. Oxburgh Hall is a beautiful moated house, built around a courtyard by the Bedingfeld family in 1482 and remodelled many times since. The entrance is guarded by a massive Tudor gatehouse. From its roof, it is possible to see for miles across the surrounding Norfolk countryside. In the courtyard, look out for the large sundial; the face was refigured in 1965. The internal rooms reflect the varied history of the house - the King's Room (so called because Henry VII stayed here in 1487) is cool and starkly furnished, the Saloon is a fine example of 18th century neoclassical opulence, and the library has a comfortable mid-Victorian feel. Don't leave without seeing the exhibition of needlework hangings, some of which were worked by Mary Queen of Scots during her captivity in England. These hangings, formerly a family heirloom, are now lent back to the house by the Victoria and Albert Museum. Outside, it's worth making a circuit of the moat before visiting the chapel, with its magnificent altarpiece, and the garden, with its orchard, beautiful herbaceous borders and immaculate French parterre.

Oxburgh Hall, Oxborough 01366 328258

Before the Black Death in the 14th century, **Oxborough** village (the Hall has adopted the shorter spelling of the name) was situated a mile away on the River Wissey and was once an important port exporting grain and agricultural produce. Today, the large green at the centre of the village is the location for three interesting buildings: Oxburgh Hall itself;

the 14th century parish church of St John the Evangelist which is famous for its 16th century early-Renaissance terra-cotta monuments in the chantry chapel; and the historic Bedingfeld Arms inn which was probably once a coach house to the Hall.

The Bedingfeld Arms is now a bustling free house owned and run by Trevor and Sue Shoat. Since taking over in 1990 they have managed to create an atmosphere which is relaxed and welcoming for both visitors and locals alike. Inside, the inn has lost none of its original character and charm. Trevor and Sue serve a first-rate pint of beer and an excellent range of meals, either in the bar or in their attractive 24-seater restaurant. In fine weather, customers can sit outside in the beer garden. Look out for the pub sign showing the family crest of the Bedingfeld family.

The Bedingfeld Arms, Oxborough 01366 21300

If you take the road out of Oxborough heading north-east towards Swaffham, you will find something rather out of the ordinary at the charming hamlet of **Cockley Cley** (pronounced 'Cly'). The original **Iron Age Village** occupied by the Iceni tribe was destroyed around 60AD, but in 1971 a reconstruction of this was built on the original site, to the south of the present village. A diverted stream forms a rectangular moat around the timber palisade, enclosing a 'village' of thatched huts and long houses. The museum complex here features a 15th century cottage and forge which houses the East Anglian Museum, and you can see a fine collection of agricultural engines and farm implements and explore the nature trail which runs alongside the stream. Incidentally, the restored St Mary's Church at Cockley Cley is thought to have been built around 628AD, which makes it one of the oldest churches in England.

There is another St Mary's at nearby **Beachamwell**, a delightful thatched church with a round Saxon tower to which an octagonal top was later added. Watch out for the column where the masons scratched the figures of a demon and a woman in the 14th century when the church was being rebuilt. To the north of the village you can see part of the 'Devil's Dyke', an ancient earthwork which is generally thought to be a territorial boundary dating back to Saxon times.

At **Fincham**, some four miles to the north-west on the A1122 Downham Market to Swaffham road, the church - yet another St Mary's! - has an unusual square Norman font. An oddity which stands resolutely on five miniature doric pillars, its somewhat crude carvings represent Adam and Eve, and the three Magi bearing gifts. The Fincham family lived in the Tudor hall which you can catch a glimpse of from the main road.

While we were in the village, we discovered **Timbers Motel.** This listed 18th century building is beautifully situated amongst mature trees, and the timber-clad walls from which it takes its name give it plenty of character. In addition to comfortable accommodation, Brian and Val Robinson offer an excellent range of meals in the restaurant and snacks are also available in the bar. The whole establishment has a very welcoming atmosphere, and a lot of care has obviously gone into making the house and gardens as attractive as possible. The first thing that struck us as we arrived at the motel were the colourful hanging baskets and the well tended borders, and this attention to detail is reflected throughout the establishment.

Timbers Motel, Shouldham Thorpe Road, Fincham 01366 47747

Further north lie the villages of **Shouldham** and **Shouldham Thorpe.** It is hard to believe that sleepy Shouldham was once a busy market town with two annual fairs and boasted a Gilbertine priory, a grammar school and the Silver Well, a famous natural spring. Today, it is a much quieter place with its collection of old dwellings, some thatched and some with red or blue pantiles, clustered round the village green. From the abundance of archaeological finds made in the immediate area, it would appear that Shouldham has been inhabited since Neolithic times.

Quite apart from the churches, religious buildings of one sort or another seem to abound in this part of the county. At **Marham** you can see the ruins of a Cistercian convent situated on a farm opposite the church, while further north at **Pentney**, the sparse remains of a 12th century Augustinian priory can still be made out in the form of a cross and a gatehouse. To the east of the A134 at Wormegay, you may noticed a distinctive grassy mound on the village green, which is all that remains of a once proud motte-and-bailey castle.

Middleton village, just over two miles south-east of King's Lynn on the A47, features a handsome brick house surrounded by a moat known as Middleton Tower, a reconstruction built in 1860. The gate tower is considerably older; dating back to the mid-15th century, it is part of the original house built by Lord Scales, the author of the first publication to be printed in England by William Caxton.

Heading east on the A47 towards Swaffham, we came to **Narborough** where you can see the remains of an Iron Age settlement in the grounds of the great Hall. Sir Henry Spelman who wrote the 'History of Sacrilege' lived at Narborough Hall and the parish church of All Saints has some splendid monuments to the Spelman family. Sir Henry was born in Congham and was High Sheriff of Norfolk in 1604. Along with several other ponderous tomes he also wrote the 'Glossarium Archaiologicum' - but we suspect more people may be familiar with his son Sir John Spelman's work on the life of King Alfred. Narborough is a charming village, enhanced by a picturesque bridge spanning the River Nar and by the old village mill which has been refurbished as a trout farm.

Just off the B1153 to the north of Narborough is **East Walton,** where there is an oven situated on the village green. However, this particular 'oven' is in fact an old wheelwright's oven, where the metal 'treads' or strips would be heated and stretched before fitting them on to the wooden waggon wheels, making them virtually indestructible. Those of you interested in the geological make-up of Norfolk will find East Walton of particular interest, as the common to the west of the village (referred to as the Ramparts) boasts distinctive physical features attributable to the Ice Age. These 'pingos' were formed when great bubbles of ice expanded, pushing the earth aside and leaving hollows and mounds when the thaw set in. This created a boggy habitat where many rare species of plant now flourish.

To the east, half way along the Peddars Way long-distance walk, stands the spectacular hillside village of **Castle Acre**, set around a green and standing within the outer Bailey of a ruined Norman Castle. (For those of you who are less energetic, it is situated three miles north of

Swaffham, just off the A1065.) In Bailey Street you will find the former pub, **The Old Red Lion,** which is unusual in that it is both a charming guest house and an independent hostel where accommodation and self-catering facilities are provided. It is privately run by Alison Loughlin, renowned for her vegetarian cooking and for her ability at creating a unique, congenial atmosphere.

The Old Red Lion, Castle Acre Staging House, Bailey Street, Castle Acre   01760 755557

Standing on the top of the hill to the east of the village, the original Castle was founded by William de Warenne, the Earl of Surrey, shortly after the Norman Conquest. At that time it was really nothing more than a robust private dwelling, and was not seriously fortified until the middle of the 12th century.

Castle Acre is generally considered to be the 'jewel' of Norfolk's many picturesque villages. The approach from the south leads you through a narrow stone gateway (built in the 13th century to defend the northern entrance to the Castle) and on to the village green. Many of the village's attractive cottages are of local flint, much of it no doubt taken from the castle when it was abandoned, and we were pleased to note that modern building has been largely sympathetic.

Eating out in Castle Acre will present no problem, for we discovered the wonderful **Castlegate Restaurant** in Stocks Green. Run by two genuine 'characters', Rex and Alan, this place is a real find. It could be said that these two gentlemen have their fingers in a lot of pies, as they sell a good range of these, all made on the premises!

Castlegate Restaurant, Stocks Green, Castle Acre   01760 755340

The restaurant commands one of the best positions in the village as it overlooks the green, near to the 18th century Ostrich Inn amidst a pleasant clutter of houses and shops. We can thoroughly recommend their pies washed down with a good hot pot of tea, but if you wish for something more substantial they have a full table d'hote menu. They are open every day for lunches - which is a relief when you are desperately looking for somewhere to eat on a Sunday - and evening meals are served from Wednesday to Saturday. It is definitely worth popping into the Castlegate Restaurant, even if all you require is a cup of coffee and a bit of cheering up!

In a grassy hollow to the west of the village is Castle Acre's other fascinating historic building, Castle Acre Priory, now in the care of English Heritage. Although now in ruins, this superb 12th century priory still creates an imposing atmosphere - especially the mighty west front of the church. Many of the original priory buildings came through the Dissolution surprisingly intact; including large parts of the church, the Prior's Lodging, various agricultural buildings and the gatehouse. We particularly enjoyed taking a stroll round the charming walled herb garden, and greatly appreciated the free personal stereo guided tour which is included in the admission price.

While we were in the village we discovered two further places well worth remembering if you are looking for accommodation here. Open all year, **Gemini House** is a cosy bed and breakfast establishment in Castle Lane, run by Gill Clarke. The house has a comfortable and relaxing atmosphere with four guest bedrooms available, one of which is en-suite. We thought from the name of the house that Mrs Clarke might have an astrological preference for guests with elements of air in their birthsigns, and as we are Capricorn and Libra, at least one of us is suitable! Whatever your horoscope, one thing that might well tempt you to stay here for a night or two is the breakfast, for Mrs Clarke serves up trout when it is in season. This is a treat that you rarely find in a Breakfast Menu, even at the larger hotels!

Gemini House, Castle Lane, Castle Acre 01760 755375

If you are looking for comfortable accommodation in a real family atmosphere, then we can unreservedly recommend **No. 5 St James Green** in North Street. Eileen and Bill Pratchett offer an excellent bed and breakfast service in their pleasant family home and you will find them to be the most genial of hosts. Two cosy rooms are available, both with colour television and tea and coffee making facilities. The situation here is quiet and peaceful, yet central to most of the attractions that Norfolk has to offer. You know that your comfort is assured the moment you step through the door and find a welcome pot of tea and biscuits ready and waiting for you. Eileen and Bill regret that pets cannot be accommodated.

No. 5 North Street, St James Green, Castle Acre 01760 755581

It was at Castle Acre that the Peddars Way crossed the River Nar via a ford, taking travellers on to Holme-next-the-Sea. (Unlikely as it may seem today, this little stream was, incidentally, once large enough for boats to navigate from the Wash.) We will meet this ancient path again in future chapters, as it starts at Knettishall in Suffolk and covers some 95 miles before arriving at the Norfolk coast. Built around 61AD, it is a text book example of the straight-as-a-die Roman road and has caused a great deal of head scratching among historians due to the fact that it seems to end rather abruptly in the Wash!

Its name is derived from the Latin word 'pedester', which means to travel on foot. A guide can be obtained from the Countryside Commission, and although you are not likely to lose your way on such a straightforward route, the guide does provide some interesting background details and gives warning of those places where the army might be training! Walkers of all ages and ability can enjoy the Peddars Way as it crosses very gentle terrain, and if you take the time to walk the whole of its length you will witness a unique cross-section of the rural delights of Norfolk and Suffolk.

Taking a lane that leads north-west from the village, we made our way across Massingham Heath to **Great Massingham**, just north of the B1145. This is a peaceful little place where time seems to stand still. We were told that the ponds on the village green where ducks now harass passers-by for titbits may well be the pools once used to stock fish for the Augustinian priory that was founded here in the 13th century. Vestiges of this building (long since disappeared) can be seen at Abbey House, and St Mary's Church is notable for its lovely 13th century south porch and 15th century hammerbeam roof.

We always enjoy a good ghost story, and were pleased to hear a rather intriguing one connected with Raynham Hall at **East Raynham,** a village on the A1065. The 'Brown Lady' is said to roam about the estate - a rather terrifying woman, elegantly dressed, but with no eyes! What is stranger is that she originally manifested herself at nearby Houghton Hall, but is thought to have moved to Raynham when the sister of Robert Walpole (who lived at Houghton) wed Viscount Townshend. She has been sighted on several occasions, including once in 1926 when a member of the family saw her drifting down the stairs, and 10 years later when she apparently posed for a photograph. However, it could be that she has since moved on, as a figure dressed in brown is reported to have been seen travelling the lanes between the villages of South and West Raynham. A well travelled spirit indeed.

Castle Rising

Custom's House, Kings Lynn

CHAPTER FOUR

North Norfolk - Babingley to Holkham

Norfolk Windmill

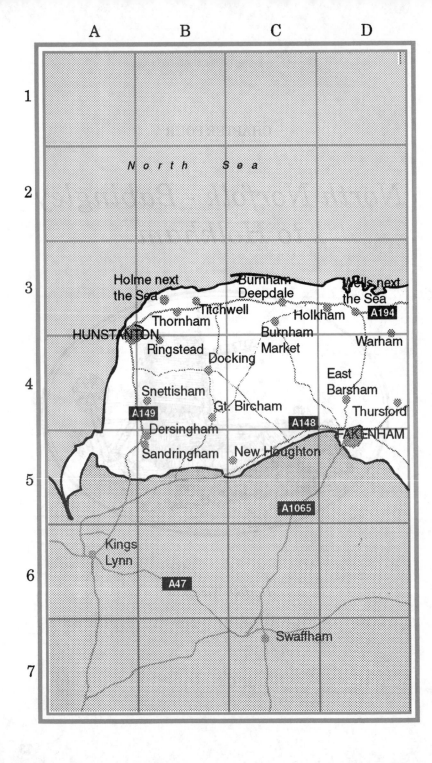

North Norfolk - Babingley to Holkham

We begin our exploration of North Norfolk one mile to the north of Castle Rising in the little village of **Babingley,** just off the A149 coast road and right on the edge of the Sandringham estate. You could be forgiven for driving straight through Babingley without noticing anything particularly remarkable about it, but one thing you should look out for is the village sign featuring a saint and a very special beaver.

In the fields to the west of the village stands the 14th century ruined church of St Felix, said to be the site of the first Christian church in East Anglia. This was founded in 630AD by St Felix, and legend has it that he crossed the sea from Burgundy in safety only to be shipwrecked in the Babingley River. The story goes that the saint was saved by beavers swimming in the river at the time, and such was his gratitude that he made their leader a bishop! The village sign at Babingley commemorates the legend most strikingly, showing St Felix and his ship with two beavers sitting above him, one of them sporting a crook and a mitre. The sign, by the way, was the work of a very talented man who we will meet again later on in this book.

Sandringham itself lies five miles to the north-east of King's Lynn on the B1440. It is of course known far and wide for its Royal connections, and no one should visit Norfolk without a closer look at one of the Royal Family's favourite residences. The Sandringham Estate was purchased for Edward VII in 1861, when he was still the Prince of Wales. Covering 7,000 acres in all, it encompasses seven villages and dominates the life and economy of the surrounding countryside. It takes its name from the sandy soils of the surrounding Country Park - it was originally known as Sand Dersingham. The house is comparatively modern, having been built between 1869-71 to replace the original Georgian building which burned down.

Sandringham became a firm favourite with the society set during the 49 years that Edward VII was in residence: he transformed it into a popular and lively place with a fine reputation for the excellence of its shooting. It has been the birthplace of several members of the Royal family: the Queen's father and her three uncles and aunt were all born at

Sandringham House

Sandringham, as was Princess Diana when her father, the late Earl Spencer, held the position of equerry. One of the few people to remain singularly unimpressed was Edward VIII: he apparently loathed the place and spent only one night there in his lifetime.

You enter the grounds through an oak door in the outer wall. The profusion of colour here during the spring and summer quite takes your breath away. Before you reach the drive leading up to the Norwich Gates (a wedding present to Edward VII from the people of Norfolk) look out for the striking and unusual 'handkerchief' tree. Another surprise is the golden Buddha who sits in contemplative splendour in the more recent part of the garden, designed by Geoffrey Jellicoe for George VI. The house itself has a cosy, friendly atmosphere about it and is open to the public except between 20th July and 8th August, when the Royal Family is in residence.

There is also a museum here with a fascinating collection of Royal photographs and vintage motor cars, and when you have had your fill of the sights there is a cafeteria to sustain you. Tucked away in a corner of the park is the tiny, medieval church of St Mary Magdalene, home church of the Royal Family. It contains many private memorial brasses, and perhaps the most memorable of its treasures is the solid silver altar and reredos, presented in 1920 by the wealthy American, Rodman Wannamaker.

An impressive list of heads of state and members of foreign royal families have stayed at Sandringham over the years, including the Kaiser, the Tsar and many others. They would have arrived at the little railway station at Wolferton, two miles to the west of the house, where their hosts waited to receive them. Wolferton Station is now an intriguing museum filled with royal memorabilia, including - of all things! - Queen Victoria's travelling bed. It is all set out on one level, and although space is fairly confined with small steps in the doorways, access to wheelchair users is possible.

The road leading northwards from Sandringham take us to the neighbouring carrstone village of Dersingham. Here in the church of St Nicholas you will find some impressive tombs and a remarkable carved chest of great antiquity, decorated with the symbols of the Evangelists. The ancient gabled tithe barn opposite the church dates back to 1671 and is now used by the county council as a storehouse for fragments from historic buildings. We only hope that they have kept up the payments on their insurance policies!

Another interesting building in Dersingham is **The Gameskeepers Lodge** in Chapel Road: a truly charming establishment with plenty of character and a friendly, relaxed atmosphere. Full credit must go to the proprietor Mr Massen, who has spent the past 18 months refurbishing the Lodge to give it a wonderful 'countryfied' feel, making it a splendid place to stop off for a drink and a meal. Mr Massen has devoted many years to his pursuit of collecting postcards from all over West Norfolk, and has even had a book published on the subject. A number of cards from his collection have been enlarged and are displayed on the wall; and quite apart from adding to the decor of the Lodge, they offer a fascinating insight into the way that Norfolk has been represented to the tourist over the years.

The restaurant here is very attractive indeed, with an excellent a la carte menu featuring a superb range of fish, meat, poultry and vegetarian dishes. One of the Chef's Specialities that particularly caught our eye was the fresh salmon and prawns cooked in butter and white wine and served in a cheese sauce - a dish described as a 'Salmon Princess', but fit for a queen in our opinion! In addition to the restaurant fare, bar snacks and daily specials are also available, and even though all the food is distinctly upmarket, the prices are very reasonable. There is a fine selection of wines to accompany your meal, and if you are looking for somewhere special to eat out as the highlight of your holiday, you need look no further. To make things even better, accommodation should also be available now, and there is no doubt that these facilities will be of the same high standard as the rest of the Lodge.

The Gamekeepers Lodge, Chapel Road, Dersingham 01485 543514

While you are in Chapel Road it is also well worth popping into **Dersingham Pottery** if you enjoy seeing skilled craftsmen at work; while the gardeners among you will probably want to pay a visit to Thaxters Garden Centre where a large selection of bulbs, heathers, ornamental trees, magnolias and many other plants can be purchased.

As you are passing through this picturesque village, the **Coach and Horses** is guaranteed to catch your eye. Mr Ashley must be exceedingly proud of this 17th century inn, which has lost none of its charm and character over the last 300 years. There are three rooms to let for those that do not wish to continue their journey after sampling the superb food and quality ale on offer. Staff extend maximum hospitality, and children are most welcome. The Coach and Horses is ideal for both the traveller and for a relaxed and friendly lunch out with the family.

The Coach and Horses Inn, 77 Manor Road, Dersingham
01485 540391

This area of sandy heathland has marvellous views of the marshes and sea, and is ideal for the cyclist with its large open vistas and excellent roads. If you would like to experience a holiday where you can leave your car behind and enjoy plenty of fresh air and healthy exercise, you could book a weekend or longer with **Norfolk Cycling Holidays**, Sandy Way, Ingoldisthorpe. The holiday comes complete with a fully equipped cycle with large panniers (or you can bring your own cycle if you like), detailed route maps, accommodation at affiliated bed and breakfast establishments, and information on the places of interest you will see on your travels. Children are welcome and parties of up to 12 people can be catered for - so why not take your mother-in-law and Great-Uncle Herbert along for a memorable holiday! Telephone (0485) 540642 for details.

Arriving at the sprawling village of **Snettisham**, our attention was immediately drawn to the medieval stone spire of St Mary's Church which soars 175ft high. St Mary's was mentioned in L.P. Hartley's charming novel, 'The Shrimp and The Anemone', which was later made into a film. It is a popular church, much loved by the locals and visitors, and we could certainly appreciate why this is so. The exquisite tracery in the magnificent west window is truly beautiful. Other interesting features of this lovely 14th century church include circular seats set around the tall pillars of the nave and an oven that was once used to bake the communion wafers.

Right in the centre of the village, all but concealed by a wall and a fine procession of limes, is the gabled Old Hall, a handsome William and Mary residence which has been given a new lease of life as a Sue Ryder Home for the disabled. As you explore the village you may notice that several of the local businesses have the word 'Torc' in their names - we found out that this is a reference to the treasure trove of Iron Age torcs or 'collar' necklaces fashioned in gold which was discovered in the area.

One of the great attractions of Snettisham is **Park Farm**, which is definitely worth setting aside a few hours to visit. This really is a super place for the children, although it has been cleverly geared to appeal to all members of the family. If you follow the blue trail with the accompanying leaflet - which is an hour long walk - you will be led on a voyage of discovery, exploring the hedgerows and fields and finding out all about how the farm operates. Near the lakes in St Thomas's meadow, you can take a safari ride and get closer to the grazing herds of red deer. The red trail guide takes you on a longer walk that will definitely appeal to the amateur naturalist; while the yellow trail will take you to the site of an Iron Age farm and to a Roman villa on a wooded rise, and just above the river are the traces of an early Saxon settlement.

The Visitor Centre contains many fascinating artifacts and lots of interesting information, and we thought that the whole venture was absolutely superb. You could spend many hours here and come away having learnt all sorts of things about our ancestors that you didn't know before. There is also a playground, a gift shop, plenty of opportunities to see the many working animals, and a tea room serving light refreshments. All this adds up to one of the best farming attractions we have come across in our travels to date.

Park Farm, Snettisham 01485 542425

Heading off westwards towards the beach we followed the tourist signs to Snettisham's charming water mill, which dates back to around 1800. Here visitors may watch the mill in action, grinding the corn at several daily demonstrations. After taking a stroll around the delightful gardens (which feature a waterfall and a picturesque millpond much loved by the resident waterfowl) you can make your way past the caravan parks and chalets to explore the R.S.P.B. nature reserve. This is set out around a disused shingle pit overlooking the Wash and gives you the opportunity to view many species of migratory birds.

As far as accommodation in the large nearby seaside village of **Heacham** is concerned, be sure to make enquiries at **Holly Lodge**, which stands in one and a half acres of land right in the heart of this picturesque village. It is a delightful 400-year-old residence with graceful Tudor chimneys rising majestically above it. Once lived in by monks, today it is owned by Mrs Piper who has provided a restful haven for weary travellers here for many years. There are six comfortable en-suite bedrooms, some with four-poster beds and all with their own individual charm. The house retains many of its original features, including a sweeping staircase with an unusual wooden and metal balustrade, a beautiful ceiling in the reception area, and an exposed brick wall in one of the bedrooms showing an old feature fireplace. A superb a la carte menu is available in the restaurant, which is also open to non-residents, and you can choose from a fine selection of wines to accompany your meal.

All the rooms at Holly Lodge are spacious and bright, and throughout the house you will find fine antiques, comfortable furniture, and tasteful pictures adorning the walls. If you are looking for a place to stay where elegant surroundings and the charm of an earlier age exist side by side with the full range of modern day comforts, we can recommend Holly Lodge most highly.

Holly Lodge, Heacham

Before you leave the village you must make a point of visiting Caley Mill, the home of **Norfolk Lavender**. It is England's only lavender farm, and to get the best out of your visit we would suggest you join one of the information tours. These take place daily from the end of May to September. The times are posted on the notice boards at the entrances. It is a most remarkable place. The National Collection of Lavenders enables you to study the different colours and sizes of the lavender varieties. Some of them have been bred at the lavender farm and others have been obtained from other gardens, nurseries or individual enthusiasts. We were told that Caley Mill aims to establish the definitive plants for each variety.

There is a wonderful herb garden, which has been laid out to show the many varieties of interesting herbs in popular use today. It includes culinary, aromatic and decorative plants. Situated on the ground floor of the 19th century water mill, there is a magnificent gift shop stocking a full range of Norfolk Lavender products, plus numerous other gifts with a countryside theme. As well as plants, the Conservatory shop also sells many attractive gifts for the keen gardener. The Miller's Cottage Tea Room, with its open log fire during the colder months, specialises in home-made cakes, biscuits, cream teas and light lunches. During the summer you can buy drinks, ice creams and other items from the Purple Kiosk. From mid-June until the end of Harvest, a mini-bus runs several times a week to take visitors up to one of the lavender fields. And during the Harvest, you can visit the distillery and see how this wonderfully aromatic fragrance is produced.

Norfolk Lavender, Caley Mill, Heacham 01485 70384

Sitting in a little valley two miles to the east of Heacham on the B1454 is the pretty village of **Sedgeford.** This is another wonderfully peaceful place, with some attractive cottages and a church that dates back mainly to the 13th century with a round Saxon tower.

While we were here we decided to pop into the **King William IV** pub for a quick bite to eat. We were lucky to find ourselves in a pub which is very popular - and no wonder, as hosts Rick and Glen East have put a lot of effort into making this a cosy place to relax. The food is great, so good in fact that many of the residents from local Bed & Breakfast establishments are advised by their hosts to come here for lunch or an evening meal, and they are never disappointed.

Very reasonable prices and an unpretentious menu means that

everyone will find something to their liking on the menu. A comprehensive wine list accompanies the food and includes a Chilean Santa Helena, which we thought might be interesting! We wondered how many of the Bed & Breakfasters come in to top up their breakfast and enjoy a King William IV late breakfast special! A fine selection of ales will please those who like trying out local brews, and a pleasant combination of locals and those passing through makes for a friendly and lively atmosphere. The King William IV has been operating as a pub since 1836, and although no accommodation is offered inside, if you come here with your tent bag under your arm you are welcome to pitch it in the field at the back of the pub.

King William IV, Sedgeford   01485 71765

Hunstanton (pronounced 'Hunston') was our next stop along the A149 coast road; a charming Victorian seaside resort (the only one in East Anglia to face west, incidentally) with a fine sandy beach and rock pools and distinctive candy-striped cliffs. A layer of white chalk, then red limestone, and finally brown and yellow stone make these 60ft high cliffs particularly interesting to geologists. At the northern end of the Promenade, next to the 1830 disused lighthouse, you will find the ruins of St Edmund's Chapel where Edmund, King of East Anglia, is reputed to have landed in 850AD.

The Sea Life Centre on the Promenade is a super place to take the children. Here you can get a really close look at the varied and often weird forms of life that inhabit our British waters, with the Ocean Tunnel giving you a unique opportunity to view this fascinating marine environment without the bother of getting wet!

Many of these creatures can be observed and handled in the 'Living Touch' rock pools, and there is also an exciting audio-visual presentation which tells the story of man's involvement with the oceans. The Centre is open throughout the year and will appeal to young and old alike.

Just three minutes walk from the centre of **Hunstanton** brought us to **Fieldsend House** in Homefields Road, a spacious carrstone house built at the turn of the century. In this magnificent house, visitors seeking bed and breakfast accommodation can spend a comfortable night or two in the tastefully decorated bedrooms, which all have central heating, hot and cold wash basins, and glorious sea views across the Wash. When you wake refreshed in the morning, you can enjoy a superb full English breakfast in the charming oak panelled Dining Room.

If self-catering accommodation is more to your taste, then you have definitely come to the right place. The holiday apartments on the ground and second floor of the house are extremely well equipped and you will find everything you need here for a most enjoyable holiday. The upper apartment offers a splendid panorama across the sea, while the lower apartment has a patio area and views over the garden. Although this is one building, entrances to both apartments are separate, so you have total privacy. Each apartment can sleep 4/5 people and is handsomely furnished, with full central heating. Another bonus is that you do not have to bring your own linen with you as it is provided, and milk and paper deliveries can be arranged too.

Children are most welcome at Fieldsend House, with cots and highchairs provided - but do note that the accommodation is not suitable for pets. This is a really first class establishment and we congratulate Sheila Tweedy-Smith for maintaining the house to an extremely high standard.

Fieldsend House Hotel and Self-Catering, Homefields Road, Hunstanton 01485 532593

Elegant villas overlook Hunstanton's green, and even though past glories such as the pier, the railway and the impressive Sandringham Hotel have disappeared, visitors are still left with a very pleasing impression of this gracious town. The local gentry for hundreds of years were the Le Strange family, who did much to develop the town. Their residence was the handsome moated Tudor Hall to the south of St Mary's church in Old Hunstanton. The family's hereditary title was Lord High Admirals of The Wash, giving them the rights to anything washed up on the shore, or found out to sea as far as they could ride a horse at low tide and throw a spear. No doubt they kept their fingers crossed that King John's jewels might reappear at some time!

Entertainment at Hunstanton is plentiful and varied, and visitors of all ages are well catered for. During the summer months you can take a boat trip out to the sandbank in the Wash known as Seal Island, where seals can sometimes be spotted sunbathing at low tide. Old Hunstanton lies half a mile to the north of the town; a lovely old fishing village, its quiet beach well protected by banks of sand dunes.

In a region which is well-stocked with excellent nature reserves, the one on Ringstead Downs to the south of Hunstanton Hall is especially rewarding. The chalky soil of the valley is the perfect element for the plants that thrive here and the beautiful butterflies they attract. **Ringstead** village itself is simply charming; with wonderfully decorative Norfolk carrstone and pink and white-washed cottages.

Ringstead Gallery, Ringstead, Hunstanton 01485 25316/25530

If you find browsing in an art gallery a fulfilling way of spending an afternoon, then you will certainly enjoy a visit to **Ringstead Gallery**. Exhibitors have include Godfrey Sayers with his beautiful, evocative paintings of the local countryside, where he hints rather than defines. Peter Barker has a completely different perception of the Norfolk coast and captures the shifting seasons to great effect. Margaret and Don

Greer's gallery is housed in a 250-year-old stable adjacent to the Gin Trap Inn. They opened the gallery in 1974 and have established a fine reputation for the high standard of the paintings they exhibit there. Open all year round every day except Sundays, it should not be missed.

The Greers also have two holiday cottages called 'Pickles Patch' and 'Tumblers' at **Sedgeford Road Farm**, just a short stroll from the Ringstead Downs with its beautiful, unspoilt woodland. The cottages are well appointed and 'Tumblers' was once an old cart shed housing 'Tumbler' carts, while 'Pickles Patch' was formerly the stables. These charming dwellings have all the modern amenities you could possibly require, and both have been thoughtfully designed to give access to wheelchair users.

The Village Stores in Ringstead High Street is run by Iris and John Lindsay, and here you may pop in for a stamp, stationary, local maps, coffee, bread, and all the essentials for a self-catering holiday. Next to the shop is the tea-room, where you can choose from a fine array of home-made cakes and scones, while a welcome cup of tea will quench your thirst. There is also self-catering accommodation in four spacious and attractive rooms above and to the rear of the Stores. This was opened in February 1991 and consists of a spacious kitchen, an elegant sitting room with colour television and hi-fi unit, and a large private garden leading to playing fields with swings and slides for the children. This would make a lovely place to stay, especially with the knowledge that all the provisions you are likely to need are literally on your doorstep!

Ringstead Village Stores, tea-room & Self-Catering, 41 High Street, Ringstead 01485 25270

While we were in the village we met up once more with the Peddars Way, so it would appear that the local claim that 'all roads lead to Ringstead' is no word of a lie! Two miles further north at Holme next the Sea, this ancient path joins the Norfolk Coast Path and leads you through the splendid heritage coast of North Norfolk, all the way to Cromer. This part of the county has quite justifiably been designated an Area of Outstanding Natural Beauty.

If you do decide to walk or bike along the path, look out for the acorn symbol which will be familiar to all those who regularly use the National Trails. Signs will give you directions to either the 'Peddars Way' or the 'Coast Path', and as we mentioned earlier, with some 95 miles to explore in all, a guide will prove to be invaluable. The Peddars Way Association (150 Armes Street, Norwich NR2 4EG) can provide you with a list of places to stay including campsites, and both walkers and bikers should set off well prepared for variable weather conditions. Pack a sweater no matter how glorious a day it might be - the sea winds can be chilly - and wear sensible footwear if you are planning to travel any distance as some parts of the path can become quite water-logged. Worth mentioning too is the fact that several sections provide good access for the elderly, wheelchair users and those with frames or sticks: these are marked on the official guide maps.

At **The White Horse** inn at **Holme next the Sea,** you have the opportunity to sample some of that succulent Norfolk Ham we hear so much about. Paul and Sue Middleton are third generation landlords and now it is 1992, the pub has been in the family for 50 years - which must surely be some sort of record! Built in the 1600s as a farm and stables, the pub has lost none of its original charm. Each of the three rooms is bright and airy, with old oak beams and plenty of character. All the food is freshly prepared, ranging from ploughmans to steaks, and the daily specials tend to favour fish dishes. There is also a children's choice for the under 12's.

The White Horse, Holme next the Sea   01485 25512

Locals still talk about that day in December 1626 when, with the wind blowing strong from the north-west, an unfortunate whale was washed up on the shore. Around 57ft long, its carcass was to make £217-6s-7d profit for the village. We are pleased to report that whale meat will definitely not appear on the White Horse's menu, although they do a very good Seafood Platter!

If you want to reach the beach at Holme you have to make your way across the golf course at Hunstanton, and from the beach road a track will take you out across the marshy shoreline to the Holme Dunes Nature Reserve and the Holme Bird Observatory. Permits for both are available from the wardens, and from here you can observe many rare species on their spring and autumn migrations.

Our next stop on the A149 is **Thornham,** a particularly charming village with its cottages of flint and chalkstone, and the tiny harbour and quiet beaches here are a wonderful place for those who enjoy exploring unspoilt coastline. If you are interested in birds, you will soon discover that this particular stretch of the coast is the habitat of a great variety of species. Whether you are here for the birdwatching, the glorious walks, or just to enjoy the peace and quiet, if you are looking for self-catering accommodation then we would strongly recommend that you take a look at the cottages at **Manor Farm.**

Manor Farm Cottages, Ringstead Road, Thornham 01485 512272

Four delightful cottages - Sandpiper, Sanderling, Little Gull and Little Tern - have been appointed to a very high standard. Everything appears to have been thought of, with modern facilities such as fitted kitchens with electric cooker, microwaves, colour television, a separate laundry room with tumble drier and a pay phone. Bed linen and tea towels are provided free of charge. Built from local chalkstone, the cottages are most attractive inside and stand in four acres of land which guests are free to explore at their leisure. Each cottage has its own patio area with barbecue, and being single storey, Little Gull and Little Tern would be ideal for someone who cannot manage stairs. Owners Michael and Anita Goddard have recently added a games room with table tennis and pool, and also a pitch and putt course.

Thornham's buildings can boast a wide variety of architectural styles; from the Red House at the southern end of the village, a mainly 18th century house with much older parts at the back, to the striking Victorian school in glorious Gothic style at the western end. One of Thornham's best known residents was the acclaimed lady blacksmith, Mrs Ames Lyde, who died in 1914. This skilled craftswoman created many fine pieces of decorative ironwork in her forge, including the garden gates at Sandringham.

Pretty **Orchard House** in Thornham is tucked away at the end of a private drive, surrounded by two acres of restful mature gardens. Behind the orchard which gives the house its name, a small wooded area has been left to mature, to encourage wildlife and birds to make it their home. The Rutlands have gone to great lengths to create a welcoming, relaxed atmosphere at Orchard House, and those guests who prefer a clean, smoke-free environment will be pleased to note that smokers, although welcome, are asked to refrain from indulging in their habit in the house. The bedrooms are spacious and tastefully decorated and provide all the usual modern conveniences, including razor points, vanity units and tea and coffee making facilities. There is also a ground floor room which would be ideal for elderly or disabled guests. In addition to a substantial breakfast, an evening meal is available by prior arrangement - or you may want to dine out at one of the three charming 'Olde Worlde' inns in the village. If you prefer self-catering accommodation, a five-berth caravan is available in the grounds from March - October.

Orchard House, Thornham 01485 26259

This particular stretch of the Norfolk coast does not tend to suffer from great hordes of holiday makers, so you should be able to enjoy a walk on the beaches in virtual isolation. Be warned, however, that when the great flocks of migratory birds rally in spring and autumn, the birdwatchers suddenly appear in their hundreds armed with binoculars and note-books!

Many of these will be making their way to **Titchwell,** the next village along from Thornham on the A149. Perhaps befitting the village's name, the church of St Mary is quite tiny, and very pretty indeed. Its round (probably Norman) tower is topped by a little 'whisker' of a spire, and inside is some fine late-19th century glass.

The Briarfields Hotel in Titchwell is a shining example of what can be done given enough time and an enormous amount of effort. When Derrick and Ros Hibbert bought this two-and-a-half acre site in 1986, all that stood here was a group of derelict barns. Apart from employing an electrician to complete the job, Derrick undertook all the building work himself, and just two years later they were able to open their doors to guests, having created the magnificent establishment we see today.

The spacious lounge area is brick walled with a handsome feature fireplace, and the original beams came from the Colemans building in Norwich. The restaurant is in a class of its own, from the leaded windows which overlook the RSPB reserve and the sea to the personal table settings. The menu offers a comprehensive choice of traditional home cooked dishes which feature locally caught fish, and plenty of fresh produce is used. We can vouch for the fact that the food is excellent, and all dishes are prepared under the personal supervision of the proprietors.

There are 15 en-suite bedrooms in all, a number of them situated outside the main building in two magnificent courtyards which are separated by wrought iron gates. The centrepiece of one of the courtyards is a fountain while the other has a decorative pond, and in the evening both are floodlit and make a magical place for a stroll. A superb wooden staircase leads to the upstairs bedrooms in the main building. All the rooms are spacious and beautifully decorated, some having four poster beds. In addition to the serviced accommodation, Derrick and Ros can also offer two self-catering cottages with all the facilities you will require for a comfortable stay, and three more cottages are currently being planned.

Whether you come to Briarfields to stay or simply to enjoy a meal, your every need is catered for from the moment you arrive to the time that you (reluctantly) depart. The Hibberts are wonderful hosts and work hard to ensure that all their guests have a memorable visit. In our opinion, they have made this establishment into one of the best on the Norfolk coast, and we wish them well with all their future plans.

Briarfields Hotel & Restaurant, Main Street, Titchwell
01485 210742

Just to the west of the village is a path that will lead you to Titchwell Marsh, a nationally important RSPB reserve comprising some 420 acres of shingle beach, reed beds, freshwater and brackish marshes and salt-marsh. These different habitats encourage a wide variety of birds to visit the area throughout the year, and many of them breed on or around the reserve. Brent geese, ringed plovers, marsh harriers, terns, waders and shore larks may all be seen, and we were pleased to note that two of the three hides available are accessible to wheelchair users.

Back on the A149 we continued eastwards through **Brancaster**, then on to **Brancaster Staithe**. Here we discovered that boats may be hired for trips out to Scolt Head Island, a remote sand and shingle bar of about three-and-a-half miles in length, separated from the mainland by a narrow tidal creek. The island is a haven for terns who flock there to breed. The nature trail takes you past the ternery (which is closed during the breeding season of May, June and July) and on to a fascinating area where a rich variety of plant and wildlife abounds: during the summer the sea asters, sea lavender and sea pinks put on a colourful display, and many different types of moths and butterflies may be observed.

Next we came to the Burnhams. We do not intend to describe each one in detail, as there are seven of them in all! There appears to be no discernible break between Brancaster Staithe and **Burnham Deepdale**, its neighbouring village on the A149. The pride of the village is undoubtedly the parish church of St Mary's, which contains what is widely held to be one of finest Norman fonts in Norfolk. Cut from a single block of stone, this square font is carved with 12 individual figures, each hard at work on a different task for each month of the year.

Just off the main road a mile and a half to the east is **Burnham Norton**, a near-perfect little village unravaged by time and modern development, which stands on a hill with views across the fields and salt-marshes to the sea. Some way to the south of the village is St Margaret's Church, where you will find the most glorious 15th century wineglass pulpit. Appearing to balance precariously on its slender stem, its colourful panels depict the four Latin Doctors, and although it is no longer in use it continues to grace the church as a beautiful object to be admired.

Across the River Burn after a sharp bend in the A149 is **Burnham Overy Staithe**, a delightful place almost solely concerned with sailing: there is an annual regatta and facilities for windsurfing too. Look out for the restored tower mill, now a private residence, which stands to the side of the main road just before you enter the village. There is a very attractive harbour here, and boat trips to Scolt Head Island are available. The harbour lies on a creek some distance from the sea - indeed, it could be said to have followed the sea northwards in a manner of speaking, as Overy Thorpe was built after the sea receded from the original port of Burnham Overy. This lies a mile to the south on the B1155 and is now referred to as Burnham Overy Town.

Phil and Barbara Conway have celebrated over 25 years at **The Hero Public House** at Burnham Overy Staithe. Over 150 years old, the building was named after Admiral Nelson, and is one of the snuggest and friendliest eating houses we have come across. The decor is rich tones of red and dark wood, while a magnificent display of burnished brass around the fireplace adds a lovely warm glow to the rooms. The centrepiece of the collection is a 1936 fireman's helmet, and our hearts went out to whoever has the task of polishing all this!

The Hero Public House, Wells Road, Burnham Overy Staithe
01328 738334

Phil and Barbara originally hailed from Oldham in Lancashire, but seem to have settled very happily in this part of Norfolk. They offer a substantial range of traditional fare, ranging from toasted sandwiches to pizzas, good hearty plates of cod, plaice and chips, salads and ploughmans - in other words, simple, tasty food that the whole family will enjoy.

Indeed, the whole pub is unpretentious, and although the exterior is plain, everything inside is cosy and very welcoming. As for your hosts, you could not wish to meet a more friendly, down to earth couple than the Conways. If you wish to stay in the area, they can provide self-catering accommodation in a three bedroomed house which is open all year round, and they also have a caravan that can be hired throughout the holiday season.

The origins of 'The Hero' himself can be found at **Burnham Thorpe** two miles south-east of here, for this is where Lord Nelson was born in 1758. His father, the Reverend Edmund Nelson, was rector of All Saint's church, and although the rectory itself was demolished in 1802, there are many mementoes of the great admiral in the church. This stands in a glorious setting on the banks of the River Burn, and among the various items of 'Nelsonia' inside, look out for the cross and lectern which were both made from timbers taken from HMS Victory. Those with a fascination for maritime history will no doubt also enjoy visiting the Lord Nelson Inn, where Burnham Thorpe's most famous son enjoyed a number of celebration dinners. Nelson was just 13 years old when he embarked upon his naval career in 1770, and became a rear admiral at the age of 39. His success at the Battle of the Nile made him a national hero, and he died at the age of 47 after his crushing defeat of the French fleet at the Battle of Trafalgar.

North-west of here is the largest of the Burnhams, Burnham Market, which now contains the parishes of Burnham Westgate, Burnham Sutton and Burnham Ulph. This newly created market town is centred around a large green surrounded by grand Georgian houses and flint cottages. Around the battlements of the church tower, those of you with excellent eyesight (or binoculars!) will be able to make out a little gallery of biblical scenes.

In the Market Place is the delightful **Fishes Restaurant** which specialises in all manner of sea food, including smoked varieties. With the coast so near, the shellfish is naturally absolutely fresh and we found some succulent dishes for those who enjoy the fruits of the sea! These include crab soup, smoked fish pate, and oysters baked or in their shell, as well as some smoked meat dishes. For the main course, there is fresh lobster when available, monkfish, salmon and halibut, and as the restaurant is licensed they stock a good range of wines to accompany your meal. Gillian Cape has run Fishes' for an amazing 18 years, and the excellent reputation that the restaurant enjoys is well deserved. With its relaxing atmosphere, comfortable cane furniture and attractive prints and paintings, this is a super place to drop into to enjoy a first class meal while visiting the town.

Fishes' Restaurant, Market Place, Burnham Market 01328 738588

Leaving the Burnhams behind us we headed south-west on the B1155 towards the **Birchams**, a smaller group of villages tucked away in a series of hollows. The first is **Bircham Tofts**, where the church of St Andrew's stands in ruins and is almost completely hidden behind a blanket of ivy. Next is **Great Bircham**, situated on the edge of the Sandringham Estate, and here we came across the **King's Head Hotel** by the side of the B1153. This fine building dates back to 1860 and despite all its modern facilities, the hotel has a dignified and traditional atmosphere about it.

Owners Iris and Isi Verrando have put heart and soul into making the King's Head a truly welcoming establishment, and we think they have succeeded admirably. There is a rather charming air about the place and it has certainly found favour with 'Them up at the Big House', for several members of the Royal Family have popped in for lunch! We cannot guarantee that you will be keeping company with a princess or a duchess if you decide to do the same, but we can tell you that the food will be first class.

The Lodge Restaurant offers a superb a la carte menu, and there are also many daily specials to choose from. Dishes such as Oak Smoked Scotch Salmon and Fillet Mignon with an excellent grain mustard sauce, accompanied by a fine range of wines, will find favour with the most discerning of guests; and if the heavenly aroma emanating from the kitchen is anything to go by, you will certainly not be disappointed.

With five well appointed en-suite bedrooms, a resident's lounge, welcoming log fires, a large garden and two comfortable bars, this would make an excellent base from which to discover the huge range of holiday attractions in this unspoilt part of the county.

The King's Head Hotel, Lynn Road, Great Bircham 01485 23265

As we mentioned earlier, it always gives us great pleasure to take time off to visit an art gallery, and in Church Lane we were delighted to find the **Bircham Art Gallery and Sculpture Garden**. Not just paintings and prints, but books, post-cards, ceramics, sculpture, watercolours and posters are all housed in a traditional brick, flint and pantile roofed cottage. Gallery owner Christopher Harrison specialises in modern British and Contemporary East Anglian Fine Art, and a visit here is sure to end in success with additions to your collection.

Bircham Art Gallery & Sculpture Garden, Church Lane, Great Bircham 01485 23604

Christopher studied fine art and art history at Leeds and Reading Universities, so the man definitely knows his art! A practising artist himself, he moved to Norfolk in 1988 and his paintings capturing the

95

Norfolk countryside are based on a more fundamental approach than simply transferring the scene to canvas. He believes in expressing the feelings that are generated from the visual senses and is a master at free expressionism in watercolour. The fantastic sculptures in the garden surrounding the gallery are an absolute delight. Sculptures in bronze, stone, wood and ceramic all have their part to play in the outdoors setting, and you will definitely feel more inspired after taking a stroll around the garden.

While you are in Great Bircham it is certainly worth taking time out to visit **Bircham Windmill**, which can be found on the B1155 about half a mile outside the village heading towards Snettisham. This is undoubtedly one of Norfolk's finest corn mills, and surrounded as it is by acres of unspoilt countryside, you could not wish for a more beautiful setting. The mill has been in use since the 1700s and if you are not afraid of heights, it is well worth climbing the five floors to see the milling machinery in action. It is certainly a long way to the top (and seems even further to the bottom!) but as you make the ascent you will find something interesting to look at on every level. On the ground floor, there are video displays and plenty of information on the history of the mill and the working of the machinery.

Another fascinating aspect of the mill is the small bakery where, on open days, you can buy bread and rolls which have been baked in the old fashioned way. The 200-year-old brick coal-fired oven was designed to bake over 100 loaves at a time, and still works today as good as new. You can also see many of the original baking utensils on display here.

After scaling the heights of the mill, it is good to come back to earth and enjoy a pot of tea with home-made cakes in the tea rooms. No ordinary tea rooms either, but Egon Ronay recommended; and as they are separate from the mill they can be enjoyed at any time, except Saturdays when they are closed. While you are here, you can also peruse the Gift table and choose from a fascinating selection of items connected with milling and baking. We thought that this would be an ideal opportunity to pick up an unusual present for a friend or a relative.

In the old days, horse and cart was the mode of transport used by the miller and baker for their deliveries, and three ponies are still kept in the stables today, with occasional pony rides available for younger visitors. A marvellous way of enjoying this peaceful countryside is by bike, and cycle hire is available from the mill at hourly, daily or weekly rates. Day routes and traffic-free green lane routes are provided, together with a range of bikes to suit all ages and requirements.

Bircham Mill is open daily from May 20th until the end of September, and from Easter on Sundays, Wednesdays and Bank Holidays. Free parking is available and coaches and school parties are welcome by prior arrangement. If you require any further information on the mill or cycle hire, the number to call is 0485 23393.

Bircham Windmill, Great Bircham 01485 23393

Just a mile to the north on the B1153 is the last of the Birchams, **Bircham Newton**. Here you will find further connections with Lord Nelson in the hauntingly beautiful Saxon church, where there is a monument on the south wall of the chancel to his grandson, the two-year-old son of his daughter Horatia.

Some three miles south-east of Great Bircham is perhaps the most magnificent house in the county, **Houghton Hall**. This was built in the 1730s for Sir Robert Walpole, Britain's first Prime Minister, who decided that Houghton village rather spoilt the view and had it relocated to the edge of the estate. He did, however, leave the church where it was - presumably not wishing to disturb the resting place of his ancestors. The Hall is neo-Palladian architecture at its very best, and the finely furnished staterooms are packed full of delights. It is one of the first houses where mahogany was used extensively throughout, and best of all is the enormous Stone Hall, undoubtedly one of the finest rooms in England.

Joining the A148 and heading east, we passed through **East Rudham** with its broad green surrounded by handsome 18th century houses and shops, then turned off the main road to Tattersett. The church here has some particularly grisly wall paintings depicting an unfortunate saint being disembowelled. In a field opposite the church you can see the scant remains of Coxford Priory, which was founded by the Augustinians.

Back on the A148, we carried on for another four or five miles to Fakenham. Famous for its National Hunt racecourse, **Fakenham** is a busy and distinctly well-to-do little market town and an important agricultural centre for the region. There are a number of fine late-18th and early-19th century brick buildings in and around the Market Place, and

97

it must surely be one of the few towns in England where the gasworks has been turned into a museum.

If you take the B1355 to the north-west of Fakenham you will shortly come to the Creakes. **South Creake** is a pretty village of flint cottages with the River Burn flowing quietly alongside the main street - some of the residents have to cross their own little wooden footbridges when entering and leaving their homes. Towering above the cottages in the centre of the village is one of South Creake's most interesting and incongruous sights: a truly hideous collection of dilapidated buildings that were originally built in the 1920s as a razor blade factory.

The factory owner was one George Theophilus Money, a London-born entrepreneur whose business sense failed to live up to the expectations of his name. It does not take a business degree to work out that the key to success in selling razor blades lies in their inherent disposability, but George would have none of this - instead, he offered to sharpen his customers' old ones! Needless to say, his factory was not in business for very long.

A mile and a half up the road is the larger of the twin villages, North Creake, and here again you will meet the little River Burn - more properly called a creek - from which both villages take their name. To the north of the village are the substantial ruins of Creake Abbey, a 12th century Augustinian monastery ravaged by fire and plague, now in the hands of English Heritage.

On the B1105 two miles north of Fakenham is **East Barsham**. As you approach the village from this direction you are rewarded with the most glorious visual feast, for here stands the magnificent East Barsham Manor. This splendid early-Tudor mansion was built by Sir Henry Fermor around 1520 and is testimony to the great skill of those 16th century brickmakers. The lavish ornamentation of moulded brick, the vertical buttresses and the embattled south front are all superb, but perhaps the most striking feature of the building is the group of 10 chimneys - all individually carved with an amazing variety of designs.

The White Horse Inn at East Barsham is a handsome, traditional pub, popular with those who are visiting Walsingham with its Anglican and Catholic shrines. Prior to the reformation, Henry VIII stayed at the neighbouring manor house before making his own royal pilgrimage to Walsingham.

Chris and Lillian Baines have run this 17th century inn for the past five years and it has been completely refurbished to maintain its original character. Low ceilings and a magnificent log burning inglenook fireplace are complemented by a pleasing clutter of memorabilia scattered about the place, including bygone farm tools, shining brassware and a fine display of dolls that many collectors would give their eye teeth for!

A small quarry-tiled flight of steps leads you from the bar area into the outstanding Stable Restaurant, where original beams and old saddles and other 'horsey' bits and pieces adorning the walls make this a cosy place to relax and enjoy some of the fine dishes of the day. An extensive menu is available seven days a week and sandwiches, steaks, chilli, home-made pies, pasta and a traditional Sunday lunch have made this a popular haunt with the locals. Here too we found the unusual 'Barsham Batters', which we had never encountered before - platters of good old 'Yorkshire Pud' filled with chicken, steak and kidney, curry or chilli, making a really tasty dish! We can also thoroughly recommend the Mississippi Mud Pie, which should satisfy those of you who share our affliction of a sweet tooth.

If you want to stay overnight, Chris and Lillian provide extremely comfortable bed and breakfast accommodation at the inn, consisting of two spacious twin-bedded rooms and a family room, all with bathroom or shower en-suite, tea and coffee making facilities, central heating, telephone and TV with satellite channel. They also have a well equipped self-catering holiday cottage which is open all year round. All in all, The White Horse is a delightful inn and well worth going out of your way to visit.

The White Horse Inn, Fakenham Road, East Barsham
01328 820645

To the east are a pair of villages whose names are a constant source of amusement and delight to visitors: **Great Snoring** and **Little Snoring**. Their atmosphere is, we suppose, quiet enough for them to be described as 'sleepy', and both have churches that are worth taking the time to visit. St Andrew's Church at Little Snoring is particularly interesting with its mish-mash of architectural styles. The detached round tower with conical cap dates back to Saxon times and in fact belongs to a slightly earlier church from the same period - no one seems to know why this was demolished after only a hundred years or so of its being built, only to be replaced by another church alongside. To the west of St Mary's Church at Great Snoring is the superb Old Rectory - the original manor house built by Sir Ralph Shelton in 1525 - opulently embellished with carved brickwork, octagonal turrets and ornamental Victorian chimneys.

Just up the B1105 from East Barsham is **Little Walsingham**, featuring a Shirehall, an Abbey and a Priory - not a bad list of attractions for a little town! It has witnessed the arrival of thousands of pilgrims since the early part of the 12th century, when the Lady of the Manor, Richelde of Fervaques, had a vision of the Virgin Mary. Transporting her in a dream to the Holy House at Nazareth where Mary had been told of the impending birth of Christ by the Archangel Gabriel, the Blessed Virgin instructed Richelde to build a replica of the house at Walsingham. An Augustinian priory was endowed around 1153 to look after the shrine, followed by a Franciscan friary in 1347, and before long a fully-fledged pilgrimage industry was underway.

Henry VIII was just one of several English monarchs to visit the shrine, barefoot and humble, although this devotion did not stop him from demolishing the priory in 1538. The largest surviving part of the priory is the splendid Gatehouse at the east side of the High Street, consisting of two slender towers supporting an arch, while just two cloisters and parts of the living quarters are all that remain of the friary, which stood just outside the village on the road to Houghton St Giles. The present Shrine of Our Lady of Walsingham, built between 1931-38 on what is purportedly the original site, can be found on the corner of Holt Road and has become a place of modern pilgrimage for believers of many denominations.

Quite apart from its main attraction, Walsingham has much more besides to keep its visitors entertained and enthralled. There are excellent shops, restaurants and inns, attractive timber-framed houses in the High Street, a market, and in Common Place, a 16th century octagonal pump house topped by a beacon brazier, a medieval well (several wells in the area were said to have curative powers) and the former Shirehall which is now a museum.

Just south of the village at **Houghton St Giles** is the restored Slipper Chapel, so called because pilgrims to Walsingham would leave their shoes here before continuing their journey barefoot. If you wish to avoid the masses you will find **Great Walsingham** a mile to the north of its sister village on the B1388. Despite its name this is the smaller of the two, and couldn't be more different in atmosphere and appearance. It is a typical rural Norfolk village with attractive cottages set around a green, and the 14th century St Peter's church with its superb window tracery and 15th century benches is quite delightful.

Three miles to the north, just off the B1105, we came to **Warham**, a fusion of two separate villages known as **Warham All Saints** and **Warham St Mary**. By virtue of the fact that there is now almost no discernible border between the two communities, the village can be said to have two medieval churches, both with plenty to recommend them. To the south of the village, an extremely well-preserved Iron Age hillfort with high banks and ramparts can be found by the side of the River Stiffkey.

The Three Horse Shoes of Warham is a step back in time for its visitors. The main bar features a beautiful inglenook fireplace and a stone floor, and is still gas-lit. A pianola stands in the Snug and an exquisite 1940s fruit machine is used generously as a fund-raiser for charity.

Ale is served from the barrel in this 18th century cottage pub, and the bygone implements which are scattered around the restaurant area are outstanding to say the least. Also among its many amenities are a family room, an extensive beer garden and a children's playroom. If you are interested in memorabilia, you should take this opportunity to view by appointment their interesting collection of old gramophones.

Vintage car rallies are an event held twice a year in Warham, and The Three Horse Shoes is the obvious meeting place. Attend the rally, then maybe dine in their excellent restaurant which serves daily specials in addition to a great variety of traditional Norfolk meals and snacks that appear on the main menu. Also available is a fine selection of desserts and a good wine list. What more could you ask for?

The Three Horse Shoes, The Street, Warham All Saints, Wells next the Sea 01328 710547

Attached to the inn you will find tastefully refurbished bed and breakfast accommodation. It boasts two single rooms (one with a luxurious four poster bed), one double room and one twin room. All are extremely comfortable with en-suite facilities.

If you continue north on the B1105 to the end of the road, you will come to **Wells-next-the-Sea**. Wells will appeal to those of you who enjoy a seaside town that has kept firmly to its origins, as its working harbour gives it great character. Mind you, the name is something of a misnomer as the harbour now stands a mile from the sea beside a creek, with a fair old walk when the tide is low! If you have the time, stroll out along the mile-long 'Bank' that was built in 1859 to prevent the harbour from silting up altogether and to provide access to the sea.

In addition to being the largest of North Norfolk's ports, with vessels from around the world mooring at the quayside to unload their cargoes, Wells is also a popular (almost-seaside) resort. There are a number of cafes on the quayside, together with stalls offering shellfish and fresh fish and chips - always so enjoyable after a walk by the sea.

Just to the east of the town you can enjoy a tranquil train ride on the Wells and Walsingham Steam Railway which takes passengers on a particularly lovely ride along the former Great Eastern Line, with halts at Warham St Mary and Wighton. The Old Station for the Great Eastern Line at Wells has a charming restored signal box which now sells souvenirs and refreshments, and we discovered that the 1986 Garratt locomotive was built specifically for this line.

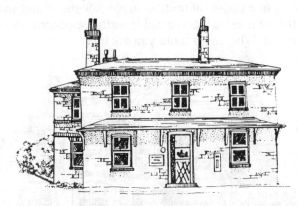

Burnham Pottery, The Old Station, 2/4 Maryland, Wells next the Sea 01328 710847

If you are a cat lover you must pop into **Burnham Pottery** which is housed in The Old Station at Wells. This is the home of the Burnham Cats - Ambrose, Bertram, Claudia, Amelia and many other cute ceramic versions of the feline world who do not need feeding and never have fleas! They reminded us of Russian ceramics with their simple cheeky characters coming in many colours and poses, and they have proved immensely popular.

Thom and Jan Borthwick started their pottery business in Burnham over 10 years ago, but moved here as things expanded! Another speciality is their range of handthrown pottery with a 'Splash' glaze, and this incorporates mugs and jugs, cups and saucers, bowls and casseroles, and some lovely jars with lids. For collectors, the range of vases with a spongeware finish are very popular and are also a good investment, as only limited editions are produced. Our favourite fellow here was Everard, caught in a pose that all cat owners will recognise.

Overlooking a tree-lined green close to the centre of Wells is **The Crown Hotel**, a grand old coaching inn that in fact dates back to Tudor times, despite its Georgian facade. In medieval times, the men of the town would have practised their bowmanship here on the green, which is known as The Buttlands. The restaurant is most impressive, with that extra special touch here and there making all the difference. The Crown can boast no less than five celebrated Chefs, who all work hard to produce cuisine of the highest standards using only the freshest of local produce.

After your meal you can relax in one of the cosy, beamed bars, where the charm and character of the furnishings is perfectly matched by the friendly atmosphere. Each of the letting rooms has its own individual character, and although no room is the same, they are all spacious, clean and tastefully decorated, with all the facilities required for a comfortable stay. Marion and Wilfred Foyers run a most pleasant establishment here at The Crown, and we thought that it would be ideal for those who want to enjoy a relaxing break at a very reasonable price.

The Crown Hotel, The Buttlands, Wells next the Sea 01328 710209

While we were in the town we made a point of visiting **Holkham**, which lies just one and a half miles west of Wells on the A149. We had read a lot about the great agricultural innovator, Thomas Coke, and how when he came into his inheritance of Holkham Hall and its three thousand acre estate, the land was a barren, sandy waste overrun by rabbits. Built in the early 18th century by Cokes' great-uncle, the Earl of Leicester, the Hall is a vast, imposing mansion designed in the style of an Italianate palace.

The Earl had successfully reclaimed much of his land from the sea, but the topsoil was poor and crop yields were low. His great-nephew (later to be dubbed 'Coke of Norfolk') was able to revitalise the soil by dragging up the lower clay level and planting turnips - a system pioneered by that other great Norfolk farmer, 'Turnip' Townsend. Rather like the rotation of crops, his scheme was to use sheep to clear the roots, and to use their manure as fertilizer. The result was greatly improved soil with abundant yields: for the first time in Norfolk, corn and wheat crops flourished and with the advent of cattle herds he had successfully devised a good basis for mixed farming. Coke encouraged farmers from all over the country to come and see for themselves just how successful his methods had proved, and his prosperity was assured as a result of his brilliant vision.

Whether you visit **Holkham Hall** to learn more about innovative farming methods or simply to enjoy the magnificent house, you will certainly not be disappointed. The mansion has had its fair share of detractors - the somewhat austere yellow brick with which it was built is not to everyone's taste - but no one could fail to be impressed by the interior. Taking more than 30 years to complete, it boasts a magnificent hall with pink marble pillars. Furniture designed by William Kent (the principal architect of the house and much of the park) features throughout, and the walls of the State rooms, which are hung with velvet and damask, make a wonderful backdrop to a superb collection of paintings by such masters as Van Dyck, Gainsborough and Rubens.

The exquisite library, richly decorated in shades of gold and white, houses hundreds of beautifully bound books, illuminated manuscripts, folios and other fascinating historic records. There is also an impressive collection of antique sculptures which Thomas Coke acquired in Italy, and it is said that the large number of ilex trees which grace the estate are attributable to the fact that these sculptures arrived at Holkham packed in ilex seeds for protection.

When you have had your fill of exploring the house, there are a number of ancillary attractions to make your visit even more rewarding. Holkham Pottery, founded by Elizabeth, Countess of Leicester in 1951, is open to visitors and you can watch the skilled team of potters at work and purchase examples of their wares. There is also a garden centre and craft centre, and in the 19th century stables you will find the Holkham Bygones Museum, a marvellous collection of Victorian and Edwardian agricultural tools and domestic equipment featuring everything from working steam engines and vintage tractors to craft tools and kitchenware. A large deer park with around 600 head of fallow deer is another feature of the estate, while a walk around the mile-long lake to see the many different species of wildfowl that have made it their home is a must.

The young Victoria was staying at Holkham Hall when she was informed that she was to be Queen of England, and the magnificent **Victoria Hotel** in Holkham, built in the early part of the 19th century, was named in her honour. This grand flint house with its magnificent, well-stocked gardens is situated in beautiful countryside, on the corner of the entrance road to Holkham Hall. Inside you will find two traditional bar areas which have been tastefully decorated in keeping with their original character. Upstairs, there are seven luxury en-suite bedrooms which have been refurbished to a very high standard. Each provides magnificent views and a full range of facilities to make your stay as comfortable as possible.

The Victoria Hotel, Park Road, Holkham 01328 710469

The restaurant is another superbly decorated room, with that extra special touch to each table. There is an open log fire at one end of the room, with comfortable seating around it where you can relax and enjoy a drink before your meal. As you can imagine, the food is indeed fit for a queen: the menu featuring such dishes as Dressed Crabmeat in the shell, Smoked Salmon and Lobster Thermidor, together with steak, chicken, lamb, and the delicious sounding Victoria Game Pie. There is also a wide selection of glorious desserts, including Treacle Tart, Bread and Butter Pudding and an excellent Chocolate Mousse. Considering the elegance of the hotel, we thought that the prices were very reasonable -

you do not need to possess the coffers of a king or a queen to enjoy an excellent meal at The Victoria Hotel!

The Holkham National Nature Reserve runs from Burnham Overy Staithe all the way along the coast to **Blakeney**, a 12-mile stretch of dunes, beaches and salt-marshes interrupted only by the harbour channel leading to Wells. As such it is the largest coastal reserve in the country, with around 10,000 acres to explore. The reserve is reached via Holkham Gap, a vast, beautiful cove of grassy dunes where pine trees, planted nearly 100 years ago to stabilise the shifting sands, sweep down almost to the sea. Access to Holkham Gap is down Lady Ann's Drive, a half-mile long driveway off the A149, which you will find opposite the main entrance to Holkham Hall. A wide variety of plant and wildlife can be observed on the reserve itself, and the beach is one of the finest in East Anglia. The sea is shallow here and safe for swimming, although bathers should be aware that the tide comes in very fast.

Steam on the North Norfolk Railway

CHAPTER FIVE

North Norfolk - Stiffkey to Foulsham

Norfolk Broads

107

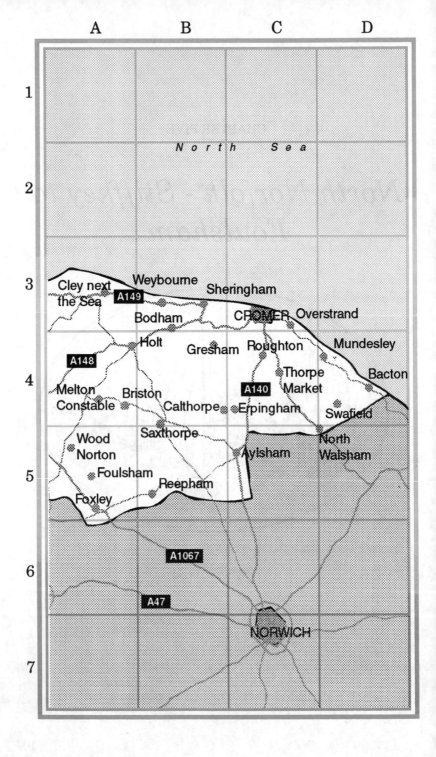

North Norfolk - Stiffkey to Foulsham

Just to the east of Wells-next-the-Sea is the straggling brick and flint village of **Stiffkey**, standing on the A149 coast road above the river of the same name. Pronounced 'Stewkey', the name means 'island of stumps' - most likely a reference to the marshy river valley of reed beds and fallen trees which indeed gives the village the appearance of an island. At the east end of the village is the church of St John the Baptist, and from the churchyard there are fine views of the river and of Stiffkey Hall to the south. All that now remains of this impressive building are the towers and one wing of the house built by the Bacon family in 1578, the 17th century gatehouse, and the stately ruins of the Great Hall - now transformed into a rose terrace and sunken garden and open to the public.

The former rectory is a grand Georgian building, famous as the residence of the Reverend Harold Davidson, rector of Stiffkey during the 1920s and 1930s. The Reverend Davidson's personal crusade for saving the 'fallen women' of London's West End caused much gossip and scandal at the time, not unlike the central character in Michael Palin's film, 'The Missionary'. Despite the fact that his notoriety regularly filled the church to capacity, he constantly fell foul of the ecclesiastical authorities and eventually lost his living. There is a bizarre ending to his story: after handing over the keys of Stiffkey Rectory he joined a travelling show and was later killed by the lion whose cage he shared!

To the north of the village are the Stiffkey Salt Marshes, a National Trust nature reserve which turns a delicate shade of purple in July when the sea lavender is in bloom. Here on the sandflats the famous 'Stewkey blues' can be found: a cockle by any other name, and considered to be a delicacy at markets all over England where they are sold. We must admit that cockles have never appealed to us personally - they always seem to have such a gritty texture - but if you are a connoisseur of such things, you will be pleased to discover that Stiffkey is also renowned for its shrimps and whelks.

The next village along the coast road is **Morston**, and from the little quay visitors are ferried over to the huge spit of sand and shingle known as Blakeney Point, where Norfolk's very first nature reserve was established. As this is the northernmost part of the county it is visited by a wide variety of migrating birds, and in winter local boatmen will take you out to see the large colony of common seals which basks on the sandbanks off the Point. Morston village itself lies about a mile south of the tidal creek which flows through the marshes between the Point and the mainland and all but dries up completely at low tide. It is a particularly pleasant little place with quiet lanes and clusters of cottages built from local cobbles. Watch out for the patched-up tower of All Saints' Church which was struck by lightning in 1743.

At the end of the creek is **Blakeney** , a commercial port until the beginning of the 20th century when the silting up of the estuary prevented anything but pleasure craft from gaining access at high tide. The old Guildhall stands on Blakeney's attractive High Street, which runs between the harbour and the A149. By the side of the main road is the beautifully restored Church of St Nicholas, its magnificent west tower standing over 100ft high and acting as a landmark for miles around. A light in the smaller turret at the east end of the chancel was once used as a beacon for guiding ships safely into Blakeney harbour.

Heading south from here on the B1388 we came to **Langham** , the home and final resting place of that well known English naval officer and novelist, Captain Frederick Marryat. After leading a fairly distinguished naval career, he went on to write a series of novels concerning life at sea, the most famous of which was 'Mr Midshipman Easy'. Although he did extremely well in his new career his extravagant lifestyle inevitably led him into financial embarrassment. In 1843 he settled on a small farm at Langham and spent the rest of his days as a gentleman farmer and writing children's stories.

The village pub in Langham is the **Langham Bluebell**, and Vic and Myrtle Newman have made this a wonderfully warm and inviting place to stop for a good pint of ale. They are both great charity workers and have managed to raise a lot of money over the years, especially for the elderly. This is the sort of place that time never changes: a truly traditional country pub where people come for a drink and a chat in friendly surroundings.

Many women are said to have a penchant for shoes, but Myrtle seems to have taken this to its extreme! In a room above the pub, she has put together an absolutely stunning collection of over 2,000 antique and ceramic shoes. Shoes made of glass, wood, coal and even lava are displayed in a permanent exhibition here, which everyone is free to look at, free of charge. Do take a look while you are here - it really is quite an eye-opener!

The Newmans also showed us a letter from a friend of theirs who had done some research on the history of the pub. It would appear that in 400 years, they are only the third family to have owned it, which is quite an achievement. We are quite sure that their customers all hope they are here for many years to come, as a more friendly and helpful couple you could not wish to meet.

Langham Bluebell, Langham

Two miles further down the road is **Binham** , with its spectacular, albeit ruined, Benedictine Priory situated above the river. Founded in 1091, this must once have been a truly magnificent building. Evidence of superb workmanship still exists in the stone columns, and the monastic church - now used as the parish church - is a rare example of Early English architecture in Norfolk. Many of the houses in the village were built from stone from the Priory, the remains of which are now in the care of English Heritage.

Taking a lane to the south of Binham, we could hardly fail to spot the landmark church of St Martin's at **Hindringham**, as it stands high above the village on a hilltop. Indeed, we imagine that both the tower of the church and the windmill at nearby **Lower Green** must make excellent navigational aids for the local birdlife!

If you take the A148 to the east of Fakenham you will come to a left-hand turning almost opposite the B1354. This will lead you to **Thursford** and **The Thursford Collection**. No one visiting East Anglia should miss out this extraordinary exhibition. Thursford might not seem the most likely place for a museum of fairgrounds and steam, but in fact East Anglia has many connections with the history of festival and its trappings, and the real Norfolk traditional art is not water-coloured painting but the practice of festival. There have been fairs all over Norfolk for over a thousand years.

Norfolk is full of folk history in which fairs were significant events for isolated communities. It is hard for us to imagine now the effect which the visit of a fair would have had on the isolated villages in Norfolk, in the late-19th and early-20th centuries. Out of the plain landscape came these exuberant vehicles and their mechanical mysteries with carved monsters and swinging chairs, all of them painted and polished in a style of power and colour. The cinema too had its beginnings in the fair, with the huge bioscopes which travelled between 1896 and 1914, some of them able to seat 1,000 people.

Above all else, the fairs brought electricity with them, at a time when most towns and villages themselves would have had only gas lighting! For many people, therefore, this would have been their first glimpse at electric light. Families would walk miles to see these things, because in a pre-television era this was the place where the truly spectacular could be experienced and, more importantly, shared.

Among the scattered groups who went to the fair was one small boy, George Cushing, who instinctively understood these things, and has retained the image of it all his life to make The Thursford Collection a show for all of us to see and enjoy.

George Cushing was caring for and collecting steam engines when most men would not have given you £5 for one. Without his perceptive honesty the museum would not exist. All the exhibits have one thing in common, which is that they are beautiful objects made by craftsmen who knew their work. George Cushing's real love for these things has a countryman's sense of the intrinsic value of the objects: to bring together this collection, to see through the blindness or carelessness which allowed traction engines, for example, to go for scrap, and to re-make for all of us one of the best arrangements of steam engines and organs in the world. More than the skill, more than the money which it has taken to finance the museum, it has required his vision and enthusiasm.

The Thursford Collection, Thursford, Fakenham 01328 878477

Thursford it's not just a museum but a total experience. Music: live music shows starring Robert Wolfe in the Wurlitzer show, plus music from nine mechanical organs. Shops: housed in renovated farm buildings, offering a wide and varied selection of goods, many locally made. Food: cream teas on the lawn, light snacks in the genuine Norfolk barn, homemade ice-cream from the parlour. And to top it all there are enough activities, including a Savage Venetian Gondola ride, to complete a wonderful visit.

After all the thrills and spills of the fairground, we were pleased to discover two superb places to stop for a meal close by.

The Thursford Crawfish is a first class public house and restaurant that can be located on the Fakenham to Cromer (A148) road at Thursford only a short mile from the famous Thursford Collection.

The Inn which was once an 18th Century coaching station has been totally modernised, but has managed to retain all its charm and character. The doors open into the bar area dominated by a roaring fire with an exquisite feature mirror above it. The seating arrangement is such that it created an intimate, cosy and relaxing atmosphere.

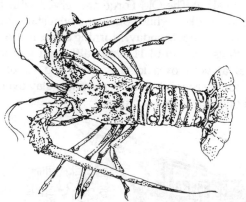

The Thursford Crawfish, Holt Road, Thursford 01328 878313

The restaurant compliments the bar, beautifully decorated with antiques and tapestries adorn the walls. The menu has a choice of six starters and an extensive selection of main meals which include steaks, home made cuisine, fish dishes, salads and a good range of appetizing desserts to finish. A bar snack menu is also available for those who just wish to have a light snack. You can accompany your meal with wine from the wine list or if you prefer a good ale a variety can be obtained from the bar. Food is served between 12.00 pm to 2.30 pm and 6.00 pm to 9.30 pm every day, except Sunday when traditional Sunday lunch is served.

During the Christmas period the nearby Thursford Collection perform their renowned Christmas concerts and the Thursford Crawfish is always delighted to provide suppers after their performances.

Anne and Seamus run the Thursford Crawfish and although they have only been in residence twelve months they have evidently put 100% effort into creating a relaxed atmosphere, comfortable meeting place and excellent cuisine in this first class establishment.

It was also on the Fakenham road that we discovered **The Old Forge Restaurant,** a former coaching station with forge and stables on the outskirts of the Thursford estate. The restaurant is well decorated throughout and has a reputation for good food. One dish that particularly caught our eye was the Asparagus Pancakes, a light and delicious combination. We were not sure if the asparagus is home-grown although it would not surprise us, as owner Chas Welch is a 'hybridist'. He specialises in growing soft and hard fruits as well as flowers and shrubs, and the trick must be finding the time to do this while running the restaurant with his wife Carol. He displays at many shows, including Chelsea, and has won many awards and introduced many new flowers and fruits.

All main meals at The Old Forge are served with five vegetables, which are freshly cooked while you wait. The restaurant is licensed and is open every day except Monday. Morning coffee is served from 9.00am and the bar stays open until 11.00pm, although you may finish your evening meal at your own leisure. Chas and Carol also have two comfortable double rooms to let if you want to stay overnight, one with en-suite and one with a shower room.

The Old Forge Restaurant, Fakenham, Thursford 01328 878345

Alternatively, if you are here on a caravanning or camping holiday let us direct you to a marvellous establishment we discovered just a mile to the south-east of Thursford. It is always a pleasure to come across a caravan and camping park which is not only attractive but has all the required amenities too, and **The Old Brick Kilns** park at **Little Barney** is one such place. Owners Tony and Tessa Gent have set their seven acre park on two levels, where the pleasant combination of wooded areas and open spaces creates a wonderfully peaceful atmosphere. The natural pond is a perfect habitat for many types of wildlife, and for the nature lovers among you, the wild bird reserves and beautiful beaches of the North Norfolk coast are only eight miles away.

There are 60 pitches in all, 52 of them providing a 10 amp electrical supply. The old brick drying shed has been converted to modern standards to provide all the main facilities of the park; and here you will find the reception area, a first aid room, and the shop, which operates a gas exchange and will supply all your basic food needs as well as homemade produce, crafts and gifts and a wide range of caravan accessories. There are luxury showers and toilets, including excellent facilities for the disabled, and other amenities include a vegetable preparation and washing-up room, a laundry room, a television room and a recreation room. Outdoor activities include fishing and boating and a safe children's play area, and there are also cycles for hire if you want to take off for an hour or two along the country lanes.

The Old Brick Kilns, Little Barney, Fakenham 01328 878305

Bearing in mind the pleasant aspect of the park and the high standard of all the facilities provided, it came as no surprise to discover that The Old Brick Kilns had been awarded the coveted 1990/91 Camp Site of the Year Award by Camping and Walking Magazine. This recognition is richly deserved, and if you would like to discover the pleasures of staying here for yourself, the park is open from the beginning of March to the end of October.

The Gents also offer superb bed and breakfast facilities throughout the year in their lovely family home, which has been converted from three brickworker's cottages. The accommodation comprises one twin, one double and one single room, all en-suite, spacious and tastefully decorated. One thing that particularly impressed us here was the size of the dining room table - even with a house full of bed and breakfast guests, it looked big enough to accommodate all the visitors staying at the caravan and camping park too!

Heading back north along the A148 from Thursford, a brief diversion along a lane to the left of the road took us to **Bale**, an attractive farming hamlet with a little green where once a cobbler had his shop in the hollow of a giant oak tree. The ancient Great Bale Oak finally gave up the ghost and was felled in 1860, and the graceful grove of ilex trees that was planted to replace it now stands proud in front of All Saints' Church.

Further along the main road, pretty **Letheringsett** came into view. 'Larnsett' (as local dialect would have it) is a truly charming place in the most delightful of settings. Set among carefully landscaped trees, it stands in the lovely Glaven valley on either bank of the river; both parts of the village linked by an ornate iron bridge which was built in 1818 by local landowner William Hardy. The great watermill by St Andrew's Church still produces flour today, and the gardens of the impressive 18th century Letheringsett Hall are open to visitors under the National Gardens Scheme.

Anne Starling and Peter Loosley are two people primarily concerned with the well being of the environment. Three years ago they introduced their Natural Surroundings, a wildlife and conservation centre in the hope of extending their views. You will find **Natural Surroundings** set in eight acres of magnificent countryside on the B1156 between Blakeney and Letheringsett.

Natural Surroundings, Bayfield Estate, Bayfield, Holt
01263 711091

The centre is divided into three areas, the shop and sales area which offers a large range of plants, shrubs and seeds, in fact just about everything you could need to become a successful gardener. A section of wildflowers, shrubs and trees all grown with the welfare of the natural habitat in mind, and finally beautiful gardens and countryside to wander around where you are able to observe many preserved wildflowers and trees sadly absent from the British countryside today. Mini-meadows and attractive ponds can be seen along the walk and there are ample spots for those who would like to picnic amongst the trees or by the river.

Natural Surroundings is open daily, with the exception of Mondays, from 10.00 am to 5.30 pm.

Further along the B1156, it is worth stopping off at **Glandford** to see the Shell Museum; a large collection housed in a fine old cottage designed in the Flemish style like several others in the village. The shells have been brought back to Norfolk from around the world and are beautifully presented in glass cases. Another interesting feature here is a striking embroidered panel created by John Craske, a Sheringham fisherman who was also renowned as an artist.

Next is **Wiveton,** at one time a thriving port on the River Glaven but now reduced to the status of quiet coastal village. Serving as reminders of its formal glory are the handsome church on the green with parts dating back to the 14th century, a medieval bridge, and Wiveton Hall to the north of the village on the edge of Cley Marshes.

If you had visited the village of **Cley-next-the-Sea** a century ago, you would have seen ships moored alongside the church! Now the sea has receded dramatically and the village could be called Cley-a-mile-away-from-the-Sea! **The Harnser** is a grand old former coaching inn dating back to the 18th century, built of traditional Norfolk flint and picturesquely situated on the edge of the marshes opposite Cley Windmill. Graham and Christine Mills have owned the restaurant for the past 20 years, enjoying what is a popular bird-watcher's paradise. Indeed, 'harnser' is a Norfolk name for the heron, and if you take a stroll across the marshes you will more than likely spot one of these elegant birds. You could work up a good appetite out on the marshes and then return to sample some of The Harnser's superb fare in what was once the bar area of the old inn. An A La Carte, Table D'Hote and Bar Snacks Menu are available, and the varied dishes include grills and the freshest of sea food, including Harbour sandeels, local mussels and Blakeney Point Whitebait. We were impressed by the fact that you can choose a meal to suit both your appetite and wallet.

The Harnser is run very much as a family concern. Judith Holman, the manageress, has assisted Graham for the past 14 years and is very popular with the customers. Judith's mother, Jean, completes the friendly staff.

If you would like to spend a few days out on the marshes with your camera, or perhaps indulge in some fishing, Graham and Christine have a number of tastefully decorated letting rooms to offer, ranging from single to family rooms, some en-suite and all very spacious with good facilities.

The Harnser, Coast Road, Cley next the Sea 01263 740776/740073

Norfolk is liberally dotted with windmills and the one situated on the old quayside at Cley is particularly fine. What is so special about this windmill is that although it is now a private residence, the owners offer bed and breakfast accommodation in the circular rooms of the mill itself, and self-catering in the outer buildings. We have always been fascinated with the idea of living in a windmill or oast house, and have often wondered how the residents cope with hanging pictures, erecting bookshelves and doing all the other D.I.Y. jobs normally associated with flat surfaces.

Cley Mill, Cley-next-the-Sea, Holt 0263-740209.

Cley (which, like Cockley Cley, is pronounced 'Cly' and means 'clay') was at one time the largest port on the Glaven estuary, but the inexorable forces of silt and land reclamation have left it high and dry and only accessible from the sea by small craft. Although the quayside remains, nothing is now left of the old harbour at the southern end of the village from which wool was once exported to the Netherlands.

The Cley and Salthouse Marshes lie between the coast road and the sea, and around 650 acres of this land is a nature reserve run by the Norfolk Naturalists' Trust. If you would like details of all the different species of birds that breed on the reserve, the Trust has a visitors' information centre just to the east of the village on the A149. There is a car park at Cley Eye if you wish to venture onto the beach, but bathing is not advisable as the shingle shelves steeply under the sea.

This striking natural feature of the coastline continues round to **Weybourne**. Here, the shingle beach known as Weybourne Hope (or Hoop) slopes so steeply that it is said that an invading fleet could bring their ships practically to the shore - giving rise to the local adage: 'He who would Old England Win, Must at Weybourne Hoop begin'. A map dated 1st May 1588 clearly shows 'Waborne Fort' opposite Weybourne Hope with an area of salt marsh dividing it from the sea. The Holt Parish Register for those times states: 'In this yeare was the town of Waborne fortified with a continuall garrison of men bothe of horse and foote with sconces (earthworks) ordinaunce and all manner of appoyntment to defend the Spannyards landing theare' - firm evidence that Weybourne would have been considered a likely landing point for the Spanish Armada.

Weybourne was also heavily defended during both World Wars, and the army camp that was established here was later to become the Anti-Aircraft Permanent Range and Radar Training Wing, providing training for national servicemen until the camp finally closed in March 1959. The site has since been returned to agricultural use, but the original NAAFI building remains and now houses **The Muckleburgh Collection**, a fascinating museum of military equipment which has seen action in battlefields all around the world. Many of the tanks, armoured cars, amphibious vehicles and pieces of artillery on display have required complete restoration, and all can be touched and examined at close hand.

Despite Weybourne's long tradition of being ready to defend itself from invasion it was in fact only attacked once, by enemy aircraft on 11th July 1940. A stick of bombs landed in the main street and badly damaged two cottages,

Sheringham lies about two-and-a-half miles further east on the A149, and a pleasant way to reach it is along the cliff path where the gorse flourishes. Have you ever examined one of the tiny, vivid yellow gorse flowers, the perfume is reminiscent of coconut.

Sheringham is a pleasant, bustling town which has undergone the transition from quiet fishing village to small-scale resort quite gracefully. It is not a resort in the unattractive sense of the word, but simply a place where everyone will find something to enjoy. The beach here is markedly different to the shingle beaches elsewhere on this part of the coast, consisting mainly of gently sloping sand; it is excellent for bathing and its adequate quota of lifeguards makes it ideal for families with children. A small fleet of fishing boats still operates from here, and it is a great pleasure to watch them leaving in the evening to go night fishing -

especially when you know that you will shortly be tucked up in bed yourself! Several original fishermen's cottages remain, some with lofts where the nets were mended, and baited pots for catching crabs are still set along the seafront as they would have been in bygone days.

Like so many other former fishing villages in England, Sheringham owes its transformation into a popular seaside resort to the coming of the railway - which in this instance arrived in 1887. And you can still enjoy an authentic full-sized passenger steam railway ride on the **North Norfolk Railway**. At one time, 64 trains a day used to steam into Sheringham station, but with the closure of the former Midland and Great Northern Joint Railway in 1967, the future of the line looked uncertain. With great efforts and enthusiasm from the M & GN Preservation Society, the full glory of the station has been maintained, and is now operated by the North Norfolk Railway Company. The Society had already bought the section of track beyond Weybourne as far as the Sheringham boundary when the Melton Constable to Sheringham line closed in 1964, and it took the opportunity of leasing the unused station in 1967. Prior to 1963, before the line had closed, the Society had formed a private company, the Norfolk Railway Company. They applied for a Light Railway Order which would grant them the status to carry fare paying passengers and by 1975 the first passengers enjoyed the rewards of all this labour.

North Norfolk Railway, Sheringham Station, Sheringham
01263 822045

Today, the company runs steam locomotives between Sheringham, Weybourne and a new station at Holt, where there are plans to develop a museum and buildings on the site. Passengers are certainly well-catered for with a buffet provided on the trains, offering light refreshments or a full meal. Sheringham Station also has a gift shop where you can

120

purchase all sorts of gifts and railway memorabilia souvenirs. Volunteers are always welcome to help restore and maintain the railways and stock, so do give them a ring on Sheringham 822045 if you feel you can offer your services. The railway opens between March - November and they have special events such as fun runs at Halloween and Santa Claus Specials.

Locals and visitors alike should give thanks to the National Trust for their policy of acquiring large parts of the heath and woodland that lie to the south of Sheringham, thereby halting the spread of suburbia so beloved by our town planners. The land here rises steeply to a sand and gravel ridge which runs parallel to the coastline from Cromer to Holt and reaches a height of more than 300ft in places. At the aptly-named Pretty Corner, which lies just to the east of the A1082 at its junction with the A148, you can park your car and enjoy superb views over the surrounding countryside. Several woodland paths are accessible from the car park, and if you decide to go for a stroll you will find a great variety of trees ranging from ash and birch to beech, pine and rowan, together with a colourful profusion of wild flowers.

To the east of the car park, a turning to the north of the A148 will lead you to **West Runton**. However, the road first takes you to 'Roman Camp' on Beacon Hill, which is actually the site of an Anglo-Saxon iron-working settlement now in the care of the National Trust. From here there are memorable views across the Cromer Ridge and out to the North Sea. At a height of 328ft above sea level it is the highest point in Norfolk, and should permanently banish any misconceptions you may have had that you are travelling through a flat and featureless county!

We were delighted to find the **North Norfolk Heavy Horse and Pony Centre** at West Runton. The great Shires demonstrate their considerable strength, intelligence and charm twice daily, and after you have enjoyed the display there is plenty more to see and a pleasant picnic area to relax in and have lunch.

If you are passing through West Runton or planning to stay a few nights there, an ideal place to dine would be the **Mirabelle Restaurant** in Station Road. Manfred has owned the Mirabelle since December in 1973 and his expereince and expertise as a chef is apparent on reading the menu and receiving your meal.

Due to Manfred's established catering abilities he has built up a good custom and reputation through North Norfolk and beyond. The exterior of the restaurant just seems like a homely domestic building but inside it transforms into a bright, stylish and beautifully decorated and furnished French restaurant with an occasionally added Austrian touch. A seasonal a la carte menu may in winter include such dishes as wienerschnizel or supreme of pheasant and wild mushrooms. The specialities are game and seafood, especially lobster. Starters range from Fresh dressed crab garnie and moules marinieres for those who enjoy seafood to honeydew melon and avocado pear vinaigrette. A good range of desserts including fresh fruits and cream and apple strudels or cheese and biscuits complements the meal.

A startling 350 wines are available from The Mirabelle, this is probably the largest list in East Anglia. The restaurant seats approximately 50 people but due to its popularity it is always advisable to book in the summer.

The Mirabelle Restaurant, Station Road, West Runton, Nr Cromer
01263 75396

West Runton beach (accessible from the north of the village down Water Lane) is safe for bathers and is worth exploring for its fossils. Fossilized sea urchins can often be found embedded in pieces of flint on the beach, and at one time the Cromer area was a rich hunting ground for amber. This is much scarcer today, and if you are lucky enough to find any it will most likely be where the shingle meets the sand, and in rock pools. The rich deposits laid down on the North Norfolk coast came from as far afield as the Rhine estuary and Scandinavia, and the wide variety of rocks and minerals to be found here include quartz, calcite, serpentine, iron pyrites and many, many more.

The beach at **East Runton** is again safe for swimming, with shingle leading to sand, and is approached over a steep ramp through East Runton Gap. This peaceful Norfolk village lies half-a-mile inland to the south of the A149 within a designated Area of Outstanding Natural Beauty; a somewhat surprising place you might think to find an excellent Greek Cypriot taverna.

The **Constantia Cottage Restaurant,** however, is well known throughout the area. Outside, the restaurant may resemble a traditional

Norfolk cottage, but inside it's more like a Greek party. The Yiasimi family (husband, wife, four sons and a daughter) have become famous for their Cypriot hospitality. As you go through the door, you are met by the sound of traditional Bouzouki music, stylish Greek decor, and a menu which is reasonably priced and very extensive. We counted a total of 27 starters and no less than 48 main courses. There is also a good value set menu with a wide range of options. The restaurant is open each day for lunch and dinner, but closed Sunday evenings and Monday lunchtimes.

Constantia Cottage Restaurant, Cromer Road, East Runton
01263 512017

For many visitors **Cromer** certainly lives up to its self-styled reputation as the 'Gem of the North Norfolk Coast' - even though you are unlikely to find any amber on the beach! It is a charming seaside town, as well-favoured now as it was in the late-18th century when the first of its grand houses were built for those seeking select bathing places in the summer - in what was then a fishing village and small port. A port of no small significance, however - evidence of Cromer's importance as far back as medieval times can be found right in the centre of town, where the magnificent tower of the 15th century church of St Peter and St Paul soars to a height of 160ft, the tallest in the county. The main development of the town came towards the end of the 19th century, and although most of the superb Edwardian hotels that once graced the seafront have since been pulled down, the splendid Hotel de Paris and the pier, which both date from this period, thankfully remain.

Of course, the Victorians made their contributions to the architecture of the town as well, and overlooking the sea at Cromer, **The Red Lion Hotel** is a excellent example of first class modernisation and impressive refurbishment. This Grand Victorian Hotel has been in Vanessa Medlers

123

family for 7 years and it is apparent that no expense has been spared in providing every modern facility and comfort for their many guests whether on a business stop over or staying a leisurely weekend.

Bedrooms are spacious, tastefully furnished with en-suite bathrooms, colour T.V, video and tea making facilities. Many have sea views allowing you to appreciate the beauty of the Norfolk coast. Amenities include a solarium, sauna, snooker room, use of a gymnasium, a residents bar and a restaurant called Galliano's which is open 7 days a week 7.00 pm to 9.30 pm. The restaurant has a magnificent fireplace and is candlelit creating an intimate atmosphere. Naturally it offers local seafood specialities as well as other appetizing meals such as Supreme of Pheasant with a whisky ginger and banana sauce. Definitely a place to dine in style. The Red Lion Hotel and Galliano's Restaurant has a English Tourist Board 3 Crowns Commendation and an AA 2 Star Rating.

The Red Lion Hotel and Galliano's Restaurant, Brook Street, Cromer 01263 514964

Speaking of local specialities, Cromer Crabs are legendary, and a dish of their succulent meat is well and truly fit for a king. Fishing may have declined somewhat over the years, yet a number of vessels still set out from here to bring back these delectable crustaceans; together with sole, plaice, mackerel and many other types of fish. The people of Cromer are also justly proud of their lifeboat, and of the many brave men who have served in her over the years. The most famous of these was Henry Blogg, coxswain of the lifeboat from 1909 to 1947, winner of many medals and honours and now commemorated by a bronze bust in North Lodge Park. The lifeboat museum stands at the foot of The Gangway, and features models and photographs illustrating the proud tradition and brave deeds of Cromer's lifeboatmen. The Cromer Museum, which is housed in a row of restored fishermen's cottages behind the church in Brook

Street, is also worth a visit to discover more about the geological, maritime and natural history of this area.

While you are in East Cromer, let us introduce you to a rare treat: a visit to **The Dolphin Free House and Restaurant** just opposite the pier at Jetty Cliff. There is no other way of describing The Dolphin except to say that it is delightful. This 17th century building has been skilfully modernised without losing any of its charm. It has eight marvellous bay windows, which overlook the sea and the pier from which the village takes its name.

At Jetty Pier you can have that rare and magical experience of watching the sun rise and set over the sea. If this is something you have never experienced before, come to The Dolphin and watch. It is an awe-inspiring sight.

Apart from being an extremely good pub, The Dolphin also has a first class restaurant offering a good range of meals from homemade Steak and Kidney Pie to Lasagne Verdi. In this area it would be foolish not to take advantage of the fruits of the sea, so you could also try their Deep Fried Plaice or Fillet of Cod in Batter, topped off by some delicious homemade Apple Pie and Cream and a fresh filter coffee. They also offer bar snacks, jacket potatoes with a choice of fillings, and a children's menu. If you happen to drop in during the winter months, you might find yourself whirling on the dance floor, as the restaurant is then closed and used for a disco.

The Dolphin Freehouse & Restaurant, Jetty Cliff, East Cromer

Cromer really is the ideal place for a family holiday. Apart from the attractions already mentioned, there is safe swimming on the sand and shingle beach, a small zoo, lovely walks, a boating lake, clubs offering family entertainment in the evenings, the Pavilion Theatre with its summer season and an excellent golf course. As you stroll around the narrow streets of the old town taking in the sights, you quickly come to appreciate the fact that you are exploring one of Norfolk's least spoilt seaside resorts.

The sandy beaches fringed by gentle cliffs on this part of the coast will no doubt tempt you to break your journey for a while to spend some hours soaking up the sun. This was a favourite place for the upper-classes to come and build their summer houses, and **Overstrand** in particular boasts some outstanding examples of that period. Overstrand Hall was built by Edwin Lutyens in 1899 for Lord Hillingdon, while The Pleasaunce, built for Lady Battersea two years earlier, boasts gardens designed by Gertrude Jekyll, who is enjoying something of a revival.

A quaint little crab fishing village which has gradually developed into a popular holiday resort with a safe, sandy beach, Overstrand can be found two miles east of Cromer on the B1159 and is built near cliffs which are fast eroding. The Church of St Martin was built to replace a much earlier church which fell into the sea in the 14th century, and east of here there is no access to the sea at all until you reach Mundesley, five miles further along the coast.

Danum House, 22 Paul's Lane, Overstrand 01263 78327

If you happen to be passing through Overstrand, do take advantage of the opportunity to spend a night at Sue Sims' lovely home. **Danum House and Gallery** was originally built as a farmhouse in 1818 but has been providing delightful bed and breakfast accommodation for the last five years. The rooms to let are beautifully decorated, spacious and all have en suite facilities. The property has original oak panelled walls in all the reception rooms and contains an old spring well in the cellar.

The property has previously been owned by notable people such as Victoria, Countess of Yarborough and Florence Barclay the renowned authoress of 'Rosary'. Her original writing desk can be found in the drawing room. A first class English breakfast will be served if required, this we stongly recommend as it is both delicious and plentiful.

A mile to the south, just west of the B1159, is the tranquil village of **Northrepps**, its buildings centred around the 15th century St Mary's Church. Verily Anderson's book, 'The Northrepps Grandchildren', vividly describes the life at Northrepps Hall, and makes excellent background reading for all visitors to the northern part of the county.

If your intention is to do a bit of sight-seeing around North Norfolk, then **Shrublands Farm** in the village is an ideal base from which to explore. This 300-acre family farm is within easy reach of the well-known bird sanctuary of Blakeney Point, close to the National Trust properties of Felbrigg, Blickling Hall and Sheringham Park, and only half an hour's drive from Norwich with its splendid cathedral, Norman castle, museum and art exhibition centre.

The house itself consists of one twin room with private bathroom, and one twin and one double room. All rooms are attractively decorated with period furniture and have tea and coffee making facilities and alarm clock radios.

Guests have access to a comfortable sitting room where they can watch TV in front of a log fire or read a variety of books which are available to borrow. Ann Youngman, who was actually born at the farm, is pleased to provide good farmhouse cooking which can be enjoyed in an elegant, spacious dining room. Every effort has been made to ensure that guests can relax in a comfortable North Norfolk atmosphere.

Shrublands Farm, Northrepps, Cromer 01263 78297

Making our way back to the B1159 coast road from here and heading south, we took a right-hand turn a mile west of Mundesley to look for the renowned **Rose Acre Riding Stables**. The stables are located within north Norfolk's Area of Outstanding Natural Beauty, just outside the quiet village of **Gimingham**. They have been run since 1985 by Mrs June Self, former member of the British show-jumping team and now a British Horse Society Qualified Instructress. June has been assisted for the last four and a half years by Julie Harding, also a fully qualified riding instructress. Together they provide hacking and tuition for riders of all ages and abilities. Small groups can take escorted rides through the quiet surrounding countryside, or for the more experienced, there are beach rides along the nearby stretch of sandy coastline. There is also an enclosed floodlit arena and sixteen acres of grounds attached to the stables. Rose Acre supplies mounts for every shape and size of rider, from a 39 inch Shetland pony to one standing over 17 hands high. The stables are open daily throughout the year (except for Sundays during the summer months).

Rose Acre Riding Stables, Back Mundesley Road, Gimingham
01263720671

After the hazards of the coastline immediately to the north, where cliffs, fields and houses have all been eroded away by the relentless sea, it is a pleasure to arrive at the quiet holiday resort of **Mundesley** with its superb sandy beach. Mundesley (pronounced 'Munsley') is totally unspoilt, yet it has all the facilities you need for a relaxing family holiday. Golf, bowling and fishing can all be enjoyed, and perhaps best of all you can swim in perfect safety while the children splash about in the many shallow pools or 'lowies' left behind by the ebbing tide.

Continuing south along the B1159 we pass by Stow Mill, an impressive tower mill complete with sails, before coming to the little hamlet of **Paston** with its enormous thatched barn to the west of the church. This superbly restored barn dates back to 1581 and is all that is left of the original home of the Paston family. Their fortune was made in the wool trade, and they are best remembered for the famous 'Paston Letters': written by several members of the family in the mid-15th century, they provide a vivid insight into how the Pastons' many estates were run during those unsettled times of the Wars of the Roses.

The coast road from here continues past the decidedly un-picturesque sight of the enormous Gas Terminal that was built to receive natural gas from the offshore wells in the North Sea; but you can soon put this unwelcome intrusion out of sight and out of mind as you arrive at the pleasant seaside community of **Bacton-on-Sea**.

To the south of the village is the ruined gateway of Bromholm Priory, which enjoyed great acclaim during the Middle Ages for its proud possession of a piece of the 'True Cross'. This relic from Calgary was purported to cure various troublesome ailments from leprosy to death, and even gets a mention in Chaucer's 'Reeve's Tale'. Bromholm was referred to many times in the 'Paston Letters', and also commanded the attention of that famous witch and prophetess, Mother Shipton, who foretold that the priory would become a farm. As it happened, she was quite correct, for that is just what it is today!

A lane to the west of Knapton will take you across the B1145 and on to **Trunch**, where the grave of Horatio, son of Lord Nelson by his mistress Lady Hamilton, can be found in the beautiful church of St Mary's. The roof here is very fine indeed, but by far the best feature of the church is the font with its splendid overhead canopy, a gloriously embellished piece of carving standing on six tall legs. We imagined that it must be quite a struggle for the vicar to negotiate the platform with a wriggling baby without bashing its head against one of the supports!

One mile northeast of North Walsham, the B1145 Mundesley road crosses the North Walsham and Dilham Canal near the charming village of **Swafield**. The canal was built around 1800 and was once the main trade route to Great Yarmouth. In a former granary on the banks of the canal, we found the **Staithe Lodge Gallery**, a fascinating establishment run by Mike and Margaret Foster. The gallery specialises in picture framing and restoration, and it also has fine displays of paintings, antique pictures, prints, local pottery, and fine examples of tapestry and embroidery. Margaret is an enthusiastic machine knitter and the gallery supplies an excellent range of machine yarns, tapestry wools and embroidery threads. She also gives tuition and produces one-off garments of her own.

Staithe Lodge Gallery, Staithe Lodge, Swafield, North Walsham
01692 402669

North Walsham is a prosperous little market town which has held a weekly market for over 700 years. Much of this prosperity came from selling the woven goods made at the nearby village of Worstead, from which the famous woollen cloth takes its name. The fine timber Market Cross with its lead-covered domed roof and lantern was rebuilt after a fire in 1602 destroyed many of the town buildings. St Nicholas' Church in Market Street dates back to the 15th century; the stump of its fallen tower (which once stood 147ft high) forming the perfect accompaniment to the tower of the earlier Saxon church just to the north. Across the square is the Paston Grammar School, founded in 1606, where Lord Nelson spent part of his schooldays.

Also in the heart of the town, appropriately situated on the opposite corner to the Black Cat Garage, we found the interesting and unusual **Cat Pottery**. Jenny Winstanley has been making her unique range of earthenware cats and dogs here for the past 30 years. Each one is individually modelled, painted and glazed, then after hard-firing, is fitted with specially-made cathedral-glass eyes. Jenny's animals come in all shapes and sizes; they are highly collectible and are sold all over the world. Her studio is a centuries-old tinsmith's workshop which she shares with her glass-sculptor husband, Ken Allen, and their son, Nick. Over the years, their workshop has become home for Nick's fascinating collection of railway memorabilia and transport curiosities which is well worth a look.

Cat Pottery, 1 Grammer School Road, North Walsham
01692 402962

On the outskirts of **North Walsham** on the Happisburgh road, White Horse Common, we called in at the **Broadland Plants Garden Centre**, an excellent place to spend an hour or so. The garden centre is run by Jim LeGrice, a real specialist in his field. He and his staff provide a fine range of quality plants, shrubs and trees, as well as helpful and informed advice on how best to care for them. For the specialist gardener, there are displays on the water garden, the bog garden and the patio garden, and

Jim also provides a skilled garden design and landscaping service which can transform even the most modest outdoor space. Broadland Plants also supply a full range of greenhouses, tools and accessories.

Broadland Plants Garden Centre, Meeting Hill Road, North Walsham 01692 500333

Passing through Scarborough Hill, a lovely area which takes its name from Sir Charles Scarborough, doctor of physics and court physician to Charles II, James II and then William III. We turned off the old Yarmouth Road to find the **Scarborough Hill House Hotel**, a very pleasant country hotel set in five acres of its own grounds. Owners Gary and Karen Dimmock have been successful in creating an exceptionally peaceful and relaxing atmosphere. There are six en-suite bedrooms, all with every facility, and an excellent range of meals available in the dining area. The hotel is renowned for its steaks, and being a free house, offering a good selection of ales.

Scarborough Hill House Hotel, Old Yarmouth Road, North Walsham 01692 402151/402149

Heading north from North Walsham on the A149, you will have the good fortune of encountering the picturesque village of **Thorpe Market**. It is here that you will find Philip Lomax's exclusive **Green Farm Hotel** and Restaurant,. This 16th Century flint faced house has been extensively refurbished and modernised to provide every service you require.

The freehouse has fine oak bar tables and pews, is ideal to visit for a drink and snack. There is a comprehensive menu and an additional selection on the blackboard ranging from sandwiches to winter warmers like Lord Suffields steak, Kidney and Guiness pie. If you fancy dinning in style enter Green Farms beautifully decorated 30 seater restaurant. A choice of traditional cordon bleu favourites are served in addition to a selection of meals unique to Green Farm including casserole of pheasant with white wine and orange and charcoal grilled sirloin steak with stilton and port wine sauce. A real treat!

Green Farm offers a blend of natural charm with homely comfort, colour T.V in all rooms, tea and coffee service trays, flowers, fruit and home made chocolates. Twin and double rooms are available and some are conveniently positioned on the ground floor for the disabled and elderly.

Green Farm is ideal for all, whether you wish to take advantage of Norfolks nearby activities or just wish to relax for a while.

Green Farm Hotel & Restaurant, North Walsham Road, Thorpe Market 01263 833602

On the edge of Gunton Park, set well back off the main road you will find the **Elderton Lodge Hotel.** This magnificent building affords unspoilt views across its six acres of country estate.

For those historians amongst you Elderton Lodge dates back to the Georgian period and was once frequented by both Edward VII and Lily Langtry. It was once part of the Gunton Estate owned by Lord Suffield who was thought to have built Gunton Station in order that Edward VII could disembark near to his home.

Today the hotel offers luxury accommodation at reasonable prices. All bedrooms have en suite facilities or washbasins, a well stocked bar provides real ales and a high standard of cuisine is available.

This hotel is conveniently positioned for both the travelling businessman and those wishing to explore the places of interest nearby. There is a large lake in the park available for fishing, and the coast, broads and local golf courses are only a short distance away.

Elderton Lodge Hotel & Restaurant, Thorpe Market, Nr Cromer
01263 79547

To the east of Thorpe Market's spacious village green, a fine avenue of trees leads to St Margaret's Church. Dating back to 1796, this is Norfolk's only example of a Gothick (or Gothic Revival) church; featuring turrets with little spires on each corner of the building, two open-work screens dividing the church into three separate parts, and two individual porches, one for the use of the priest and the other for the congregation.

A mile or two to the south-west is the lovely little church of St Andrew in Gunton Park. Built by Robert Adam in 1769, it features a Doric portico of great Tuscan columns at the west entrance, and resembles a temple rather than a church. Gunton Hall has been largely restored, though parts of the house - which was badly damaged by fire in 1882 - stand in ruins in a lovely formal garden.

North-west of Thorpe Market at the junction of the A140 and B1436 is **Roughton**, where St Mary's Church with its Saxon round tower stands at one end of the long village street.

Heading south from here on the A140 we came to a fascinating working crafts complex which is housed in a well-restored group of brick and flint farm buildings. Here you will find **Alby Gardens** with its

133

comprehensive range of wild and wetland plants, together with the **Alby Lace Museum** where you can see a stunning collection of lace - some of it over 300 years old - and watch the intricate art of bobbin lace being made. Handmade lace, lacemakers' requisites and books on the subject can all be purchased at the shop. Here too is the Charles Matts Furniture Showroom, where you can buy or commission beautifully crafted furniture made from locally grown hardwoods in a great variety of original designs. Alby Crafts seems to have something for everyone who is interested in traditional crafts, and as you stroll around the centre you will also see woodcarvers, sculptors, stained glass designers, glass engravers, a silversmith and a ceramics expert hard at work.

To the west of Alby Crafts, just off the main road, lies the village of **Erpingham**. Just in case you missed the sign and are wondering where you are, the name of the village is spelt out around the parapet of the tall 15th century tower of St Mary's Church!

The Ark, a restaurant started in the home of Mike and Sheila Kidd has now been open eight and half years. Much restoration has been carried out over the years and two en-suite rooms have now been finished. If you enjoy being pampered, away from it all, this is the place to try.

All the food is produced by Sheila and her daughter Becky, starting with the bread and finishing with the chocolates. Mostly local produce, much of their own produced vegetables, free range eggs, local and Lowestoft fresh fish all add to a short, constantly changing menu. Mainly British cooking, but with leanings to French and Italian. Vegetarian dishes are a speciality, with plenty of variety, including home made pasta. The dining room and bedrooms are non smoking.

The Ark Hotel & Restaurant, The Street, Erpingham 01263 761535

The surrounding gardens are beautiful and eating in them is a possibility in the summer and Wednesday to Saturday evening in winter.

134

Sunday lunch is served throughout the year. They are now expecting guests any time of the week and it may be worth giving them a call to see whether they are open outside these times.

Small wedding parties and private luncheons or dinners can always be arranged.

Half a mile further east is **Calthorpe**. In the main street you will find Paul and Penny Jackson are the proud owners of the **Calthorpe Workshop** located on the Aldborough Road. Anyone within driving distance of this exquisite, unique workshop are strongly recommended to call in. Both Penny and Paul have outstanding artistic abilities and are accepted members of the East Anglian Pottery Association. In 1977 they set up their first ceramic workshop in Sheringham together, and have held numerous exhibitions in the years that followed before moving to Calthorpe and opening their new workshop in May of 1988. It is here that you will get the opportunity to meet Oscar and Bertie bear, the inspiration behind the whole range of products including door plaques, coat hooks, jigsaws, tins and greeting cards. The two bears, dating back to 1918 and 1920 respectively, sit proudly in the workshop, Bertie is almost bald with the exception of a few whiskers under his chin, and Oscar (named after Oscar Wilde) sports a big bow tie. Toy manufacturers, Monkey Puzzle famed for their 3-D stand up jigsaw puzzles expressed great interest in marketing a range of products based on the bears so Paul busied himself in designing and the Oscar and Bertie range was born.

Calthorpe Workshop, Corner House, Aldborough Road, Calthorpe
01263 768346

Not all of Paul's time is dedicated to his fluffy friends, he is also busy sculpting intricate little fairytale pieces comprising the fantasy theme section of the workshop. Fairies, kings, dragons and dreams feature amongst his excellent range of ceramic figurines each formed with great care and attention to detail.

Penny is also a talented artist. Her Edwardian theme contains little clay miniatures of houses and shops. She also produces ceramic teddy bears, brooches and hand painted fabrics which are used to make hats, waistcoats and other items of clothing.

The opening hours are October 1st to June 30th, Wednesday, Friday and Saturday, 10.00 am to 5.00 pm and July 1st to September 30th, everyday except Monday. Call in and be delighted by this couples fine example of talented art.

About two miles to the south, just off the B1354 and a mile-and-a-half north-west of Aylsham, stands the great National Trust property **Blickling Hall.** This magnificent redbrick mansion was built on the site of a late-medieval moated house purchased in 1616 by Sir Henry Hobart. He commissioned the architect of Hatfield House, Robert Lyminge, to design his new country residence and in 1628 Blickling was completed. Inside, you will find the Great Hall with its carved Jacobean double-flight staircase, the magnificent library in the Long Gallery, and the Peter the Great Room which is dominated by a massive tapestry of the Battle of Poltawa. This was given by the Empress Catherine the Great to John Hobart, the Second Earl of Buckinghamshire, whilst ambassador to the Russian court.

Blickling Hall, Blicking, Nr Norwich 01263 733471

In the grounds you will find an 18th century orangery, an extensive parterre, a delightful secret garden, and huge yew hedges originally planted in the 17th century. In late spring, the garden is ablaze with rhododendrons and azaleas; in high summer, the large exotic herbaceous borders dominate. The parks and woods contain several miles of footpaths, a mile long crescent-shaped lake and the unusual pyramidal mausoleum of the Second Earl of Buckinghamshire. Look out for special events and guided walks throughout the year. Adjacent to Blickling, and within the National Trust estate, stands the famous Buckinghamshire Arms public house, itself a Grade II listed building and an ideal stopping place for those wanting good food and drink in genuinely historc surroundings.

Standing 45ft high, the pyramid at Blickling is undoubtedly the finest of its kind in England. It is strikingly different to its Egyptian relatives in that it has a large portico at the main entrance to the mausoleum, which is surmounted by the Earl of Buckinghamshire's arms. Its builder was one Ignatius Bonomi, an architect with a definite penchant for the Egyptian style - he is also renowned as the builder of a particularly splendid mill in Yorkshire, where his 'Egypt-mania' was given full rein.

One resident of the original house at Blickling was Sir John Fastolf, and it only required a minor change of his name to give Shakespeare one of his most endearing characters. Sir John sold the house to Geoffrey Boleyn, the great-grandfather of Anne Boleyn, and it is possible that she was in fact born here. Poor Anne, the great love of Henry VIII until it became evident that she would never be able to give him an heir. If only Henry had known that her daughter Elizabeth would become one of England's greatest monarchs!

Anne was executed on 19th May 1536 on a charge of treason and adultery, and it is reported that on the anniversary of her death, a coach drawn by headless horses drives up to Blickling Hall with the unfortunate Anne clutching her disembodied head inside. The phantom traffic on the roads around the estate must get quite congested at this time of year, as it is said that on the same evening her father, Thomas Boleyn, can also be spotted charging along the lanes in his coach - his task to cross over 40 of Norfolk's bridges as penance for his betrayal of the King.

To the south-west of Blickling, by the side of the B1149 and close to its junction with the B1145 near Cawston, there is a large stone ball on a plinth called the Duelling Stone. It commemorates a duel fought between Sir Henry Hobart and Oliver La Neve in 1698, and the National Trust plaque states that their quarrel arose from words spoken in anger during an election campaign. Sir Henry was mortally wounded and died at Blickling the following day, while La Neve fled to Holland then later returned to stand trial and was acquitted. La Neve came from nearby Great Witchingham Hall, better known today perhaps as the original H.Q. of one of Norfolk's more famous sons, Bernard Matthews CBE - he of 'bootiful' turkey-roll fame!

For those looking for a rather special caravan park, it's well worth finding the Haveringland Hall Caravan Park, near Cawston. Well-hidden, eight miles north-west of Norwich and a mile west of the B1149, it may be necessary to phone the park manager, Mr Ken Rustidge on

Cromer Pier and Seafront

(0603) 871302, for directions. The caravan park was established in 1953 in the grounds of Haveringland Hall, now demolished, but formerly the residence of Baron de Ramsey. There is a well-stocked 14 acre lake which can be fished by caravan park residents, many beautiful woodland walks and an arboretum filled with specimen trees. This truly is the perfect place for peace and relaxation. An interesting feature of Haveringland is its medieval stocks. Haveringland Hall Caravan Park provides an ideal base for exploring the beautiful Norfolk countryside and many nearby places of interest.

Haveringland Hall Caravan Park, Cawston, Nr Norwich
01603 871302

The most memorable thing about Cawston itself is the impressive Church of St Agnes with its stunning hammerbeam roof and 120ft high tower that soars above the houses of this little town. Perhaps even better is the massive 15th century Church of St Peter and St Paul in the little village of **Salle** (pronounced 'Saul'), which lies a couple of miles north-west of Cawston. Thanks must go to three great local families - the Briggs, the Fountaines and the Boleyns - for providing such a tiny village with such a magnificent place of worship. Much could be said of the treasures inside: from the Seven Sacrament font complete with original beam and pulley to lift the cover, to the three-decker pulpit, medieval stained glass and abundance of wonderful carvings and brasses - this is without doubt one of Norfolk's most glorious churches and outstanding in every way. It is also interesting to note that a number of people insist that this is Anne Boleyn's final resting place, and not the Tower of London as the history books would have us believe.

If you have a particular passion for exploring English churches, then you really should make your way to the little market town of **Reepham**, which can be found to the west of Cawston on the B1145. Here you will find not one, not two, but three parish churches, all sharing the same churchyard! All Saints Church, which belonged to the old parish of Hackford, was destroyed by fire in 1543 and only a part of the tower wall remains. The surviving churches, St Mary's and St Michael's, are linked by a common choir vestry. The explanation for this veritable warren of churches is that this is the place where the parish boundaries of Reepham, Hackford and Whitwell met; each village insisted on having its own church, and perhaps it was deemed more economical to build all three on the same site. As it transpired, the three villages were to be merged into the market town of Reepham, so in hindsight one church would have sufficed!

Quite apart from its churches, Reepham has a number of fine old buildings that will catch your eye as you explore the town. One of the best of these is known locally as the Dial House due to a sun-dial above its portico, which is inscribed with the words: 'I do not count the hours unless they are sunny/happy'.

St Andrew's Church at **Saxthorpe**, which can be found about four-and-a-half miles north-east of Reepham on the B1149/B1354 crossroads. Here a delightful story concerns the 17th century altar rails, which have unusually large knobs on the posts. It appears that the knobs are in fact so large that they have actually been confirmed on several occasions by short-sighted bishops!

A lane to the north of the village then takes us to **Little Barningham,** where the tiny St Mary's Church has a particularly fine example of the type of off-beat humour sometimes to be found in English churches. On the corner post of a box pew stands the wooden carving of a skeleton decked out Grim Reaper-style, complete with shroud, hour-glass and scythe. The pew was dedicated by one Stephen Crosbie in 1640, and the inscription reads: 'As you are now, even so was I, Remember death for ye must dye'. This otherwise conventional message is given a somewhat macabre twist by an additional inscription on the back of the pew, which states: 'For couples joined in wedlock this seat did I intend'.

Just to the south of Little Barningham village you will find **Mannington Hall Gardens**, which are well worth a visit. The Rose Gardens, which were created from an acre of walled kitchen garden, feature roses in small gardens reflecting their period of origin. Lord and Lady Walpole have provided 20 miles of way-marked footpaths, including nature, local history and farm trails. These are open every day with just a small parking fee. There is access for wheelchair users, over a boardwalk, across a traditional wet meadow, and light refreshments are available when the gardens are open.

About a mile to the east, Lord and Lady Walpole are also busily restoring their home, Wolterton Hall, to its former splendour. The Old

Brew House is being opened as a Visitor Centre, and Wolterton is the centre for the Hawk and Owl Trust. A number of musical events and lectures are held in the saloon of the handsome red-brick house, which was built by Horatio Walpole (with Thomas Ripley as architect) in 1741. Information on both of these estates can be obtained from Mannington Hall (Telephone: 026 387 4175).

Two 'castles' lie a few miles to the north of here; not really castles at all in the accepted sense, but fortified moated manor houses built by two other important local families. The first is Baconsthorpe Castle, built by the Heydons in the 15th century and pulled down in 1654; some of its stone to be used at Felbrigg Hall further east - of which more later. Its remains are now in the hands of English Heritage. The other is Gresham Castle, one of the Paston family's many properties, the ruins of which can be seen in the fields to the south of Gresham village.

It was here that you will find a very talented couple, Andrew and Joanna Young, who started **A. & J. Young Pottery** in Hunworth before moving to their present premises at Common Farm in **Lower Gresham**. Once part of the Felbrigg estate, their house has been converted from derelict cottages and their workshop from the old cow sheds.

This couple have been either learning or practising the art of making pottery for most of their lives and have won many awards, including the Crafts Council Ruskin Award in 1988. They use their skills to produce an interesting and versatile range of pots, that are specifically designed to stand up to the rigours of everyday use. In addition to their kitchen range, they also make garden pots and decorative items, and if you visit their shop at Common Farm you will find a selection of non-standard pots which are unavailable elsewhere.

A. & J. Young Pottery, Common Farm, Sustead Road, Lower Gresham, Norwich 01263 77548

The Youngs produce their own clay, glazes and designs, and because their work sells all over the country and overseas as well, they have had to take on extra staff to cope with the demand. They designed a small range of pots for Next Interiors in 1988, and there is a permanent exhibition of their work at Norwich Castle. Their shop is open from 9.00am - 5.00pm every day from Easter until the end of September, and if you want to visit during the winter months, it is advisable to ring beforehand for details of opening times on Matlaske (026 377) 548.

Over to the east at **Aylmerton** there have been several sightings of an unhappy ghost who is seen walking around The Shrieking Pits, a series of round depressions in the ground which are thought to be the sites of prehistoric dwellings or possibly flint mines. This unfortunate soul, a woman dressed in white, seems doomed to perpetual misery as she clasps her hands in despair and shrieks into the pits. No one knows who she is or what ails her, but her frequent appearances certainly put the wind up the locals!

Two miles south of Cromer, and just to the west of **Felbrigg** Village on the B1436, we visited the National Trust property, **Felbrigg Hall**. This 17th century country mansion was built by the Windham family on the site of an earlier manor house. The mid 17th century saw a revolution in English architecture and the extraordinary contrast between the south and west wings of Felbrigg, separated by only 60 years, provides a clear illustration of this. The architect of the Jacobean south front was almost certainly the master mason Robert Lyminge, who, in the early 1620s, was also rebuilding Blickling for Sir Henry Hobart. The west wing was added in the 1680s; it was designed by William Samwell and still contains some sumptuous plasterwork of the period.

Felbrigg Hall & Sheringham Park, Felbrigg 01263 837444

The interior of the house was extensively remodelled in the 18th

142

century, and the internal decorations reflect this more consistent opulent style. Look out for the elegant library and the beautiful wallpaper in the Chinese bedroom which dates from the 1750s. In the grounds, be sure to visit the orangery, which was added in 1705, and the wonderful walled garden with its huge herbaceous borders, greenhouses and magnificent octagonal dovecote.

A few miles to the west of Felbrigg Hall on the B1157 at Upper Sheringham, lies Sheringham Park, 770 acres of National Trust parkland originally designed by Humphrey Repton in 1812. Visitors can follow waymarked trails through large areas of species rhododendrons and azaleas (at their best in late May and early June) and on towards the coastline. Magnificent views of the Norfolk coast and countryside can be obtained by climbing specially constructed viewing towers.

From here we join up with the A148 and head west. The first village we came to was **Bodham** , where Colin and Sally Graver have been at the **Red Hart Inn** for the past two years. Although this charming 200-year-old inn has been updated over the years, its original character remains unchanged. It is set back off the Cromer to Fakenham road by a couple of hundred yards or so, and although it would be easy to drive straight by, that very small detour will be well worth while.

The Red Hart Inn, Bodham 01263 70270

They serve a good selection of ales and some very tasty pub meals, but what caught our eye especially were the extremely tempting desserts! We all have to shuffle off this mortal coil at some time or another, and 'Death by Chocolate' sounds to us like the perfect way to go! Consisting of cake, mousse, fudge sauce and solid chocolate topped with chocolate chips it is, as they say, 'indescribably delicious' - and we will not argue with that. They also serve an excellent range of salads, including a cooked chicken half salad at a very reasonable price, as well as lasagne, curry, bolognaise and chilli - all firm favourites with those who want a hearty meal with no stinting on the portions! The daily blackboard specials are also worth looking out for, and on the day we were there the choice was homemade chicken and mushroom pie or traditional roast beef with all the trimmings.

To relax in front of the magnificent feature beamed fireplace in the bar, with a drink in your hand and the knowledge that a tasty meal is being prepared for you, must be one of the best ways of enjoying your holiday!

It is just a short drive from here to **Holt**, an attractive market town whose more interesting houses are of the Georgian era - most of the town having been destroyed in a great fire in 1708.

Gresham's School was founded in 1555 as a grammar school by Sir John Gresham, then Lord Mayor of London. The original building was rebuilt Tudor-style in 1858 and still stands in the market place, but the school itself was relocated to the eastern outskirts in 1900 and became a public school. One of Holt's most unusual buildings is Home Place, designed and built in 1903-5 by E.S. Prior, an architect of the Arts and Crafts movement, the building's exterior is completely clad in local pebbles.

Arts and Crafts of a different kind can be found at **Picturecraft**, which refers to itself as 'North Norfolk's Art Centre' - a title that it richly deserves, as it offers a comprehensive service in every area where art and art materials are concerned. This is no small scale venture either, but one of the largest, private-owned galleries in England. We found the gallery in Lees Courtyard, just off Bull Stree, and it is well worth setting aside an hour or two to visit this fascinating place.

Owner Michael Hill and his family pride themselves on the close contact they have between the artists they represent and those of us who wish to purchase a print or a painting. After you have made your choice from the large selection available, you will be taken to the Framing Shop where frames of every description are displayed. Every assistance is given in choosing the right frame for your purchase and the decor of the room in which it will hang, and the most modern techniques and machinery are used to ensure that all pictures are correctly mounted and framed.

The main gallery is light and airy and paintings are shown to good advantage in alcoves along the walls, with plenty of information about the exhibiting artists. The exhibitions change frequently too, so if you are in the area for more than three weeks, it is worth revisiting them to see new works being displayed. The reputation of the gallery is such that exhibiting artists get a considerable boost from their work being shown here, and this helps to generate a higher level of commissioned work.

Having a number of friends in the painting profession, we were at first amazed to discover that the gallery does not charge commission on sales made, which we thought was rare indeed! We then learnt that the preferred method here is that the artist rents the alcove in which his painting is displayed, and so knows from the outset what the charge will be, how long his pictures will be exhibited, and most importantly, that they will be displayed as a group.

Picturecraft also stocks an excellent range of artists' materials - one of the largest of its kind in the whole of East Anglia - and helpful advice is always at hand, whether you are looking for paints, paper, nibs, pens, or whatever. One of the most fascinating rooms at the gallery houses a superb collection of antiquarian and decorative prints, including hand-coloured engravings and antique maps, all beautifully displayed and painstakingly catalogued. An extension of this side of the business is the Valuation and Restoration Service which Picturecraft offers its clients, which could come in handy if you discover an original painting whilst rummaging through your attic one day!

Picturecraft is a true Aladdin's Cave for anyone with an interest in art, and yet the thing that struck us even more forcibly than the amazing range of products and services available was the friendliness and dedication of the people who work here. Knowing that you can always rely on expert guidance and courteous service whenever you come to make a purchase encourages you to return. We are certainly looking forward to our next visit.

Picturecraft, Lees Courtyard, off Bull Street, Holt 01263 713259

Still on the subject of crafts, we were also delighted to come across **Wansbeck Dolls Houses**, which is situated within the Old Chapel in the centre of Holt.

Jill Swift, the friendly owner of the business has been specialising in

Dolls Houses for the previous three years. They have always been a personal hobby of hers and she is delighted to be able to extend her interest to others.

This year she is introducing two new houses, one Edwardian and the other Regency and three new shops. The houses and shops come either assembled or in kit form depending on your personal predilection. Wansbeck Dolls Houses will be only too pleased to decorate and furnish your house in the style of your choice. Conversely, if you prefer to decorate yourself there is a superb range of miniature furniture to choose from in varying colours and styles. Some particularly appealing items include a chaise longue upholstered with white silk, a chiffonier, available in both mahogany and walnut and a four poster bed with salmon pink brocade.

For the younger members of the family, the 'Selecta House' made in Germany is ideal. it is attractive, tough and accessible with its own set of furniture. A real treat for your kids!

Whether a collector or not, this shop is definitely worth a visit. You will find it open between 9 am and 5 pm, Monday to Saturday take a look around, you won't be disappointed!

Wansbeck Dolls Houses, Old Chapel, Holt

Holt's mixture of grand Georgian and Victorian houses, colour-washed buildings around the market place and traditional Norfolk Flint cottages off the pretty main street makes for a very pleasant, often picturesque, combination of styles. Small wonder that the town has been designated a Conservation Area. Another interesting feature to look out for is the large obelisk-cum-milestone surmounted by a pineapple, which can be found at the north end of town at the top of Letheringsett Hill. It was apparently a former gatepost from Melton Constable Park, and bearing in mind that Melton Constable lies some four miles to the south-west of Holt, it is obvious that the original inscriptions on the column showing distances to all the local villages are somewhat unreliable!

The Hall at **Melton Constable** stands in a beautiful park with a lake and was the home of the Astley family for over 700 years, from 1236 to 1956. The present building, which dates back to the late 17th century, has been used as a set in various films, including 'The Go-Between' with Julie Christie and Alan Bates.

Although neglected for many years after it was sold, Melton Hall's current owners have embarked upon a long campaign of restoration to bring the house back to its former glory. From the B1110 to the north-west of the village you can see the tall tower surmounted by a glass observatory that was built by the Astleys in 1588. It was used then as a look-out post to warn of the approach of the Armada, and for similar purposes during the Napoleonic Wars and both World Wars.

A mile to the east of Melton Constable, just south of the B1354, is the village of **Briston**. This was once the centre of the Midland & Great Northern Joint Railway, its lines linking Norfolk to the Midlands, but no trace of the lines or the station remain today. What we did find here, however, is an excellent pub which we would happily recommend to any traveller passing through.

It is always nice to see a family-run concern, and **The Green Man,** situated on the outskirts of Briston, is a fine example of this. Doug, Pat and their son Stephen have been running this first-class freehouse for the past five-and-a-half years. The inn dates back to the 18th century, and the additional modern facilities do not affect its character or traditional atmosphere.

The Green Man, Hall Street, Briston   01263 860993

An 'olde worlde' style is reflected in low-beamed ceilings and a huge roaring fire under an original inglenook fireplace.

147

A special attraction for pool fans is the exceptional pool room positioned at one end of the inn. This room and its table is reminiscent of a gentleman's snooker room, and is one of the best we have ever seen. On Sunday lunchtimes, the room is transformed into a superb dining area where traditional Sunday dinners are served.

Bar meals are available every lunchtime and evening, except Sundays. There is a set menu comprising a good range of starters, main meals, snacks and desserts, and an additional daily specials board tempting you with mouthwatering dishes such as homemade beef casserole, barbecued spare ribs, honey roast ham and rump steak. Delicious!

Open all day, everyday, except Sunday (when normal licensing hours apply), with a weekday happy hour between 6.00pm and 7.00pm, this really is the ideal venue for all occasions. All in all, it is a very classy inn with friendly, efficient owners, and is beautifully decorated throughout. Definitely worth a visit.

Accommodation can be found at **Hulverhill House**, which is situated in the heart of magnificent countryside on the B1110 near **Wood Norton**, eight miles south of Holt and nine miles north of Dereham. Originally, it was built in the 18th century as a public house called the 'Three Horseshoes' but for the last few years Diana and Stan Smith have had great pleasure in offering bed and breakfast accomodation to weary travellers. On arriving at Hulverhill House, Diana and Stan succeed in making you feel at home right away. A tray of tea and coffee awaits you and if you are lucky, you may get the opportunity to try Diana's home-made coffee cake.

Hulverhill House, Holt Road, Wood Norton, Dereham 01362 84826

Downstairs the lounge, dining room and conservatory are all tastefully decorated. The conservatory offers a beautiful view of the well stocked and carefully tended gardens. Upstairs there are three spacious, first

148

class bedrooms, two double rooms and one family room which has en-suite facilities. Don't forget to take a peek at Stan's impressive display of R.A.C. badgeswhich take pride of place on the upstairs landing.

Full English breakfast is provided and evening meals are available by prior arrangement, all served with home-grown vegetables.

A mile to the east of the A1067 we stopped at the inappropriately-named village of **Foulsham**. The attractive market place was rebuilt after a devastating fire in 1771, and its imposing Georgian houses are dominated by the 15th century tower of Holy Innocents' Church.

The Queens Head in Foulsham dates back in parts to the 17th century and is full of character, both inside and out. Colin Rowe and his partner Dorothy Deadman have been here for 10 years and have worked hard to produce a truly outstanding establishment. The interior is charming, with low beams, feature fireplaces and a pleasant clutter of antiques and knick-knacks giving it a cosy and intriguing atmosphere. All meals are prepared using fresh local produce and the menu offers an excellent range. You can choose from sandwiches with great fillings, to juicy steaks and some interesting vegetarian dishes such as the tasty cauliflower cheese with a dash of white wine. A children's menu is available too, and all prices are extremely reasonable.

Children can let off steam in the large garden, which is also a super place to sit out and relax when weather permits. One of Colin and Dorothy's latest improvements has been to refurbish an old stable block to a very high standard; and this now provides a comfortable function room for meetings and parties of all kinds. A wide range of buffet menus are available here to suit different occasions, and a television is provided. The Queens Head is also a great place to visit over the festive season, for what could be better than enjoying traditional Christmas Fayre in the friendly atmosphere of a lively village pub?

The Queens Head, High Street, Foulsham, Dereham 01362 84339

Blicking Hall, Blicking

CHAPTER SIX

Central Norfolk

Norwich Castle Keep

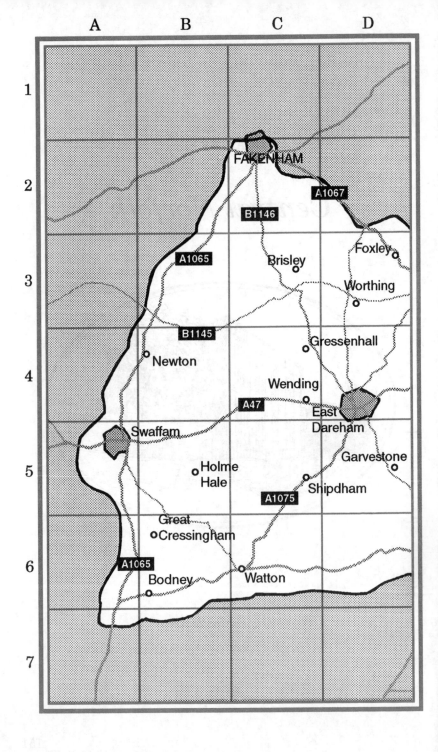

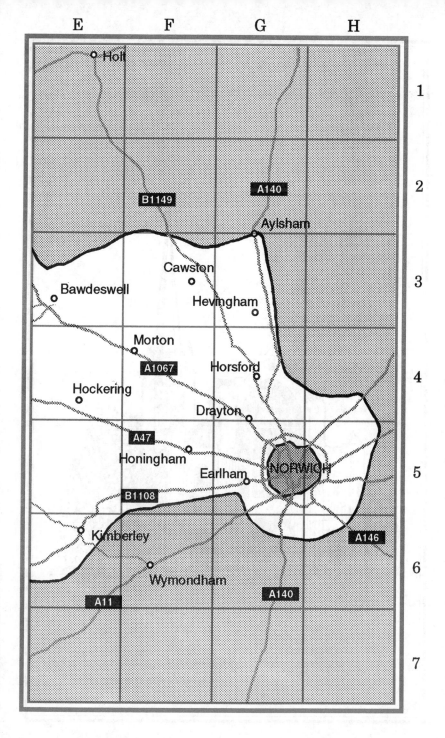

Norwich Cathedral

Central Norfolk

As you begin to explore the inland heart of Norfolk, you quickly get the feeling that the countryside here has changed very little over the years. The coming of the railway opened up much of this land to the outsider, though the discontinuation of local lines due to supposed 'under-use' has meant that the car remains the chief method of exploring the county. With the large open vistas and long stretches of often quiet road before you, it is tempting, perhaps, to overlook the pleasant aspects that lie over the nearest hedgerow, intent instead on clocking up the miles with your eyes set firmly on the horizon. Thankfully, the visitor who wants to see more can still get well away from the main arterial roads and onto the secret lanes leading to hidden villages set deep in the Norfolk countryside.

The first stop for this particular part of our tour, however, is the village of **Foxley**, which can be found on the A1067 some six miles northeast of Dereham. If you are passing through **Foxley West**, do take the time to visit The **Silver Jubilee** in Chapel Road for a drink.

The Silver Jubilee, Chapel Road, Foxley West 01362 88304

Previously the village supermarket, it earned its name from the fact that it was converted into a pub in 1977 - the year of Queen Elizabeth II's silver jubilee. It is a small, cosy pub, tucked away in a cul-de-sac in the village, and Gilly and Bruce Saker have been running it for the past four years. They are a very friendly couple, and have created the sort of atmosphere where visitors will feel just as at home as the locals.

As you walk through the door, a crackling log fire and subdued lighting set the scene. We felt that this made a refreshing change from so many of the pubs we visit on our travels, where the glare of the lights positively discourages intimate tete a tetes! Two restaurants are thoughtfully provided - one for those who like to smoke after a meal, and one for those who prefer a clearer atmosphere! In addition to the comprehensive menu, Gilly offers some of her fine home cooked meals, and there is also a good selection of beers to choose from. Those of you who like a bit of sporting activity with your drink will find two good sized pool tables in the games room.

Close by, a mile to the east of where the B1145 King's Lynn to Aylsham road bridges the River Wensum, we reached the pleasant village of **Billingford**. Here, we called in at the attractive inn, **The Forge**, run by Mr J Shirley. The building is a former blacksmith's cottage and workshop. It is believed to have been built around 1500 and was once owned by the Earl of Leicester. On the outside walls it is still possible to see the rings where horses were tethered whilst waiting to be shod. Today, The Forge has a 28-seater restaurant, a games room and an attractive beer garden. Look out for the ghost of the original blacksmith which is said to appear once the customers have gone.

The Forge, Bintree Road, Billingford, Dereham 01362 668980

St Peter's Church at Billingford is notable for its octagonal tower and a most impressive eagle lectern which dates back to the 15th century.

Having crossed the bridge on the B1145, we stopped in the lovely village of **Worthing**. The village stands in the valley of the River Wensum, a couple of miles downstream from the remains of a Saxon cathedral. Those looking for exceptional bed and breakfast accommodation in this

156

beautiful part of central Norfolk could find none better than that run by Belinda and George Eve at **Tannery House**. The accommodation is located in a tastefully converted first-floor winery, and has en-suite shower/WC, television and tea/coffee making facilities. Guests are free to stroll around the lovely three-acre grounds which contain an outdoor swimming pool (heated in summer) and 250 yards of superb river frontage where guests can fish free of charge.

Tannery House, Worthing, Dereham   0362 668202

Our final view of this exceptionally pretty village was of the tiny Saxon church of St Margaret's with its round tower and Norman door, standing in lonely isolation by the river.

On a completely different scale are the dramatic ruins of the Saxon cathedral which can be found opposite the park entrance of Elmham House at **North Elmham**. This sprawling village straggles along for nearly half a mile on both sides of the B1110, some of its larger houses hidden from passers-by behind the tall flint and brick walls that line the main street. The grounds at Elmham House are now open to the public under the National Gardens Scheme and together with the large park they also feature vineyards and a wild garden which are well worth seeing. Lovers of the grape will also find a rather fine winery and vineyard in the village, run by Robin Don.

The cathedral ruins to the north of St Mary's Church are together with those at South Elmham in Suffolk the only visible Saxon cathedral remains in England. In the 7th century, North Elmham was the centre of the diocese of the North Folk, while South Elmham served that of the South Folk. The North Folk see moved to Thetford in 1072 after the Danish invasions, then the two dioceses were combined in 1093 and transferred to Norwich. Over 120ft long and with twin towers, the cathedral at North Elmham was a very impressive building indeed for

157

those times; but today the remains, though extensive, stand only 10ft high. The reason that the building has survived at all is that the Bishop of Norwich, Henry le Despenser, converted the abandoned cathedral into a hunting lodge in the late-14th century. From the number of jugs and drinking vessels excavated at the site, it would appear that Henry was certainly a 'dispenser' of merriment and good cheer.

Sight-seers with a taste for more modern buildings will enjoy a visit to the County School Station, where the former railway station has been converted to a Visitor Centre surrounded by pleasant country walks and a picnic area. The station, half a mile north of the village, was built in 1873 specifically to provide a service for the County School and was in use up until 1953. There is plenty to see, with maps and photographs recalling those bygone days, and the line now operates a diesel train and brake van run by the Fakenham and Dereham Railway Society.

We discovered some excellent literature here on the many Wensum Valley walks available in the area; one walk in particular (which is conveniently circular) will take you alongside a section of the old railway line through a glorious mixture of grassland and woodland. Look out for the ruins of the old Bishop's Chapel en-route, and if you haven't already done so, do take some time to see the lovely 14th century St Mary's Church with its painted rood screen and beautiful stained glass.

Further west on the B1145 is **Brisley,** with its moated Tudor manor house and barns, and houses clustered around the handsome 14th century church of St Bartholomew and large village green. A sweeping, semi-circled stone driveway leads up to **The Brisley Bell,** which stands proud on The Green, surrounded by open countryside. The building dates back to 1511 and it has been an alehouse for over 200 years. This lovely old inn exudes charm and character both inside and out, from its gabled end which was made from clay lumps from local ponds to the beamed interior, stone walls and feature fireplace. Chris and Anne Carter have been here less than two years, but they have already stamped their own personalities on the inn and a more friendly couple you could not wish to meet.

Their pride and joy is the wonderful seafood restaurant, which is beautifully decorated and has a truly welcoming atmosphere. To say that the menu is extensive would be an understatement indeed: with a minimum of 18 starters and 20 main meals to choose from, no one could possibly leave here feeling hungry or dissatisfied. All the food is brought daily from the coastal fish markets, so you are guaranteed that everything you eat is freshly prepared as well as being attractively presented and cooked to perfection. The restaurant is open Tuesday to Saturday from 7.00pm - 10.00pm, with traditional Sunday lunches served from 12.00am - 3.00pm.

To the rear of the inn is a cottage which Chris and Anne have completely refurbished. It was here that Richard Taverner translated the Bible from Latin into English in 1570. And on a lighter note, The Brisley Bell has also been used as a location by the BBC when some of the sketches in the comedy series 'You Rang, M'Lord?' were filmed here. In our opinion, this is a 5-Star inn with 5-Star hosts, and it will be our pleasure to patronise it again.

The Brisley Bell Inn & Restaurant, The Green, Brisley, Nr Dereham
01362 668686

While we were in Brisley we were told of the deserted village of **Godwick** nearby, one of a staggering 200 'lost' villages in Norfolk, and the only one that is open to the public. To find it, turn north onto the B1146 after Brisley, heading towards Fakenham, then after about a mile, take the left-hand turning to Whissonsett. From here, head south-west towards Tittleshall and a turning to your left will take you to Godwick Hall Farm and the parking area.

We certainly had no idea what to expect, but when we arrived we found a fascinating site that has long lain undisturbed; it owes its preservation to the fact that this has always been grazing land and has remained untouched by the plough over the centuries. The Saxons were the first to settle here and the village continued to be lived in right up until the 17th century; it was eventually to become absorbed into the parish of **Tittleshall** in the 19th century. The decline of the village was not marked by a sudden exodus brought about by plague, famine or war - it was just an inevitable fact of nature where poor harvests and an unyielding clay soil meant that the villagers simply could not eke out a living from the land.

A leaflet is available showing how the village was once laid out with church, streets, 'tofts' (individual homesteads) and even a watermill and millpond. The great house here was Godwick Manor, a handsome brick manor house built in 1585 for Sir Edward Coke, and though its ruins were demolished in 1962 its outline can still just be made out if you know where to look. The great Barn has stood the test of time; it is a fine building in its own right, with surprisingly ornate features such as the elaborate windows which were never in fact designed for anyone to look out of! The 13th century church was pulled down some time during the 17th century, and the ruined tower was then used as the base of a folly which was built in its place. Sir Edward and his wife now lie in the mausoleum in Tittleshall church, where you will also find many monuments to other members of the Coke family including Thomas 'Coke of Norfolk', the renowned agriculturalist.

The Godwick site is now managed and preserved by English Heritage, and the landowner has kindly consented to allow visitors to park their cars in the farmyard so that we may all enjoy this special piece of local history. If you happen to have brought your dog along with you, please remember to keep it on a lead as this is a working environment.

South of here on the B1145 is the straggling village of **Mileham**, which, although still very much alive in contrast to Godwick, shares a similar sense of history. Its main features of interest are the remains of Mileham Castle - a Norman fortification of the motte-and-bailey variety - the 14th century church of St John the Baptist with its outstanding stained glass, and nearby Burghwood Hall which occupies the site of Burghwood Manor, the birthplace of Sir Edward Coke. A precious relic in the form of a 10th century Viking sword was discovered here and is now on display in the museum at Norwich.

Two miles further west on the B1145 we came to **Litcham**; more than a village and yet not quite a town, but a pleasant enough place whatever you decide to call it. The attractive Georgian houses that line the main street and the 17th century tower of All Saints' Church are of red brick, and the 18th century farmhouse that includes the remains of the former priory at the southern end of the village was once the home of Matthew Hulcott, who financed the building of the church. The common land surrounding Litcham has been turned into a 60-acre nature reserve and provides a superb natural habitat for wetland creatures and plants.

Beeston lies about two miles south-east of here, and anyone looking for a respite from the rigours of travelling and sight-seeing is bound to find the solitary church of St Mary appealing. Standing rather forlorn in the fields, its notable features include a superb hammerbeam roof, a painted rood screen and two elaborate parclose screens. In contrast to the special atmosphere of the place, you may be amused to find a memorial in the churchyard to Jem Mace, a one-time bare-fisted boxing world champion who was apparently born in the village!

160

Over to the east, a couple of miles off the B1110 to the northwest of East Dereham, we found the **Norfolk Rural Life Museum** at **Gressenhall**. The museum is housed in a former 'house of industry', i.e. a workhouse, which was built in 1777 to house up to 700 people. When workhouses were abolished in 1930, Norfolk County Council took over the building and used it as an old people's home until 1975. A year later the museum was founded which over the years has grown to its present size. The purpose of the museum is to preserve a sense of the past 150 years of rural Norfolk life. Agriculture has always formed an important part of the county's economy, and so farm machinery and utensils form the central exhibits. These are displayed according to the months of the year, starting in October when farm tenancies changed hands and winter work began. In 1990, Union Farm was incorporated in the museum. This fifty acre working farm was originally cultivated by the inmates of the workhouse. The farm now operates the traditional 'Norfolk four course' system of crop rotation and makes use of two Suffolk heavy horses. Also to be seen on the farm are examples local rare breeds. Look out for Cherry Tree Cottage and its adjacent Edwardian cottage garden. Inside, we can see how a farm cottage would have looked around 1910. There is also a wildlife garden, a network of nature trails leading through beautiful riverside meadows, a gift shop selling locally made products, and a cafeteria serving light lunches and local home-made specialities. The Museum is open from Easter until the end of October.

Norfolk Rural Life Museum, Beech House, Gressenhall, Dereham
01362 860563

While we are on the subject of rural life and crafts, you may like to take a short detour from here to the village of **Beetley** - about one-and-a-half miles north-east across the B1146 - and seek out the home of a very talented lady called Debbie Booth. Debbie devotes her time to producing the most beautiful handmade English willow baskets, made to order in a great variety of shapes and sizes and ideal to take back as a gift for a friend or relative or to decorate your own home.

If you feel in need of sustenance at this stage of your journey, we suggest that you head south-west from Gressenhall and go in search of **Greenbanks** , a licensed Country Restaurant with accommodation, situated just off the A47 at the **Wendling** turn-off. Originally a Coaching Inn dating back to 1722, it is set in eight acres of meadows with lakes, an enclosed courtyard and garden, complete with its own well. When Brian Lovesay and Jenny Lock bought the property some years ago, it was virtually derelict; their careful renovations have now brought it back to life and all its former character and charm has been retained. In short, they have turned a motley collection of old buildings into a first class establishment that deserves to do well.

The restaurant offers the best of home cooking, using plenty of local produce when available. Travellers, who are weary of the standard chicken and chips fare they are used to being served when touring, will be delighted to find well presented meals accompanied by a range of excellent wines - and all good value for money too. The restaurant is open to non-residents from Tuesday evening to Saturday inclusive, and in addition to Dinner, Lunch and Sunday Lunch, you can also enjoy morning coffee and afternoon teas with delicious home-made cakes. If you want to stay for a night or two, double, single and family rooms are available. All the rooms are elegant but extremely comfortable and offer private bathroom, colour television and tea and coffee making facilities. Whether you come here to stay or simply to enjoy a meal, we hope you will be as delighted with Greenbanks as we were.

Greenbanks Restaurant and Accommodation, Swaffham Road, Wendling

We joined the A47 from here and headed west, and after about seven or eight miles turned south onto the A1065 and made our way to **Swaffham**. Having spent so much time exploring the quiet rural villages of the region, we really felt that we had come back to civilisation once more when we arrived at this charming, but increasingly busy market town.

The hub of the town is its large wedge-shaped market place, where many fine Georgian houses attest to the fact that Swaffham was a popular centre for Norfolk's gentry during that graceful era. Their main gathering place and the centre of the town's social life at that time was the Assembly Room at the northern end of the market place, which dates back to 1817. Nearby is the former Headmaster's House (now the Sixth Form Centre), Oakley House, the Corn Exchange and Plowright Place, a collection of old workshops which has been transformed into a delightful shopping precinct.

The main focus of the market place is the so-called Butter Cross (from the fact that beneath it, butter-sellers once displayed their wares), which was presented to the town by the Earl of Orford in 1783. It is not a cross at all, in fact, but a classical lead-covered dome standing on eight pillars, surmounted by a life-sized statue of Ceres, the Roman goddess of agriculture. An appropriate symbol indeed for a market town that has long relied upon the rewards which a good harvest would bring! She is obviously a popular divinity here, as the local bookshop in London Street is called Ceres Bookshop, and is one of the best in the area.

In contrast to Ceres and her pagan associations, you will find the quite magnificent 15th century church of St Peter and St Paul to the east of the market place, approached along a beautiful avenue of tall trees. Its tower dates back to the early 1500s and features a fine lead and timber Georgian spire crowned by a copper ball. Inside is one of the very best double hammerbeam roofs in the county, strikingly embellished with many angels. Here too are some carved bench-ends representing a little man and a dog on a chain, a figure that has also been incorporated into the town's coat of arms. This is a reference to John Chapman, the legendary 'Pedlar of Swaffham', whose change in fortune was to prove so beneficial to the church.

The story goes that Chapman, an impoverished tinker who lived in Swaffham some time during the 15th century, had a dream which foretold that if he were to make his way to London Bridge he would meet a man who would make him rich. So, in true Dick Whittington style, he set off with his faithful dog and tramped all the way to London to make his fortune. There on old London Bridge he met a shopkeeper who told him that he too had had a strange dream - in which a pedlar from Swaffham discovered gold buried in his garden! Returning back home post-haste (and no doubt rueing the fact that if his own dream had been more specific he would have been spared all this exercise), Chapman was nevertheless amply rewarded for his labours when he unearthed two large pots of gold coins beneath a tree in his garden. In thanks for this welcome turn-around in his financial state of affairs, he donated a generous part of his fortune to the church and the north aisle was built as a consequence.

John Chapman and his dog are further commemorated in the town sign, which stands just beyond the market place. The sign here was carved by the same talented craftsman who carved the 'Bishop Beaver' featured in the village sign at Babingley, a schoolmaster called Harry Carter who was in fact a Swaffham man. Harry rose to prominence during the 1950s when the villages of Norfolk, particularly those on the Sandringham Estate, felt the need to commemorate the Queen's Coronation in a way that would be both visually striking and permanent.

Today, beautifully carved and brightly painted signs can be found all over the county; many of them created by Harry himself, and others by the craftsmen of the Queen's Carving School at Sandringham who carried on his good work. As well as the name of the village or town in which it stands, each sign depicts the history of the place by reference to a local personality or legend. One of the great pleasures of exploring the county is that you continually come across yet another of these memorable landmarks as you drive around.

Saturday is market day in Swaffham, and the famous open-air market and public auction held here each week has attracted thousands of visitors over the years. Nearby you will find Swaffham Museum at the Town Hall in London Street, and it is worth keeping an eye on the ever-changing exhibitions there for a fascinating insight into the life and history of the town.

Did You Know...

There is a full list of
Tourist Information Centres
at the back of the book?

You will no doubt feel in need of refreshment after a busy morning or afternoon's sight-seeing, and Swaffham has an excellent choice of restaurants and tea rooms. After visiting the museum, we found a super licensed restaurant in London Street called **Haydn's**. Proprietors Neil Burton and Noreen Eagle offer a very friendly personal service and delicious freshly prepared food. A full a la carte menu is available in the evening, with lunches and cream teas being served during the day. Sunday lunches are also very popular at Haydn's and it is an ideal place to take a break from the rigours of exploring the town.

We left Swaffham with the feeling that it had definitely earned its one-time title of 'the Montpelier of England' - indeed, one of the most graceful buildings in the market place is Montpelier House, where it is said that Lady Nelson stayed whenever she visited the town. Lord Nelson was also a regular visitor, as was Lady Hamilton.

From here we headed south on the A1065 Swaffham-Brandon road. If you feel in need of a good meal or just a refreshing drink, we recommend that you call in at **The Windmill Inn** which is situated on the edge of **Great Cressingham,** just off the main road. This first class country Inn with its real oak beams and roaring log fires has all the charm of years gone by.

There are three bars which hold a good selection of real ales including Adnams, Broadside, Sam Smiths, Bass, Charrington and a guest variety. There is also a good selection of bar meals, snacks for those wanting a light lunch and dinners for those needing something a little more filling.

Children are very well catered for, having access to a play area with a pony, two family rooms, games room and conservatory. If the sun is shining you may want to eat and drink in the Windmill's large beer garden while watching the children play.

The Windmill Inn, Water End, Great Cressingham, Thetford
01760 6232

165

Great Cressingham lies some six miles to the south-east of Swaffham in the lovely valley of the River Wissey. About a quarter of a mile to the north of St Michael's Church stand the remains of Great Cressingham Priory, a fine brick house that dates back to around 1545, now merged into the fabric of the farmhouse that occupies the site. The original south front survives, with its terracotta panelling and elaborate moulded brickwork.

Some two miles further on, just off the B1108, is the pretty village of **Little Cressingham**, which stands on a tributary of the Wissey. Here we were delighted to discover the old windmill and miller's house, now faithfully restored by the Norfolk Windmill Trust. Across the fields is Clermont Hall, a handsome 18th century country house built in 1812 by William Pilkington and once owned by the Second Duke of Wellington. Visitors to St Andrew's Church enter dramatically through the massive, ruined west tower and arcade - a great storm which raged across the region in the 18th century is thought to have toppled the tower, and the part of the nave on which it fell still remains without a roof today.

North-east of the Cressinghams on the B1077 is the oddly-named **Saham Toney**, a village built around a large mere surrounded by trees. Peat was once extracted here in large quantities, and the resulting hole filled with water to become a much needed natural reservoir, as well as one of the prettiest meres in Breckland.

Joining the A1075 we headed north, and midway between Watton and East Dereham, we came to the interesting village of **Shipdham**. Look out here for the church tower with its unique wooden cupola. At the brown tourist 'bed' sign, we turned southeast and found the **Pound Green Hotel**, a modern family-run hotel owned by Jennie Davies and her son, John.

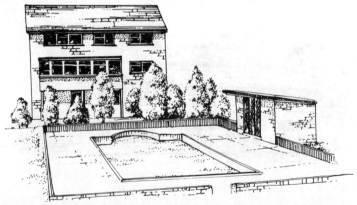

Pound Green Hotel, Pound Green Lane, Shipdham 01362 820165

The hotel's acre of secluded grounds contain a patio and a large heated swimming pool. Most of the fourteen bedrooms are en suite, and all have colour televisions and tea/coffee making facilities. Head chef Paul Abendroth provides a first-class menu which includes vegetarian dishes and children's specialities. This is an excellent location for exploring the many attractions of the surrounding countryside and coast.

It is hard to believe, but the village once boasted no less than 27 public houses and inns and four bakeries. From the inclusion of the odd word 'Drynkkings' on the village sign, you could be forgiven for assuming that they were a decidedly boosey lot here in the past. However 'drynkkings' were relatively harmless affairs where mainly tea was consumed - they were popular social gatherings that took place here around the 16th century and were roughly equivalent to our present-day garden fetes or tea parties.

The handsome parish church of All Saints' is quite a landmark in the area, and besides its cupola it also features a superb wooden lectern carved with Tudor roses. This dates back to around 1500 and is one of the best examples of its kind in the country.

In the churchyard is a plaque commemorating the American airmen of the 44th Bomber group, who came to Shipdham in 1942 and flew their final mission from here on 25th April 1945. 'The Flying Eightballs', as they were known, flew numerous sorties over Europe and fought some of the bloodiest air battles of the war, losing 153 aircraft in their 343 missions. Some of the veterans of the group returned to Shipdham with their families in September 1983, to dedicate the plaque in honour of their fallen comrades. 'The Flying Eightballs' certainly left their mark on the life of the village, and both the living and the dead are remembered by the locals with a touching combination of pride and affection.

From Shipdham it is just a short distance of three miles or so to **East Dereham,** which is right in the geographical centre of the county. The town's origins go way back to 654 AD, when St Withburga, a daughter of Anna, King of the East Angles, founded a convent here. Local legend has it that the nuns were kept alive during a famine by the milk of two deer, who providently appeared in response to Withburga's prayers.

It is thought that Dereham derives its name from this miraculous event, and the legend was quickly seized upon by Harry Carter as the theme of the town sign; spanning the High Street, it is the largest and perhaps most ambitious of his works. Withburga was buried in the churchyard of St Nicholas' Church, and her shrine was said to have been the scene of a number of miracles. Unscrupulous monks removed her bones several hundred years later to lay them next to those of her sister, Etheldreda, who had founded their own community at Ely. The intention was, of course, to divert the steady stream of pilgrims from Dereham to

Ely, but the monks' plan backfired: the desecrated grave filled with water which was discovered to have miraculous properties, it was promptly dubbed 'St Withburga's Well', and Dereham became even more popular than before despite its recently vacated resident!

Another resident of the churchyard is the poet, William Cowper. Known for his deeply melancholic nature, he attempted suicide at one stage before eventually dying here of natural causes in 1800. He left a legacy of several much-loved hymns, poems such as the brilliant 'Castaway' and 'The Task' which looks at the everyday life of rural folk, and a number of translations of Milton and the works of Homer.

Another local writer was George Borrow, who was born in the nearby hamlet of **Dumpling Green** in 1803. His great love of travelling led to such works as 'The Zencali, or an account of the Gypsies in Spain', 'The Romany Rye', and 'The Word-book of the English-Gypsy Language'.

To the east of St Nicholas' Church is an exquisite row of thatched cottages called Bishop Bonner's Cottages, named after the 16th century rector who resided there and later became Bishop of London. The cottages now house a museum, and the delightful pargetry work which forms a frieze of flower and fruit designs below the eaves is extremely rare in Norfolk. Such beauty is in fact completely at odds with Bishop Bonner's character: 'Bloody Bonner', they called him, and he was responsible for sending many unfortunate Protestants to the stake during Mary Tudor's reign.

Did You Know...
There is a full

Town and Village Index

at the back of the book?

If you are looking for bed and breakfast accommodation in Dereham, do try **Fern House** at 25 Commercial Road. Mrs Marion Winn has two letting rooms available at her 1810 Georgian house, one with en-suite facilities and the other with an adjacent bathroom. Both are very comfortable and well-appointed. The garden is exceptional, and in summer it is possible to take afternoon tea whilst enjoying the lovely flowers and shrubs. Mrs Winn is a cheerful person who guarantees a warm and friendly welcome, and she is happy to provide evening meals by arrangement.

The little village of **Yaxham**, which lies on the B1135 just to the south of Dereham, boasts a simple and gracious church dedicated to St Peter and features a round Saxon tower and a fine 14th century font. In the chancel is a memorial to the Reverend Dr John Johnson, who looked after his cousin William Cowper in the poet's declining years. Cowper referred to him fondly as 'Johnny of Norfolk'.

As we made our way north-east from here towards the A47, we were reminded of the fact that the local lanes must once have been fairly choked with sheep, for these were the routes used for the old sheep droves into the pretty little market town of **Mattishall**, once an important wool trading centre. Indeed, it was thanks to the wealth from this trade that the handsome church of All Saints received its fine hammerbeam roof.

A good stopping-off point on the busy A47 King's Lynn to Norwich road is the small village of **Hockering**, its wide village street lined with a number of attractive houses. We continued eastwards on the A47 for several miles then took a turning to the south and came to **Bawburgh**, which lies four miles west of Norwich. This pretty village enjoys a picturesque setting on the River Yare, on one side of which is a former 19th century water mill, now a private house. The mill which previously stood on the same site was once owned by a local miller called Jeremiah Colman - he who later went on to found the mustard dynasty of Norwich.

Unlikely as it may seem today, this quiet spot was one of England's most popular pilgrimage centres during the Middle Ages. The individual responsible was a humble farmhand named Walstan, who died here in 1016. When he was buried, one of those familiar 'miraculous' springs erupted from his grave, and soon pilgrims from around the world were flocking to Bawburgh to catch a glimpse of St Walstan's Well and the shrine that was built alongside. Parts of the well can still be seen today in a farmyard near the little village church, which is dedicated to St Mary and St Walstan.

This is really the perfect setting to stop a while and take stock of your travel plans: the lovely river meadows flanking the Yare and the charming old triple-arched bridge that spans it are quite enchanting.

Making our way back to the A47 then heading north along a lane that took us over the River Wensum, we found **Taverham** just to the south of the A1067 Norwich to Fakenham road. A smiling St Walstan is depicted in Harry Carter's village sign here, complete with scythe to commemorate his years of toil in the fields. Apparently this was once a quiet little hamlet, but due to its close proximity to Norwich has suffered from a bad case of 'galloping development' - an all-too-familiar story these days! However, we had our destination in mind, and we found it by taking a right-hand turn off the A1067 heading towards Felthorpe.

The main enterprise here is the famous **Taverham Garden Centre**, owned by Ken Dye. You will find an astonishing range of plants, trees and garden accessories covering a 15-acre site, and everything is so colourful and well-presented that we were not surprised to learn that this is one of Norfolk's most popular attractions for gardening enthusiasts. Over 100,000 visitors come here each year, and we are sure that this number will increase once people get to know about the latest venture, the Craft Centre. The 10 purpose-built workshops encompass a wide range of crafts including wood-turning, pottery, embroidery and lacemaking, and we were pleased to see that visitors are encouraged to ask the craftspeople about their work as they demonstrate their skills. Admission to both the Garden Centre and the Craft Centre is free, and there is also an excellent pet shop on site and a tea room where you can enjoy a cup of tea or freshly ground coffee together with home-made snacks.

A few miles to the north-east on the B1149 Holt road, we stopped off at the **Marsham Arms Hotel** near **Hevingham**. Inside this handsome 19th century inn, we found a delightful entrance bar with an open fireplace and original timber beams.

Marsham Arms Hotel, Holt Road, Hevingham, Norwich
01605 48268

Nearby, there is a tastefully refurbished restaurant and freehouse which offers a good choice of beers and wines, and a menu which includes dishes ranging from simple bar snacks to more adventurous a la carte specialities. Dishes are home-cooked and make use of local produce wherever possible. The present owners, Nigel and Anne Bradley, have transformed this delightful roadside pub in recent years and are now able to offer high standard accommodation. There are eight twin studio-bedrooms available, each centrally heated and provided with colour television, bathroom, compact kitchen, kettle and fridge. The Marsham Arms Hotel is located in the heart of the tranquil Norfolk countryside and provides an excellent base for many nearby places of interest.

Just to the east of the A140 Norwich to Cromer road, we came to the ancient village of **Horsham St Faith.** At Abbey Farm, next to the 15th century church of St Mary and St Andrew, are the ruins of the Priory of St Faith, a Benedictine priory founded in 1105. Parts of the cloister and chapter house are still in evidence, together with the Norman door of the refectory which is now part of the farmhouse. While this building was being restored in recent years, a series of 13th century wall paintings was discovered. They illustrate scenes from the life of one Robert Fitzwilliam who, so legend has it, was returning with his wife from a pilgrimage to Rome when they were imprisoned. Prayers to St Faith secured their release, and they showed their gratitude by founding the monastery when they arrived safely back home.

In the heart of the village we found the **Elm Farm Chalet Hotel,** an ideal base for those looking for superb accommodation in this part of Norfolk. Walter, Ada and Pam Parker have lived at St. Faith and farmed there for over 30 years and in 1978 began a major programme of alterations on one-and-a-half acres of the premises.

Elm Farm Chalet Hotel, Horsham St Faith, Norwich 01603 898366

Their first task was to convert some of the 17th-century farm buildings into chalets, then in 1986 they added a dining room overlooking the pond and gardens. More recently the barn has been converted into six large

171

bedrooms. All rooms are tastefully furnished and equipped with every facility. The restaurant specialises in traditional English dishes using local and home-grown ingredients.

And so we came to the county town of Norfolk, and the capital of all East Anglia. **Norwich** is a lively and exciting city whose unique character has, in the main, been sensitively preserved.

The earliest known reference to Norwich is on coins struck during the reign of King Athelstan - as far back as 930 AD - and by the time of the Norman Conquest it was one of the largest towns in England. The arrival of the Normans heralded a period of continued expansion which would see an increase in overseas trade and a steady influx of immigrants, many of them craftsmen who would leave their mark on the architecture of the town. The building of the castle and the transfer of the Seat of the Bishops of East Anglia from Thetford to Norwich obviously did much to sustain this growth. By the end of the 14th century the population had grown to around 6,000, and the town's prosperity was firmly bound up in the wool trade; the Rivers Wensum and Yare providing a convenient link with the coast from which the raw material was then exported to the Low Countries.

The only way to even begin to appreciate the many sights and attractions of Norwich is to park your car as quickly as possible and start to explore the city on foot. You would be well advised to arm yourself with a street map before you set off, as the city is a maze of narrow streets and passages and the enthusiastic newcomer could quite easily lose his or her bearings!

A good place to start is at the colourful Market Place, which has been trading now for over 500 years and is one of the largest permanent markets in England. It has an almost Continental feel to it with its many stalls set out under bright canvas awnings known locally as 'tilts', and as you walk up and down the narrow aisles looking for a bargain, you will frequently hear the accents of visitors from abroad.

The Market Place is surrounded by noteworthy buildings, both old and modern. At one end is the impressive City Hall with its soaring 202ft-high clock tower, opened by George VI in 1938; on the right as you face the City Hall is the Guildhall, built of flint at the beginning of the 15th century in a striking chequerboard design, once the seat of local government and now housing the Tourist Information Centre.

And on the south side of the Market Place is St Peter Mancroft, one of England's largest and finest medieval parish churches. It was built between 1430 and 1455 and is a superb example of the Perpendicular style, its ornate stone tower crowned with turrets and a graceful but slightly incongruous Gothick spirelet. The many delights of the interior include an impressive 15th century font canopy (albeit largely rebuilt in

Norwich Castle Keep

1887), the boss-studded hammerbeam roof, and the beautiful east window with its superb collection of 15th century glass illustrating the lives of the saints.

This is just one of over 30 medieval churches that still survive in Norwich today, yet it is of course the Cathedral that really draws the crowds. The main entrances to the Cathedral Close are the Erpingham and St Ethelbert Gates which lie at either end of Tombland, a cobbled thoroughfare lined with delightful old houses and trees, and the site of the original Saxon market place. It takes its name from the table tops from which the merchants sold their wares. The magnificent Erpingham Gate was presented to the city in 1420 by that famous hero of the Battle of Agincourt, Sir Thomas Erpingham - his kneeling figure can be seen in a recess at the top of its tall arch.

Once you enter the old monastic precinct of the Cathedral Close, the noise and bustle of the city itself seems far away - it is almost like stepping back in time into the heart of a medieval village. It is divided into Upper Close, where a statue of Horatio Nelson now watches over the old 14th century Grammar School he attended as a boy; and Lower Close, which leads down to Pull's Ferry on the River Wensum. The grey flint gateway here with its picturesque arch has guarded the river approach to the Cathedral since the 15th century, and it was from this spot that a little canal was dug to ship building materials direct to the Cathedral site. This would have included the beautiful white Caen stone of the Cathedral's exterior, which was off-loaded at Pull's Ferry after its journey from Normandy via Great Yarmouth and the Wensum. Today, you can stroll down to the river along the quiet lane which follows the course of the old canal, and turn back for a memorable view of the Cathedral.

Norwich Cathedral, or to give it its full and proper title, the Cathedral Church of the Holy and Undivided Trinity, was begun in 1096 by Bishop Herbert de Losinga, two years after he transferred the see from Thetford. Its turbulent history is a catalogue of fires, riots and natural disasters which all inflicted various degrees of damage; yet each succeeding period of rebuilding and restoration has improved upon the original, making this, the mother church of all East Anglia, one of England's finest cathedrals.

The wonderful nave roof - added in the 15th and 16th centuries after the original had been destroyed by fire - is undoubtedly the crowning glory of Norwich. Supported by the soaring trunks of the flying buttresses, its coloured and gilded bosses (now beautifully restored) are carved with a series of biblical scenes illustrating the story of man from the Creation to the Last Judgement. There are 2,000 in all, and those in the cloister, which is among the largest of any cathedral in the country, have a variety of themes and can be studied closely with ease. Another addition at the end of the 15th century was Norwich's famous cathedral spire, which at 315ft is the tallest in England apart from Salisbury.

Around the apse are a number of small chapels which were desecrated at the time of the Dissolution, but faithfully restored during the 1930s. They are quite delightfully furnished and offer the visitor an opportunity to sit peacefully and enjoy a moment or two of quiet contemplation whilst studying the impressive display of rare medieval painted panels. Best of these is the reredos in St Luke's Chapel, which was commissioned by Bishop Henry le Despenser in 1381 and is said to be the finest work of the Norwich School of painters.

Before we move on we must mention two special women who are commemorated here. The first is Edith Louisa Cavell, whose simple grave can be found outside the east end of the great south transept. This English nurse, a daughter of the rector of Swardeston to the south of Norwich, was one of the great heroines of the First World War. Working at a Red Cross hospital in occupied Brussels, she helped around 200 Allied prisoners to escape to neutral Holland - for which selfless act of bravery she was court-martialled and executed by the Germans in 1915.

The other woman of note, who is commemorated in the Cathedral on 8th May each year, is Julian (or Juliana) of Norwich, an anchoress who lived in a cell attached to the chancel. Born around 1342, this English mystic had a series of visions on 8th May 1373, and her written account of these, including her interpretations of their significance (published as 'Revelations of Divine Love') constitutes the first book to be written in the English language by a woman. As such, you would think that her name would be widely known - but who has heard of her today?

The other great Norman building here is the Castle, which dates from the beginning of the 12th century (replacing an earlier wooden fort) and is Norwich's second most significant landmark. The huge stone keep - one of the largest in England - dominates the skyline from the castle mound, and no visit would be complete without climbing the stairs to take a walk around the battlements and enjoy the superb views of the city below. The Castle was used as the county gaol for over 600 years of its life, and if you dare to gleam some idea of what it was like to be incarcerated in such a place, you can visit the dungeons to see the instruments of torture and the death masks of some of the prisoners who were executed here. One of the most famous characters in Norfolk's history, Robert Kett, was hanged from the walls of the Castle in 1549 - but more of him later in this book.

The keep now houses one of the best provincial museums in the country, and its varied attractions include a superb, though rather sad array of stuffed birds, a fine collection of Lowestoft porcelain, and an art gallery featuring many works by members of the Norwich School of painters. A brand new attraction is the Castle Mall. This will consist of a vast shopping complex with car parks under the Castle Bailey, and a large park and conservatory above.

Art lovers should also make a point of visiting the Sainsbury Centre, which is based in the grounds of the somewhat utilitarian University of East Anglia, three miles to the west of the city centre. This modern, purpose-built gallery opened in 1978, and although Norman Foster's building may resemble an aircraft hangar from the outside, the interior is extremely restful and must surely be one of the best laid out galleries around. It makes an excellent setting for the intriguingly diverse range of styles on display, which includes everything from ethnic and modernist works of art to the substantial creations of Henry Moore. Thanks must go to Sir Robert and Lady Sainsbury for donating such a unique collection for us all to enjoy.

Norwich is of course the main shopping centre for the region, and all the familiar national stores can be found in the city centre. However, if like us you fail to get excited by the prospect of tramping round major department stores and prefer something a little different when you are looking for a gift or souvenir to take back home, there are plenty of interesting alternatives. Antique shops and craft shops abound, and we were delighted to discover one particular shop that is quite unique.

On February 15th 1823, Jeremiah Colman took his nephew James into partnership, and created the famous firm of J. & J. Colman.

To mark the anniversary of this event, **Colmans** opened a **Mustard Shop**, the only one of its kind in Britain, in 1973. The shop can be found in 18th century quarters in Bridewell Alley, one of the attractive little alleyways in the old centre of Norwich which are wonderful to explore.

The Mustard Shop, Bridewell Alley, Norwich 01603 660166

The shop has now become a major tourist attraction for both overseas and British tourists visiting East Anglia. Its fame and popularity has become worldwide. The premises have been extensively restored and decorated in late 19th century style. The shop houses a mustard museum, which takes the form of a series of displays illustrating the history of Colman's mustard from the early years to the present day. Many of the articles offered for sale are based on old designs taken from the company's archives, and are unique to the shop.

Further along Bridewell Alley is another museum, the Bridewell Museum, with exhibits on local crafts and industries throughout the city's history, such as fishing, weaving and brewing. The latter, incidentally, is something that Norwich knows a lot about: it is said that at one time, the city had enough pubs for you to drink in a different one every day of the year!

This may or may not still be the case, but if you want to quaff a pint in one of the oldest pubs in Norwich, we can recommend that you head for the Dutch-gabled Adam and Eve in Bishopsgate, which purportedly dates back in parts some 700 years.

Another hostelry with plenty of history is the Maid's Head Hotel, the oldest inn in East Anglia and referred to as such as early as 1287. Among its more famous guests were Queen Elizabeth I and the Black Prince, and it was from here that 'The Norwich Machine', the city's first stage coach, left for London in 1762.

From here it is just a short distance to the bottom of Elm Hill, a charming, narrow cobbled street of timber-framed and colour-washed Tudor and Georgian buildings, which was thankfully saved from the threat of demolition through the determined efforts of a local conservation group, the Norwich Society. It is very atmospheric at any time, but if you can, take a stroll here at night and enjoy the magical effects of the award-winning street lighting.

The thatched Briton's Arms at the top of the street was the only house to survive the fire of 1507 which destroyed all its neighbours; but alas, the nearby elm tree from which the street takes its name fell victim to Dutch elm disease and is no more.

Historic Elm Hill is known for its specialist retailers, at number 18 is **The Bear Shop**, a delightful and unusual gift shop specialising in every conceivable type of teddy bear. Owner Robert Stone carefully selects his stock from over 60 different manufacturers most of them British, in styles ranging from the traditional teddy with built-in growler to handmade collectors' bears. Sizes range from the one inch miniature to the five foot giant. Teddy bears are among the best-loved toys in the world and are much in demand as collectors' items, good luck mascots and of course as children's toys. For the bear buff, Robert's shops (he has another in Colchester) are not to be missed.

The Bear Shop, 18 Elm Hill, Norwich 01603 766866

At number 30 Elm Hill, we found the fascinating jewellers and goldsmiths, **Timgems**, a wonderful establishment which is run by pleasantly eccentric proprietor, Tim Snelling. The building is in complete keeping with its surroundings and has windows which are a delight to behold and which seem to attract passers-by like a magnet.

Timgems, 30 Elm Hill, Norwich 01603 623296

Not only is this one of the few jewellers in Norwich to have a goldsmith actually working on the premises, but it also boasts an unrivalled collection of second-hand and antique jewellery and silver which Tim has carefully selected over the years. Although his stock tends to change continually, on the day we visited it contained a number of interesting items which are worth a mention. These included a pair of delicate Georgian rose-cut diamond-set earrings, a pair of heavy gentleman's 18-carat gold cufflinks by Cartier, a 1787 silver wine ewer by Henry Chawner, and a fine selection of Art Nouveau and Art Deco silver pieces. Over the years, Tim has built up an excellent reputation for buying and selling antique jewellery at prices which are known to be keenly competitive.

We have only skimmed the surface here of everything that Norwich has to offer, and as whole books have been written on the subject the best we can hope to do is encourage you to make your own discoveries with this brief glimpse into its appeal. Among the many other buildings we think you will enjoy seeing, the following are of the 'not-to-be-missed' variety. There is the Music House in Rouen Road, the Assembly House, Carnery College to the right of the western front of the Cathedral, the Bishop's Palace at Palace Plain, the Great Hospital, the Regency houses of Quayside, the Roman Catholic Cathedral of St John on the way to the University, and over at Whitefriars Bridge, the imposing 19th century Yarn Mill hidden under its thickets of creeper.

We would certainly recommend that anyone planning to come here should budget for an overnight stay if they can - this will give you adequate time for sight-seeing and make your visit a lot more pleasurable. If you do decide to stay over and want an alternative to Norwich's many pubs for your evening's entertainment, why not visit one of the city's excellent theatres? You will find the Theatre Royal next door to the Assembly House. Its two predecessors were both destroyed by fire, and the present building, erected in 1936, was extensively altered in 1970. Today it is one of the leading theatres in the provinces, with a constantly changing programme of first-class productions.

For sheer diversity, the Maddermarket Theatre is hard to beat. This building was converted into an Elizabethan-style theatre in 1926, and the Norwich Players - mostly amateur, but with a professional producer and designer - give enthusiastic and lively performances of plays ranging from Restoration comedies to modern works from around the world. Next door is the fascinating Stranger's Hall Museum, a rambling medieval house with exhibits of domestic life and furniture from Tudor to Victorian times.

Finally, if by this time you are footsore and physically exhausted from walking around - but have still only managed to take in a fraction of the sights on your itinerary - why not take a boat trip around the city? This will provide an excellent opportunity to see a good selection of Norwich's historic buildings, and with a running commentary from your professional guide on both the past and the future of this great city, there is no better way of experiencing something of its character.

The Pedler on Swaffham's Town Sign

CHAPTER SEVEN

North-East Norfolk

Beeston Hall, Nr Neatishead

181

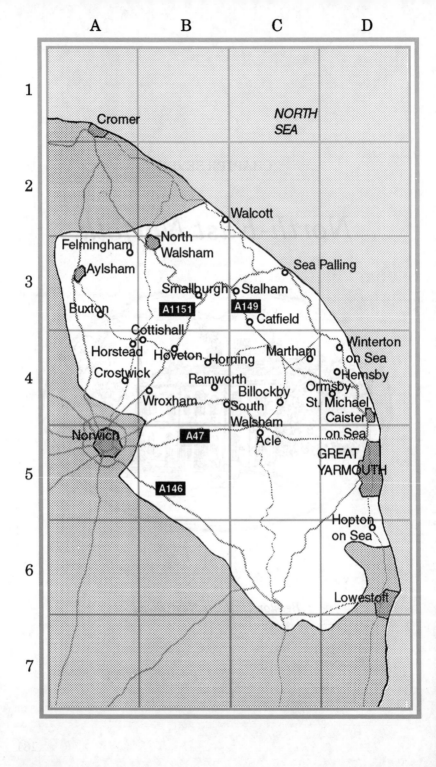

North-East Norfolk

Heading out from Norwich on the A140, the first stop on our tour of North-east Norfolk is the lovely market town of **Aylsham**. Recorded in the Domesday Book as 'Elesham', the town's origins go back to before the Norman Conquest. In 1372 its long-term prosperity was assured when, along with several other Norfolk manors and estates, Edward III presented the town to his son, John of Gaunt. This enthusiastic landowner was determined to put Aylsham firmly on the map, and its steady development into one of Norfolk's most flourishing markets dates from this time.

It is a stalwart place of red brick and flint, with some of its most handsome buildings grouped around the town's centrepiece, its splendid Market Place. From here we set off to explore the surrounding streets, and in Red Lion Street we were delighted to find that the majority of buildings still retain their original shop fronts.

It was here that we met local artist Anthony Butler and his family, who run the **Red Lion Gallery.** They stock a superb range of oil paintings, watercolours, pastels and prints as well as ceramics, carvings and other art forms.

Did You Know...

There is a full list of
Tourist Information Centres
at the back of the book?

Red Lion Gallery, Red Lion Street, Aylsham 01263 732115

It is well worth browsing around, as many East Anglian artists are represented here and it is a wonderful chance to see how they have interpreted the seasons and landscape of Norfolk with its marvellous light and space. We found the Gallery not only interesting, but 'visitor-friendly' - unlike some we have come across, which tend to make people feel a little intrusive. So do feel free to drop in and browse, and Anthony and his wife will be happy to offer any advice you may need. Anthony himself specialises in house portraits and landscapes captured in gentle washes of watercolour, and the Butlers hope soon to set up special painting weekends by liaising with another local couple who offer bed and breakfast facilities.

Aylsham's affluence first came about through the manufacture of linen, then of wool and worstead in the 16th century. Bearing in mind the town's strong associations with the woollen industry, we were not surprised to find a most unusual shop in located in Penfold Street. **Black Sheep Limited** stock absolutely everything to do with the woollen and sheep trade, including fine knitwear, yarns ranging from black to a warm rusty brown and a paler grey, knitting machines, mugs, hats and leather goods all carrying the Black Sheep logo, as well as other gift ideas with a country theme.

If black sheep have been traditionally associated with a shady past they are fully vindicated here, as the company has been running for more than ten successful years. The wool actually comes from the Black Welsh Mountain breed, but the company's parent farm at Ingworth proves that sheep do not need high ground and Welsh air on which to thrive! Visitors are very welcome at the farm shop there and after admiring the distinctive sheep, you can purchase a wide range of items.

Owner Clare Hoare has certainly had an eventful life, having been a poultry farmer, a pilot, a tennis coach, a Foreign Office worker and a shepherdess - just to name a few of her professions! She founded Black Sheep Limited in 1980 and the success of the company to date owes much to her lively, outgoing spirit.

Black Sheep Ltd, 9 Penfold Street, Aylsham 01263 733142

The prosperity of any town can normally be gauged by the appearance of its church. St Michael's in Aylsham provides ample evidence of a place that was quite prepared to channel a significant part of its wealth into building an imposing edifice which would transcend the mundane. This 14th and 15th century flint-faced parish church with its tall west tower was much restored in 1824, and has a fine pulpit dating back to 1637. Humphry Repton, that great landscape gardener who was responsible for designing many of our best late-18th century country parks, was buried here in 1818. It was his love of the informal, the 'picturesque', that heralded the final demise of the old concept of gardens as formal layouts; bringing a more relaxed view to the way in which the design of a garden was perceived.

Visitors looking for somewhere really special to stay in the area would be well advised to seek out the magnificent **Sankence Lodge Hotel** on Cawston Road, which has been in the Young family for over a century. This listed Georgian house provides very stylish and elegant accommodation and really captures the flavour of country house living. Yet despite the obvious luxury of the furnishings, we were immediately impressed by the welcoming atmosphere of the place and the fact that Miss Young pays such close attention to the wishes of her guests.

Sankence Lodge is situated on a 300-acre working farm, although the farming side is kept quite separate - you will not have to wade through mud in your wellies to enter this fine house! If we may be excused using the word 'classy', then this epitomises the four letting rooms, which are beautifully furnished and decorated. They are all en-suite with every luxury facility you could possibly require for your comfort, and one boasts a magnificent four-poster bed.

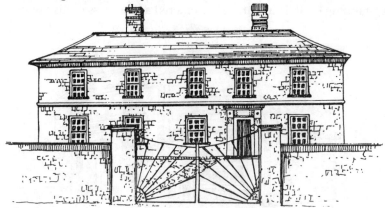

Sankence Lodge Hotel & Restaurant, Cawston Road, Aylsham
01263 734120

The restaurant specialises in first class a la carte cuisine at reasonable prices, or alternatively, if you prefer a more informal setting, you may enjoy an excellent meal in the Watering Hole Wine Bar. Either way, the French chef and his team prepare superb freshly cooked meals, using plenty of good local produce. As you will appreciate when you see it, the Watering Hole takes its name from the African Safari theme which has been created here by the artistic decor and the huge Cape Buffalo head mounted on the wall. Although we did not have a chance to ask if one of the earlier Young's had brought this back from his or her travels, we suspect that there may well have been a Big Game Hunter in the family at one time!

If you have time to stop for a drink after exploring Aylsham and are fond of memorabilia, then **The Feathers** - also on Cawston Road on the edge of the town - is well worth a visit.

This Georgian brick and flint inn dates back to the late-18th century and is an ideal setting for all the antiques and trinkets scattered within. On entering the bar area you are met by a roaring open fire, a good atmosphere enhanced by the local football and darts team's spirit, and to top it all, an extremely good range of beers, wines and spirits. The walls and ceilings are adorned with copper pots, traps, brass and old guns, and to your left, another room is modelled on the British Empire Exhibition held at Wembley in 1924. Everything from spoons and badges to porcelain is exhibited in this room, and it has to be seen to be believed. A real eye-opener!

Roland and Shelley seem to have settled in remarkably well, even though they have only been here for 12 months. Roland took over the pub after having been a teacher for 20 years - and it seems to us that with this outstanding establishment, he has entered a new class of his own!

The Feathers, 54 Cawston Road, Aylsham 01263 732314

From 1792 until the beginning of this century, the River Bure was navigable from Coltishall to Aylsham, and the area known as Millgate was a bustling place with shallow-bottomed wherries making their way to the harbour from Norwich and Yarmouth. But the coming of the railway and a devastating flood in 1912 which caused the channel to silt up put paid to Millgate's future as a working harbour. Now it is a quiet residential area, with just its handsome 18th century houses and large mill as a reminder of busier days.

For us, one of the best reasons for visiting Aylsham must be the **Bure Valley Railway** , evocative of those famous books by Rev Audrey concerning the exploits of Thomas the Tank Engine! The older generation was brought up during the Steam Age, and modern children can still share with grans and grandads and mums and dads the fascination that these little engines inspire. Opened in 1990, this particular line operates on 15-inch gauge and runs along the former East Norfolk Railway line between Aylsham and Wroxham. The return trip will take around two hours, and you will have the chance of speeding across the River Bure and enjoying the lovely Broadland countryside. Adjacent to this is the British Rail line and you can be sitting having a nostalgic ride on one of the little carriages, when a lumbering diesel speeds past.

The Bure Valley Railway, Norwich Road, Aylsham   01263 733858

Two special trips offered by the Railway particularly caught our eye. The first was the Broadland Boat-Train, which leaves Aylsham Station at 10.15am every day between 10th May and 5th September. Once you arrive at Wroxham Station it is just a short walk to Wroxham Bridge where the Boat will take you on a most enjoyable one-and-a-half hour cruise on the beautiful Norfolk Broads. The other trip is The Blickling Link, where the train departs from Wroxham Station at 11.15am every Wednesday from 13th May until 15th July, and every Tuesday and

Bure Valley Railway

Wednesday from 21st July until 2nd September. Upon arrival at Blickling, a free coach will take you to nearby Blickling Hall (which we visited in Chapter 3) for a tour of the House and Gardens. This is a marvellous way of enjoying two of the best attractions in the area on the same day.

There is an excellent souvenir shop at Aylsham Station, where we recommend that you buy one of their informative guides concerning the history of the line. After an exhilarating ride courtesy of 'Sian', 'Sandy River' or 'Wroxham Broad' locomotives, we suggest that you retire to the cafe for a welcome cup of tea and a good read through the brochure.

On the B1145 between Aylsham and North Walsham, we came to the picturesque village of **Felmingham.** Dominating the village is the 16th century tower of St Andrew's Church, although the rest of the building was rebuilt in 1742 after a fire. Right next to the church is **Belaugh Pottery**, a fascinating place to visit. Bridget Graver and George Simmons set up their studio here in 1975 (before that it was situated eight miles to the south in the village of Belaugh - hence the name). You can watch them at work throwing, glazing and preparing their work for the kiln, which is housed within the stables of a former 18th century inn. Everything they make is hand-thrown, and they specialise in domestic oven-to-table stoneware. Much of the work on view is for sale, and special items can also be made to order. Belaugh Pottery is open from 10.00am to 4.00pm daily and closed on Sundays and Bank Holidays.

Belaugh Pottery, Church Road, Felmingham, North Walsham
01692 403967

Two miles south of Aylsham on the A140 Norwich to Cromer road is the village of **Marsham,** where Marsham Hall and Bolwick Hall stand on either side of the Mermaid Stream. It is worth paying a quick visit to pretty All Saints' Church to see its fine 15th century hammerbeam roof and Seven-Sacrament font.

Also in Marsham St Andrew's Church has a moving monument to a little girl called Mary Ann Kent, who died in 1773 at the age of four, following a small pox vaccination. A plaque on the chancel wall relates that '...her fond Parents, deluded by prevalent Custom, suffered the rough officious hand of Art to wound the flourishing root of Nature, and rob the little innocent of the gracious Gift of Life'.

Feeling somewhat subdued and in need of good cheer, we decided to drop in at the **Black Lion Inn**, run since 1991 by Glenda and Nigel Booth. Glenda has lived in Buxton all her life. She serves an excellent pint of beer and prides herself on giving the warmest of welcomes to locals and visitors alike. There is a good selection of beers and spirits, and bar snacks are available six days a week. The inn was built in the early 18th century and has been a centre of the local community ever since. The interior of this traditional village pub is relaxed and welcoming, and there is a good selection of pub games to keep customers amused. Outside, there is a popular beer garden and an unusual feature - a bowling green.

The Black Lion Inn, Lion Road, Buxton, Nr Marsham
01603 279313

The Bure Valley Steam Railway runs through the village and trains stop here en route from Aylsham to the Broads Centre at Wroxham. There is also excellent fishing nearby and many miles of country walks including Dudwick Park with its resident herd of deer.

Joining the B1354 and heading south-east, we soon arrived at **Horstead,** a most attractive village on the B1150 Norwich to North Walsham road. We rather liked Horstead: a cheerful and unpretentious place with some fine 19th century houses flanking the street like soldiers on parade!

For those stopping here for refreshment, we will continue with this military theme by suggesting the excellent pub and restaurant, **The Recruiting Sergeant**, which is run by Matthew and Nicola Colchester.

There has been an alehouse on the site since the days of the Domesday Book, and more recently (probably during World War I), the building was used as a recruitment centre. Inside, the wood-panelled bar is decorated with coaching and military memorabilia. There is a separate restaurant which offers a good value set menu, a vegetarian dish of the day and daily specials on the blackboard. Portions are generous and prices very fair.

The Recruiting Sergeant, Norwich Road, Horstead 01603 737077

And so we made our way from 'horses' to 'colts' - as our next stop was at **Coltishall**, just across the River Bure from Horstead, back on the B1354. Glad to leave the car behind and stretch our legs for a while, we walked across the meadows from the main street and spent an hour or so watching the bustle of the traffic on the river. We were not short of company that day: from the scores of anglers casting their lines from the riverbank, to the proud owners of launches and more hardy types messing about in small dinghies; it seemed that half the population of the county was out and about, taking advantage of the fine weather! There is a glorious sense of aimlessness in watching the many different scenarios being acted out on the water; just enjoying others enjoying themselves.

John the Baptist was another individual who spent a lot of his time in rivers, so perhaps it is appropriate that the village church - a thatched building with a 15th century tower and porch - is dedicated to him.

Whenever we visit somewhere for the first time, we normally like to seek out one or two places to stop for a drink or a bite to eat that we can recommend to our readers. This sometimes takes more effort than you may imagine, but in Coltishall we were well and truly spoilt for choice!

First we found the **Red Lion Inn**, an exceptional pub and restaurant which stands opposite the church, 400 metres up the hill from the Staithe. The original inn building was built in the early 1700s as an alehouse with three separate adjoining alms houses. Over the years, these cottages have been incorporated into the pub and they now form the kitchens and lower bar area. The restaurant was added in the early 1980s but was carefully designed to blend in with the original architecture. The Red Lion now operates on two levels - there is an upper bar and restaurant and a short flight of stairs which leads down to the lower bar area. Inside there are beams, wood-panelled walls and feature fireplaces; the walls are decorated with Norfolk memorabilia including a collection of sepia and black and white photographs and prints, many of which are for sale. There is also an interesting collection of pewter tankards in the lower bar.

The Red Lion has been run for the last two years by Andrew and Monica Burrell-Saward. We found them friendly and welcoming, and the food and drink they serve is excellent. They offer an exceptional choice of top quality bar meals (examples from the menu include swordfish steak, wild Greenland salmon and home-cured Norfolk ham) and their cask conditioned ales are excellent. On the day we visited, there were six beers available including the famous 'Couteshall Weasel' brewed exclusively for the Red Lion by the award-winning brewers, Woodfordes of Woodbastwick. Outside in the garden is a children's play area which includes a large play fort and adjoining the pub is a sun-trap patio area, which overlooks the large car park.

The Red Lion Inn, Church Street, Coltishall 01603 737402

Also on the edge of Coltishall, alongside the River Bure, we called in at the fine pub and restaurant, the **King's Head** run by Adele and Brian Wadsworth.

The King's Head, Coltishall Common, Wroxham Road, Coltishall
01603 737426

The building was once an old coaching inn and parts of it, including an elegant courtyard, date back to 1640. The restaurant offers an excellent choice of grills and house specialities and has wonderful views towards the river. There are also six letting rooms, two of which are in the beautifully renovated stables in the old courtyard.

Having thoroughly spoilt our readers with a fine selection of local pubs to choose from, we thought we would try to find some suitable accommodation for those who may wish to prolong their stay in Coltishall. A few enquiries of the locals soon led us to the **Norfolk Mead Hotel** on the banks of the River Bure, and we immediately knew that we had found just what we were looking for. This outstanding country house hotel and restaurant stands within 12 acres of landscaped grounds which gently slope towards a long frontage on the river's edge. This is truly a beautiful place for a stroll along the river or around the fishing lake. There is a slipway and off-river mooring for those bringing their own boats, and towing dinghies are available for use by hotel guests. Within the walled gardens, there is also a large swimming pool which is heated in suitable weather between June and mid-September.

The hotel building was originally a manor house dating from 1740. During its recent renovation, great care was taken to preserve its Georgian character, and inside the public rooms have been decorated and furnished to the very highest standards. (Look out for the superb staircase). The hotel has ten beautifully furnished bedrooms, all with en-suite bath or shower, colour television and tea/coffee making facilities, and a restaurant which is renowned for the outstanding quality and presentation of its dishes. On the day we visited, the choice of main course included steamed fillet of salmon with oyster mushrooms in a cream sauce. Special half-board rates are available for short or weekend breaks.

The Norfolk Mead Hotel, Coltishall 01603 737531

To the north of Coltishall is the famous RAF station where Spitfires

193

and Hurricanes of Fighter Command were based during the Second World War. That great war hero, Sir Douglas Bader, spent part of the war years here during the Battle of Britain, and the story of the brave fighter pilot who was determined to fly again and serve his country despite losing both his legs in a flying accident was a great inspiration to many. His tireless endeavours after the war to improve the quality of life for the disabled earned him a CBE in 1956, and he was knighted 20 years later.

The riverside village of **Wroxham**, linked to its twin **Hoveton** by a hump-backed bridge over the River Bure, is the self-styled 'capital' of the Norfolk Broads. As such, it gets extremely busy here during the summer, with visitors jostling for elbow room in the pubs by the river, and those who have come for a boating holiday quickly becoming acquainted with the workings of their hired craft. The banks of the river are chock-a-block with boatyards full of cruisers of all shapes and sizes, and this is the place to come to choose your boat and decide how long you wish to forsake the land in favour of the waterways. As an alternative to hiring a boat yourself for a matter of weeks or days, you may prefer to opt for a piloted river trip of an hour or two and hand the navigation over to an expert while you relax and enjoy the scenery.

Despite the crowds, Wroxham enjoys an extremely pleasant setting and is the logical place from which to set off on your exploration of the Broads. It is also the main shopping centre for holidaymakers in the area, and here you will find just about everything you could possibly need at Roy's, with its proud boast of being 'the largest village store in the world'. If you find all the excitement of this lively village a little too much, take a few moments respite by visiting the 15th century St Mary's Church with its splendid south doorway - a Norman showpiece of quite magnificent ornamental carvings.

Garden House Hotel & Restaurant, Salhouse Road, Rackheath
01603 581974

A couple of miles to the south-west, on a minor road between the A1151 Wroxham to Norwich road and the B1140, we came to the attractive village of **Rackheath**, unusual in that it used to stand approximately one mile from its present location. All that remains of the original village is the church, the rest having been lost in the great plague. Those looking for a good meal or first-rate accommodation should try the **Garden House Hotel and Restaurant.** The reputation of this charming family run hotel has been built up over the last 13 years by John and Jill Smart. There are eight letting rooms available, all with en-suite facilities, and the conservatory restaurant looks out over secluded gardens. Besides the good value set menu, delicious daily specials (such as 'slips' - baby Dover Soles) are available.

We came across a very special attraction just to the north of Wroxham on the Tunstead Road, Hoveton. Set in 10 acres of Norfolk parkland, **Wroxham Barns** houses a collection of traditional 18th century barns which provide the setting for probably the finest centre of rural crafts in East Anglia.

It was discovered as a disused dairy in 1982 by three Norfolk businessmen; Ian Russell, Rupert Latham and Jack Chippendale who decided that it would be the ideal location for a craft centre. After much hard work and a grant from the English Tourist Board, Wroxham Barns opened to the public on 24th May 1983.

Jack Chippendale has been operating his Chippendale Craft at Wroxham for nearly a decade now. In 1985 he built the 35ft Storm, reputed to be the largest wooden cruiser built for The Broads in 15 years.

Other craft workshops that visitors will be interested to see are Charollais Originals a range of hand dyed 'Designer Knitwear' from the wool of pedigree Charollais sheep. They hold a terrific selection of leisure wear and sweaters in pure lambswool in plain or floral designs. Garments are mainly unisex but there is a large stock of mens sweaters, hats, ties and scarves.

Norfolk born Terry George runs his own grass engraving workshop. Terry produces commemorative pieces each year such as The Royal Weddings, Anniversary of The Battle of Britain and Halley's Comet. A variety of items are on display covering a wide range of pieces, but virtually anything can be engraved on request.

Chris Hutchins arrived at Wroxham Barns in 1984 and now exhibits a wide range of local prints. He has worked on numerous commissions, including drawings for the National Trust and Canterbury Cathedral. This range also includes greeting cards, notelets and writing paper.

Bill and Debbie Ross are the husband and wife team that produce 'Capricorn Jewellery'. Bill produces unique designs including earrings, pendants and crucifixes many of them in jet and amber. Debbie complements Bill's work by manufacturing imaginative necklaces and earrings from gemstone beads. The couple also keep a wide range of rocks, minerals and crystals.

Chris Bradshaw opened his booking binding workshop at Wroxham Barns in 1988. A large portion of his work consists of rebinding old volumes but he also produces a range of notebooks and albums bound in cloth and marbled paper for you to purchase from his workshop.

Adeline Ford's hand painted, flower decorated collections of furniture and artifacts is another main source of attraction for visitors. Adeline has the enthusiastic patronage of many collectors, some of whom she suspects have as many pieces as herself.

Stained glass can be made into a lampshade, window, showcase of anything else you desire. Ian de Ath will be willing to oblige.

In addition to other workshops you can look at there is a delightful Old Barn Tea Room for you to take refreshments. This carefully restored barn overlooks the courtyard and will serve morning coffee, a light lunch or delicious cream teas.

A traditional fair which contains a unique collection of amusements including a swingboat and beautifully restored children's roundabout is sure to be a favourite with younger visitors.

Wroxham Barns is open to visitors from 10.00 am to 5.00 pm, seven days a week, all year round.

Wroxham Barns, Tunstead Road, Hoveton

Half a mile to the east at the tiny village of **Ashmanhaugh**, we discovered what is reputedly the smallest church tower in England and certainly the smallest in Norfolk. The other point of interest at St Swithin's is the tomb of Honor Bacon, a young bride who died in 1591 on the eve of her wedding.

Picturesque **Worstead**, which lies north of here some four miles from the Broads and seven miles from the coast, was a busy industrial town during the Middle Ages. Today it has dwindled in size to become little more than a quiet village with some fine Jacobean houses grouped around its square. Worstead lent its name to the tough woollen cloth produced in the region, and many of the original weavers' cottages can still be seen in the narrow side streets. Worsted cloth, woven from tightly twisted yarn, was introduced by Flemish weavers and became popular throughout England from the 13th century onwards. These immigrants settled happily into the East Anglian way of life and seem to have influenced its architecture almost as strongly as its weaving industry.

The lovely 14th century church of St Mary provides ample evidence of Worstead's former prosperity. Its many treasures include a fine hammerbeam roof, the chancel screen with its remarkable painted dado, and a magnificent traceried font complete with cover. The village has an annual weekend of events to raise money for the continuing restoration of the church, and the 'glory days' are kept very much alive by the presence of a still-functioning Guild of Weavers. Looms stand in the north aisle of St Mary's and you can watch the weavers demonstrating their skills at certain times.

We now begin our exploration of the North-east Norfolk coastline, and our first stop was at the pleasant seaside village of **Walcott**, situated between Happisburgh and Mundesley on the scenic B1159 coast road. Here, there are long stretches of fine sandy beaches that are ideal for swimming and coastal walks. For those wishing to stay in the area, first-rate chalets and letting bungalows are available at **Ostend Place Chalet Park.** With its direct access to the golden sands, safe bathing and fine sea fishing, this is an ideal place for a quiet family holiday. The aim of the owners, Mr and Mrs Treacy, is to give their guests and informal, carefree and enjoyable stay.

Ostend Place Chalet Park, Walcott 01692 650462

Residents stay in detached six-berth brick bungalows (consisting of three large bedrooms, lounge/dining room, fully fitted kitchen, bathroom and separate WC), or in semi-detached four-berth cedar chalets (consisting of two bedrooms, lounge/kitchenette, shower room and WC). All chalets have superb views of the sea and are provided with cooker, fridge, television and a grassed area in front for recreation. There is also a selection of smaller two-berth flats in the main house. Ostend Place lies within easy driving distance of the Norfolk Broads and the many other beauty spots and attractions which stand along this dramatic stretch of North Norfolk coast. Regular guests return year after year, so book early to secure a place.

All Saints' Church in Walcott is yet another place with Nelson connections. It was heavily restored in Victorian times, and much of the finance for this was attributable to the Reverend Horatio Nelson William Comyn, a godson of Lord Nelson and actually baptised on board the 'Victory'. It seems that Reverend Comyn would do just about anything to raise money for his beloved church, even trotting around the countryside hawking wares from his pony and trap!

The coastal waters off **Happisburgh** (or 'Hazeborough' to give it its unlikely but correct pronunciation) have been the setting of many shipwrecks over the centuries, and the unfortunate victims of these lie buried in the churchyard. We were told that the large grassy mound which lies to the north side of St Mary's Church contains the bodies of the ill-fated crew of HMS 'Invincible', which was wrecked on the treacherous sandbanks in 1801. The ship was on its way to join up with Nelson's fleet at Copenhagen when tragedy struck and resulted in the death of 119 crew members. Happisburgh's distinctive lighthouse - built in 1791 and striped like a barber's pole - certainly proved ineffectual in this instance; as did the soaring 110ft-high tower of the church itself, which could normally be relied upon to act as a 'back-up' warning to mariners.

Inside the church is a splendid 15th century octagonal font carved with the figures of lions, satyrs, musicians and the Evangelists; and embedded in pillars along the aisle, you can still make out the shrapnel from German bombs which were dropped on the village in 1940.

Between the lighthouse and the wide, sandy beach (one of the top 20 in Britain) we found **Cliff House**, a very pleasant guest house run by Jill Morris and Diana Wrightson. They have four rooms available, all with tea/coffee making facilities, central heating, hot and cold water and electric blankets on each bed. In summer (and during winter weekends), Cliff House is also a tea shop and restaurant, open until 7pm and serving a good selection of home-cooked meals including vegetarian dishes and cream teas. Look out for the delicious home-baked bread and cakes. Jill and Diana also have a detached flint and thatched house, the Pyghtle, which has been divided into three attractive self-catering flats.

Cliff House, Beach Road, Happisburgh   01692 650775

Happisburgh is also the stomping ground of a particularly gruesome smuggler who is said to haunt the area. Legless, with his head dangling down his back on a strip of skin, he must present a pretty unprepossessing sight as he emerges from the sea, 'heading off' (as it were) towards Well Corner with a large sack in his arms! Local farmers first spotted him sometime around 1800, and arranged a nightly vigil to find out what he was up to. For several nights they watched him drop his bundle down a well which then stood on the site, then jump in (or perhaps roll in?) himself. When they investigated the well, they discovered the mutilated torso of a man with his legs and head stuffed into a sack nearby. It seems likely that he was murdered by his fellow smugglers, probably following an argument over how to split their ill-gotten gains.

Further south on the coast road we came to **Lessingham**, where a lane will take you down to the southern end of Eccles Beach. The dunes here look spectacular, the tough marram grass creating a firm anchor for the sand which would otherwise be blown inland. A little further north is Cart Gap, which provides the only official parking place on this stretch of coast before you reach **Sea Palling**. The beach at Cart Gap is particularly well suited to families as the sands slope gradually down to the sea, while **Eccles on Sea** is a rather odd little place hidden behind the dunes, with its rows of beach huts and houses (which one assumes are only lived in for part of the year) creating a rather dispirited atmosphere when the season is over.

Sea Palling is again an excellent place to bathe, but the dunes have been declared off-limits to the public to allow the marram grass to flourish. Some eight miles of sea defences from Happisburgh to Winterton

199

were prompted by the floods of January 1953, and the natural sea wall of marram grass seems to provide a pretty effective barrier against the ravages of the North Sea.

Just outside Sea Palling lies the tiny village of **Waxham** , where we were surprised to see trees firmly rooted in the dunes - which here have reached a most impressive height. By the derelict church of St John are the remains of a Tudor wall with corner turrets and a splendid 15th century gatehouse. This was once part of Waxham Hall, now a farmhouse, which is reputedly haunted by several members of the Brograve family - each of whom died a violent death during some of the most famous wars and battles in English history.

Still heading south on the coast road, the next place we came to was the little hamlet of **Horsey,** which lies on the marshes about a mile from the sea. Standing little more than three feet above sea level, the village has survived against great odds since Roman times, and still fights its constant battle with the sea. The battle was almost lost in 1938 when Horsey was flooded and became completely cut off for over four months, the villagers having to be evacuated until the waters receded. In the village we found a super old inn called the Nelson's Head, and the delightful thatched church of All Saints' hidden away beneath the trees surrounding its overgrown churchyard.

To the west of Horsey is Horsey Mere, one of the outermost and least spoiled of the Norfolk Broads. Now owned by the National Trust, it covers around 120 acres, and many visitors to the Broads manage to find their way here to moor their boats at Horsey staithe. Overlooking the staithe is an impressive four-storey brick-built windmill, built in 1912 to pump water from drainage ditches into the mere. The National Trust has done a splendid restoration job on the building, and if you scale the heights to the viewing gallery you will enjoy an unrivalled view across the mere and over the surrounding marshland.

While we were there we spotted a number of different species of wildfowl bobbing up and down on the water, competing for space with a veritable flotilla of sailing boats - but some say that, sometimes, there is just as much activity below the water as on it. A strange but moving local legend relates that the Romans would place the bodies of their dead children into the mere, and on one particular night of the year it is transformed into a garden where all the children ever laid to rest there can be seen at play.

Next along the B1159 are **West** and **East Somerton**. West Somerton is a pleasant little village with access to Martham Broad and the River Thurne - popular with sailors as the flat, open countryside it traverses offers little resistance to the sea breezes that fill their sails.

The village was the birthplace of the 'Norfolk Giant', Robert Hales, who stood 7ft 8in tall in his stockinged feet and weighed in at 32 stone. He used his great size to good advantage, faring pretty well from touring both England and America, and later became a publican in London where he was presented to Queen Victoria. Hales died in Great Yarmouth in 1863 at the age of 43, and his grave and memorial can be seen in the churchyard of St Mary the Virgin here in the village - but we wondered where his sister Mary, the 'Norfolk Giantess', ended up. She grew to a very respectable 7ft herself!

You certainly could not miss the landmark church tower at **Winterton-on-Sea**, for it soars to a height of 132ft - positively a high-rise building in this low-lying landscape. Inside Holy Trinity Church is the so-called 'Fisherman's Corner', a striking tribute to all those who have lost their lives in these waters, with ropes, nets, a ship's lantern and an anchor - even the cross is fashioned from the timbers of a ship. This memorial was conceived and set up by the Reverend Clarence Porter, who, ironically enough, was himself drowned whilst rescuing a young choirboy from the sea.

Indeed, many of the houses in the village in the early part of the 18th century were said to be built from timbers washed ashore from the wrecks. We caught a glimpse of some even stranger looking dwellings close to the beach - round thatched buildings which evoke an impression of the African plains. The Hotel Humanus has very bravely modelled its guest accommodation on the mud huts of South Africa, and it must be great fun to stay in one.

The beach at Winterton is wide and sandy, and at low tide youngsters will delight in the numerous rock pools that form there with their little underwater worlds. However, do be wary of the very real dangers of drowning - markers are set out to warn you of the area to be avoided, and notices insist that children should be accompanied by an adult at all times.

Just to the south of Winterton on the B1159 coast road is the popular holiday resort of **Hemsby**. Two miles inland from Hemsby on the B1152, we stopped at the lovely village of **Martham**, with its attractive Georgian houses and cottages surrounding the village green and the massive west tower of St Mary's Church dominating the northern end. Here you will find the Countryside Collection, a working museum of rural life and bygones where craftsmen such as a wheelwright and a blacksmith demonstrate their skills and, during the summer months, heavy horses can be seen hard at work in the fields.

While we were here, we also called in at **Grange Farm Riding School**, which can be found within a 270 acre arable farm on the outskirts of the village. This first-class riding school has been operating here for the past 16 years, and for the last 12 of those, Frances Burgess has been their chief instructor. There is an indoor riding area, an all-weather outdoor arena, and provision for jumping and longer-distance hacks. The school caters for all ages and levels of ability, and on certain days, makes special provision for disabled riders. The riding school is open all year round. Please phone for further details, or to let them know you're coming.

Grange Farm Riding School, Martham, Great Yarmouth
01493 740245

Three miles to the south-east of Martham, you will find animals of a different kind at the **Norfolk Rare Breeds Centre** of **Ormesby St Michael**, just half a mile off the A149 travelling from Great Yarmouth in the direction of North Walsham.

Norfolk Rare Breeds Centre, Decoy Farm House, Ormesby St
Michael, Great Yarmouth 01493 732990

Mr and Mrs Lanham decided to dedicate 15 acres of their 700 acre farm into providing the first Norfolk Rare Breeds Centre. This grew out of a personal hobby of collecting rare breeds of animal but due to the growing interest of outsiders it was felt that the Centre was called for.

Upon entering the Centre there is a large pond to the left, with wildfowl of every variety. Although regularly fed they appreciate the titbits offered by visitors that can be bought from the refreshment kiosk. Adjacent to the pond are The Old Stables which have now been converted into an indoor piggery, housing various breeds of pig ranging from the Apple Orchard to the Pug Nosed Middle White. From here you can stroll down to the paddocks to see all the different types of sheep, cattle and goats. Not to be missed is Chester the little white bull. In the incubation centre you can watch chicks being hatched and reared under a brooder lamp. The farm is open to the public from Easter until the end of September every day except Saturday from 11.00 am to 5.00 pm.

Heading west from Ormesby, the A149 crosses scenic Ormesby Broad. From the bridge, fine views can be had of this section of Norfolk's inland waterways system - indeed, the views from the two-and-a-half-mile stretch of road between Ormesby and Rollesby are arguably the best to be found anywhere in Broadland. It is also an interesting area from an archaeological point of view, as metal pots found in nearby barrows would suggest that a community of Beaker Folk inhabited the vicinity around 2000 BC.

Pleasant **Rollesby** village lies a mile further on from the bridge, and here you will find an attractive row of thatched cottages and the Norman church of St George, which has a round tower and dates back mainly to the 14th century. A mile to the south-east of the village is the 200-acre Rollesby Broad which, together with Ormesby, is one of the largest of the Broads.

The Horse and Groom, Main Road (A149), Marsham, Nr Aylsham
01493 740624

Beeston Hall

Caistor Castle

While we were in the village, we called in at the **Horse and Groom,** a freehouse, steak and seafood restaurant recently opened by Chris and Anne Carter. Inside the decor furniture and carpets have been carefully chosen to create surroundings which are relaxed, friendly and of a very high standard. Chris and Anne are the type of people who make their customers feel instantly at home, and they successfully create an atmosphere which is warm and welcoming. They offer a wide selection of ales and wines, and the food is first-class too. The menu contains an excellent choice of steaks, grills and the house speciality - seafood. The local fishing fleet is based only a few minutes drive away from this busy roadside pub and restaurant, so mouthwatering fresh fish and shellfish always features strongly on the menu.

Before heading further inland, we decided to back-track along the A149 to the coast and pay a quick visit to **Caister-on-Sea**. The Romans settled here in the 2nd century (the name is derived from the Latin 'castra', meaning a 'camp' or 'fortress') and excavations have verified the town's importance as a Roman port. Before the Romans came, saw and conquered, however, Caister was an important town of the Iceni tribe, once led by Boudicca, the great warrior queen.

A mile to the west of the town is the splendid ruin of Caister Castle, which we were surprised to discover was the first castle to be built of brick in England - and indeed one of the earliest brick buildings of any kind in this country. The 90ft tower survives, together with much of the moated wall and gatehouse, lapped by still waters and with ivy relentlessly encroaching. It may look like the sort of place where only bats and owls should dwell, but it is in fact open to the public during the summer. As an additional attraction to visitors, the castle grounds house an impressive collection of motor vehicles, including a car used in the film of Ian Fleming's 'Chitty-Chitty-Bang-Bang'.

Caister Castle was built between 1432-5 by Sir John Fastolf, who we met earlier at Blickling. Though there is the possibility of Sir John being the prototype of Shakespeare's boisterous character, Falstaff, purists would probably insist that he was in fact based on Sir John Oldcastle, the despised heretic and leader of the English Lollards. Whether Fastolf deserves this distinction or not, he was certainly the hero of the hour not just at Agincourt, but also during the so-called 'Battle of the Herrings' in 1429. This may conjure up visions of the 'Monty Python' team dressed up as armoured knights bashing each other with dead fish, but in fact it refers to a clever tactic employed by Sir John during the Seige of Orleans, when his convoy of ships taking supplies to the English army formed a laager of herring barrels and beat off the French.

Rather than taking the easy (and perhaps logical) option of heading straight into Great Yarmouth from here, our journey continues westwards from the castle to explore some of the other villages in the heart of Broadland.

Midway between Caister and Acle on the A1064, we reach the picturesque village of **Filby** on Filby Broad. Here, we dropped in at the **King's head**, a traditional Norfolk pub run for the last two years by Lou and June Curson. The pub building dates from the 17th century and inside the atmosphere is friendly and intimate. There is an open log fire, historic pictures and memorabilia on the walls, and a massive timber beam in the bar which holds the low sloping ceiling in place. Lou and June are experienced hosts and provide their customers with an excellent selection of drinks and good value bar meals. There is also a spacious games room and a piano in the bar.

The King's Head Inn & Restaurant, Main Road, Filby
01463 730992

We turned down the side road from Filby towards **Thrigby,** passing by some very attractive cottages and orchards on the way. It was also in this area that we spotted the large, sprawling flower that grows along the verges, known as the Alexander. It looks rather like a yellow-hued cow-parsley, and we had seen the same plant growing around the lanes near the old Roman fort at Reculver on the Kent coast. It is in fact a descendant of a plant which the Romans brought over from Macedonia - they used it in salads and it is said that it tastes rather like celery.

The present **Thrigby Hall** was built in 1876 on the remains of a previous mansion. This country building stands in old landscaped grounds amid an interesting collection of Asian wildlife. The gardens are one of the top attractions in Norfolk, set between Norwich and the Great Yarmouth coast, they are the ideal place to visit and an exciting outing for all the family.

Other features include a tree house overlooking the willow pattern garden, childrens adventure playground and ample picnic spots. The fine gift shop and cafe are open from Easter until late October.

Another popular place with visitors of all ages is **The Bygone Village,** which is easy to find on the A1064 in **Fleggburgh** - also known as **Burgh St Margaret.** Set in over 40 acres of glorious Norfolk countryside, this unique Heritage Village holds a wealth of nostalgic memories and offers so much for visitors to see and do.

A narrow gauge railway built in 1988 enables you to take one of several locos along a specially designed track to show you as many of the village's attractions as possible. The train will take you through the pets' paddock, where you will see all types of birds including rare Snowy Owls, as well as rabbits and guinea pigs and Buster and Graceful the black pot-bellied pigs - a firm favourite with children.

Enthusiasts of the steam age will be delighted by the extensive collection of unusual engines on display in the main exhibition hall, and those who love music will be interested to see the beautifully restored Compton Cinema Organ, built in 1932. The resident organist is always pleased to play requests.

Other attractions include an adventure playground and fairground for children, country craft and gift shops, glass making demonstrations six days a week, and several refreshment areas and picnic spots. Open every day from 10.00am to 6.00pm, this diverse attraction is just too good to miss.

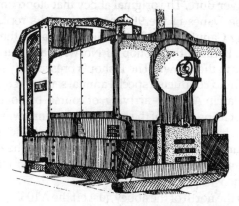

The Bygone Village, Fleggburgh

Taking a minor road across the B1152 from Fleggburgh, we came to the quiet village of **Thurne** about three miles further on; next to the river of the same name and just upstream from where it joins the Bure at Thurne Mouth. A few hundred yards from the riverbank, we found the first-rate pub and eating house, **The Lion Inn,** which has been run since

1989 by Royston and Vanessa Hart. The inn stands within three acres of attractive gardens containing a lily pond, a children's play area and a lively pet's corner. The Lion offers a range of first-class snacks in the bar and a full á la carte menu in the separate dining room. Sunday lunches are a speciality, and there is also a family room and a room offering pool and other amusements. Free moorings are available for patrons.

The Lion Inn, Thurne, Great Yarmouth 01692 670796

About a mile to the south-west of Thurne, and only approachable by boat or on foot, stands the decidedly odd-looking ruin of St Benet's Abbey by the River Bure. The original abbey that stood on this site was destroyed by the Danes in the 9th century, and its replacement was founded by King Canute in 1020. It fell into ruin after the Dissolution, when the abbot became the Bishop of Norwich and surrendered the episcopal estates to the Crown. The Bishop's present-day successor still holds both titles, and conducts a special annual service at the abbey ruins on the first Sunday in August - arriving, of course, by boat. Seen from a distance, our first impression of the outline of the ruins was that an army of giant termites had decided to set up camp there! The reality is only slightly less bizarre - the 'termite hill' rising up from the middle of the gatehouse is actually the stump of an 18th century brick windmill which was built into the walls.

Two miles to the north of the abbey, just off the A1062, is the beautiful Broadland village of **Ludham** , very popular with the boating fraternity but still unspoilt by the crowds. Rows of picturesque thatched cottages, handsome 18th century houses around the market place, and the 14th and 15th century church dedicated to St Catherine make up the heart of this attractive village, while the surrounding marshland is a wonderful place to stretch your legs after hours of travelling by car or boat. After you have seen the ruins of St Benet's Abbey and the splendidly restored painted screens in the church, make your way to **How Hill** where you will find the unusual open-framed timber-built windpump known as Boardman's Mill, which is open every day to visitors.

If you head east on the A1062 from Ludham you will soon rejoin the A149, and across the road from the junction is **Potter Heigham**. You may not be intimate with the village itself, but all those who have ever been for a boating holiday on the Norfolk Broads will be familiar with the name - courtesy of its notoriously low bridge. This medieval hump-backed bridge spanning the River Thurne has a headroom of only seven feet, and still puts the fear of God into all novice sailors who attempt to negotiate it without the recommended professional pilot to guide them safely through.

Essentially, an entirely new village has sprung up around the old bridge, the hub of it being the Broads Haven Marina which caters for all the needs of the tourist afloat. Potter Heigham proper lies a good mile further north, and its name is said to derive from the fact that a Roman pottery once stood here. If you want to get away from the crowds, it is certainly worth visiting the old village to see St Nicholas' Church. It is mainly 14th century, with a thatched nave, a circular tower supporting a 15th century octagonal belfry and, inside, a unique brick-built font.

However, it must be said that far and away the most intriguing of Potter Heigham's architectural offerings is the peculiar building that can be seen on the riverbank a few hundred yards downstream from the bridge. At first glance it resembles a somewhat stunted windmill upon which someone has draped an old sou'wester to shield it from the elements, but the more discerning among you may recognise it for what it really is - the top section of a helter-skelter! Lopped off and transplanted here as a holiday cottage, it originally stood on the Britannia Pier at Great Yarmouth and must have been an even more impressive sight in its working days.

At **Catfield Common**, half a mile east of the A149 on the Hickling road, we made a point of calling in at Myrtle Farm, home of the **Jacques Daniels Ornamental Pheasants and Crafts Centre**. Jacques is a naturalist, and over the years he and his wife have built up a unique collection of pheasants and wildfowl from all over the world. Many species are bred here for reintroduction to the wild, both in this country and overseas. The birds are well cared for and can be viewed in the lovely grounds of the Daniels' old farmhouse. Look out also for the renovated stables which contain a fascinating display of crafts of every description, and for Jacques' collection of caged birds.

Helter-Skelter House, Potter Heigham

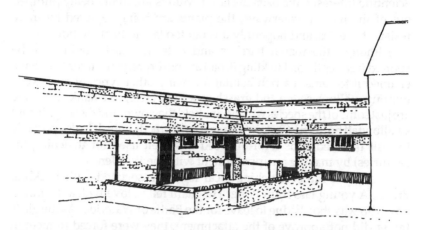

Jacques Daniels Ornamental Pheasants and Crafts Centre, Myrtle Farm, Catfield Common, Great Yarmouth 01692 670862

To the east lies Hickling Broad, the largest and least spoilt of all the Norfolk Broads. It now forms part of a 1,400-acre national nature reserve (one of the first to be established in England), managed by the Norfolk Naturalists Trust, and those exploring it by boat must keep strictly within the markers.

It is worth reminding ourselves that the Broads and surrounding wetlands are a fragile environment, having been under threat from the increasing amount of water traffic over the years. The wash from motor-boats has eroded the banks of rivers and broads at an alarming rate, the mud settling on the bottom and gradually filling in the waterways. This is not the only cause for concern, however. Much has been written on the problem of pollution here, with nitrates from fertilisers and phosphates from sewage and detergents causing the spread of algae, and the subsequent choking of the indigenous plant life as its light is blocked out and its oxygen stolen. Once familiar sights such as the massive wild water-lily meadows have virtually disappeared, and the death of aquatic plants has affected the entire food chain - insects, fish and birds have all suffered the consequences. There are 46 Broads altogether in the region, and today, only four of these have perfectly clear water and only half a dozen or so have any plant life at all. The rest are sterile wastes.

Many of the Broads may now be beyond help, but the future of the region is not totally one of doom. Whether or not the conservationists have their way and motor-boats become a thing of the past, the Broads Authority and the various conservation bodies are implementing other measures to ensure the survival of this unique place. Broadland has finally been designated a National Park, and over 20 Sites of Special

211

Scientific Interest have been declared. Mud is gradually being pumped out of the barren waterways, the plants are being replaced by more resistant species, and hopefully it is not too late to turn the tide.

Although the marsh harriers and bitterns which could once be spotted frequently on Hickling Broad are now rare, careful controls have enabled it to remain a rich habitat for many other types of bird. Reed bunting, willow, sedge and grasshopper warblers, redshank and snipe are just some of the species which have held their own, and the magnificent swallowtail butterfly (Britain's largest) still breeds here. It is also possible to visit the reed beds (Norfolk reed has been used for thatching for centuries) by making an appointment with the Warden.

There is a rather touching local legend associated with Hickling Broad. A young lass from Potter Heigham fell in love with a drummer boy who was shortly due to leave for the Battle of Waterloo. As the girl's father did not approve of the attachment, they were forced to meet in secret at a place called Swim Coots on the Heigham side of the Broad, the young soldier skating across the winter ice to join his sweetheart. One evening the ice gave way and the boy was drowned, but they say that his ghost can sometimes still be seen on winter evenings, scudding across the ice and beating his drum as he faithfully maintains his tryst.

Hickling village itself lies to the north of the Broad, and the best approach to it is via **The Pleasure Boat Inn** on the water's edge at Hickling Staithe. Surrounded by a most attractive group of buildings, this is a popular meeting place for the sailing fraternity.

The Pleasure Boat Inn, Hickling Staithe

The Inn is over 150 years old and used to be the rendezvous point of the wherries, which would drop their cargoes and collect local produce to transport to Great Yarmouth. Today, The Pleasure Boat is run by

Andrew and Jenny Haylett, who have been providing an excellent service for their many customers over their last two years in residence.

The Inn is very tastefully decorated and has a dining area that boasts magnificent views over the Broads. A comprehensive set menu contains many varied dishes, including vegetarian and a good selection of children's meals. Daily specials always include a roast dinner, and for those who like a drink with their meal a good wine list is available.

On a warm day you can sit outside with your drink, watching the numerous breeds of bird and taking in the scenery, and perhaps enjoy a delicious salad from the amply stocked salad bar.

Two miles southeast of Stalham, and just to the east of the A149 Great Yarmouth to Cromer road, we made a point of visiting **Sutton Windmill** and the **Broads Museum** at **Sutton**. The historic windmill (the tallest in Britain) was constructed in the 18th century and remained in use until 1940. In recent years, a lengthy programme of restoration work has been carried out by the present owners, the Nunn family, using authentic materials wherever possible. Their ultimate aim is to restore the sails of this nine-storey windmill to working order. Visitors are welcome to view the historic corn-milling machinery with its four sets of millstones, and to experience the superb views from the top. Over the past 30 years, the Nunn family have also built up a fascinating private collection of artifacts which reflect the social history of England since World War I. These are on show in the family's privately-owned Broads Museum and include many interesting examples of domestic and kitchen appliances, banknotes, cigarette packets, razors and leather- and barrel-making tools.

The Broads Museum & Sutton Windmill, Sutton 01692 581195

The ancient market town of **Stalham**, lying three miles inland just off the A149, provides an excellent base for exploring the northern reaches of the Norfolk Broads. From Stalham Staithe, boats can be hired for day trips along the River Ant and beyond, or water tours can be taken to the beautiful gardens at How Hill. Hickling Broad with its nature reserve is only two miles away and is popular with bird watchers. For those more interested in walking, the famous Weavers Way passes through Stalham on its route from Great Yarmouth to Cromer.

A short walk from Stalham Staithe in the centre of the town, we found the impressive **Kingfisher Hotel,** run since 1987 by the resident Williams family. This modern hotel has 16 tastefully furnished bedrooms, all centrally heated and equipped with en-suite bathroom, colour television, direct dial telephone and tea-coffee making facilities. The restaurant has a relaxed atmosphere and offers a good selection of reasonably priced wines. A number of local seafood dishes feature on the extensive a la carte menu. Alternatively, a wide range of bar meals and real ales is offered in the lounge bar. (Vegetarian dishes are always available). Mrs Williams, her sons Nigel and Roger and their staff provide their guests with an excellent centre for a relaxing stay in this, one of the most lovely parts of the country. Enquire about their specially-priced two and three day bargain breaks.

The Kingfisher Hotel & Restaurant, High Street, Stalham
01692 581974

Two miles along the A149 to the west of Stalham, we cross the beautiful River Ant at Wayford Bridge. Here, there is a water sports and cycle hire centre, and an attractive riverside pub, the **Woodfarm Inn.** The original pub building was built as a farmhouse in the early 18th century and remained so until the early 1960s. It has been added to in the years since then, and now boasts a large in-pub children's room, games room and a spacious lounge and restaurant. Outside there is a tranquil beer garden, a barbecue cabin and five acres of beautiful Broadland grounds. Keith Bedford has run the Woodfarm Inn since 1984. He is quite a character and sure to make your visit welcoming and enjoyable. Over the years, he has successfully retained the original character of the building (look out for the historic farm tools in the old bars) and has built up a fine inn serving good food and ales in very pleasant surroundings.

Woodfarm Inn, Wayford Bridge, Nr Smallburgh 01692 582414

South of here, a mile to the east of the A1151 and close to Beeston Hall, lies the charming village of **Neatishead**. Limekiln Dyke runs down from here to the western side of Barton Broad, and although its cottages and farms are fairly spread out, the heart of the village is centred around the main village street with its late Georgian houses. If you want to visit **Beeston Hall**, it is normally open in the afternoons during the summer. Standing just half a mile to the north-west of Neatishead, it is a charming building of the 18th century with flint facade and laudable Gothic pretensions. Much of the charm of a house of this calibre comes from the fact that it is still very much a family home, and the Prestons have lived here for centuries.

A minor road from Cangate led us south to **Horning** , which lies just off the A1062 between Wroxham and Ludham on the River Bure. Although it is now a popular boating centre, Horning does not yet suffer from the same degree of commercialisation as Wroxham. With its pretty reed- thatched cottages, the main street of this ancient village runs parallel to the river for almost a mile, and the trim lawns of half-timbered Edwardian houses sweep down to thatched boathouses on the water's edge.

Many of the pubs and hotels along the river offer mooring space, one of them being the 15th century Old Ferry Inn. This historic inn stands at the point of the river where the old chain ferry once transported its passengers from one bank to the other, and was at one time used as a mead storehouse for St Benet's Abbey. It seems that more than one kind of spirit can be found at the inn, for it is said to be haunted by the ghost of a young woman dressed in a flowing green cloak, sometimes seen walking through the bar before sinking into the river. The story goes that she was raped and murdered by monks from the abbey who went on a drunken rampage, then tried to hide the corpse in the river.

Another place at Horning that we would particularly like to recommend is **Petersfield House Hotel**, an excellent three-star hotel and restaurant catering for those looking for a first-rate meal or well above average-accommodation. The hotel is set in two acres of landscaped grounds and has its own water frontage and moorings on the River Bure. An extraordinary feature of the garden is a 19th century moon-gate, a large circular aperture let low into the wall which separates the formal gardens from steps leading to a woodland glade. This rare example of once highly-fashioned garden Chinoiserie is doubly unusual in that, while most moon-gates in Britain were built of brickwork, this one is constructed of Norfolk flint with only the inside of the archway being lined with brick.

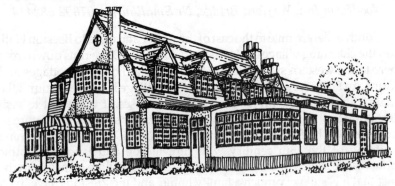

Petersfield House Hotel & Restaurant, Lower Street, Horning
01692 630741

During the Second World War, Petersfield House was requisitioned by the Air Ministry for use as an officers' mess, then in the 1960s it was enlarged to its present size and converted to an 18 bedroomed hotel. The present owners, Philip and Gwen Crouch and their son Robin, took over the hotel in 1985. Robin is now manager, and he and his staff provide a high standard of comfort, service and cuisine. The 80 seater restaurant overlooks the lily pond and fountain in the landscaped garden and has a menu which is both excellent and adventurous. In addition to the good value set menu, there is a range of more exotic options available at a modest extra charge. On the day we visited, we could have opted for

Couquelles St Jacque (scallops blended in a cheese sauce, topped with parmesan) as a starter, or as a main course, Lobster Americaine (halved lobster shell filled with lobster meat, flamed in calvados and coated with a creamy tomato and onion sauce). There is a dinner dance every Saturday evening.

Before you leave Horning, do pay a quick visit to St Benedict's Church, which stands on a hill outside the village. Its soaring 14th century tower has the Four Evangelists on its pinnacles, and inside there are some unusual medieval bench-ends - one of a particularly horrific nature depicting the Devil pushing a man into the fiery mouth of a dragon.

Two miles to the south-east of Horning, between the River Bure and South Walsham on the B1140 Norwich to Acle 'back' road, is the beautiful Broadland village of **Ranworth**, famous for its church and its position on the Ranworth Marshes. From the top of St Helen's church tower it is possible to see five Norfolk Broads, Horsey Mill and the sea at Great Yarmouth. Inside, you will find a 15th century service book and one of the finest rood-screens in the country. The church is open daily and visitors are welcome.

The Norfolk Naturalist's Trust chose to locate the Broadland Conservation Centre at the nearby nature reserve. An exhibition on the Broads, past and present, can be found here, as well as a quarter-mile nature trail which starts in the village. For those approaching by boat, there are 24-hour public moorings at the entrance to Ranworth Broad, although no land access to the village is possible from here. Alternatively, it is possible to anchor in Malthouse Broad where landings can be made at the village staithe. The staithe was once a thriving mooring for the old Norfolk trading wherries. These would sail into Ranworth to unload their cargoes of coal and barley for the maltings, and reload with locally produced wool and woven cloth. (Remember that the famous woollen town of Worstead is only a few miles away to the north). The wherries ceased trading in 1950 and little has changed here since. There are still magnificent views across Ranworth Marshes and a solitary disused wherry resting by the quay.

Adjacent to the staithe, we found the **Granary Stores and Old Granary Steakhouse** which have been run for the last three years by Barry and Mollie Pring. The numerous moorings nearby make this a thriving establishment during the summer season. Here, the traveller can purchase groceries and provisions, dairy goods, fresh meats and locally grown fruit and vegetables. It is also possible to choose from over 100 different wines, beers and spirits at the off-license counter. There is also a section offering gifts, toys, paintings and local crafts. Adjoining the stores is the Old Granary Steakhouse which is open for business from mid-March to the end of November each year. An excellent range of starters and main courses is available here, including roast duckling, lemon sole and prime beef steaks. At lunchtime, jacket potatoes with assorted fillings and ploughman's lunches can be ordered. There is a separate children's menu, and special dishes available at Sunday lunchtimes. Barry and Mollie also provide luxury all-weather day launches for hire, either by the hour of by the day. A small tourist information centre is open at Ranworth staithe from Easter to October.

The Granary Stores, Restaurant and Boat Hire, Ranworth Staithe, Ranworth 01605 49432

There are few places in England where at all times of the year you can find an innate beauty and tranquillity, which forms an idyllic escape from the hustle and bustle of daily life. To find one, just travel along the road into **South Walsham** and the **Fairhaven Garden Trust**. Be prepared to spend many happy hours there.

The village was first recorded in history during the reign of King Harold. After the battle of Hastings, William the Conqueror took over the land, and gave the manor of South Walsham to the Earl of Norfolk, later to become the Duke of Norfolk. There is much of interest to see, and we should have drawn your attention in the beginning to the 15th century rood screen and carved poppy heads on the pews in St Mary's church. The fine 18th century organ in the church was originally built for the Assembly House, Norwich, but was donated to St Mary's by the late Lord Fairhaven.

About a mile to the north lies Malthouse Broad, leading to Ranworth Broad and its Nature Reserve. To the north east there is road access to the public South Walsham Outer Broad; this leads through a narrow channel called "The Weirs" into the private Inner Broad, which forms part of the Fairhaven Garden Trust.

Lord Fairhaven was not only a gardener, but also a naturalist. He purchased the South Walsham Estate in 1947, and the whole garden was a wilderness. The dykes of the present garden existed, but the whole area presented an impenetrable jungle of fallen trees, brambles and nettles. Inspired by his friend, Sir Eric Savill, creator of one of the first woodland gardens in the world, Lord Fairhaven conceived the idea of a woodland garden in Norfolk. The jungle was slowly cleared, and as each new area was conquered, shade and water-loving plants were introduced, primulas by the thousand, Lysichitum Americanum, which now grows in almost wild profusion, camellias and rhododendrons were just a few of the plants chosen.

What you see today took 15 years to create, and Lord Fairhaven achieved it with the help of a single woodman, Jack Debbage. Since then there has always been a Debbage at Fairhaven. The head gardener and resident warden is now George Debbage.

The Fairhaven Garden Trust property covers about 170 acres including the Inner Broad, and a further 60 acres comprising the bird sanctuary to the west of Ranworth Road. There have been 92 varieties of birds in the woods around South Walsham, and the bird sanctuary may be visited by prior arrangement with the warden. So much more could be written about the Fairhaven Garden Trust, but seeing is better than reading, so do go and experience this enchantment for yourselves.

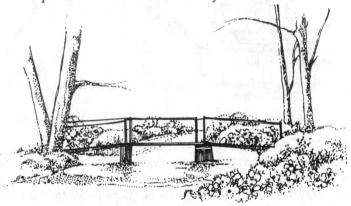

Fairhaven Garden Trust, Woodland and Water Garden, South Walsham 01605 49449

South Walsham Hall, on the northern edge of this lovely Broadland village, is now an exceptional hotel, restaurant and country club which has been run for the last 10 years by Swiss-born Alex Suss and his staff. The present house dates from the Elizabethan era and was added to in Georgian, Victorian and Edwardian times. It is set in 30 acres of private grounds with sloping lawns, beautiful lakes and many specimen trees and shrubs. Inside, a magnificent carved staircase leads to the 10 luxurious bedrooms; all have en-suite bath/shower and every modern facility. To the rear, a further seven rooms are located in the tastefully-converted gun room, carriage house and blacksmith's workshop.

If you are looking for somewhere in the village to go for a drink and a bite to eat after you have visited Fairhaven, we can heartily recommend **The Ship**, a first-rate pub and restaurant run for the last few years by Sara and John Lind. The Ship is now a listed building with parts dating back to the 17th century. The oldest section, now an excellent restaurant, has oak beams, an original archway, and great character. Look out for the good-value set menu and the wide range of vegetarian dishes and specials on the blackboard. At lunchtimes, freshly made ploughman's lunches and sandwiches are also available. The bar area, also with a low-beamed ceiling, features a fine selection of guest beers, and there is a separate childrens's room and a good play area outside.

The Ship, The Street, South Walsham 01605 49553

If you head east from South Walsham on the B1140, after about three miles you will arrive at the attractive village of **Acle**, now thankfully by-passed by the busy A47 Norwich to Great Yarmouth road. The River Bure and its large marina at Acle Bridge are only a mile away to the north-east, so Acle gets its fair share of summer holidaymakers stocking up on essentials. The bridge that once stood here was apparently the scene of numerous executions, with victims hung on the parapet and left to dangle over the Bure and rot - though it is hard to imagine such grisly events today!

Those looking for comfortable accommodation or a first-rate meal in this part of Norfolk should call in at the **East Norwich Inn** near the centre of the village. Formerly municipal offices, this grand and stylish building was converted to an inn, hotel and restaurant in 1979. Locally called 'The Cabin' it is now owned and personally run by Liz and Robin Graves-Morris. There are nine spacious en-suite bedrooms available and an elegant restaurant which offers a good selection of excellently-priced dishes including a choice for vegetarians. The bar has an inviting log fire and a fine selection of ales.

East Norwich Inn & Hotel, Acle Old Road, Acle 01493 751112

If you carry on down the A47 heading for Yarmouth you cannot fail to miss the Stracey Arms Windpump, which was built of brick in 1883 and stands close to the pub of the same name. Its function was to draw off surplus water from the surrounding marshland and pump it into the Bure. It has now been fully restored by the Norfolk Windmills Trust, and visitors can also see an educational exhibition of photographs outlining the history of windpumps in the region.

However - still putting off our visit to Great Yarmouth until we had seen all that we wanted to see - we headed south from Acle on the B1140 to explore the area to the west and south of the town. A glance at a road map will show you the incredible number of windmills or windpumps in this area In the area from Norwich to Caister and down to the Suffolk border, there are nearly 40 in all, with a heavy concentration of them around the Halvergate Marshes.

East of **Halvergate** and **Wickhampton** is a maze of fields and dykes, where many of the old windpumps have been restored (though not necessarily to working order) and are now open to visitors. Footpaths from both villages will take you across the marshes to the tallest and best restored marsh mill on the Broads (this one in full working order), Berney Arms Mill. Standing 70ft high, the present mill was built in the 1860s to grind cement and was later converted to a pumping mill. It is now owned and run by English Heritage.

Close by, the Berney Arms public house must be one of the most isolated pubs in the country, with no access by road at all. To reach it you must come by footpath, or by train from Yarmouth or Reedham (the halt is half a mile away over the fields), or by boat. Holidaymakers who start their boating holiday in Beccles and chug up the River Waveney to visit Yarmouth often take advantage of the safe mooring place here, before venturing onto the tidal waters of Breydon Water.

Back at Wickhampton, which lies a mile to the east of the B1140, we discovered two very old, and rather strange effigies in the chancel of St Andrew's Church. The figures have been badly defaced over the centuries, but they represent Sir William Gerbygge and his wife, who originally both clasped a small stone heart to their chests - presumably signifying their devotion to God or perhaps their love for one another. However, local folklore gives a quite different identity to the figures and a far more disturbing reason for their presence. Parents of fractious children would tell them that this couple were actually two brothers named Hampton, who argued fiercely following a dispute over local parish boundaries and tore each other's hearts out! They were then turned to stone by the wrath of God (said the parents, threateningly) and left in the church as a warning to all those who are in the habit of losing their temper!

It is essential to visit **Reedham** if you wish to explore the countryside to the south of the River Yare, as its chain ferry provides the sole crossing for vehicles over the river between Yarmouth and Norwich. St John the Baptist's Church in the village was almost totally destroyed by fire in 1981, but a programme of restoration was begun at once, and rather like the tiny plants that shoot up from the ashes of a forest fire, something good can be said to have come from the disaster. As the ruined plaster was being chiselled off the wall of the nave, a glorious pattern of alternating herringbone and horizontal tiles was revealed.

Reedham is also the home of the enterprising 'Hales Snails' which, as you would guess, is the place to go for edible snails. These gastronomic delights are, believe it or not, even exported to France. The snail centre is not open to visitors so you can't try any samples, but if you would like to watch other things getting stuffed, you can visit 'Pettitts', the local taxidermy firm! Besides seeing the experts at work on new commissions (they number many film and theatre companies amongst their clients), there is also a display of previous works in the form of various stuffed animals and birds. If you prefer your wildlife alive and kicking, you may be surprised to learn that the company is also involved with breeding the delightful Falabella miniature horses.

To reach the last destination before our final port of call for this chapter, we had to set off on a fairly long-winded route, down the B1140 past Thurlton, then east on the B1136 to join up with the A143. This led us north-east through **Haddiscoe** (where St Mary's Church boasts a fine Saxon round tower and two splendid Norman doorways), across the bridge over the railway line and the New Cut (an 18th century drainage and navigational channel), then across the bridge over the River Waveney and on to the remote hamlet of **St Olaves,** where you can see the ruins of the Augustinian St Olaves' Priory and a lovely little boarded trestle mill called Priory Mill. The A143 then led us through the village of Fritton (of which more in Chapter 9), and two miles further on we took the left-hand turning through Belton and on to **Burgh Castle.**

The village itself has little to offer apart from its caravan sites, but just to the south are the impressive ruins of the old Roman fortress of Gariannonum, three of its flint and brick walls still standing today to a height of 15ft. One of a chain of forts on the south-east coast, it was built during the 3rd century as a defence against Saxon marauders who would sail across the North Sea on their frequent raids. Although this site now lies over three miles from the sea on flat marshland at the southern end of Breydon Water, things were very different in Roman times. The fort would then have stood on one bank of a huge estuary, looking across to Caister on the opposite shore and commanding a vital position at the head of a vast river which would take enemies deep into the heart of East Anglia.

The river has now dwindled to become Breydon Water - although those of a nervous disposition who come here on a boating holiday for the first time would claim that it is quite large enough as it is, as they gingerly steer their craft between the 'telegraph poles' marking the route to take if you wish to avoid the mudflats! Excavations at Burgh Castle also point to the fact that a monastery was established here around 635 AD by the Irish missionary, St Fursa, and it is likely that the Normans built a timber fort on the site. So much history, combined with the varied wildlife of Breydon Water and the haunting peace of the surrounding marshes make a lasting impression on most visitors.

And so we come at last to **Great Yarmouth.** The River Yare, from which the town takes its name, is the largest in Broadland, and sea-going cargo ships sail from here to Norwich along with pleasure boats, yachts, dinghies and the rest. After meeting the River Bure and widening out into Breydon Water, the river then takes a sharp turn to the south, forming a three-mile-long peninsula between its eastern bank and the sea. It was here that the old town of Yarmouth was built, somewhat surprisingly facing inland, and later spread along the west bank of the Yare as it developed. When Henry III granted Yarmouth its charter in 1272, the 'Great' was proudly added to its name, and throughout the Middle Ages and beyond, the town became known as a harbour and shipbuilding centre. The herring industry brought great prosperity to the town for many centuries too, and when overfishing led to its decline after the two World Wars, Yarmouth was given a new lease of life by the discovery of North Sea oil.

Visitors soon discover that much of Yarmouth's special character comes from its unique blend of the old and the new. Certainly it is one of our most popular seaside resorts, with five miles of sandy beach, two piers, and an impressive range of holiday amenities and entertainments; yet at the same time it has one of the most complete medieval town walls in the country and many outstanding historic buildings going right back to the Middle Ages. The 13th century Tolhouse in Tolhouse Street is one example that springs to mind: once the town's courthouse and gaol, it is said to be the oldest civic building in Britain. Its dungeons are now open to the public and it also houses a fascinating museum of local history.

While you are in the area, look out for the fascinating **Great Yarmouth Pottery** situated close to the city walls in Blackfriars Towers. The pottery inhabits a 300-year-old former herring smokehouse. Visitors can still see the blackened walls of the original smoke rooms and smell the lingering aroma of smoking kippers. (At one time up to 64 girls, many of them migrant workers from Scotland, were employed in a single smoke room). The modern pottery has been in operation for over 20 years and specialises in the production of superb limited-edition mugs. Visitors can watch Mr and Mrs Childs and their staff at work and view their fine display of pottery mugs, some of which are now valued at over £400.

Please Don't Forget...

To tell people that you read about them in

The Hidden Places

Great Yarmouth Pottery, Blackfriars Towers, Blackfriars Road,
Great Yarmouth 01493 850585

The broad Market Place is one of the largest in England (you will find that Yarmouth claims many places in the record books!) and is crammed with stalls on Wednesdays and Saturdays, and on Fridays during the summer. At its northern end is the splendidly restored 12th century

Church of St Nicholas. Badly damaged by fire during the Second World War, it was rebuilt between 1957-60, its original medieval form being perfectly preserved. It also claims (naturally enough!) to be the largest parish church in England. To the south of the church is a delightful group of handsome Georgian houses, and among them you will find the half-timbered town house where Anna Sewell, the author of 'Black Beauty', was born. St George's Church, at the opposite end of the Market Place to St Nicholas', now serves as a theatre and arts centre; while on the north-east corner is the delightfully-named Hospital for Decayed Fishermen, now dedicated to retired seafarers.

Some of Yarmouth's best buildings can be found in The Rows, a network of narrow alleys and courts whose alignment has not been changed since medieval times. Many of these were destroyed when the town was bombed during the war, but some survived and a number of the more historic buildings have been restored.

Other places of interest that we can recommend here must (for want of space, not enthusiasm!) be kept to a minimum. The Marina Centre is a 'must', as is the exciting new Sealife Centre, where you can venture underwater without the bother of squeezing into a wet-suit! The Maritime Museum on Marine Parade was once a home for shipwrecked sailors, but today houses a superb collection of model vessels and tells you exactly how modern trawlers operate. We were amazed to discover that old-style life jackets were made from cork!

South Quay, with its elegant mixture of Tudor, Georgian and Victorian merchants' houses, must be seen - especially Number 4, which is now the Elizabethan House Museum, a museum of domestic life containing a number of oak-panelled Elizabethan rooms with superb plasterwork ceilings. In total opposition to such elegance and charm, these houses look across to the port itself, a tough, noisy, working environment, stretching for nearly two miles along the River Yare.

Finally, may we suggest that you make your way about a mile to the south of Old Yarmouth where, behind South Beach and now surrounded by factories, you will find the Norfolk Pillar. This landmark monument to Lord Nelson was erected in 1819 to commemorate the Admiral's landings at Yarmouth following his victories at the Battles of the Nile and Copenhagen. Standing at the top of the 144ft column is not Nelson himself (his figure was reserved for the more famous column in Trafalgar Square 10 years later), but our very own Britannia. To climb the 217 steps to the viewing platform is an awesome experience, only to be attempted if you don't get winded easily (and in fact only allowed during July and August) - but what a view! A perfect way to look down over the town and back across to some of the places we have been exploring in this chapter!

Sailing on the Broads

South Norfolk

Village of Eye

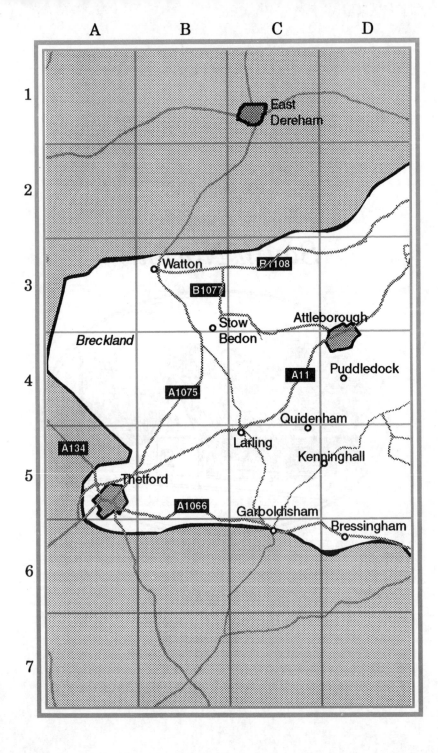

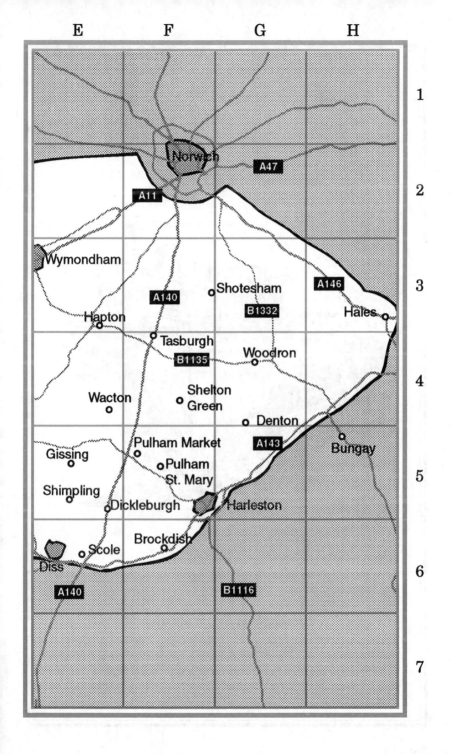

Bressingham Steam Museum

South Norfolk

One of the most famous episodes in Norfolk's history was Kett's Rebellion, an event which shattered the peace of the countryside around **Wymondham** in the mid-16th century. At that time peasants all over England were rising in protest against unscrupulous landowners who were fencing off large areas of common land for their own use and profit. In July 1549, an angry mob at Wymondham voiced their grievances by tearing down the offending fences put up by the local squire. They were confronted by one Robert Kett, who although a landowner himself, had been born the son of a humble tanner and listened sympathetically to the peasants' side of the story. Deciding that their cause was just, Kett and his brother William marched on Norwich, the size of their rebel army swelling to over 16,000 by the time they established their camp outside the city on Mousehold Heath.

The King offered a free pardon for all if the rebels would agree to surrender before any blood was spilt, but Kett's army responded by launching a full-scale attack and capturing the city. After an unsuccessful attempt by the Marquis of Northampton to drive them out, the Earl of Warwick arrived on the scene with 12,000 soldiers and recaptured Norwich, forcing the rebels back to Mousehold. Kett then made the fatal mistake of quitting this relatively safe position in favour of lower ground closer to the city, and when Warwick attacked the new camp on 27th August, the peasant army was promptly defeated. Those who fled for their lives were mercilessly hunted down and executed, and the Kett brothers were both hanged for their part in the revolt - Robert from the walls of Norwich Castle and William from one of the towers of Wymondham Abbey.

The two towers at Wymondham Abbey (where the nave has been preserved as the parish church) were the subject of fierce local dispute for many years. It was intended right from the start that both the Benedictine monks and the people of Wymondham should share the building between them, but predictably enough, there was much argument over who should make use of what space inside! Eventually, an interior wall was built to divide the church in two, and the parishioners - not to be bested by the monks' octagonal tower (which now stands at the east end of the church) - erected their own 142ft tower at the west end sometime around 1450. Though now ruined, the monastic tower has been carefully restored, and both towers offer an impressive sight as you turn the corner of Church Street in the town.

Inside, the hammerbeam roof above the Norman nave is resplendent with angels and starry bosses; there is a superb font with carvings of lions, wild men and angels; and perhaps best of all is the beautiful reredos and tester provided by Sir Ninian Comper as a memorial to local men who lost their lives in the First World War.

Wymondham (pronounced 'Wyndham', by the way) boasts a number of other attractive historic buildings spanning the centuries: medieval buildings sit comfortably with brick-built houses and elegant Georgian and Victorian residences, with only a slight jarring note from modern housing. An ancient Bridewell or gaol can be seen in Bridewell Street, with some of its windows still barred, and the handsome 14th century chapel dedicated to Thomas a Becket stands next to one of the oldest pubs in England, the half-timbered Green Dragon Inn. The chapel now houses the county library, and although rumours of a tunnel connecting this building to the Abbey have persisted for many years, it is likely that this is nothing more exciting than part of the disused Victorian sewage system!

Many of Wymondham's oldest buildings were lost in 1615 when a fire raged through the town, destroying more than 300 houses. Most of the townsfolk were at church when the fire occurred, so loss of life was not so dreadful as it might have been. The picturesque octagonal Market Cross that stands in the town centre was rebuilt two years after the fire. Crowned by a pyramid roof, this attractive timber-framed building is open on all sides on the ground floor, with an outside stairway leading up to the room on the first floor.

Just a few yards from the Market Cross and close to the splendid 12th century Abbey, you will find the **Sinclair Hotel,** a spacious Victorian building which has recently been converted to provide every comfort for the modern traveller. Very much a family concern with Paul and Josie Hawkins at the helm, guests can expect to receive a warm welcome on arrival and to be treated to the friendliest of service throughout their stay.

Of the 20 available bedrooms, six are situated on the ground floor, making them ideal for the elderly or infirm. All the rooms have en-suite bathrooms, hairdryers, colour television, direct dial telephone and tea and coffee making facilities. Both table d'hote and a la carte menus are available to guests and non-residents in the Licensed Chandlers Restaurant, which takes its name from the candle-makers who sold their wares in the street behind the hotel in medieval times. Up to 40 people can be accommodated in the restaurant, where you can also enjoy the chef's monthly speciality of European Cuisine. Smaller function rooms are available for meetings and private parties of all kinds, and after a meal guests can relax in comfort in the private residents lounge.

Sinclair Hotel, 28 Market Street, Wymondham 01953 606721

Steve and Mary Bell recently celebrated eight years behind the bar at **The Windmill** in Wymondham, and in that time they have established a reputation for good beer and satisfying, inexpensive food. The pub dates back over 500 years and its original name was 'The Windmill Sails', due to the close proximity of a now forgotten windmill in the area. In those far-off days, this was an inn used by coachmen and drovers. In more recent times, the pub was owned by the Canon Clarke Brewery of Norwich, but they were literally bombed out of business during the Second World War and sadly, all records relating to The Windmill at that time were lost. Today, The Windmill is a Free House, where locals and visitors alike can enjoy a good pint and a tasty meal in the friendly surroundings of a traditional village pub.

The Windmill, 3 Norwich Road, Wymondham 01953 602131

For railway buffs, we can also highly recommend a visit to the Brief Encounter tearooms at Wymondham Station. This provides pleasant and interesting surroundings in which to linger over a pot of tea and a snack - although there is no guarantee that visitors will experience a romantic interlude there!

On the B1172 three miles north-east of Wymondham is the large village of **Hethersett**, which has developed steadily over the years to become a popular residential suburb of Norwich. It was here that we discovered an exceptional hotel which is determined to keep abreast with the times by providing the very best of modern amenities.

Park Farm Hotel in Hethersett has long enjoyed an excellent reputation as a secluded Georgian country house hotel, and we are convinced that the wide range of additional facilities now completed will spread its fame even wider. Peter and Helene Gowing run this beautiful hotel, while their son David manages the family farm. In April 1991, work commenced to extend and improve the conference facilities offered at the hotel, and to build a major new leisure club. Membership of the Club started in January 1992 and includes an indoor heated swimming pool, sauna, solarium, jaccuzi, steam room and a superb custom equipped gym. The complex in which the leisure club is housed has been sympathetically designed to complement the architecture of the existing building.

In addition to this, the expansion of the existing conference facilities means that a total of five conference rooms of varying size, style and character are available, including a purpose built centre which seats up to 120 delegates theatre style. Boardroom and classroom style rooms are also provided, together with all the latest equipment necessary for the smooth running of a successful conference.

Park Farm Hotel & Restaurant, Heathersett 01603 810264

All these improvements will undoubtedly result in Park Farm

becoming one of the premiere small hotels for leisure or business in East Anglia. However, we can assure our readers that this does not mean that the Gowings have lost sight of the friendly touch! Park Farm has always been renowned for its welcoming atmosphere and personal service, and this is one thing that definitely will not be changing. The telephone number for the hotel is (0603) 810264, and you can reach them by FAX on (0603) 812104.

Two and a half miles south-east of Wymondham on the B1135, we came to the village of **Ashwellthorpe.** If you take the time to visit All Saints Church, the first thing you will notice is that you step down into the chancel as opposed to up. Here you will find the striking alabaster tomb and effigies of Sir Edmund de Thorpe and his wife; he dressed in full armour and his Lady wearing a fine example of the great 'horned' headdress that we associate with noble-women of the Middle Ages.

Gerry and Caroline Bloor have been running **The White Horse** public house in Ashwellthorpe for just under two years now, and in that time they have turned it into a really comfortable place to stop off for a drink and a meal. Caroline's cooking needs to be experienced to be fully appreciated, but basically she provides an excellent range of meals in what she calls her 'Mother's Cooking' style. We will probably suffer the consequences for saying so, but our mothers never cooked as well as this!

The White Horse, Ashwellthorpe

This is still very much a traditional village pub, and together with the excellent food, good ale and friendly company, this makes it a popular haunt with locals and visitors alike. You will also find a large, pleasant beer garden where you can sit out and enjoy a drink and a bite to eat in the summer months, and even a bowling green. Gerry and Caroline are busy making improvements to the pub all the time, and they have lots of interesting ideas for the future. We certainly intend to pop in again to see what's on offer then, and of course to re-acquaint our taste buds with some more of Caroline's delicious food!

Continuing south-east on the B1135 for several miles, a minor road then led us to **Tasburgh**, just west of the A140. Here we payed a visit to the exquisite gardens at Rainthorpe Hall, through which the River Tas winds its way northwards towards Norwich. Together with its superb Elizabethan garden, Rainthorpe is also notable for its range of bamboo plants that have adapted so well to the Norfolk climate. The Hall itself dates back to the 16th century and is timber-framed - something of a rarity for a Norfolk great house - and it also features an impressive collection of medieval stained glass in its windows. The gardens are open to the public on Sundays throughout the summer months.

Tasburgh village is especially appealing as it nestles at the base of a hill which was used as an encampment during the Iron Age. Today, the Church of St Mary sits up on the hillside enjoying the view; a charming little building with an early Saxon tower.

Further evidence of Saxon settlement in the area can be deduced from the local village names of **Saxlingham Thorpe**, **Saxlingham Nethergate** and **Saxlingham Green**. Each has its own particular charm: Thorpe with its church a virtual ruin, situated in a lonely pasture; Green with its quaint reed-thatched cottages; and Nethergate, whose Church of St Mary boasts a fine collection of Norwich stained glass from the 13th to 15th centuries. Indeed, this part of the county is particularly rich in churches, **Shotesham** alone having four within its parish boundaries. Admittedly, St Martin's and St Botolph's are now both ruins, but All Saints Church still stands proud high up on a hill above the delightful village of **Shotesham All Saints**. The tower of the church has an unusual exterior staircase made of iron, and the views from the churchyard are quite superb. Down below, a tributary of the Tas winds its way north-westwards, flanked by charming thatched cottages and willow trees and crossed at intervals by a series of little white bridges.

The village is hidden away in a very rural area south of Norwich and, together with its church, features several other interesting buildings. A number of these used to be pubs which are now closed, but one of them, standing at the edge of the village, is still very much 'alive and kicking'. **The Globe Inn** dates back to the 17th century and is a genuine, down-to-earth village pub with a marvellous traditional atmosphere. We often come across old-fashioned pubs which their owners have turned into the modern 'restaurant with bar' type of establishment, but Stewart and Kathie Steel have not succumbed to this with The Globe.

They have decided to let the pub function as it always has done: as a place for both locals and visitors to drop in to catch up with the local gossip over a glass or two of ale and a good meal of wholesome, sensibly priced food. We think they have made the right decision, as so often these days you walk into a pub which has been transformed into an up-market eatery, designed purely for those who do not object to spending a small fortune on food. The bar food here is varied but inexpensive, making it a great place to stop if you have children with you. Stewart told us that a fair amount of walkers and shooting parties frequent The Globe, and when the BBC was filming in the area recently, many of the crew stopped by for refreshments - which certainly boosted the day's takings!

The Globe Inn, Shotesham All Saints

We joined the B1332 to the east of Shotesham and headed south, and five miles further on came to **Ditchingham**. The Hall here dates from the early Georgian period and is open to visitors in the summer. It stands next to a lake in a park that was designed by Capability Brown. In the north aisle of St Mary's Church we found a memorial window to Sir (Henry) Rider Haggard, who was born in Bradenham Hall near Shipdham and lived at Ditchingham House. Two of his wonderful adventure stories, 'King Solomon's Mines' and the hauntingly romantic 'She', are the stuff of 'Boy's Own' fantasies and have both been made into films.

If you are intent on taking a look at as many Halls as possible in a short space of time, then you are certainly in the right area. Head south-west from Ditchingham on the A143 and a turning to the north will take you to Coldham Hall at **Alburgh**. To the south of this is Gawdy Hall, and to the west Starston Hall which lies just over a mile north of **Starston** village on the B1134. Further up the road from Starston are the Pulhams, two extremely attractive villages lying in the valley of the River Waveney. **Pulham St Mary** is the smaller of the two. An avenue of lime trees leads down to the splendid 15th century church of St Mary the Virgin, which was exceptionally well restored in 1886. Carvings on the parapets depict the story of St Edmund, the local king and saint who took refuge in one of the local churches before he was captured and killed by the Danes. He is also remembered in the name of the village pub, the Kings Head, which was originally called the King Edmund.

Pulham Market, from the Saxon 'village of pools', has a long history. In the 16th and 17th centuries it was a thriving place, famous for its cottage industries, manufacturing linen cloth for hangings, carpets and vestments. The old houses remaining in the village are far more numerous than in any surrounding parish. Old country masonry, clay walls, and tiny lantern windows abound.

The Old Bakery is a listed 400-year-old house in the heart of Pulham Market, a conservation village which has won the 'best kept village in Norfolk' award in 1990 and 1991. The house is oak-framed and studded, the original timbers and spiral staircases lending warmth and charm with a sense of well preserved history. It stands on Church Walk which crosses the village green and is surrounded by fine old thatched houses.

Visitors will find comfortable rooms, tastefully furnished in sympathy with the timbered construction, the bedrooms having modern en-suite facilities. The lounge has a splendid welcoming log-burning fireplace with inglenooks and you may wish to relax here, perhaps with a glass of mulled wine. If an evening meal is required this can be arranged to suit your needs. All meals will be cooked by your host, a member of the World Master Chefs Society. Breakfasts can range from a simple continental style to a more traditional English Breakfast.

The Old Bakery, Church Walk, Pulham Market, Diss
01379 676492

Jean and Martin welcome you to come and stay in their charming period home offering good and comfortable accommodation in Pulham Market, which is conveniently situated for those wishing to visit the numerous attractions of both Norfolk and Suffolk. The Old Bakery, which is a licensed premises, also offers Gourmet Weekends for those wishing to celebrate special occasions.

A short stay here will be a welcome break and will also provide an excellent opportunity to enjoy a walk around a picturesque historic village.

Pulham Market and neighbouring Pulham St Mary once gained fame as the home of the Airships. Most of us probably think of airships today as somewhat unreliable bags of gas: entertaining novelties at air shows and useful as airborne advertising hoardings, but not to be taken seriously in terms of 'real' aviation. During the First World War, however, they were to play an important role in the defence of the British coast. In 1912, the surveyors and land agents Thomas Gaze and Son acquired land at Pulham St Mary and Rushall on behalf of the Admiralty, and Pulham Air Station was established here as part of a chain of such stations along the east coast. Because of the low-lying landscape and relative lack of trees in the area, coupled with the fact that the site was well inland and out of range of the German guns, Pulham made an ideal base.

The airships were used mainly to detect submarines and mines and to aid shipping. These 'Pulham Pigs' - so-called due to their 'bloated' appearance and buff-coloured 'skin' - became a familiar sight over the Norfolk coast. The first operational vessels were powered by a 'car' made up of two aeroplane fuselages mounted back to back, providing an engine at both ends of the ship. They patrolled an area from Margate to Dunkirk in the south and from Mablethorpe to Holland in the north, and proved to be an effective way of keeping an eye on enemy activities.

If you are interested in learning more about these fascinating craft, we recommend that you obtain a copy of the excellent booklet produced by the Pulham Market Society, entitled 'The Story of Pulham and its Airships'. This covers in some detail the early prototypes, life on the station at Pulham, the coming of the 'rigid' airships and their adventures and accomplishments during and after the war until their eventual decline. The Society has also produced another booklet called 'A Village Walk', which provides a good insight into the history of Pulham Market and takes you on a special 'guided' tour of the village and its many fascinating houses and buildings.

Airship travel may appeal to the more adventurous among you, but a quite different form of transport is now available in the area. Many of have at some time or other dreamt about taking a horse drawn caravan holiday, and at **Waveney Valley Horse Holidays** at Airstation Farm near Pulham St. Mary, this could become a reality. From the comfort of a lovely, gaily painted caravan, you can plod along the quiet country lanes, taking this unique opportunity of enjoying the Norfolk countryside at the most leisurely pace imaginable. The 'Open Road' beckons everyone and if you wish to sample a Romany Holiday for one or two weeks, your caravan will come equipped with all you need.

Do not be afraid that you might lack the necessary handling skills, for Mr Wall and his staff provide full instructions on harnessing, driving and taking care of your horse. Of course, the most important person in your team will be the one with four legs, as he is not only going to provide the horsepower, but as an old hand will know all the ropes. Once you have stowed your gear and harnessed up, then you can set off on your travels, either returning to the base every night, or staying at specially designated country inns which appear on the optional planned route which is supplied.

Alternatively, you could choose to stay in a static gypsy caravan or mobile home, and Airstation Farm is superbly equipped with all the facilities you will need to make this a truly memorable holiday. If you would like to receive a brochure with full details, you can ring Waveney Valley Horse Holidays on Diss (0379) 741228 or 741690.

Waveney Valley Horse Holidays, Airstation Farm, Pulham St Mary, Diss 01379 741228/741690

The pretty market town of **Harleston** lies just to the south-east of the Pulhams and Starston, and is now by-passed by the A143. It is notable for its attractive Georgian houses (particularly Candlers House at the northern end of town - a favourite of that renowned authority on English architecture, Nikolaus Pevsner) and the original shop fronts on either side of the town's main streets.

Another splendid building is **The Swan Hotel** at the southern end of the town, which dates back to the 1550s and was built by Robert Cook, a devout follower of the rebel William Kett. It was one of the first Norfolk inns to take advantage of the increasingly fashionable activity of travelling. It is likely that the rebuilding of The Swan into the fine Georgian inn we see today occurred after the Turnpike Act of 1755, which resulted in a dramatic increase in the volume of road traffic and a corresponding demand for good roadside inns. As far back as King Charles II's time, The Swan was an important stopping place on the Yarmouth to London runs. It would then have taken a traveller around three days to complete his journey by coach, compared to today's leisurely five hour trip!

The Swan has a wealth of interesting architectural features, and we were especially impressed by the two Elizabethan wings at the rear of the inn, which partly enclose the large courtyard. There is also a splendid Assembly Room with Georgian panelling, where the local gentry would have enjoyed their banquets, balls, musical soirees and all manner of social events throughout the social season. At one time, the inn was the headquarters of the Savings Bank, and so played another important role in the affairs of the town. Today, The Swan is owned by Jackie and Alan Walker, a friendly couple who have made their own particular contribution to the reputation of this fine hostelry, which has seen so many interesting landlords over the centuries.

The Swan Hotel, 19 The Thoroughfare, Harleston   01379 852221

Some three miles to the south-west of town on the A134 is the lovely little village of **Brockdish**, with many of its pretty houses standing on the banks of the River Waveney. Its name means 'pasture by the brook'.

It is always gratifying to be able to recommend a good self-catering establishment in areas which we particularly like, and we have no hesitation in referring to **The Olde Coach House** in Brockdish as a superb holiday home. This Grade II listed property dates back to the early 17th century and has plenty of character, with oak beams and inglenooks throughout. It is beautifully furnished and we were particularly impressed with the lovely two acre garden, which features its own summer house and leads down to the banks of the river. This would definitely suit anyone who would like to try their skill with rod and tackle.

There are three bedrooms and the house can sleep up to six people in all. The kitchen is very well equipped, including a microwave, and the large, comfortably furnished open-plan lounge cum dining room is the perfect place in which to relax. John Spooner has done all the renovation work himself, and he and his wife Jackie will be undertaking the renovation of two further properties over the next few months.

This would make a lovely place to escape to at Christmas time, and included in the price during the festive season is a Christmas Tree and decorations, which we thought was a lovely idea. Children will love this warm, cosy house and pets are also welcome. Plenty of thought has gone into making the house as comfortable as possible for guests, and those with very young children will find cot, cradle, high chair and even a baby's bath available. Full credit must go to the Spooners for being so caring of their small guests' needs!

The Olde Coach House Holiday Cottages & Craft Centre,
Brockdish, Diss 01379 758146

Among the many places of interest which are easily accessible from the village are the Air Museum at **Thorpe Abbots** , and further along the A143 lie Billingford and Scole on the approach road into Diss. At **Billingford** there is a fine five-storey windmill which is open to visitors at weekends in the summer, and at **Scole** you will find the superb White Hart (now the Scole Inn), more like a mansion than an inn with its Dutch gables, giant pilasters and towering chimney stacks. Built in 1655 of red brick, this was the most important of the old coaching inns on the main road between Ipswich and Norwich, and is without doubt one of the finest examples surviving in England today.

Also on the Ipswich Road in Scole and older still is **Crossways** hotel,

242

which dates back to the 16th century and is one of the oldest buildings in the area. Peter Black bought it in 1983 and converted it from a pub to the comfortable hotel and restaurant we see today. The accommodation comprises five comfortable bedrooms, all with en-suite facilities, and the most obvious features of this charming residence are the large fireplace, original beams and the splendid oak panelled hallway.

Peter is justifiably proud of his restaurant, particularly the fine selection of wines he has selected to accompany the menu. He has not taken to serving cider in a big way so far, although legend has it that an old lady who lived in the house about 100 years ago was fond of brewing the amber nectar. Word soon got out, and apparently it wasn't very long before the whole village was reeling about from the effects of her potent brew. It is also believed that secret underground passageways lead from the house under the road, but for what purpose and to what destination, no one knows. Peter certainly hasn't discovered them yet, but perhaps it would be worth taking along some echo-sounding equipment if you decide to stay for a night or two!

Crossways Hotel & Restaurant, Ipswich Road, Scole, Nr Diss
01379 740638

Leaving Scole on the A140 we headed north for **Dickleburgh**, birthplace of the 19th century painter George Cattermole, who is perhaps best known for his illustrations in Sir Walter Scott's 'Waverley Novels'.

Close to Dickleburgh Moors, Brenda Vargeson runs a small bed and breakfast establishment called **Moor House**, a place where guests are made to feel part of the family as opposed to part of the furniture! Chatting to one of her guests convinced us while we were there, as he was full of praise for Brenda's welcoming hospitality. Her delightful home was built in 1810 and has a rather romantic feel about it - anyone who has read of Jane Eyre's encounter with Rochester knows that there is a special sort of magic about a moorland residence!

Brenda prides herself on her cooking which is first class, and her evening meals are the perfect thing to round off the day. Most people who come to Moor House do so by recommendation, and it is definitely the type of establishment you will want to tell your friends about.

Moor House, Dickleburgh

Less than a mile to the north-west is **Shimpling,** on the other side of the Norwich road. Here, St George's Church commands an idyllic position looking across to the woods, and over the fields is Shimpling Place, a handsome moated Tudor manor house which was once the home of the Shardelow family. Further to the north-west and just five miles north of Diss is the village of **Gissing,** which we will always remember for its glorious oaks and chestnut trees. St Mary's Church with its Saxon round tower and two Norman doorways is well worth seeing - the double hammerbeam roof to the nave is quite exquisite.

Winfarthing lies to the west on the B1077, where an abundance of yet more majestic trees points to the fact that this area was once part of an ancient forest. As we looked around the church of St Mary here, we noticed a window depicting a sword. The 'Winfarthing Sword', or 'Sword of the Good Thief' as it later came to be known, has since been lost, but it was said to have been left here when a thief sought sanctuary in the church.

We were unable to find out anything more about this mysterious weapon - why its whereabouts are unknown, why the thief was 'good', or why indeed the sword should be commemorated in a modern window - it all seems rather a puzzle. Local folklore relates that village women who had had enough of their husbands held the sword in great esteem, but we have no idea whether this was simply with a view to using it as a cold instrument of dispatch, or if perhaps the sword had some other more subtle properties which would grant them what they desired.

Heading south on the B1077 towards Diss, we first came to **Shelfanger**, whose name derives from two Old English words meaning 'wood on sloping ground'. For simply first class accommodation in this area, we would have no hesitation in recommending **Shelfanger Hall**, a splendid farmhouse that dates back to the 15th century. The house has been in the Butler family for the past 20 years, and Deborah and Bill have one of the finest homes it has ever been our pleasure to visit.

The main farmhouse is surrounded by a moat, and views from the bedrooms are over the most breathtakingly beautiful countryside, making this a perfect place to escape the world and its cares. Three rooms are available in the main house for bed and breakfast guests and as they have been so superbly furnished, these would not be suitable for children. However, the Butlers also have two self-catering cottages on their working farm, one of which has two bathrooms and sleeps up to six guests, making it ideal for families. The other sleeps two and would be suitable for elderly guests as all the accommodation is on one floor. The large gardens are really lovely and would be the perfect spot to relax on sunny days under the shade of the trees.

Shelfanger Hall Farmhouse & Self-Catering, Shelfanger, Diss
01379 642094

Many visitors find **Diss** to be one of the most attractive country towns in this part of the county. The fascination of the place lies in its pleasing mixture of Tudor, Georgian and Victorian houses, grouped around the six-acre mere from which the name of the town is derived - 'place of the ditch, or dyke'. At the lower end of Mere Street is a public park where you can sit and watch the antics of the water birds who flock here to feed each day, then you can make your way uphill along the tortuously narrow street to where it opens out into the small market place at its northern end.

This former poultry market is dominated by the somewhat over-restored St Mary's Church. The church was built over 700 years ago, though the windows in the nave date from the 19th century. The St Nicholas Chapel is particularly enjoyable, with its wonderful corbels, angels in the roof and gargoyles - this part is many centuries old. Also here is the delightful Victorian Shambles with its cast-iron veranda and small museum inside. From Market Place you can walk along a number of streets and narrow alleyways, taking in a wealth of fine half-timbered houses; and just to the north of the church stands the Georgian Manor House with its semi-circular porch supported by Corinthian columns. Small wonder that John Betjeman voted Diss his favourite Norfolk town!

Those looking for a quiet place to stay in Diss would do well to seek out **'Crossways'**, a real hidden treasure of a house that may be found tucked away behind tall trees along Roydon Road, close to the centre of town. Accommodation is offered here, and owner Daphne Batrum has gone to a great deal of trouble to make sure that her guests are provided with extremely comfortable surroundings.

There is a lawn tennis court which guests may use and lovely gardens in which to stroll. The house has been described as an 'ideal home of 1929', and indeed the art deco interior has been retained so that none of the original charm of the building has been lost. As we tend to stay in a lot of places with beams and inglenooks, it made rather a refreshing change to visit a house of this elegant period. While we were there, the decorators were preparing the outside of the house for another busy season - 'Crossways' is often fully booked, so it is well worth booking in advance to be sure of a room for the night.

'Crossways', 41 Roydon Road, Diss 01379 642653

Two-and-a-half miles west of Diss on the A1066 Thetford road, we come to the village of **Bressingham,** home of the famous **Bressingham Steam Museum.** From those with a casual interest to serious steam enthusiasts, people of all ages will find a day out here to be a fascinating and rewarding experience. Bressingham has one of the world's finest collections of British and Continental locomotives, perhaps the most famous being the 'Royal Scot'. A number of locomotives on display here are on loan from the National Railway Museum at York. All are housed under cover in the museum's extensive locomotive sheds, which also contain a large collection of steam-driven industrial engines, traction engines, and a recently opened exhibition entitled 'A Journey Back to Steam'. Visitors can view the interior of the Royal Coach and admire the many fine examples of these mighty machines from the golden age of steam.

The Fire Museum has a collection of fire engines and fire fighting equipment which could form a complete museum in its own right. Exhibits range from hand-pumped and horse-drawn machines to the one used on the royal estate at Sandringham until the 1960s. There are four different gauges of railway within the grounds and visitors can ride along five miles of track through the woods and gardens. Bressingham has six acres of internationally famous landscaped grounds. Beautiful trees, shrubs and flowers can be enjoyed in the superb Dell Garden which was created by Alan Bloom, Bressingham's founder. A two-acre plant centre adjoins the gardens where thousands of plant specimens, many of them rare, are available for visitors to purchase.

Bressingham Steam Museum, Bressingham, Diss 01379 58382

Bressingham is renowned for its 'special days' when engines can be seen in full steam on the three narrow gauge lines, and talks and footplate rides are given on the standard gauge locomotives. There are also

247

demonstrations of traction and industrial engines, and rides on the magnificent steam-driven 'Gallopers' roundabout with musical accompaniment from the Chiappa organ. 'Special days' are every Sunday, Thursday and Bank Holiday, plus every Wednesday in July and August.

Refreshments can be found in the 'Gallopers' restaurant, on the terrace, or in the picnic area. There is also the 'Garden Seat' coffee shop and a complete set of souvenirs available in the museum's 'Goods Depot'. Alan Bloom now also welcomes guests for short bed and breakfast breaks at Bressingham Hall. The museum is open daily from 10.00am to 5.30pm.

If all that steam has developed your thirst nearby there is a wonderful 14th century Inn, **The Old Garden House**, which has a wealth of timber beams, inglenook fireplaces, flagstone floors and all you could ever wish for in a country inn.

The food is freshly prepared from local produce and people travel miles to visit what can only be described as one of the finest country inns in Norfolk. It has an outstanding menu, both lunchtime and evening with fish a speciality. A fine wine list and good range of real ales, including locally brewed specials.

A large car park and garden. Children and families are most welcome. Well worth a visit - you will not be disappointed.

The Old Garden House, Thetford Road, Bressingham 0379 88405

Some four-and-a-half miles further west along the A1066 we came to **Garboldisham** (pronounced 'Garblesham'), where we saw some fine pre-Raphaelite glass in the church of St Mary the Virgin. Just west of the village lies part of the Devil's Dyke, an ancient earthwork whose origins are still the subject of debate amongst archaeologists. Some argue that it was erected by the Romans as a defence against Anglo-Saxon invaders, while others insist that the Saxons themselves built the dyke to mark out the boundary of their newly conquered territory. Both arguments were thrown into doubt by the excavations of 1924, which indicated that the dyke was in fact more likely to have been built by the East Anglian people in the 8th century as a defence against the neighbouring kingdom of Mercia.

We were to discover further evidence of the area's ancient history at the next place we visited. **Ingleneuk Lodge** in Garboldisham would be a very pleasant place to stay for a quiet break, and as this is a single storey building, it is particularly suitable for disabled guests.

Ingleneuk Lodge, Hopton Road, Garboldisham, Nr Diss
01953 81541

Connie and Doug Atkins told us that the present building has grown around their original bungalow, which is now the reception area. The bedrooms have been set out as smoking and non-smoking wings and each room is identified by the name of an animal or bird - so you could be staying in the Hedgehog Room or the Kingfisher Room, and so on. All the rooms are extremely comfortable, with the full range of modern facilities. Connie and Doug, along with their daughter Leigh, pride themselves on running an efficient establishment without losing sight of the human approach; we found them to be warm and friendly and the atmosphere here is very much that of a happy, family home.

Ingleneuk Lodge is surrounded by peaceful wooded countryside, and while you are out exploring, you may be lucky enough to find some ancient 'treasures'. The Atkins's showed us their collection of flint tools which they discovered in the garden, and we were amazed to learn that they are an incredible 60,000 years old! They also have several other artifacts such as clay pipes, keys and coins from more recent history.

Heading north from here towards East Harling, we then turn right onto the B1114, and joining the B1113 some three miles further on come to the lovely village of **Kenninghall.** The houses here are full of interest, with plenty of timber and plasterwork giving the village real character.

It is easy to imagine how it must have looked in the days when Mary Tudor came here to stay at Kenninghall Place, still owned today by the Duke of Norfolk. Mary hastened on to Framlingham Castle in Suffolk where she was proclaimed Queen, little knowing that her reign would last a mere five years. She died in 1558, childless, ravaged by sickness and grief at the cruelty of her husband, Phillip II of Spain; and although it is dubious whether she was directly responsible for all the persecutions carried out in her name, she would be forever remembered in history as 'Bloody Mary'. On her death, her younger half-sister, Elizabeth I, took the throne, and in St Mary's Church you can see a rare and quite superb example of Elizabeth's coat of arms.

Next to the church is a chapel which has remained virtually unchanged since it was first built in 1807. It would be well worth a visit in its own right, but what makes it even more interesting is that it now houses **The Particular Pottery.** You could be forgiven for thinking that the name derives from the care and attention with which the potters here produce their range of beautiful hand-thrown, reduction-fired porcelain and stoneware - but there is in fact a more specific reason for it.

The Walters and the Andersons arrived in this country from South Africa several years ago, and as soon as they discovered the chapel they realised its fantastic potential as a workshop and gallery. For the first 150 years or so of its life, the building was, in fact, the Particular Baptist Chapel of Kenninghall; and as well as retaining the name for their new venture, these skilled craftspeople ensured that the essential fabric of the place was altered as little as possible.

The Particular Pottery, Church Street, Kenninghall 01953 878476

The Particular Pottery has enjoyed great success, and has proved very popular with visitors who come to watch these two gifted couples at work and to purchase the results of their labours. The collection is excellent, and in addition to the finely crafted porcelain and stoneware, you will also find ceramic sculptures, hand-built pots and some beautiful wooden carvings. The prices, by the way, are extremely reasonable.

Outside the Pottery, there is a listed, early-19th century walled garden that you can visit. You will also find a number of old tombstones in the garden, and as a classic example of bizarre coincidence at work, the inscriptions on a couple of these reveal that the deceased parties were named 'Potter'!

The White Horse, Market Place, Kenninghall 01953 87379

Just across the road from the pottery you will find **The White Horse**, a fine traditional village pub with a good local trade, where visitors are also made more than welcome. Diane and Shaun Lee are a young, lively couple who offer good beer, good food and good company.

You could certainly make a good day out of it hereabouts, for after a visit to the pottery and a meal and a drink at the pub, you can make your way a couple of miles further up the road to **Banham**, where you will find both the Banham Motor Museum and Banham Zoo. Quite apart from the zoo's fine collection of rare and endangered species from around the world (including otters, exotic monkeys, seals and snow leopards), many other attractions for the whole family to enjoy can be found in the adjoining 'Appleyard' Craft Courtyard.

A superb range of cane ware, fresh plants and silk flowers can be purchased at 'Barbara's' craft shop, which is housed in the old dairy parlour, while other locally-made crafts and curios are on display in the former fruit barn. Banham has been an important centre for the Norfolk cider industry for centuries, and here at Banham Cidery, the Burnard family continue to produce high quality cider using traditional methods.

251

Visitors can watch the whole process from the viewing gallery, then make their purchases of the local brew (together with other traditional ciders and speciality wines) from the Cidery shop. There is also an excellent farm shop which is as well stocked as any village store, and 'Pantiles' Bistro & Bakery offers all sorts of freshly baked delicacies and refreshments.

Banham itself is a lovely old place, built around a rectangular village green. The brick kilns that once stood at neighbouring Hunt's Green supplied the brick and tile for a number of interesting local houses. These include the 19th century Norfolk House, the timber-framed Guildhall, and a handsome Georgian house with Dutch gables called the Priory.

Two miles to the north on the B1077 between Diss and Attleborough, **Old Buckenham** boasts a simply massive village green - it looked big enough to us to host the next Olympic Games!

Old Buckenham wins the prize for some of the oddest street names you are likely to come across in your travels. 'Hog's Snout' and 'Loos Wroo' are two favourites, and we couldn't even begin to guess the origin of the latter! A mile to the south-east on the B1113 is New Buckenham, which despite its name dates back to 1146. It was then that the son of William d'Albini abandoned his father's castle at the original village (no trace of that building now remains) and built a new round keep on this site - the earliest example of its kind in the country. The orderly system of streets, the market place (now the village green) and St Mary's Chapel (New Buckenham's first church and now part of a barn) all survive to this day, and together they form a superb 'living' example of Norman town planning. Thatched and timber-framed cottages line the streets, and on the green stands the Court House, a fine 16th century building with Tuscan columns.

West of the Buckenhams is a fine moated Elizabethan house called Wilby Hall, and a little further on, between the railway line and the A11 Thetford to Norwich road, we came to **Eccles Road**. The village name derives from the word 'ecclesiastical', and this is an area which has proved to be of great interest to archaeologists. Many weapons of the Romans and Early Britons have been discovered here, and the story goes that a hoard of treasure is buried somewhere in the vicinity. Eccles seems peaceful enough today, but apparently it was not always so - during the Middle Ages, they say that soldiers marched here from Norwich, sacked the village and hanged the vicar!

Deciding to pay a visit to the local pub, we found that there is something about **The Old Railway Tavern** in Station Road that makes you feel as if you have popped into a neighbour's house for a quick pint! This feeling is probably due to the friendly approach of the lovely couple who run the pub, Pat and John Blaney. They have been here since 1978, and John has established quite a reputation for his selection of real ales. Known locally as 'The Eccles Tap', the building dates back to the 16th century and has been in business as an inn since 1845.

Chatting to the Blaneys, we learnt about their resident ghost, thought to be a local lady by the name of Brindy Cook. She was apparently run down by a herd of sheep right outside the pub - which seemed to us a rather ignominious end! If you want to find out more about the ways in which she makes herself known, just ask Pat about 'the lady in the cloak'.

The Old Railway Tavern, Station Road, Eccles, Quidenham

While we were having a drink, we noticed a photograph of one of the 'heros' of World War II, a 'Flying Fortress'. The photograph features the signatures of all the crew, who used the Tavern as their local when they were stationed locally during the war. John told us that several of the survivors have popped in to see the old place and have a chat about the 'good old days'.

The small town of **Attleborough** lies three miles north-east of Eccles, just to the east of the A11. It was men from this town who cast down the fences and set Kett's rebellion rolling in 1549. The impressive church of St Mary dominates the centre of town, and in the churchyard we discovered another of those strange memorial pyramids. Nowhere near as imposing as the one at Blickling Hall, this one is far more modest in size, standing about six feet high. It was erected in 1929 to mark the grave of a local solicitor with the rather splendid name of Melancthon William Henry Brooke, or 'Lawyer' Brooke as he was more familiarly known. Apparently, Brooke was most particular about the precise measurements of the pyramid, and left detailed instructions regarding its construction in his will - possibly an attempt to preserve his bones by replicating the supposed magical properties of those fabled Egyptian pyramids!

Do take the time to see the interior of the church while you are here, as it contains one of Norfolk's most outstanding chancel screens. Stretching the width of the church, this huge 15th century screen is beautifully embellished and is one of the few to survive the Reformation intact.

We were delighted by the little market town of **Hingham**, which lies four miles north-west of here on the B1108 and conjures up the gentility of 18th century England at its very best. The Market Place is flanked by elegant Georgian houses, and the impressive White Hart is one of the finest coaching inns we have come across so far. Hingham can boast a very influential (if not exactly famous) son, a weaver called Samuel Lincoln who was baptised in the church in 1622.

During the first half of the 17th century, many local people emigrated to America and founded a colony in Massachusetts called Bare Cove - an event which is aptly commemorated in Harry Carter's village sign. Samuel set out to make a new life for himself there in 1637, and though he didn't know it at the time, his great-great-great-great-grandson would turn out to be the 16th American President, Abraham Lincoln! Bare Cove was later renamed Hingham, and the two towns retain strong links to this day. A bronze bust of Abraham Lincoln can be seen in St Andrew's Church, which also features a superb 15th century monument to Lord Morley.

About seven miles to the west of Hingham on the B1108 is another small market town called **Watton** , and it was from here and from the neighbouring village of **Griston** that a local legend arose which would later inspire that famous nursery story, 'Babes in the Wood'.

The legend, which dates from the 16th century, relates how, as poor Arthur Truelove lay dying, he decided that the only hope for his two children was to leave them in the care of their uncle. Unfortunately, the uncle decided to help himself to their inheritance and paid two men to take the children into nearby Wayland Wood and kill them. In a moment of compassion, one of the men decided that he couldn't do the dreadful deed, so he disposed of his accomplice instead and abandoned the children in the wood to suffer whatever fate befell them. Sadly, unlike the nursery tale where the children find their way back home and live happily ever after, this unfortunate brother and sister perished, and their ghosts are said to wander lonely through the woods to this day.

Outside the 17th century Clock Tower in Watton, the striking bronze town sign depicts the story of the 'Babes', and we learnt that their sad tale is further remembered in the name of the wood itself - Wayland being a corruption of 'wailing'. The wood is now owned by the Norfolk Naturalist Trust and is said to be one of the oldest in England. Griston Hall, a Grade II listed ancient manor house which stands half a mile south of Wayland Wood and one mile from Watton on the A1075, was reputedly the home of the 'Wicked Uncle'. Today, it is part of Hall Farm and offers excellent bed and breakfast facilities.

Every once in a while we come across a superlative country house hotel and in **Stow Bedon**, we were privileged to visit one of the finest houses in the county. **Stow Bedon House** is situated just off the A11 on the Thetford to Watton road, close to Thetford Forest. Built in 1725 as the Rectory for St Bartolph Church in Stow Bedon, perhaps its most famous inhabitant was the Reverend Redgrave, the last Rector of Stow Bedon and uncle of that great British actor, Sir Michael Redgrave.

The Rectory was sold to the great grandson of the artist William Morris in 1964, who had great plans to renovate the house, but was unfortunately prevented from doing so when he suffered a serious accident. As a result, the house fell into disrepair during the 11 years of his occupation, until it was bought by Peter and Hope Earle in 1975. The Earles made many improvements over the next few years and, following the death of Mrs Earle in 1986, the house was turned into a Country House Hotel and Restaurant with indoor heated swimming pool, and opened as **Earles'** in October 1988.

The comfort and style of this beautiful house is greatly enhanced by the wealth of antique furniture to be found in all the rooms. This was collected by the Earle family over many generations, and perhaps the most interesting piece is the tester bed which came from Claydon House in Buckinghamshire and belonged to Florence Nightingale following her return from Istanbul.

Earles', Stow Bedon House, Stow Bedon, Attleborough
01953 383284

When you stay at Earles', you are welcomed very much as a family guest. The beautifully furnished bedrooms all have en-suite showers or baths, together with colour television, telephone and tea and coffee

Wymondham Market Cross

making facilities. In the Restaurant, you can choose from a varied menu of interesting dishes which are all freshly prepared. One that immediately caught our eye was Steak Balmoral, said to be a favourite dish of Queen Victoria. The recipe was apparently handed down to the Earles by one of their ancestors who was Lady in Waiting to the Queen.

Other amenities include a cosy Bar (converted from the old wine cellar) which leads on to a south-facing terrace overlooking the two acre gardens. The sports facilities comprise an indoor heated swimming pool, sunbeds and sauna. Those of you who like to keep fit can take advantage of the keep fit classes run by Heather Earle, or you could try 'Swimfit', which we understand to be basically the same thing but in the water! All sports facilities are available to non-residents, and the hotel offers its own membership scheme with all sorts of benefits and discounts.

Whether you come to Earles' for a relaxing holiday, to have Dinner or a bar snack, swim in the pool or simply to have a drink, we can guarantee that you will receive the warmest of welcomes.

There is a marvellous country walk along the disused railway line between Stow Bedon and **Great Hockham**, which is known as the Pingo Trail. The eight-mile circular walk is renowned for the many species of birds that can be seen en route. To the north-west of Great Hockham is Cranberry Rough, a reserve owned by the Norfolk Naturalists Trust, where you may well have the good fortune to spot one of the rare White Admiral butterflies that breed there. If you are travelling with your caravan, by the way, we can recommend an excellent site in Great Hockham right on the edge of Thetford Forest, at Puddledock Farm. It is admirably sited for exploring the forest and the Pingo Trail, and for those wishing to enjoy all the regular events organised by the Forestry Commission.

This part of Norfolk offers visitors a great variety of interesting walks, including the Hockham Forest Walk, the East Wretham Heath Nature Reserve and Trail, and the Devil's Punch Bowl Forest Walk. East Wretham Heath really typifies the eerie beauty of the Breckland countryside with its scrub and heath and natural woodland, offering some relief from the regimented rows of pines to the west. The meres that are dotted about the area bristle with reeds, and the soft sound of the wind soughing through them gives this quiet place a rather haunting atmosphere. It is a natural habitat for many different species of water birds, including waders and sand pipers, and everywhere ducks, ducks and more ducks, dipping and diving 'up tails all'!

This strange landscape with its chalky band covered by a sandy layer does not make for fertile soil. As man attempted to plough the earth, flints would be thrown up, and this churned and broken land became the 'breck' which now encompasses an area of some 300 square miles. Apart from the phenomena of its vanishing and reappearing meres (which we mentioned in an earlier chapter), another feature of Breckland for which it was once notorious were the problems caused by wind-blown sand.

In 1668 the village of **Santon Downham**, four miles north-west of Thetford, was swamped by sand that blew in from the wastes of Breckland in a ten-mile wide band, temporarily choking the Little Ouse river as well. This catastrophe was the direct result of centuries of cultivation followed by over-grazing. After visiting the area several years later, the diarist John Evelyn (famous for his treatise on air pollution in 17th century London) said of the disaster that it reminded him of 'the sands in the deserts of Libya'. The planting of trees to hold down the light sandy soil of Breckland and prevent further disasters of this type began as far back as 1805.

The Little Ouse meets the River Thet at **Thetford**, an important settlement for well over 1,000 years. When the Normans arrived here they found a prosperous community with its own mint and an extremely successful pottery industry. It remained the seat of the Bishop of East Anglia until 1094 when the see was transferred to Norwich, and there is no doubt that until this event, Thetford was the most important town in the region and among the top six in England.

Thetford's first castle was probably built sometime around the 8th century, and the Norman motte that replaced it was demolished in 1173. This was built to defend the place where the Icknield Way crosses the rivers Little Ouse and Thet, and energetic visitors may enjoy fine views of the town and surrounding countryside by climbing up the steep banks of the huge mound that dominates the site - this is all that remains of the castle today.

The decline of the town began in the mid-16th century after the Dissolution of the Monasteries; it once boasted 24 medieval churches, but only three of these still survive. Of particular interest are the remains of the 12th century Cluniac priory which was founded by the Norman knight John Bigod. He was a poor warrior who acquired the earldom of Norfolk from King Stephen in 1136; an earldom which would become extinct less than 200 years later. The priory ruins can be found near the railway station and are maintained by English Heritage.

Thetford made a number of unsuccessful attempts to ward off its steady decline. In 1700 it became a port, with an eye to regaining the lucrative wool trade from the towns and villages on the east coast. The plan was doomed from the start, and its failure was compounded with the coming of the railways in the mid-19th century. More surprisingly, Thetford also had aspirations to become a flourishing spa town after a medicinal spring was discovered here in 1746. Its attempts to lure the fashionable elite of London society were, however, largely unsuccessful, although the Pump Room that was built in 1819 can still be seen in Spring Walk.

Thetford remained a quiet market town with a steadily dwindling population up until the 1960s, when its status was altered dramatically by its becoming an overspill town for London. Housing and industrial estates became to spring up on the edges of town, and it was during excavations for one such estate in the 1980s that an extensive Iron Age enclosure was discovered - so extensive, in fact, that they have led many experts to believe that Thetford may well have been the capital of the redoubtable Iceni tribe.

Anyone with an interest in local history and artifacts should not miss out on the chance to visit the Ancient House Museum in White Hart Street - particularly for the many items relating to Breckland's ancient flint-knapping 'industry'. The building itself is quite magnificent: a half-timbered, early Tudor house with superb carved oak ceilings. It has been admirably restored throughout, and if you should need another good excuse for visiting it, it also acts as the local Tourist Information Centre.

Thetford's most famous son was that great champion of human rights, Thomas Paine, who emigrated to America in 1774 where he edited the 'Pennsylvania Gazette'. He was an ardent supporter of both the American and French Revolutions and called for the overthrow of the British monarchy, and on his return to England in 1787 he published his most famous work, 'The Rights of Man'. A statue of this brave and outspoken man, who died ostracized and penniless on his farm in New York State, stands in front of King's House in King Street.

For younger and old alike may we also recommend a visit to the Childhood Treasures Museum in Raymond Street. A precious collection of old toys, dolls and their private residences, much loved and much coveted by younger visitors; this is a very pleasant place to spend an hour or so. The Charles Burrell Steam Museum in Minstergate is one of Thetford's newest attractions, and a 'must' for all those who are fascinated by the age of steam. An impressive collection of steam engines and recreated workshops is housed here in the former paint finishing shop of Charles Burrell and Sons, a company that was at one time famous throughout the world for its construction of steam traction and threshing engines.

Notwithstanding the spread of modern housing and factories which the overspill agreement brought to the town - and the fact that a shopping precinct built in the 1970s dominates the town centre - the ancient heart of Thetford still survives, and medieval and Georgian buildings can be found nearly every way you turn. The town also seems to have more than its fair share of legends too; an ancient palace with a glorious treasure is said to lie deep beneath the castle mound. Others believe that the mound is the hiding place for six silver bells from the Priory; secreted there at the time of the Dissolution to prevent Henry VIII from getting his hands on them. Castle Hill has also been associated with sun worship, and one of the more fanciful legends claims that the hill is in fact no more than the scrapings of mud from Old Nick's boots, left there in a pile after he had finished digging the Devil's Pits at Weeting!

We end our tour of Norfolk as far away from the crowds as possible, deep in the heart of Thetford Forest. Covering an area of some 83 square miles, this is the largest lowland forest in Britain. The Forestry Commission began planting in 1922, and although it is largely given over to conifers, with Scots and Corsican Pine and Douglas Fir predominating, oak, sycamore and beech can also be seen throughout. There is a particularly varied trail which leads from the Forestry Commission Information Centre at Santon Downham, and if you venture off the track into the deepest parts of the forest you may be lucky enough to spot a roe deer - although this calls for some extremely quiet footwork! Other creatures to look out for are squirrels, grass snakes and lizards, as well as a wide variety of birds and butterflies. If you wish to see things from a different perspective it is possible to explore parts of the forest on horse-back, and permits can also be obtained for carriage driving.

Two miles north-west of Thetford on the B1107 Brandon road, you can see the ruins of the 14th century Thetford Warren Lodge, where the Prior's gamekeeper once kept a wary eye open for poachers who dared to take liberties in the Priory's hunting grounds. Exploring the forest at different times of the year can also prove very rewarding, as its atmosphere and appearance alters dramatically with the changing of the seasons. The heart of Thetford Forest is dissected by the county boundary, and whether your visit here gives you your final glimpse of Norfolk or your first sight of Suffolk, its quiet beauty is sure to make a lasting impression on you.

CHAPTER NINE

West Suffolk

Friary Gate

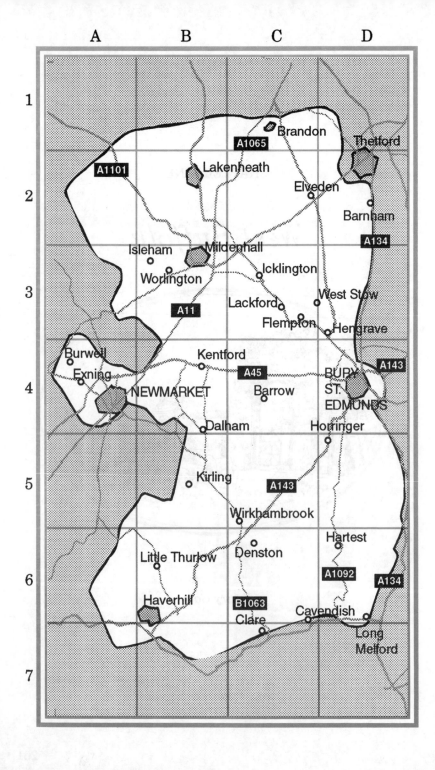

CHAPTER NINE

West Suffolk

Suffolk is a county that surprisingly few people know well, those who come here for the first time are often drawn back again and again, and some are so caught up in its spell that they eventually settle here.

Much of the land has a chalk foundation over London Clay; a fossil-enriched soil, particularly around the heathlands. The countryside is similar in many ways to that of Norfolk, with wide open spaces broken by gentle hills, making it a paradise for the keen walker. Our first glimpse of Suffolk is just over the border from its northern neighbour at Thetford Forest; and as our journey takes us deeper into the heart of the county, we will discover many sites of archaeological and historical interest and countless scenes of incomparable rural beauty. It comes as no surprise to find that one of Britain's foremost landscape painters, John Constable, was a Suffolk man.

Our first stop was at the lovely village of **Barnham**, which is situated right on the border with Norfolk, adjacent to the A134 Thetford to Bury road. While we were here we paid a visit to the **Grafton Arms** . The Grafton Estate had many acres of parkland, and so the public house has ample car parking facilities as well as the village bowling green within its grounds.

The Grafton Arms, Bury Road, Barnham, Thetford 01842 890200

Wendy Grove, the proprietress, has a wealth of experience serving customers in the hotel and catering trade, and her expertise is evident in this splendid hostelry. The ales and beers are cared for and dispensed to the highest standards and the wine list is excellent, offering little known vintages at very reasonable prices.

The cooking is based on French cuisine, and Wendy's staff provide excellent service accompanied by good humour and professionalism. The Grafton Arms offers good ale and first class food in a relaxed atmosphere and lovely surroundings, which makes a visit here truly worthwhile.

If you are looking for somewhere to stay in the area, East Farm at Barnham offers very comfortable bed and breakfast accommodation in friendly surroundings. The facilities here include heated and spacious rooms with en-suite bathrooms, a full English breakfast made from fresh local produce, and glorious views of the surrounding countryside. Telephone Mrs Margaret Heading for reservations and enquiries on (01842) 890231.

Just to the east of Barnham is the pretty little village of **Euston**, on the A1088 Thetford to Ixworth road. Euston Hall, which is open to the public on Thursdays during the summer months, has been the seat of the Dukes of Grafton for around 300 years. Originally built in 1666, the Hall was rebuilt in 1902 after a fire and features a fine collection of family portraits by such artists as Van Dyck and Stubbs. It stands in a great park with gardens landscaped by William Kent and Capability Brown, and the garden created by the present Duke is renowned for its creative use of colour.

Euston village itself has only been in its present position since the 17th century, when it was moved outside the gates of the park because it 'spoilt the view' from the Hall - a fate which has befallen several other villages around the British Isles. Only St Genevieve's Church was left undisturbed, and if you take the time to visit it, look out for the delicate wood carving throughout which is attributed to Grinling Gibbons. There is also an attractive ice-house disguised as an Italianate temple within the grounds.

Taking the minor road leading west from Barnham, we turned south on the A11 and came to **Elveden**. Elveden Hall is remembered as the one-time home of Prince Duleep Singh of the Punjab, he who was 'persuaded' to hand over the famous Koh-i-Noor diamond to Queen Victoria. Deposed from his kingdom and exiled to England for his part in the Sikh wars, the young prince was nevertheless granted a handsome pension and bought the Georgian house at Elveden in 1813.

His enormous wealth enabled him to later transform it into a stunning replica of an oriental palace, to remind him of those he had left behind at Delhi and Lahore. So extravagant was this rebuilding and refurbishment (which included a copper dome and literally tons of Italian marble) that the prince died a bankrupt. The Hall was then bought by Lord Iveagh, of the Guinness family, who added even more lavish adornments to the place including a replica Taj Mahal, and also rebuilt the village and the church in 1904-6. The present Earl of Iveagh sold off the contents of the house in 1984, and it now stands empty.

During the First World War the quiet countryside hereabouts resounded to the sounds of the first training exercises of the then most secret tanks. The area is also particularly rich in Neolithic sites - in 1888, Sir Arthur Evans, who excavated the ancient Cretan city of Knossos, was brought in to throw light on the discovery of an Iron Age burial site at Elveden. All in all, this proved to be quite a diverse place to visit!

From here, the B1106 led us north-west across Wangford Warren to the attractive border town of **Brandon**. The Brandon Heritage Centre in George Street has excellent exhibits relating to the Stone Age, the story of the early flint-knappers, and much information ranging from the Neolithic period to modern times. The town is largely built of flint, and we learnt that Brandon flints were renowned throughout the world for their use in the old flintlock guns. The industry guaranteed steady employment in the area for centuries, and still survives in a small way to this day.

With the close proximity of the warrens and their incumbent rabbit population, another important industry here was the production of felt for hats from rabbit pelts. In the warrens near Thetford, a local legend relates how a White Rabbit with blazing eyes haunted the area and was said to be a harbinger of death. The hunting of rabbits and game up on the warrens may well have encouraged Prince Duleep to settle at Elveden, as he was a most enthusiastic sportsman. If you have not already done so you can take time out to explore Thetford Forest from here, while Brandon Country Park offers 30 acres of woodland and beautifully laid out gardens in which to stretch your legs.

St Mary's Church at **Lakenheath** - a sprawling village four miles south-west of Brandon on the B1112 - is renowned for its fine wall paintings and 13th century font, and if you wish to see inside, look at the notice board in the porch for details of where to pick up the key. Lakenheath was the setting for Charles Wesley's first Methodist sermon in the region in 1754, and the ancestors of Lord Kitchener are buried in the churchyard.

The 15th century bench-ends here are exquisite; they are carved with imaginative scenes portraying acrobats and fishes, together with the unusual image of a tiger gazing vainly into a mirror. The humour and eccentricity of these designs is quite captivating, and it is thought that the carvers here were also responsible for those at the church of St Mary and St Andrew at **Mildenhall** to the south. Indeed, the great dragons that peer down from the hammerbeam roof of Mildenhall's beautiful church seemed to be a distinctly pagan image to find in a Christian place of worship.

The ancient Suffolk town of Mildenhall has proved to be an important centre of archaeological discovery over the years. Nearby excavations in 1988 revealed what is believed to be the earliest site of human occupation in this country, and over 2,000 flint tools and other artifacts have been discovered on the site of an ancient lake that existed some 500,000 years ago. The remains of extinct species of elephant, horse and rhinoceros were also found - the tooth of the latter being around 400,000 years old. A previous exciting discovery came in 1946, when a ploughman uncovered what was to become known as the Mildenhall Treasure. This was a remarkable collection of silver dishes, goblets and baptismal spoons - over 30 pieces in all - left behind by the Romans when they pulled out of Britain at the end of the 4th century. The collection can now be viewed in the British Museum, while the Mildenhall and District Museum in King Street has many other local artifacts on display.

The parish of Mildenhall is the largest in Suffolk and one of the largest in England, covering some 14,000 acres. The Bunburys were lords of the manor here from 1747 to 1933, and were it not for an unlucky gamble, their name would now be immortalised in one of our most famous horse races. This occurred in 1780, when Sir Thomas Bunbury and Lord Derby flipped a coin to decide who should lend their name to a new annual race at Epsom. Lord Derby won the toss, but ironically, it was Sir Thomas' horse Diomed who came first past the post on that premiere of Derby Day.

The Riverside Hotel stands on the banks of the River Lark in an idyllic setting in the heart of the town. Resident owners John and Carolyn Child and Keith and Alison Lardner have a wealth of experience between them in the hotel profession - the family having, in fact, owned and managed The Bell Hotel in Mildenhall for over 60 years before moving to this most impressive establishment by the river. This elegant, early Georgian residence is perfectly set off by mature trees and spacious lawns which sweep down to the riverbank; a setting which can be especially enjoyed whilst enjoying a meal in the newly restored hotel restaurant, with its fine views over the gardens. Largely due to the imagination and skills of the resident Chef, Gerrard, the restaurant has established an excellent local and regional reputation for the superb quality of the food it serves. Local game, fowl and fish are a regular feature of the menu and venison offers a truly royal alternative to roast beef.

The hotel is renowned for providing special Bridge Weekends, which can be enjoyed by enthusiasts and beginners alike, and keen anglers can also fish in the hotel's own private stretch of the river. If you decide to try your luck, you may even land old 'Monty', the resident giant pike who patrols the waters of the Lark. His ferocity is graphically illustrated by the sight of a one-legged duck called 'Nelson' who now hops around the grounds, having had too close an encounter with the Lord of the River one day! In fact, you are likely to see a number of convalescing creatures during your stay, as Alison is a great animal lover and devotes a lot of her time to looking after orphaned, ill or injured geese, cats, ducks, birds and anything else that is brought to her. We can vouch for the fact that the care and attention received by human residents is every bit as special, and we would strongly urge our readers to sample the hospitality of the Riverside Hotel for themselves.

The Riverside Hotel, Mill Street, Mildenhall 01638 717274

Both Mildenhall and Lakenheath are situated on the edge of massive U.S. Air Force bases, and at RAF Lakenheath guided tours for 12 to 50 visitors can be arranged. If you want to know more, contact the base public affairs office for details on (01638) 522151. 1992 was the 50th anniversary of the U.S. Air Force arriving in this country. During the war, airfields were put up in quick succession all over East Anglia, 19 of them being established in Suffolk alone. Films such as 'Yanks' and 'Memphis Belle' have documented the initial reservations felt by the locals on meeting these glamorous American heroes, who seemed determined to lure away every young woman they encountered. However, the truth is that, romantic conquests aside, great friendships sprang up from this coming together of the Old and New Worlds; friendships that have endured to this day, with American veterans coming back to relive their experiences in Suffolk and to be reunited with the acquaintances they made here.

One mile south-west of Mildenhall on the B1102, we come to the village of **Worlington**. Here, we made a point of visiting **Worlington Hall Country House Hotel,** a splendid hotel set within five acres of grounds leading down to the River Lark. The original house was built in 1570, the Queen Anne facade being added early in the 18th century when the building became a manor house. Today, the interior has been carefully restored to reflect the building's history. The lounge bar has 16th century carved-wood panelling and a traditional fireplace with roaring log fire. There is also a bistro, a la carte restaurant and eight bedrooms which have been individually designed and equipped with every modern facility.

Worlington Hall Country House Hotel, Worlington, Nr Mildenhall
01638 712237

About three miles to the west on the B1104, just over the border into Cambridgeshire and approximately half way between Ely and Newmarket, we came upon the delightful village of **Isleham,** complete with its village green where cricket is played every Sunday during the summer months.

The Red House, 45 Mill Street, Isleham, Cambs 01638 780453

Overlooking the green we found **The Red House**, a fine restaurant owned and run by John and Belinda Betham which is housed in a handsome redbrick Regency building, built in 1848 and now Grade II listed. John and Belinda met whilst training in hotel and catering management. John is in charge of all food preparation and cooking, whilst Belinda manages the restaurant and bar. The restaurant seats up to 60 people and the menu is varied, imaginative and of outstanding quality. Look out for the excellent selection of vegetarian dishes and the popular traditional Sunday lunch.

South-east of Mildenhall on the A1101 is **Icklingham** , which lies on the north bank of the River Lark. St James's is now the parish church, but more interesting to us was the simple and rather lovely thatched church of All Saints, now redundant. Note the medieval tiles on the chancel floor and the beautiful east windows in the south aisle. Further down the road is **Lackford** and its Wildfowl Reserve; former gravel pits which have been restored to provide a habitat for wildfowl and waders. There is access to two hides, one being suitable for wheelchair users, and groups of 10 or more should contact the warden or ring the Suffolk Wildlife Trust for details on Saxmundham 3765.

The Greyhound, The Green, Flempton, Bury St Edmunds
01284 728400

Four miles north-west of Bury St Edmundson the A1101 Mildenhall road lies the picturesque Suffolk village of **Flempton**. Standing on the village green and opposite a row of thatched cottages we found **The Greyhound**, a traditional village pub set in this, the most English of settings. Inside you will find the surroundings genuinely welcoming, especially the lounge with its warm, mellow atmosphere. David and Jenny Nunn have been running The Greyhound for the past three years and have built up a reputation for offering their customers, both local and

Abbey Gate, Bury St Edmunds

Norman Tower, Bury St Edmunds

visiting, the very best in food and drink. If you have a request for something special, please don't be shy to ask. They also offer bed and breakfast accommodation throughout the year in rooms which couldn't be more pleasant. David told us that guests return to the Greyhound again and again. Having been told about his Suffolk breakfasts, we think we know why.

If you carry on down the A1101 you will next come to **Hengrave**, where the Hall is now a religious retreat centre and open to the public by appointment only. It was built during the period 1535-38 and was visited in 1578 by Elizabeth I and her court. The tiny church of St John Lateran which stands adjacent to the Hall completes the idyllic setting within this beautiful parkland.

However, we take the minor road north-east of Flempton to visit the Anglo-Saxon Village at **West Stow**. It was the discovery of an Anglo-Saxon cemetery in 1849 that first put West Stow on the map. In 1940 Roman kilns were also found here, and in 1947, the actual layout of the original Anglo-Saxon village was revealed. A Trust was set up to discover more about the Anglo-Saxon way of life and the building and craft techniques employed by this ancient farming community, which is known to have existed here from 420-650 AD. Using the tools and techniques of those times, a group of thatched wooden houses and a communal hall were reconstructed on the site, each one testing different ideas. This unique attraction is open daily from 10.00am - 5.00pm, and a choice of cassette-tape guides are available.

The Village lies within the **West Stow Country Park**, which encompasses 125 acres of woodland, marshes and heath, as well as a large lake and a beautiful stretch of the River Lark. All are linked by paths and a five-mile nature trail, which gives you plenty of opportunity to study the abundance of plants, birds and wildlife that thrive in this particular part of Breckland. There is an excellent Visitor Centre with plenty of written information and audio-visual displays, as well as an adventure playground for the children, picnic tables, toilet facilities and a large car park.

Heading back to Flempton and taking the road leading south-west from the village we came to **Risby** , just to the north of the A45 dual carriageway. While we were here we called in at **Risby Place,** an English manor house dating back to the 15th century. In recent years, the house has been carefully restored to its former glory and is now a Grade II listed building. Here, guests can stay in the most beautiful and luxurious of surroundings. The house is surrounded by 10 acres of grounds which contain dozens of specimen shrubs, an outdoor swimming pool, two grass tennis courts, a squash court ad a croquet lawn. There is also a delightful summer house where guests can have breakfast and relax in the morning sunlight. Inside, there is a medieval hall, panelled reception rooms, and bedrooms which have been decorated in the most sumptuous style. Mrs Jayne Tracey and here staff believe in caring for their guests in the grand manner, so you can be sure that a stay at Risby Place will be exceptionally comfortable and relaxed.

Risby Place, Risby

Mrs Tracey also organises country house language courses here (please telephone for further details). Also, be sure to drop in at **Risby Barn Antique Centre**, a medieval thatched tithe barn which houses 28 antique dealers, tea rooms and a garden centre.

Situated just off the A45, **The White Horse** is a 17th century inn offering accommodation, good food and ale in very romantic furnishings, with candlelit dining room, open fire and soft background music.

The White Horse Inn and Accommodation, Newmarket Road, Risby
0284-810686

Whether it be a lunchtime snack or an evening meal, the locally purchased fresh produce is always available. It also has an excellent wine list and the accommodation, which has just been refurbished, at very competitive rates. This Inn is well worth the visit.

To the south of the A45 is **Barrow**, home of the Tropical Butterfly Garden. This is open from April to October from 10.00am - 5.00pm daily, and provides a good opportunity to warm yourself up in the humid butterfly houses if the weather turns chill. If you head west on the A45 towards **Kentford**, you may spot a sad memorial to a young suicide at a crossroads about a mile and a half before the village.

This is known simply as 'The Boy's Grave', and marks the spot where a shepherd boy was buried after hanging himself when he was accused of sheep stealing. No one knows whether he took his own life out of remorse or as a preferable alternative to the horrors of transportation, but his grave is still tended and adorned with fresh flowers to this day. Suicides were traditionally buried at crossroads to prevent their unfortunate spirits from wandering, and strange stories have been told of this particular grave by cyclists who have apparently felt an unseen force preventing them from riding past it.

Carrying on past Kentford on the B1506, we joined the A1304 and made our way into **Newmarket**. This is, of course, the headquarters of British horse racing and bloodstock breeding, with two of the most famous racecourses in the world. On either side of the town are four square miles of land used to train the horses who have such vast amounts of cash hanging on their performances. There are something like 60 training stables and 50 stud farms within the area, and Newmarket is without doubt the premier place to purchase pure bred racehorses in Britain.

It is said that Boudicca herself enjoyed the spirit of horse racing, although the shaggy ponies that pulled the ancient Iceni chariots are a far cry from the long-legged equine beauties that grace the paddocks of Newmarket today. **The National Horse Racing Museum** in the High Street is a tribute to the men and the rules that have fashioned this modern 300-year-old sport, and most importantly to the horses themselves - without whom none of it would be possible. By arrangement, you can also enjoy guided tours around the training areas, the Jockey Club and the National Stud.

As far as we are aware, Newmarket has the only racecourse in the world which is haunted. A phantom rider has often been spotted joining his colleagues on the turf, occasionally making the other horses shy. Jockeys say that the spirit is obviously taking part in the races, as it tends to keep well up in front with the leaders! Some reckon that it could be the ghost of Fred Archer, who won the Derby on four occasions before his death in 1886 at the age of 29.

James I is thought to have been the first monarch to enjoy the sporting grounds of the heathland surrounding the town; he was so taken by it that he chose to revisit the town on many occasions to watch the hare coursing events. But it was Charles II who firmly established Newmarket as the place for horse racing, taking part in many races himself. His mistress Nell Gwynne used to stay at a house in Palace Street which can still be seen today. Newmarket's largest racecourse is called 'The Rowley Mile', a tribute to Charles whose favourite horse was a stallion called 'Old Rowley' - a name also used by the king himself when he went off on his nocturnal adventures!

Another famous lady associated with Newmarket was the actress who dominated the Victorian stage, Lillie Langtry. She owned the house in Gazeley Road which is now the Langtry Hotel. So often it seems that those with the chastest origins attain the dizzy heights, for she was born Emilie le Breton in 1853, daughter of the Dean of Jersey. She would later become the mistress of Edward VII, and Oscar Wilde (despite his personal predilections) declared of her: 'Lillie's beauty has no meaning, her charm, her wit, and her mouth - what a mouth - are far more formidable than weapons!'

Stretching across the Heath is a massive, six-mile long fortification known as the Devil's Ditch. It was probably built sometime during the 7th century, although there may have been an earlier fortification here as the Iceni are known to have had a settlement at nearby **Exning** . Plague forced them to move their community to what is now Newmarket in the first century. We also learnt that the Iceni coinage bore the picture of a horse - an animal that was obviously much loved and revered by this ancient tribe.

Heading out beyond Exning, which lies two miles north-west of Newmarket on the B1103, we crossed over the border into Cambridgeshire and stopped in the fenland village of **Burwell**. For those of you looking for well-appointed bed and breakfast accommodation at a competitive cost, call in on Mrs Hilary Marsh at the **Meadow House**. A very warm welcome is guaranteed at this modern detached house which provides a good base for reaching many nearby places of interest.

The Meadow House Hotel & Self-Catering, 2A High Street, Burwell,
Cambs 01638 741926

To the east of Newmarket on the B1085 is **Moulton** , where a fine medieval hump-backed packhorse bridge spans the River Kennett. Today's traffic, however, crosses over a more mundane by-road which fords the river, while the old bridge marks the ancient route between Cambridge and Bury St Edmunds. This peaceful spot has a tendency to flood in winter, although perversely, like many of our English rivers, the Kennett can also run dry in summer.

The road runs south from Moulton to **Dalham,** a pretty village nestled among gentle wooded hills, where the residents of thatched and white-washed cottages have to cross little footbridges over the Kennett to reach their homes. The Duke of Wellington lived at Dalham Hall for several years, and the estate was later bought by Cecil Rhodes for his retirement. As it transpired, he died in 1902 and never returned to England.

Joining the B1063 to the south of Dalham, a turning to the right led us over the border into Cambridgeshire once more, and about two miles further on we came to **Kirtling** . A splendid tower gatehouse here is all that is left of the 15th century mansion that once belonged to Henry VIII's Chancellor, Lord North, who was at one time the jailer of Elizabeth I before she took the throne.

It was here too, within easy access of Bury St Edmunds, Cambridge and Newmarket, and just five miles from the A45, that we came across a beautiful old farmhouse dating back 400 years. Mrs Ann Bailey, proprietor of **'Hill Farm'** , is renowned for her hospitality and her ability as a wonderful hostess and chef. Ann has had plenty of practice, having been in the 'Public House' and catering business for many years, once holding the position of head chef at the Egon Ronay recommended Queens Head in Kirtling.

A wonderful historic atmosphere is preserved here, yet the bedrooms have en-suite and service tray facilities. Bar billiards and darts can be played in the 'Hill Farm' games room which is equipped with its own little bar, or you can relax and watch television in the superbly decorated lounge.

The luxury of open wood fires, the splendid rural views and the excellent cuisine make staying here a pleasurable experience.

Hill Farm, Kirtling, Nr Newmarket 01638 730253

Back on the B1063 and heading south, we came to **Wickhambrook,** where in All Saints' Church we saw the fine carved statue of Sir Thomas Heigham. One of his ancestors built nearby Gifford's Hall, a gabled, timber-framed house whose moat-enclosed grounds are open to the public under the National Gardens Scheme.

Also worth a visit is the church of St Nicholas, a mile and a half to the south-east at **Denston.** Built during the 15th century, this is one of the finest medieval churches in Suffolk. It is one of 18 churches dedicated to St Nicholas, the patron saint of sailors, and it seemed rather odd to us to find him so far inland.

There is plenty to admire here, including the medieval glass, the beautiful tracery work throughout, and some particularly fine carvings. The crane clasping a stone in its claw recalls the legend that when a flock of cranes flew down to rest at nightfall, one of them would stand guard just so, and the stone would drop with a loud clunk and wake him if he inadvertently fell asleep on the job! Animal carvings feature everywhere; a fascinating menagerie of mythical as well as more familiar beasts. The unicorn is said to symbolise the Incarnation, while a stag represents the image of a good Christian. We also spotted a rather odd carving of an elephant that looks more like a pig with a trailing snout!

Some five miles to the south-west, the twin villages of **Little Thurlow** and **Great Thurlow** merge to become one large, sprawling community on the west bank of the River Stour. The pretty Hall, its walls festooned with rambling roses in high summer, is open under the National Gardens Scheme, and the views along the grassy riverbanks are quite delightful. Some of the most attractive buildings are in the main street, including a school house founded in 1614 by a former Lord Mayor of London, Sir Stephen Soame.

Ignoring the turn-off to Haverhill, an uninspiring town to the south of the Thurlows, we carry on to the end of the B1061 then headed east on the A604. At Baythorn End we join the A1092 and passed through **Stoke by Clare** , a picturesque little village huddled around its green and flanked by some spectacular oak trees.

A mile further on lies the small town of **Clare,** whose name has rather a charming origin - the River Stour flows through Clare Country Park, and some believe that the clarity of its waters gave the town its name. This stretch of the river still seems pretty well looked after, if the swans who inhabit it are anything to go by. As the town was known to have extensive vineyards at the time of the Domesday Book, it has also been suggested that it may have given its name to that popular tipple, Claret.

The ruins of **Clare Castle** with its 13th century keep and 100ft high motte make an attractive landmark, and if you carry on along the footpath by the river you will come to the remains of a Priory that was founded by the Austin Friars in 1249. This was abandoned at the time of the Dissolution, but the order returned some 400 years later in 1953 and still maintain the Priory (converted into a house in 1604) to this day. To the north of the town, the remnants of an Iron Age hill-fort offer further evidence of Clare's ancient heritage.

The wool trade brought great wealth to Clare, and the magnificent Church of St Peter and St Paul stands as a testament to the town's prosperity from the 15th century onwards. The carvings on the Jacobean choirstalls are superb, some of the woodwork being commissioned by Katherine of Aragon. Her symbol was the pomegranate of Aragon, which can be seen in a crest above the rood screen where the letters 'H' and 'K' are linked. We thought this was rather a touching sight, as it shows the love that Henry VIII and Katherine must once have felt for one another - before the barren years which were to prove her downfall. It seems particularly ironic that the pomegranate is a traditional symbol of fertility. Henry presented Katherine with a number of estates around the town, and with great generosity she gave 60 acres of her lands to the poor to use for grazing at a peppercorn rent. This land was later purchased by the town and has since been absorbed into the Common.

While we were looking for accommodation to recommend to our readers, we called in at the **Ship Stores** in Callis Street, which turned out not only to be a general store, but also a bakery, tearoom and bed and breakfast. This handsome 15th century building (now Grade II listed) is the home of Colin and Debra Bowles. They have three en-suite double rooms available, all well-decorated and appointed to three crown standard. Guests wake up to the wonderful smell of freshly baked bread, and the choice of fresh croissants makes breakfast time unforgettable.

Did You Know...
There is a full
Town and Village Index
at the back of the book?

Ship Stores B&B, 22 Callis Street, Clare 01787 277834

There are a number of attractive houses in Clare which you should definitely take the time to see, perhaps the best of them being the Ancient House to the south of the churchyard. Built in 1473 as a priest's house it is now the town museum, and its lavish swirls of plasterwork or 'pargetting' irresistibly conjours up the image of royal icing on a wedding cake! Also worth seeing are Nethergate House on Nethergate Street, once the working place of weavers, dyers and spinners; and the Old Maltings to the north of the church, whose surviving timbered wing once housed the public library.

From Clare we continued north-eastwards on the A1092 towards **Cavendish**, a pleasant route along the Stour valley with its water meadows stretching out around us. Cavendish offers one of those quintessential portraits of the English rural village: a picturesque group of candy-pink thatched cottages clustered beneath the medieval tower of St Mary's Church on the edge of the broad village green. It comes as no surprise to learn that the village has been the proud winner of the 'best-kept village in Suffolk' award.

The Sue Ryder Foundation has taken over the Old Rectory, a 16th century timber-framed house close to the village pond. This now houses a museum illustrating the origins of the Foundation and the hard work it does on behalf of the sick and the disabled. Sue Ryder's formal title is Baroness Ryder of Warsaw and Cavendish, and she gained her nurse's training in occupied Europe during World War II.

The Foundation was established here at Cavendish in 1953 to ease the plight of sick and injured war veterans and refugees, and now serves as an H.Q. linking 80 centres throughout the world. Lady Ryder was married to that other great philanthropist and war hero, Leonard Cheshire - who founded the famous Cheshire Homes for the incurably sick. The museum is open all year round from 10.30am to 5.30pm, and a cafeteria is available for refreshments.

In 1381, Sir John Cavendish was in attendance at Wat Tyler's conference with Richard II at Smithfield, when the leader of the Peasants' Revolt was struck down by the Lord Mayor of London and stabbed by Sir John's son. When a number of Tyler's enraged supporters came after Sir John swearing vengeance, he stashed away his valuables in the belfry of St Mary's Church at Cavendish and fled. They later caught up with him near Lakenheath and beheaded him, which ironically enough was the same fate that befell their leader.

The Countrymen Restaurant at the Black Lion Hotel in Long Melford overlooks the village green on the A1092 between the A604 Cambridge road, and the A134 Bury St Edmunds to Sudbury road. Records show that a previous Black Lion stood on approximately the same site in 1580. The cellars of the original building run under cottages known as Church Walk, reference to which is made on the map of the Manor of Melford

278

Hall dated 1580. A fire destroyed the original building, which was replaced in the mid 1830's by the present Black Lion.

Countrymen Restaurant at the Black Lion Hotel, The Green, Long Melford 01787 312356

This fine establishment is a family-run concern. Stephen and Janet Errington welcome you to the Countrymen Restaurant which seats 50 people comfortably, with a spacious lounge area and a well-stocked bar. There is no a la carte menu; instead there are two fixed price menus for lunch and dinner. Menus are changed each month to offer variety and prices are inclusive with no hidden extras.

Stephen trained at the Dorchester in London and takes responsibility for the gastronomic delights served in the restaurant, where Janet ensures that things run smoothly.

The restaurant offers a superb wine list, and the bar, which is run by Janet's father Selwyn, offers a large selection of after dinner liqueurs, excellent cognacs and a superb selection of single malt whiskeys.

Mary Humphreys, Janet's mother, is responsible for the smooth running of the hotel, which has nine double rooms, all furnished with antiques and equipped with all modern amenities including en-suite bathroom, colour television, direct dial telephones and tea and coffee hospitality trays.

The hotel has premier rooms with brass bedsteads or four poster beds. There is also a library of books to borrow from and a large selection of games for children and adults to play.

The Cock & Bell is a beautiful 15th century Coaching Inn situated in the centre of Long Melford, is open all day every day from 10.00am for morning coffee, lunch, cream teas and dinner.

The house is full of character; it's warm and has a very friendly feel.

You can sit at one of the tables in front of the house, enjoy a drink or a snack, and just watch the world go by.

All produce is purchased locally which enables the chef to prepare some of the finest food in the county.

The Cock & Bell, Hall Street, Long Melford 0787 379807

Long Melford could not be more aptly named; its tree-lined main street seems to go on and on, covering a distance of three miles in all. Guide books tend to refer to Melford as a town, but it has more the feel of a very large, spacious village. A lot of visitors come here specifically to browse around Melford's surprisingly large number of antique shops, most of which lie dotted about the main street with its timber-framed and Georgian houses. Another regular feature of the village, popular with visitors and locals alike, are its book fairs and musical concerts.

The beautiful 15th century Holy Trinity Church stands on a rise above Melford's green. It is renowned far and wide for its striking tower, its magnificent display of flushwork, and the incredible number of windows in the 150ft nave and chancel which give the interior such a sense of light and space.

On the other side of the green is Melford Hall, built during the 1570s and once used by the Abbot of Bury St Edmunds as his country retreat, where he could enjoy venison from the deer park. Now a National Trust property, this mellow red-brick house with its 'pepperpot' towers is full of fine paintings, furniture and porcelain for the public to enjoy; but what interested us especially was the charming collection of water colours by Beatrix Potter. She was related to the Parker family who bought the house in the 18th century, and somehow her pictures seem more quintessentially English than those of our greatest landscape painters!

In search of a drink and a meal in these pleasant surroundings, we then called in at the splendid village pub and eating house, **The Hare Inn,**

280

run by John and Jill Pipe. The inn has a handsome Georgian façade and a traditional interior divided into three attractive bars. In cold weather, blazing log fires and relaxed lighting help to add to the cosy and welcoming atmosphere.

The Hare Inn & Restaurant, High Street, Long Melford
01787 310379

The Hare Inn is renowned for its traditional country cooking and offers a superb range of freshly prepared dishes including east coast fish and prime Suffolk beef. The inn participates in the 'Taste of Suffolk' scheme with ingredients largely being sourced from the local area. The menu is changed with the season and at times features such local delicacies as pigeon casserole and rabbit pie. As well as its á la carte menu, the Hare offers bar snacks, roast Sunday lunches and traditional Greene King ales.

Outside, there is a large lawn and patio area with tubs and hanging baskets overflowing with flowers in summer. At lunchtimes barbecues are served in the open air and in the evenings the garden is illuminated. Children are welcome in the family dining room which offers special children's portions on request. The Hare Inn has been featured in the 'Best Inns in East Anglia' and has twice been runner-up in the Greene King 'In Bloom' competition. Easy access for the disabled.

Opposite the Hare Inn at the northern end of the village, we turned into the impressive tree-lined drive which is the entrance to **Kentwell Hall.** Kentwell is an elegant redbrick Tudor manor house which stands within a splendid brick-lined moat. It was built between 1520 and 1550 by the Clopton family on wealth derived from the wool trade. Since then, the interior has been remodelled on several occasions, in particular by architect Thomas Hopper in the early 19th-century. In 1971, Kentwell was acquired by Patrick Phillips who began a continuous programme of restoration and improvement, including the realignment of the main staircase, the refurbishment of the State bedroom, the creation of a Roman-style bathroom, and perhaps most ambitious of all, the building of a unique brick-mosaic maze in the main courtyard.

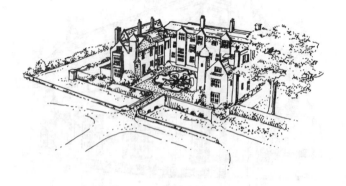

Kentwell Hall, Long Melford   01787 310207

Perched on the edge of the moat is the superb 15th-century moat house, a remnant from the earlier house which stood on the site. Now fully restored, this magical building has its own great hall and solar. The moat gives Kentwell its unique character and surrounds not only the house, but also a large area of beautiful formal gardens which were laid out in the 17th century. A short distance from the main house, a home farm has been created using relocated and newly built timber-framed buildings. This fascinating working farm contains a wide variety of rare breeds and an interesting collection of farm tools and carts.

Special summer events at Kentwell include their famous 'historical re-creations', days involving over 200 people who dress, speak and behave in Tudor style to create an impression of everyday life at the manor in the 16th century. For details of opening times and special events, telephone (0787) 310207. Delicious home-produced refreshments are available when the house is open.

Just over three miles to the north-west of Kentwell Hall we came to **Hartest**, a pleasant little village sheltered in a valley, with colour-washed houses and chestnut trees on the village green. Here we found a vineyard with a difference. In addition to the free wine tasting on offer, Gifford's Hall (not to be confused with the house at Wickhambrook) also provides a host of other things to see and purchase, including wild flower meadows, rare breeds of sheep and chickens, organic vegetables, cut flowers and a rose garden - all within a 33-acre site. The Hall is open every day from 12.00am - 6.00pm from Easter through to the end of October. There is a shop and tea room, and wheelchair access is provided.

Making our way along the lanes to the east of Hartest, through Shimpling with its agricultural college, then Shimpling Street, we turned north on the A134 and headed towards our final destination for this chapter.

Coaching House Carvery, Cockfield

Further up the A134, midway between Bury St. Edmunds and Sudbury, we called in at the unusual roadside restaurant, the **Coaching House Carvery**, near **Cockfield**. The pleasant pink-washed exterior of this former coaching house gives customers little idea of the truly eccentric welcome that awaits them inside. Proprietor Dave Upton has gone to great lengths to create an atmosphere which is unconventional and out of the ordinary. The corners of the dimly-lit restaurant have been decorated with Halloween cobwebs, and instead of a menu, there is a verbal list. The emphasis here is on good English fare which is prepared by Binz, the highly-qualified chef. The Coaching House is ideal for those who like their food off-the-bone and their atmosphere off-the-wall.

Speaking of eccentricity, what do you make of an odd village name like **Bradfield Combust**? It apparently derives from the fact that the local hall was burnt to the ground in the 14th century, during riots against the Abbot of St Edmundsbury.

From here it is just a four-mile drive to **Bury St Edmunds,** widely held to be the jewel of Suffolk's towns and rich in archaeological treasures and places of great historical interest. It has long been known as one of the least spoilt towns in England; a reputation that has been greatly enhanced by the building of the A45 by-pass.

The town takes its name from St Edmund, who was born in Nuremberg in 841 AD and arrived on these shores 14 years later to become King of

East Anglia. He was a renowned soldier and a fervent Christian. The latter was to prove his undoing, for when he was captured by the Danes in 870 AD he refused to deny his Christianity, and was brutally murdered by being tied to a tree, shot full of arrows and beheaded.

At this point, legend mingles with fact, for it is said that although his body was recovered, his head could not be found. His men searched desperately for it for 40 days, then heard his voice directing them to it from the depths of a wood, where they discovered it lying protected between the paws of a wolf. When the head was taken back to his body they were miraculously joined, with no apparent signs of damage. To commemorate the wolf's benign influence, the crest of the town's armorial bearings depicts a wolf with a man's head.

Edmund was buried first at Hoxne - the site of his martyrdom - but when he was canonised some 30 years later his remains were transferred to the monastery at what was then called Beodricksworth. The town changed its name to St Edmundsbury, and a shrine was built here in his honour, later to be incorporated into the Normans' Abbey Church after the monastery was granted abbey status by King Canute in 1032. It became a place of international pilgrimage, and the monks were quick to realise its potential by stocking the abbey with an imaginative array of relics. Edmund was the patron saint of England for many years, later to be 'deposed' by St George - this seems a bit hard, considering that the 'historical' George is little more than a myth.

Further history was made here on 20th November 1214, when on St Edmund's Feast Day, the Archbishop of Canterbury, Simon Langton, met with a gathering of barons and swore on Edmund's shrine to uphold the Magna Carta and to make certain that King John would honour its proposals. With Edmund's burial here and the ratification of this important historical document, Bury well deserves its motto of: 'Shrine of a King; Cradle of the Law'.

All that remains of the abbey and its church today are the romantic ruins which stand within the beautiful municipal park known as the Abbey Gardens. These can be reached from the broad thoroughfare (or medieval 'square') called Angel Hill by going through the superb Abbey Gate. This was originally built for defensive purposes and once led into the monastery courtyard.

Angel Hill itself is full of interest. Firstly, there is the impressive Norman Tower, the original gateway to the Abbey Church which was built by Abbot Anselm in the 12th century. It now serves as a belfry for the cathedral church of St James which stands alongside. St James's was rebuilt in the 16th century and was elevated to the status of cathedral when the diocese of St Edmundsbury and Ipswich was created in 1914. To the south on Crown Street is the 15th century St Mary's Church,

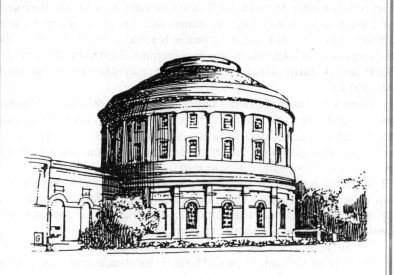

Ickworth House, Nr Bury St Edmunds

Moyes Hall Museum, Bury St Edmunds

renowned for its wonderful oak roof and famous as the burial place of Henry VIII's sister, Mary Tudor. To the west is the Athenaeum, the centre of Bury's social life in Regency times, and the place where Charles Dickens gave two of his stirring public readings. He also stayed at the adjacent Angel Hotel, which was to be immortalised as the place where Mr Pickwick learns of the intended lawsuit against him by the 'spurned' Mrs Bardell.

The lovely Abbey Gardens were created in 1831, their central feature being a one acre circle filled with flower beds, set out along the lines of the Royal Botanic Gardens in Brussels. This had been transferred to its new site from Nathaniel Hodson's original garden to the east of the Abbey Churchyard, and it is estimated that some 2,000 plants were used. This botanic garden was conceived strictly as a scientific establishment, with native flowers and herbs laid out in their botanical orders; but ornamental plants were later introduced so that the fee-paying public could take over the financing of the project.

Today, you can still see some of those original ornamental trees, such as the Tree of Heaven, Turkish Hazel, False Acacia and Fern Leaved Beech; and many other features that were introduced at a later date can be enjoyed. These include a garden for the blind (combining a range of particularly fragrant plants), the Water Garden and the John Appleby Rose Garden; while splendid shows of shrub roses, ferns, heather banks and hostas (now making a big comeback) all add to the stunning picture. The pretty River Lark flows through the Abbey grounds and converges with the smaller River Linnet at the place where Bury's first monastery was built - these are surely two of the most charmingly named rivers in the country. The Gardens also have a most unusual tribute to our American allies in the form of a park bench made entirely from the metal framework of a 'Flying Fortress' bomber.

There is so much to see and do in Bury that it is quite difficult to condense it down into just a few paragraphs. In addition to those places 'not to be missed' the following are well worth discovering for yourselves..

No visitor should miss the opportunity of taking a leisurely stroll along Abbeygate Street, which leads you up from Angel Hill and features a fascinating and diverse variety of old shop fronts. Near the top of the street you can turn right into The Traverse, past the Victorian Corn Exchange and on to the charming Nutshell - which claims to be the smallest pub in England and belies its name by offering large-scale hospitality. Further along is the handsome Cupola House, a fine old inn that was built in 1693 and reputedly numbered Daniel Defoe amongst its guests. At the end of The Traverse and facing Cornhill is the Market Cross, originally built as a market hall and theatre combined (note the tell-tale masks of tragedy and comedy), later to become the town hall, and now housing an art gallery on its upper storey.

Moyses Hall Museum in the Butter Market is said to be the oldest stone domestic building in England. Although its precise origins are unclear, it is thought to have been built sometime around 1180 - of flint and limestone in a town whose secular buildings were strictly made of wood. The fact that these materials would have been transported from quarries more than 70 miles away implies that whoever it was built for must have been a person of no small distinction. The Hall has served various functions over the centuries; it has been a prison and a workhouse, a police station and a railway office, and in 1899 it became the Borough museum - which it remains to this day. With around 10,000 objects on display, this unique building makes a wonderful setting for such diverse exhibits as Anglo-Saxon grave jewellery, Roman pottery and a 19th century doll's house. It seems particularly ironic that one of the town's most recent developments, the Cornhill Shopping Centre in Brentgovel Street, stands alongside Bury's oldest house. A curious juxtaposition of the old and new indeed!

For the horologists among you, the Manor House Museum on Honey Hill is devoted to timepieces of all shapes and sizes; from clocks and watches to sundials and a replica of a 15th century planetarium. Around 200 exhibits from the Gershom Parkington Collection are displayed - formerly housed at the Clock Museum on Angel Hill - and in addition, there are some fine works of art by such painters as James Tissot and Joshua Reynolds.

Not far from here, at the junction of Crown Street and Westgate Street, evidence of Regency patronage can be seen in the handsome architecture of the Theatre Royal, now in the care of the National Trust, though still a working theatre. It was built in 1819 by William Wilkins - also the architect of the National Gallery - and can claim the distinction of being the first theatre in the world to premiere 'Charley's Aunt', apparently before an audience of five!

A visit to Bury St Edmunds is definitely one of the highlights of a tour of Suffolk. It is a charming town of great character, and yet unlike other historic towns, it is still very much alive with plenty of modern entertainments and facilities. High on this particular list would be 'Rollerbury', the National Rollerskating Rink; the superb Sports & Leisure Centre on Beetons Way; and the annual Bury St Edmunds Festival in May, when the town plays host to both national and international artists from the world of the performing arts.

With so much to enjoy it is patently impossible to 'do' Bury in a day, and we would suggest that you make a point of finding somewhere to stay for a night or two if budget allows. The choice of accommodation is wide both in and around the town, but we would particularly like to recommend an establishment not too far away from the Suffolk Regimental Museum on Out Risbygate.

Holly Lodge is a delightful little guest house surrounded by its own gardens along Albert Street. It is ideal for those who would like to relax in a friendly, comfortable atmosphere and appreciate a good, hearty Suffolk breakfast cooked by one of the co-proprietors, Dick Lee-Stamper alias 'The Master Breakfast Chef'. Dick is not the only one with talent as his wife Audrey is a musician who teaches the piano from a rather pleasant music room.

Holly Lodge, 7 Albert Street, Bury St Edmunds 01284 752458

Dick and Audrey have carefully restored this spacious Victorian building to its present condition and have endeavoured to provide every modern comfort their guests could require. Arrangements can be made with Dick to be escorted to and from local eating places and other interesting venues if required, as part of the hospitality.

Holly Lodge has picturesque gardens with a fine display of Victorian horticulture, and a warm atmosphere ensuring a welcome stay for all.

Another local attraction not to be missed is **Ickworth House**, owned by the National Trust and easily found in Horringer Village, three miles south-west of Bury St Edmunds on the A143. Ickworth's spectacular elliptical rotunda makes this one of the most extraordinary mansions in England. The design was inspired by Belle Isle, a house built on an island in Lake Windermere in the mid-18th century. Construction of Ickworth got underway in 1795, but because of technical problems and the death of Frederick, 4th Earl of Bristol and Bishop of Derry in 1803, it wasn't completed until 1829. The Earl-Bishop's son even considered demolishing his father's highly impractical house before deciding that the state rooms in the rotunda would make an excellent setting for the family's extensive art collection. Works now on view include those by Titian, Velasquez, Gainsborough, Hogarth and Reynolds. Inside, the state rooms are spectacular. The hall, dining room, library and drawing room follow the same grandiose style and are furnished with late-Regency and 18th century French furniture. Be sure not to miss the collection of Georgian silver, one of the finest private collections ever assembled. Outside, the grounds are arranged as a semi-formal Italian garden. Here we suggest a visit to the orangery and a walk along the terrace which overlooks the park beyond. In the park, there are several miles of way marked trails, including a seven mile Grand Tour which includes some fabulous views of the rotunda.

Ickworth House, Horringer, Bury St Edmunds 01284 88270

Adjacent to the park is the Community Centre, where Horringer Crafts 'open their door' to the public every Sunday and Bank Holiday Monday from 2.00 - 6.00pm. There is a small admission charge although accompanied children are free, and you can spend a pleasant hour or so watching the local artists and craftsmen at work before making your selection from the wide range of high quality, individually made items available for sale. The group emphasises that they are more than happy to demonstrate their skills and discuss their work in detail with you, so do feel free to ask questions! To round off a pleasant and interesting afternoon in their company, they can also provide you with afternoon tea. Any local craftspeople who would like to join the group should phone (01284) 766326 for details.

289

Racing at Newmarket

Central Suffolk

Lavenham Guildhall

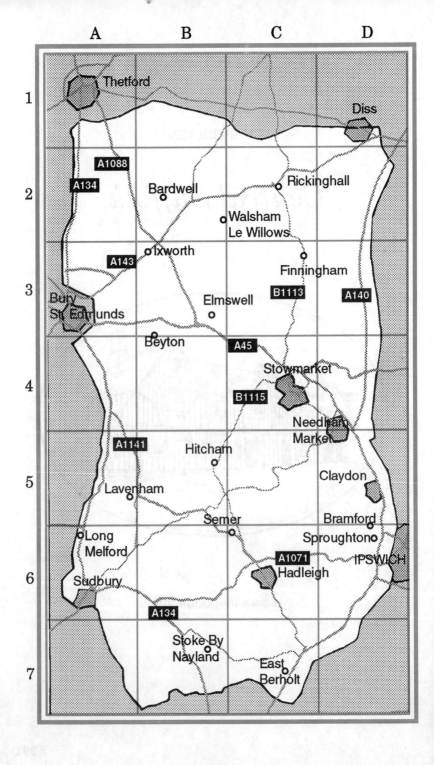

CHAPTER TEN

Central Suffolk

Situated just six miles north-east of Bury St Edmunds, off the A143 and south of the village of Ixworth, you will find a fine 18th century working mill. When approaching from the south-west on the A143, follow the signs from **Pakenham**. The mill is signed from the village centre. It was built around 1816 on a site which had a considerable and interesting history. Domesday Survey records have proven that there had been a watermill on this site since 1086, thus corn has definitely been ground here for the past 900 years. However, excavations of a nearby Roman site have suggested that there could have been a watermill here as far back as 43-60 AD.

The mill was purchased by the Suffolk Preservation Society in 1981. With the help of a small group of volunteers, they lovingly restored this magnificent watermill to its present condition and rightfully accepted a European Award in 1982 for their sympathetic and talented renovation.

The water which powers the mill comes from Pakenham Fen: about 60-70,000 gallons of treated water are fed into the Fen area each day. A steep drop in the stream of approximately 10ft is necessary to power a watermill. This drop is made by creating built-up banks and damming the stream to form a millpond. Thus outlets leave the millpond. One is known as the spillway gate, which allows excess water to by-pass the mill; the other is called the shut and its purpose is to direct water onto the waterwheel.

A tour of the mill will give you greater insight into the everyday life of a Miller, and will allow you to study the mechanisms used.

One article of particular interest is that of the 'Tattersall Midget Roller Mill'. Towards the end of the 19th century, fine white flour was being produced with more efficiency by new roller mills. A few watermills tried to install roller milling machinery, but found it far too expensive. As a compromise, the 'Tattersall Midget Roller Mill' was introduced, which actively combined rollers and separators in one large machine. The Tattersall exhibited at Pakenham is dated around 1913. Unfortunately for the country watermills, even with the aid of this new-found invention they still found it difficult to compete, and those that survived only produced animal feed.

Even today, huge overheads comprising of maintenance and insurance quickly absorb profits, and many mills, including Pakenham's, are kept running solely due to the efforts of volunteers, who work hard towards improving, maintaining or staffing the mill.

The Blackbourne stream flowing down to Pakenham Fen with its willows and riverbank recreation park is a beautiful setting for visitors just to walk, rest, have a picnic, or enjoy tea and refreshments at the tea rooms provided adjoining the pump room of the mill.

As a working mill the atmosphere is resonant of the past, and there is so much for all the family to see in such a small area that you will want to spend a good half a day here, savouring this unique Suffolk watermill which is set in surroundings reminiscent of a landscape painting.

Pakenham Watermill & Wildlife Park, Grimestone End, Pakenham
01787 247179

What makes Pakenham so unique is that it has two working mills, for to the west of the watermill, near Fulmer Bridge, stands a magnificent five-storey tower windmill; darkly tarred and dramatic enough to have 'starred' in a host of television programmes, including 'Campion'. Pakenham Fen used to be known as 'fowl mere' (from which the bridge takes its name) and was used extensively for the cultivation of reeds for thatching. There are some splendid buildings in the village, including the 17th century Nether Hall, built on the site of an earlier house which belonged to the Pakenham family of which Lord Longford is a descendant.

A circular walk around the village takes you close by the house across spectacular parkland, and also en route is Newe House from the same period, a handsome Jacobean building with Dutch gables and a two-storey porch. Above the village stands the lovely St Mary's Church, with its striking octagonal crossing tower and beautifully carved Perpendicular font. As you walk up The Street, look out for the ancient chalk pit known locally as the Dell, which in spring makes a pretty picture when the snowdrops and aconites are in bloom.

Ixworth, just to the north of Pakenham, is a veritable treasure-trove of beautiful timber-framed buildings standing side-by-side with later houses boasting Georgian facades. Just west of St Mary's Church, a footpath leads to 'The Abbey', and although this Georgian house may seem an unlikely place to bear such a name, the building does indeed incorporate the 12th and 13th century remains of an Augustinian priory that was founded here in 1170. In the church is an effigy to Sir Richard Codington, who was made lord of the manor at Ixworth by Henry VIII in recompense for handing over Codington Manor in Surrey - which was then transformed into the Palace of Nonesuch for Anne Boleyn. Alas, that romantically named showpiece is no more.

Those interested in wildfowl conservation should make a point of finding the **Priory Waterfowl Farm** on the River Blackbourne at Ixworth. The farm was established over 70 years ago by Reginald Appleyard who achieved international fame showing domestic waterfowl. After World War II, it was purchased by Lieutenant-Colonel Johnson and the emphasis changed to the conservation of wild birds with many being used to stock Peter Scott's Wildfowl Trust at Slimbridge. Today, Priory Waterfowl Farm is owned and run by Mr J Copsey and boasts over a 100 different species of ducks, swans, geese, pheasants and peafowl, many of which are supplied to zoos, parks and bird gardens. The collection can be viewed, though by appointment only.

The Priory Waterfowl Farm, Ixworth, Bury St Edmunds
01359 31122

Some four miles east of Ixworth is **Walsham le Willows**, a name that conjours up thoughts of picnics and boats and lazy summer afternoons. So named the village might not live up to such an idyllic ideal- but not a bit of it. Walsham is simply lovely, with weatherboarded and timber-framed cottages fronting the tributary of the Little Ouse which flows through the village, fringed by the willows from which it takes its name. This is English 'riverscape' at its best.

St Mary's Church is no less pleasing to the eye, with its sturdy western tower and handsome windows in the Perpendicular style. Of particular interest inside is the superb tie and hammerbeam roof of the nave, and (unique in Suffolk and very rare elsewhere) a tiny circular medallion which hangs suspended from the nave wall, known as a 'Maiden's Garland' or 'Virgin's Crant'. These marked the pew seats of unmarried girls who had passed away, and the old custom was for the young men of the village to hang garlands of flowers from them on the anniversary of the girl's death. This particular example celebrates the virginity of one Mary Boyce, who died (so the inscription says) of a broken heart in 1685, just 20 years old. While you are here, also see if you can spot the carving on the rood screen which looks rather like the face of a wolf: this may well be a reference to the benevolent creature that plays such an important role in the legend of St Edmund.

It was in this delightful village that we found the charming self-catering holiday cottage which is owned by a local doctor's wife, Hilary Russell. **Bridge Cottage** stands behind the church in the centre of the village and is reached from the road by crossing a delightful curved oak bridge which spans a little stream (the stream is said to be occasionally visited by kingfishers). The building is surrounded by a charming country cottage-garden. Mrs Russell's garden close by, opens to the public during summer in aid of the church restoration fund. Inside, the holiday cottage is beautifully appointed yet it still manages to retain its traditional country charm.

Bridge Cottage, The Beeches, Walsham-le-Willows, Nr Bury St Edmunds 01359 259227

Heading north-west from here through Stanton, we came to the enchanting village of **Bardwell** just to the west of the A143. **The Six Bells Inn** can be found tucked away off the village green alongside the ancient London to Norwich coaching road.

Carol and Richard have turned the clock back 400 years and restored this lovely old Inn to its former glory.

The old barn and stables have recently been converted into outstandingly decorated chalet bedrooms. Each room is furnished in pine wood and all have en-suite shower rooms. Facilities include a colour T.V, complimentary tea and coffee trays, direct dial telephones and a well-lit quaint writing desk for those on business.

As regional finalists in the Pub Caterer of the Year competition in 1988, 1989 and 1990 The Six Bells Inn has gained an excellent reputation and is highly acclaimed both locally and regionally.

Carol and Richard's meals are truly superb, they offer a wide choice of menu in both bar and restaurant, which Carol prepares daily from local produce.

Light dishes include grilled sardines in lemon juice and king prawns in garlic to specialities such as salmon trout in champagne sauce and a good variety of steaks, grilled or served in one of many delicious sauces. To finish, those with a sweet tooth will love the selection from the dessert menu which ranges from home-made chocolate profiteroles served with fresh cream to home-made apricot and almond crumble, and don't forget to choose a wine to compliment your meal.

There is also plenty of space for parking and extensive play areas for the children.

In all, The Six Bells Inn provides you with delicious meals, convivial company, a genuine welcome and superb relaxing accommodation.

The Six Bells Inn, The Green, Bardwell, Bury St Edmunds
01359 50820

The fine 19th century tower windmill at the northern end of the village is now owned by Geoffrey and Enid Wheeler and their colleague Simon Wooster. Unfortunately, the mill lost its sails during those dreadful storms of 1987, so electricity is now the power source used to produce the stoneground flour on offer here. Bread made from this flour is also for sale in the small bakery attached to the mill, and do note that the flour is organic. The three partners are keen to undertake a full restoration job on the mill, but as they have less than 20,000 visitors a year, no grants are forthcoming. So if you want to do them a really good 'turn' (and let a new set of sails do the same), pay them a visit and help boost the figures!

Two miles to the north-west on the A1088 is **Honington**, birthplace of the poet Robert Bloomfield, author of the 'The Farmer's Boy' and 'Rural Tales'. Although he received patronage from the Duke of Grafton, he died half-blind and impoverished in 1823.

There is some beautiful countryside for walkers around here, notably **Knettishall Heath Country Park** to the north-east with its 400 acres of prime Breckland terrain. The Heath has been designated a Site of Special Scientific Interest, and there are circular waymarked walks, picnic areas and facilities for horse riding. This is the official starting place of both the Peddars Way National Trail and the Angles Way Path, the latter stretching for 77 miles from here to Great Yarmouth and taking in the peaceful scenery of the Little Ouse and Waveney valleys.

A few miles to the east, just a mile north of **Redgrave** and a mile south of South Lopham in Norfolk, the sources of both rivers can be found. The ditch to the west of the B1113 is the source of the Little Ouse, while the ditch to the east of the road is that of the Waveney; the rivers flow from here in opposite directions and form the county boundary between Norfolk and Suffolk. There is access from the road to the 360-acre valley fen reserve of Redgrave and Lopham Fens, an internationally important wetland site of reed and sedge beds on either side of the Waveney. Among the many small invertebrates that make their home here is the unique Great Raft Spider, though you can cast aside the terrible vision of a giant pole-wielding arachnid, punting through the fens on the lookout for somewhere to string up his unfortunate victims.

A mile to the south of Redgrave, the B1113 joins the A143. If you head west you come immediately to the attractive village of **Botesdale**, which was once an important thoroughfare in the old coaching days. We assumed that its name was derived from St Botolph as there is a chapel dedicated to him here, but other sources site a local tribal chief called Botwulf. Over the hill are the Rickinghalls, in essence one village that has been neatly divided in two by the boundary between East and West Suffolk. Presumably, the inhabitants of **Rickinghall Inferior** have now come to terms with the fact that this imaginary line so cruelly distinguishes them from their neighbours at **Rickinghall Superior.** We wondered whether a coin was tossed to decide which part of the village should be bestowed with the more desirable of the two suffixes - as there appears to be no particularly significant reason for the choice. The churches of both villages are dedicated to St Mary, and each is rich in fine flushwork and tracery.

If you make your way back east on the A143 to **Wortham**, you will find yet another church of St Mary, this one instantly recognisable by the breadth of its round tower. It is, in fact, the broadest round church tower in England, and may well have been used as a lookout station to warn of invaders. The Waveney was a known route used by Scandinavian marauders on their way to plunder the towns and villages of East Anglia, and appropriately enough, its name means 'troubled water'.

Three miles to the south-east, just off the A140, lovers of unusual church artifacts will find something of particular interest in the beautiful 400-year-old church at **Yaxley**, which is dedicated to none other than - St Mary! The item in question is an extremely rare Sexton's Wheel, which hangs above the south door and was used in medieval times to select fast days in honour of the Virgin - or Lady Fasts, as they were known. When a pair of iron wheels were spun on their axle, strings attached to the outer wheel would catch on the inner one, stopping the rotation of both and denoting the 'chosen' day. This is one of only two surviving Sexton's Wheels in England, the other being at Long Stratton in Norfolk. Also worth seeing at Yaxley's church is the sumptuously carved 17th century pulpit, which is widely held to be the finest of its kind in the country.

Turnings off the A140 to the south of Yaxley will lead you to the Thornhams. The tiny, thatched church at **Thornham Parva** stands in the middle of a field and features the most exquisite medieval altar painting (known as a retable), its central panel depicting the Crucifixion, with four saints on each of the side panels. It dates back to around 1300 and is in remarkably good condition. Like so many of these magnificent relics, nothing is known for sure about the artists responsible; although there is some evidence to suggest that it may have originated in the Royal Workshops at Westminster Abbey and that it was made specifically for Thetford Priory.

It is only by chance that this immensely valuable painting rose again to see the light of day, for it was discovered in 1927 amongst a pile of jumble bought at a farm auction in nearby Stradbroke - it still carries the auctioneers tag to this day! Add to this the splendour of the recently restored 15th century wall paintings here, and you have a place that is well worth visiting. Unfortunately, this simple little church needs to be kept securely locked to guard its main treasure, but if you wish to feast your eyes on it you may obtain the key from the house nearest the church.

A mile further south at **Thornham Magna** is a delightful, traditional inn called the Four Horseshoes, which has been offering hospitality to travellers since 1150. The food is excellent, and despite the antiquity of the inn, the bedrooms are particularly luxurious and provide today's visitors with every comfort. If you would like to contact the owners for further details, the telephone number is (01379) 71777.

The Thornham Estate has been home to the Henniker family since 1756. Thornham Hall burnt down in 1955, but today, visitors can enjoy the 2,500 acres of working farmland, ancient woodland, parkland and wetland that makes up the estate. Thornham Walks have been opened up allowing public access to some 12 miles of footpaths, taking you deep into countryside where deer and orchids may be seen, together with a colourful profusion of primroses in the spring. A Field Study Centre has been set up at Red House Yard, helping visitors to appreciate the countryside and rural life by providing a range of courses, activities and guided walks. All types of groups are catered for, and there are excellent facilities for the disabled. There is a charge for any group using the Estate, to cover use of the facilities and insurance.

Those wishing to take full advantage of everything on offer here may like to arrange a short or long stay at Thornham Cabins, overlooking the Parkland in Old Blacksmith's Field. The two purpose-built Swedish cabins provide excellent accommodation (each sleeping up to 14 people) and prove that the descendants of those marauding Scandinavians we mentioned earlier had a few good ideas! Meals can be provided at the Forge Tearooms across the road, and you will find a number of excellent hostelries nearby. Alternatively, self-catering can be arranged for groups using the Field Study Centre. The cabins also cater admirably for the needs of disabled visitors, and prices - including full board - are very reasonable. For further details on Thornham Cabins and the Field Study Centre, write or phone: Thornham Field Centre, Red House Yard, Thornham Magna, Eye, Suffolk IP23 8HH Tel: (01379) 838153.

Just to the south are the Wickhams, and at **Wickham Skeith**, a treasure-trove of coins dating back to the reigns of King Harold and Edward the Confessor was discovered under an oak tree at Wizard Farm. The coins can now be seen in the British Museum. 'Skeith' comes from a Scandinavian word meaning 'race-course', which would be appropriate with Newmarket not so many miles away.

There was also magic in the air at this place, for in 1825 the village witnessed the 'trial by swimming' of a local witch - one of the last recorded cases of such an event in the county. A poor pedlar called Isaac Stebbing was accused of driving two local inhabitants mad, presumably by evil curses. As a consequence, his feet and hands were bound together and he was thrown into the village pond three times to see how he would fare. Isaac floated like a log on each occasion, which meant of course that he was guilty, and it was only the intervention of the parson that saved him from the vengeance of the locals.

Two miles to the south-west, just off the B1113, you will find the fascinating Mechanical Music Museum at **Cotton** . This is a 'must' for those of you who remember and love the great Wurlitzer Theatre Organ, seen here in a reconstructed cinema setting. Street organs, gramophones, musical boxes and dolls are just some of the items on display in the museum's extensive collection - there is even a musical chair and fruit-bowl! The museum is open from June to September, and good access is provided for the disabled.

Over at **Mendlesham**, towards the A140, you can hardly fail to notice the massive mast of the television transmitter that was erected to the south-east of the village in 1959 by the IBA. Standing 1,000ft high, it now connects these isolated villages to the outside world. Less impressive in stature, but infinitely more agreeable in form, Mendlesham's church boasts some fine carvings and a splendid collection of armour dating back to 1470.

From here we make our way some five miles south-west to **Haughley**, just to the north of the A45. All that now remains of the huge motte and bailey castle built by Hugh de Montfort is a mound behind the church. Nevertheless it is an imposing mound, standing 80ft high - this was the largest Norman motte and bailey in Suffolk. To find Haughley Park, ignore the signs to the village from the A45 and continue westwards for a mile and a half until you come to the magnificent park and handsome manor house. Andrew Sulyard - who held the presumably enviable title of 'esquire of the body' to Mary Tudor - was granted the manor in 1538, and following the queen's death in 1558, it went to his nephew, Sir John.

The handsome red-brick mansion we see today was built by the third Sir John Sulyard in 1620. In 1961, a major fire destroyed the Jacobean staircase, but this has now been meticulously recreated in oak. The fireplace in the hall was carved in 1964 by the firm of Hallidays of Dorchester, their young carver having taken only two weeks to complete his work. The eight acres of gardens and surrounding woodland are lovely, with masses of flowering shrubs and herbaceous plants, and some splendid trees - one magnolia is 40ft wide, while the oldest oak tree has stood here for 1,000 years. Exploring the many woodland paths will take you past a half-mile stretch of rhododendrons, and bluebells and lilies of the valley create their own special magic in the spring. Haughley Park is now the private residence of Mr & Mrs A.J. Williams, who open their doors to the public from May to September on Tuesday afternoons from 3.00pm to 6.00pm.

Further to the west is **Woolpit**, whose name, surprisingly enough, has nothing to do with the woollen industry. It comes from the Old English 'wulf-pytt', or 'pit for trapping wolves', and the Domesday Survey indicates that these creatures were still terrorising the locality as late as the 11th century. The unusual white bricks that were once produced here in great numbers are in evidence in many of the village houses, and at the height of their popularity they were exported as far afield as Washington in the United States - where they were used to build the Senate Wing of the Capitol. The bricks were much favoured by builders from the 17th century onwards because they had the appearance of stone, but time was to prove that they weathered badly.

In the centre of the village, medieval and Tudor houses surround the green with its roofed-over village pump, and the 400-year-old Swan Inn features an archway and yard once used by the stage coaches that pulled up here on their way to Bury St Edmunds. At the northern end of the village is the beautiful flint and stone church of St Mary the Virgin, the earliest parts of which date back to the 11th century. Its landmark steeple with flying buttresses was rebuilt in 1853 and soars to a height of 140ft.

Inside, there are some fine carved bench-ends depicting a varied assortment of allegorical animals, and a splendid brass eagle lectern presented by Elizabeth I. However, the crowning glory here is the host of feathered angels that decorate the beam ends of the magnificent double hammerbeam roof - a tribute to the restorers who replaced them after these and many of the church's other treasures were destroyed in the 17th century by order of a puritanical Parliament. Close by the church is a Lady's Well, which pilgrims visited regularly right up until the beginning of this century. Water from the well was said to be most efficacious in the treatment of eye complaints, and those hopeful pilgrims are remembered on a banner in the church which features a woman with bandaged eyes.

Woolpit also has a most interesting legend. The story goes that, in the 12th century, a boy and a girl with green skin were spotted climbing out of one of the old wolf-pits, dressed in clothes made from an unknown material. The kindly villagers adopted them and cared for them, and although the boy died young, the girl survived and gradually learnt to speak the English language. She told the villagers that she and her brother came from a twilight land called St Martin on the other side of a great river, and that they had been tending their father's sheep when a mysterious ringing of bells had led them into a cavern. They were led deeper and deeper underground, until they eventually emerged at the wolf-pits, to be discovered by the villagers in this strange new land. It is said that the girl lived a long and happy life - her skin took on a more human colour, and she grew up to marry a man from King's Lynn.

Two and a half miles further to the west, is the lovely **Old Rectory** in the village of Beyton. Mrs Charlesworth, the lively hostess is (more than willing to show you around the modernised rooms and splendid gardens while sharing with you her enthusiasm for local history and her extensive knowledge of Bury St Edmunds.

Did You Know...

There is a full list of

Tourist Information Centres

at the back of the book?

The Old Rectory, Church Road, Beyton, Bury St Edmunds
01359 70335

Keep an eye out for the old church next door with its round Saxon tower. A sight rarely seen outside Norfolk and Suffolk.

If you take the time to visit All Saints Church, look up at the flint-faced tower and you may notice that bricks from Woolpit have been used here to line the windows. Inside, the medieval octagonal font is quite plain, but this is more than compensated for by the 19th century pulpit with its intricate carvings and by the menagerie of beasts that decorates the choir stalls.

As befits a church dedicated to the King of East Anglia, St Ethelbert's in nearby **Hessett** is a splendid flint building which is obviously well-kept up by the parishioners. It has been described as a 'museum church' due to its many notable features, perhaps the best of them being some beautiful 16th century glass and a remarkable set of wall paintings that escaped the desecrations of the iconoclasts in 1643.

A glance at our map indicated the nearby rake factory at **Little Welnetham;** not as strange as it may first sound, as the local Monkspark and Felshamhall Woods at Bradfield are used to grow coppice. Trees are carefully cut or 'pollarded' to encourage branches to grow straight up like poles, which local woodworkers then transform into brooms, fence posts, scythe handles, and of course - rakes! Apparently, these ancient woodlands have been coppiced in this fashion since 1252, and if you are interested in finding out more about the process, there is a Visitor Centre here with plenty of useful information.

A few miles to the south, St Mary's Church in **Thorpe Morieux** is situated in as pleasant a setting as you could wish to find. With water meadows, ponds, a stream and a fine Tudor farmhouse to set it off, this 14th century church presents a memorable picture of old England. If you have had your fill of church interiors for a while - though St Mary's has much to interest the enthusiast - then at least take the time to wander around the peaceful churchyard here with its glorious profusion of aconites in early springtime, followed by the colourful flowering of limes and chestnuts in the summer.

Three miles to the south-east we came to the lovely village of **Hitcham,** which can be found midway between Sudbury and Stowmarket on the B1115. The racehorses of Newmarket may be well beyond the reach of the average purse, but here at the northern end of the village, we discovered a place where you can purchase a horse that requires minimal upkeep - just a quick polish every now and then!

This is Elm Tree Workshops, where fine rocking horses are made using traditional Victorian methods. At **Hitcham Horses,** each rocking horse is individually crafted from top quality hardwoods, finished with real horsehair mane and tail and leather tack made by a local master saddler. Visitors (who are asked to 'phone before they visit) are able to see the range of rocking horses and learn about the loving care which goes into creating each one. Antique rocking horses can often be seen undergoing restoration. New horses are usually available from stock, or special orders can be undertaken.

Hitcham Horses, Elm Tree Workshops, Hitcham 01449 740211

Just off the B1115 is the hamlet of Nedging, 4 miles North of Hadleigh, and **The Old Rectory,** the home of Rupert and Tess Chetwynd. This elegant Georgian building has been carefully restored, and each of the bedrooms, which are beautifully decorated, has its own bathroom;

dinner is available if you wish. There are reductions for people staying 3 nights or more. The house is non smoking, and pets are not allowed. There are 2 acres of delightful gardens at The Old Rectory, and for those of you who prefer self -catering, the Chetwynds have just converted an old stable with the same care and attention into a delightful retreat . Both the house and barn are open all year and you can be assured of a warm welcome from these charming hosts.

The Old Rectory, Nedging, Nr. Hadleigh, Suffolk. 0449 740745

Continuing south on the B1115, we passed through **Bildeston** with its long, winding High Street lined with 16th century timber-framed houses, then came to **Chelsworth**. Here, a picturesque two-arched bridge crosses the River Brett, which flows close by All Saints Church then makes its way through the parkland of Chelsworth Hall. The centre of the village is a vision of timber-framed, thatched houses, and once a year, almost every property in the village opens its colourful gardens to the public.

The Peacock Inn & Rooms, The Street, Chelsworth 0449 740758

305

Dating back to the 14th century, **The Peacock Inn** is a genuine oak timbered inn with inglenook fireplaces and its own unique character.

Across the road from the banks of the River Brett, the Peacock Inn is a prominent feature of the picturesque village of Chelsworth.

The Peacock Inn prides itself on imaginative freshly homecooked meals available seven days a week, with a selection of real ales and fine wines. They also have quaint letting rooms which makes this village inn the ideal traveller's rest.

From here we joined the A1141 and headed west, and at **Monks Eleigh**. Here, we called in at the fascinating dried flower centre, craft shop and tearoom, **Corncraft**, which was established nearly twenty years ago by Win and Royston Gage. On this seventy acre site, they grow a wide assortment of dried flowers and the strain of wheat known as 'Masterpiece' which is used in the ancient craft of 'corn-dolly' making. (Traditionally, the last sheaf of the harvest is preserved as a corn-dolly in order to keep alive the spirit of the corn.) Corn-dollies are available for visitors to purchase, along with pottery, prints, preserves and a good selection of traditional crafts.

Corncraft, Monks Eleigh, Nr Ipswich

Monks Eleigh is a perfect example of the traditional English village, with colour-washed thatched houses and a 14th century church grouped around the village green and pump. So picturesque is the setting, in fact, that it featured regularly on railway posters at one time to lure visitors to this beautiful corner of England.

Heading north-west from here on the A1141 and following the twisting course of the River Brett, we arrive at a place regarded by many to be the jewel in Suffolk's crown. **Lavenham** proudly claims to be the finest surviving medieval town in England, and once you have spent some time wandering through its twisting streets and marvelling at the wealth of magnificent buildings on every corner, you will find it hard to disagree.

From the 14th to 16th centuries, Lavenham flourished as one of the foremost and wealthiest wool and cloth-making centres in the country, specialising in blue broadcloth. The demise of this industry and the steady decline in the town's fortunes began in the second half of the 16th century, and ironically, it is largely due to the fact that Lavenham never found another industry to reverse its fall from prosperity that it remains such an attractive and fascinating town today. Unlike other places in Suffolk that saw an energetic program of rebuilding and redevelopment during the 18th century, there is no sweeping evidence of a Georgian 'invasion' as far as Lavenham's architecture is concerned - it was simply not rich enough at that time to make such a thing possible.

And so, centuries later, we find a delightful medieval and Tudor town which has remained almost untouched by later styles; firmly rooted in its ancient traditions, yet at the same time no mouldering museum piece but a thriving little town with much to offer today's visitors. The residents here have gone to great lengths to maintain the original character of the town: telegraph poles were removed in 1967 and cables buried underground, and even such familiar sights as television aerials have been hidden away in the attics of the houses!

Lavenham's medieval street pattern is still in existence today, complete with the market place and market cross - erected in 1501 and thought to have originally been a preaching cross. This was used as a setting in that wonderful old horror film: 'Witchfinder General'. Although the market place is almost entirely surrounded by timber-framed buildings (Lavenham has more than 300 buildings which are officially listed as being of architectural and historical interest) perhaps the finest of them all is the Guildhall. Dating from the early part of the 16th century, this was originally the meeting hall of the Guild of Corpus Christi, an organisation that regulated the production of local wool. It has since served many purposes, and has at various times been a prison, workhouse, almshouse and woolstore. It is now owned by the National Trust and houses a museum of local history, with a fascinating exhibition covering seven centuries of the cloth industry.

Also in the market place is the Little Hall, a 15th century former Hall House and now headquarters of the Suffolk Preservation Society. Both the house and its lovely enclosed garden are open to the public during the summer. Dating back originally to the 13th century, the Priory in Water Street was first the home of Benedictine monks, and was bought by a wealthy clothier after the Dissolution. The entire building as we see it today was completed by 1600. It contains medieval and Jacobean staircases,

Guildhall, Lavenham

The Crooked House, Lavenham

a Tudor brick fireplace, mullioned windows and the best examples of pargeting to be found anywhere in the town.

Now a private house, the Priory is open to visitors from Easter to the end of October, and you can also explore nearly four acres of grounds at the rear of the building, which feature a kitchen garden, a herb garden, a pond and a fascinating derelict building which illustrates the condition the property was in when the present owners took it over. Guided tours for groups can be arranged, and there is also a restaurant serving morning coffee, home-made lunches and afternoon teas, and a gift shop with a most unusual selection of gifts and crafts including woven tapestries and plants from the herb garden.

Across the road, the Wool Hall was built in 1464 and was originally the hall of Our Lady's Guild. It now forms part of the splendid Swan Hotel, but was nearly lost altogether in 1911 when the Duchess of Argyll decided to 'up timbers', dismantle the entire building and remove it to Ascot. Local feeling ran so high that the plan was abandoned, and the hall was returned to the town and re-erected in its rightful place. Lavenham also has its connections with the Arts: John Constable attended the Old Grammar School in Barn Street, and Shilling Grange in Shilling Street was once the home of Jane Taylor. Her name may not ring any bells at first, until you learn that she wrote that immortal nursery rhyme, familiar to us all, 'Twinkle Twinkle Little Star.'

Its here too that we called in at the **Bank House Tea Shop**, an attractive teahouse serving delicious home-made soups, salads and cakes. The oldest part of the building dates from the 16th-century and was originally used as a wool dyeing hall. Traces of wode can still be seen on some of the bricks in what is now the owners' part of the house. (They can sometimes be persuaded to let visitors view this area.)

Bank House Tea Shop, 95 High Street, Lavenham 01787 247154

When young children are in the house, the ghost of a very young girl sometimes appears on the landing. Nicknamed Emily, she is happily accepted by any children who encounter her.

John and Jean also have three letting rooms available which are located in the 17th-century part of the house. The two which are situated in the uppermost part of the building (mind your head on the sloping ceilings) have superb views of the famous Crooked House, and the third has a fine brass double bed. All three rooms share two bathrooms and have colour televisions, videos, hair dryers and tea/coffee making facilities.

Many of Lavenham's half-timbered houses stand at such crazy angles that you wonder what is actually stopping them from giving in to gravity and sliding down the streets - a good example being the Crooked House in the historic High Street.

The magnificent church of St Peter and St Paul stands on a hill above the town, completely dominating the view. Regarded as the greatest of all the 'wool churches' in East Anglia and declared by the 19th century architect August Pugin to be the finest example of Late Perpendicular in the world, it owes its cathedral-like appearance principally to the generosity of two great families, the Springs and the de Veres, Earls of Oxford. It was built during the late 15th and early 16th centuries to celebrate the end of the Wars of the Roses in 1485. Sadly, its original stained glass fell victim to the Puritan zealot William Dowsing, who was responsible for so much destruction in his role as 'Parliamentary Visitor to the Churches of Suffolk' - so the glass we see today is coloured Victorian. That aside, the interior has much for the visitor to enjoy, and if you are feeling especially fit you can even climb up the massive 140ft flint tower and take in the glorious views over Lavenham and the surrounding countryside.

Heading south from Lavenham on the B1071, we join the B1115 and travelled the last few miles into **Sudbury.** This ancient market town is situated in the Stour valley; the river flows around the town in a great loop, and the combination of picturesque watermeadows and gentle, rolling countryside makes for a very pleasant setting.

It is easy to see how such scenes of rural beauty must have inspired Sudbury's most famous son, Thomas Gainsborough. The painter was born here in 1727, and his birthplace and home for many years can be found in Gainsborough Street, just off Market Hill. It is now a museum housing a unique collection of Gainsborough's work, as well as that of a number of his contemporaries like Frost and Dupont. The museum is open most weekdays from 10.00am - 5.00pm and on Sundays from 2.00pm - 5.00pm, and do note that wheelchair access is limited to the ground floor. The gift shop sells prints and postcards of Gainsborough's work, and if you are planning on a longer stay in Sudbury, look out for details of the Print Workshop, set up in 1977 to run courses on printmaking. You can telephone (0787) 72958 for further information.

Sudbury's origins go right back to Saxon times, and its market was first mentioned in the Domesday Survey of 1086. In those days, the market was held between School Street and Stour Street, whereas today it is held at the bottom of Market Hill, every Thursday and Saturday. This was the largest of Suffolk's wool towns (with silk production coming later), and unlike Lavenham it kept its industry because it was a port.

One consequence of this was that it saw far greater changes in its architectural styles than its declining neighbour, and today's visitors can enjoy a wealth of historic buildings from many different periods. Among these are the mid-19th century Corn Exchange on Market Hill, now the public library; Salter's Hall (a merchant's house) and the Old Moot Hall in Stour Street - both 15th century timber-framed houses with ornate carving and oriel windows; and the remains of the Dominican Priory in Friars Street, which was founded in 1248 and now survives in parts as the Priory Gate and the Ship and Star inn.

In the heart of this lovely Suffolk town, we called in at the **Old Bull and Trivets**, a first-rate guest house and restaurant situated at the junction of Church and Cross Streets. This 16th century former coaching inn has been carefully restored so as to retain much of its original character. The charming guest rooms are now appointed to the highest modern standards, with most having en-suite facilities. The Old Bull is situated within easy reach of superb riverside walks and the Quay Theatre, and is an ideal base for exploring the surrounding Suffolk villages and countryside.

The Old Bull & Trivet, Church Street, Sudbury 01787 74120

The best of the afore-mentioned walks is the three-mile Valley Walk,

311

which takes you alongside the river through the watermeadows, following the course of the old Stour Valley railway line. Alternatively, if you feel like exploring the area from the river itself, look out for Sudbury Boathouse at Ballingdon Bridge, where rowing boats can be hired in the summer. Remember to take your sketch pad with you!

Standing beside the river and overlooking Friars' Meadow, the Quay is definitely the place to go for your evening's entertainment. This 200-year-old converted granary is considered to be one of East Anglia's most exciting arts centres, with cabaret, theatre, cinema, musical concerts and arts and crafts classes on offer here throughout the year.

Finally, those of you who enjoy visiting churches will need to set aside a few hours to indulge in your favourite pastime here, for there is much to see. All Saints Church in Church Street dates back to the 15th century and has a glorious carved tracery pulpit and screens; the 14th century St Gregory's, which stands to the north of the town on the Croft, boasts one of the finest medieval font covers in England; and St Peter's at the top of Market Hill has some wonderful painted screen panels and a splendid piece of 15th century embroidery on velvet, known as the 'Sudbury Pall'. Now a redundant church, St Peter's is used mainly as a concert hall, and outside stands a bronze statue of Sudbury's most famous son.

From Sudbury we make our way south on the B1508, following the course of the River Stour down as far as **Bures.** There, the river turns sharply to the east and heads off towards the coast, creating the natural boundary between Suffolk and North Essex. Straddling the Stour, this little town lies partly in Essex and partly in Suffolk, and on the Suffolk side of the river brick and half-timbered houses cling to a hillside overlooking the market place and St Mary's Church. Half a mile to the north-east on the road to Boxford, look out for the signpost to St Stephen's Chapel, which was consecrated in 1218 to commemorate the place where St Edmund was crowned King of East Anglia - on Christmas Day, 855 AD. From here you can make your way to the Arger Fen nature reserve, a pleasant stretch of varied woodland renowned for its springtime flowers.

Bures is also the headquarters of Blackwater Boats, who offer visitors the chance to take a traditional narrowboat holiday, cruising through the rural Essex countryside along the Chelmer and Blackwater Canal. We can think of no better way to enjoy yourself: lazing about on deck, drink in hand, gazing at the world going by on this quiet, willow-fringed waterway For details of short breaks and longer holidays, telephone (01787) 227823.

The narrow lane leading east from Bures is a sheer delight. Quickly dispelling any ideas you may have had that Suffolk is flat, this twisting road leads you deep into the heart of 'Constable country', high above the

Stoke by Nayland

River Stour, with green meadows dotted with solitary houses stretching out on either side.

The lane continues for about four miles until it joins the A134, where we crossed over onto the B1087 and came to the pretty village of **Nayland**. The narrow winding streets of Nayland are full of picturesque colour-washed houses with overhanging timbers, and right in the centre of the village are Alston Court - a 15th century house with mullioned windows and a large hooded 17th century door - and the parish church of St James, which dates from 1400. The chief treasure of the church is Constable's 'Christ's blessing of the Bread and Wine', which he painted in 1809. It hangs above the altar and is one of only two paintings by him to have a religious theme.

One of the most memorable views over the Stour valley can be enjoyed by taking the B1087 north-east of the village to neighbouring **Stoke-by-Nayland**.

This delightful village stands on a bluff of land which rises above the meadows of Dedham Vale. The Vale contains many country lanes and footpaths which are ideal for exploring on foot or by bicycle, and the village church with its 120ft tower appears in several Constable landscapes. At the crossroads in the centre of the village (the junction of the B1068 and B1087), we called in at the **Angel Inn**, a truly superb establishment run by Mr R Wright and his staff. The magnificent restaurant is situated in a converted barn which has a gallery and an unusual 40ft well. The menu features such specialities as red sea bream and Tournedos of beef in filo pastry, and traditional roast lunches are served on Sundays. In the bar, an extensive chalkboard menu is available at lunchtimes and in the evenings. The Angel also has six well-appointed guest rooms available, all with en suite facilities, colour televisions, direct dial telephones and tea/coffee making facilities.

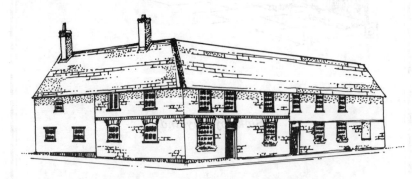

The Angel Inn, Stoke-by-Nayland, 01206 263245

314

The massive church of St Mary the Virgin seems almost preposterously large for a village of this size. Among the many impressive brasses and memorials inside is a 16th century brass of Lady Howard, an ancestor of two of Henry VIII's wives, Catherine Howard and Anne Boleyn. On a wooded hillside to the south of the church stands a neat little row of timbered almshouses, while a short stroll from the church into School Street leads you to two extremely fine 16th century half-timbered buildings, the Guildhall and the Maltings - now converted into cottages.

Stoke-by-Nayland stands just a short distance from the River Stour within an Area of Outstanding Natural Beauty,

Just over a mile to the north is **Polstead**, scene of the notorious 'Red Barn Murder'. It was here in 1827 that a young girl called Maria Marten was brutally murdered by William Corder, her lover and the father of her illegitimate child. It was widely thought that Maria had eloped with Corder to London and married him there, but her stepmother dreamed three times that she had in fact been murdered and buried in the barn. Pressed by his wife, Maria's father dug at the floor of the barn and found her body buried there. Corder was eventually tracked down to Middlesex, where he was married to a woman he had met through a matrimonial advertisement. He was found guilty of Maria's murder and hanged, and his skin was used to bind a copy of the trial proceedings. Together with Corder's scalp, this grisly document can be seen at Moyses Hall in Bury St Edmunds.

Those visitors who want to see the local scenes associated with this dreadful crime will find an excellent guide to the village in the church. The barn itself burned down shortly after the event, and the approximate site of Maria's grave is now marked by a sign - her tombstone having been chipped away over the years by souvenir hunters, eager for fragments to display on their mantle-pieces! The thatched cottage which was Maria's home still stands in what is now called Marten's Lane, as does the farm in the centre of the village where Corder lived - now known as Corder's Farm.

In stark contrast to all this unpleasantness, Polstead is in fact an extremely pretty village, nestling in wooded, hilly countryside and surrounded by cherry orchards - the 'Polstead Black' is regarded very highly by those who know their cherries! Thatched and colour-washed cottages surround the village green at the top of Polstead Hill, and as befits a place whose name means 'place of pools', a broad duck pond fringed with trees dominates the centre of the village at the bottom of the hill. Standing on a rise above the pond are Polstead Hall and the 12th century St Mary's Church, the latter being notable for its unusual brickwork. At this time, brick-making was almost unheard of in England, but the brickwork of the arches and windows suggests that the Norman builders here had perfected the craft which elsewhere was forgotten when the Romans left our shores.

Two miles north-west of Polstead, just to the north of the A1071, you will find yet another glorious example of an unspoilt Suffolk village. Surrounded by the peaceful watermeadows of the River Box, **Boxford** is a traditional weaving village with some of the most highly colourful houses to be found anywhere in the area. St Mary's Church dates back to the 14th century, and its wooden north porch is said to be the oldest one of its kind in the county, if not in England.

From here it is just a short drive along the A1071 into the pleasant market town of **Hadleigh**, with its comprehensive variety of architectural styles. Making your way down the mile-long High Street, you will find a wealth of timber-framed buildings still standing today as a reminder of the prosperity that came from the wool trade in the 14th to 16th centuries. Unlike Lavenham, however, there is also an abundance of plasterwork (some of it pargetted) together with fine houses from the Regency and Victorian periods. The 135ft broach spire of St Mary's Church soars above the town, and providing an interesting contrast alongside is the red-brick Deanery Tower, built by Archdeacon William Pykenham in 1495 and now a Grade I listed building. Opposite St Mary's in Church Square is a splendid group of medieval buildings which includes the timber-framed Guildhall with its two overhanging upper storeys, and backing on to this are the 19th century Town Hall and Corn Exchange.

There are two good walks from the town, the first being along the banks of the River Brett with access from the 500-year-old red-brick Toppesfield Bridge. This is said to be one of the oldest bridges in England still in use, and nearby you will find Toppesfield Hall, beautifully restored and now the headquarters of the East Anglia Tourist Board. Alternatively, you could choose to walk along the disused railway line between Hadleigh Old Station and Raydon, a distance of about two and a half miles through peaceful countryside full of wild flowers and birdlife.

Those looking for excellent bed and breakfast accommodation in the heart of rural Suffolk should make a point of finding **Ash Street Farm** in the domesday hamlet of Ash Street, near **Semer**. Situated in the lanes to the north of Hadleigh, please telephone the owners, Miranda and Edward Sprot (0449) 741493, for directions. The house stands in pretty country in the Brett valley. It has a fine, early timber frame, circa 1450, and has been sympathetically modernised. Both bedrooms have en-suite/private facilities and are well appointed. They have lovely views overlooking the garden which is partly formal and partly unadulterated meadow abundant with wild life. The Sprots happily welcome children and dogs and claim to cater for most eccentricities! Ash Street Farm is open all year and evening meals are available by arrangement.

Ash Street Farm, Ash Tree, Hadleigh, Nr Semer 01449 741493

Kersey, just off the A1141 two miles to the north-west of Hadleigh, is another picture-postcard village that you will definitely not want to miss. Nestling in the steep-sided valley of a tributary of the Brett, this delightful village seems completely transfixed in time. If you approach from the direction of Lavenham, the first thing you will see is the massive church of St Mary standing proud on its hilltop, then all of a sudden the village itself comes into view as you turn the corner into The Street. Making your way down the hill you pass by a glorious collection of medieval merchants' houses and weavers' cottages - their red-tiled roofs weathered with age and covered with lichen - until you reach the water-splash at the bottom.

The road then takes you steeply up Church Hill, where the sheer size of the church points to the prosperity the village once enjoyed through its production of tough Kersey broadcloth. St Mary's suffered greatly at the hands of iconoclasts at the time of the Reformation, and a number of headless angels and mutilated carvings bear witness to the havoc that was wreaked during that dark period in history. Nevertheless, some of its oldest treasures are still intact, and we particularly enjoyed the ornate flushwork of the 15th century south porch, with its roof of 16 traceried wooden panels inside.

Known to be one of the most photographed village inns in the country, **The Bell** dates back to 1320. A timber framed Tudor type property with open fires, a mass of timber beams and character like you've never seen before.

Whether it be morning coffee, lunch, afternoon cream tea or an evening meal, The Bell can offer you the finest. All locally purchased produce enables our chef to produce excellent creative and very tasty food. Whether it be a bar snack or a meal in our restaurant, you will not be disappointed.

A fine range of cask conditioned ales and wines, a large car park, a patio, families and children are welcome. This has to be one of the most beautiful country inns in Suffolk

The Bell Inn, Kersey 0473 823229

Two miles to the east of Hadleigh on the A1071 is Wolves Wood; and if the name brings to mind a dark and sinister place with wild creatures lurking behind every tree, nothing could be further from the truth. This is actually an R.S.P.B. reserve with woodland nature trails, well known for its spring orchids and nightingales in summer. The wood is open all year round at all times, and entry is free.

Further along the A1071 on the outskirts of Ipswich lies **Hintlesham** and Hintlesham Hall. The Hall was originally the Elizabethan home of the Timperley family, but was much altered during the 18th century. More recently, it was owned by that doyen of good taste and good food, Robert Carrier, and although it has since passed into different hands, it still maintains its excellent reputation for fine cuisine. If you wish to admire the exquisite Elizabethan plasterwork ceilings today, you will have to indulge in a meal; although the public footpath that passes through the grounds will afford you a glimpse of the handsome Georgian facade for free!

Three miles west of Ipswich, the A1100 connects the A12 to the A45. Near the village of **Sproughton**, midway between these two major routes, we found the first-rate freehouse, the **Beagle**. The house which was originally four 18th century farm cottages, was purchased in 1986 by William and Nicola Freeth. They set to work and after a great deal of toil and careful renovation, the Beagle was ready for opening the following year. Inside, the two bars have exposed beams and an atmosphere which is friendly and relaxed. As well as an excellent selection of beers, William and Nicola serve mouthwatering home-cooked meals such as pheasant casserole and pork and apricot pie. Lunches are served Monday to Saturday inclusive from 12 noon - 2.00 pm. There is also an attractive conservatory and beer garden.

The Beagle, Old Hadleigh Road, Sproughton, Ipswich
01473 730455

A mile further north, just two miles north-west of Ipswich, the B1067 crosses the River Orwell near the pleasant village of **Bramford** . The pretty little church of St Mary's and a fine collection of 16th and 17th century cottages gives this place plenty of character.

In the heart of the village, we stopped at the former coaching house, **The Angel Inn**, which was originally constructed in 1757.

Angel Inn Hotel & Restaurant, Bramford, Ipswich 01473 743402

Inside, the bar is decorated with many fine examples of historic memorabilia, much of it relating to a sporting theme. The restaurant is renowned for its food, most notably its steaks, vegetarian dishes and traditional Sunday lunches. A wide selection of bar snacks is also served. The Angel also has four comfortable guest rooms available, all of which have hot and cold washbasins and colour televisions. Outside, there is an attractive floodlit garden with a large children's play area.

Opposite the church, a 10-acre meadow adjacent to the River Gipping provides a lovely spot for a picnic, and fishing platforms have been erected here especially for the disabled. It also gives access to the Gipping River Path, a 17-mile walk along the old towpath of the river between Ipswich and Stowmarket. Those of you who are keen on watersports may prefer to make your way to the nearby Suffolk Water Park, where windsurfing and canoeing are available on the lake. Craft may be hired, and tuition is also provided.

North of Bramford is **Little Blakenham**, where the five-acre bluebell wood is thick with camellias, azaleas, rhododendrons, hydrangeas and climbing roses, and is open to the public from April to September on Wednesdays, Thursdays, Sundays and Bank Holidays from 1.00pm - 5.00pm.

From here we joined the B1113 and headed north. After passing through Great Blakenham our next stop was at **Needham Market**, where we must recommend that you take the time to visit the church of St John the Baptist.

Even if you are not normally moved by church architecture, we defy you not to be amazed by the magnificent roof here. From the outside the church looks unremarkable, but once you step inside, the strategically placed skylights give the massive hammerbeam roof a glorious infusion of light and allows you to fully appreciate the tremendous skills of those 15th century carpenters. It is so huge, in fact, that if it were to be removed and placed upon the ground, it would be as high as the walls of the church itself. On a less positive note, it is perhaps just as well that you automatically cast your eyes heavenwards as you enter the building, for the church is rather sparsely adorned otherwise and has little to commend it apart from its famous roof.

The River Gipping flows to the east of Needham's High Street, and bordering this is a 25-acre picnic site containing a large lake. You can reach this either from the town centre or from the junction of the A45/A140, and if you want to indulge in either fishing or watersport activities you will need to obtain a permit, as the lake is also used as a wildlife and wetland habitat.

Our last stop on this part of our tour was at the little country town of **Stowmarket**. You will find no buildings of any particular architectural merit here; but what you will find is a lively place with a refreshingly bustling atmosphere, especially on market days. Stowmarket enjoyed a rapid period of growth when the River Gipping was navigable between here and Ipswich, and although that particular trade is now a thing of the past, the town continues to prosper as the main shopping centre for a wide agricultural region.

Far and away the most popular attraction here is the excellent Museum of East Anglian Life, which is situated in the centre of town to the west of the market place, in a 70-acre meadow-land site on the old Abbot's Hall estate. The displays here cover a wide variety of subjects from domestic and working life to rural crafts, agriculture and the industrial heritage of the region, and there is a continually changing programme of craft demonstrations and special events throughout the year. Just to give you an idea of what you may expect to see during your visit, the annual programme would typically include everything from coopering, candle making, sheep shearing and spinning, to blacksmithing, saddlery, basket making, tractor ploughing, hedge laying and folk dancing - and much, much more!

In addition to all this, part of the open-air section features several historic buildings from around the region which have been carefully re-erected on site. These include an engineering workshop that dates from the 1870s, part of a 14th century farmhouse, and a working watermill and windpump - from Alton and Eastbridge respectively. The Museum also has a collection of steam engines which can be seen at work at various times of the year - as can 'Remus', the Museum's Suffolk Punch horse, just one of various local breeds of farm animal on display. If you plan to eat while you are here, the restaurant serves hot and cold meals and snacks, or alternatively, you can walk down to the banks of the Rattlesden River and enjoy a picnic in peace and quiet.

Many visitors who come here intending to stay just a few hours end up making a day of it; but however long your visit you will find plenty to hold your interest and that you will promise yourself a return trip one day.

Pakenham Windmill

CHAPTER ELEVEN

North-East Suffolk

Orford Church

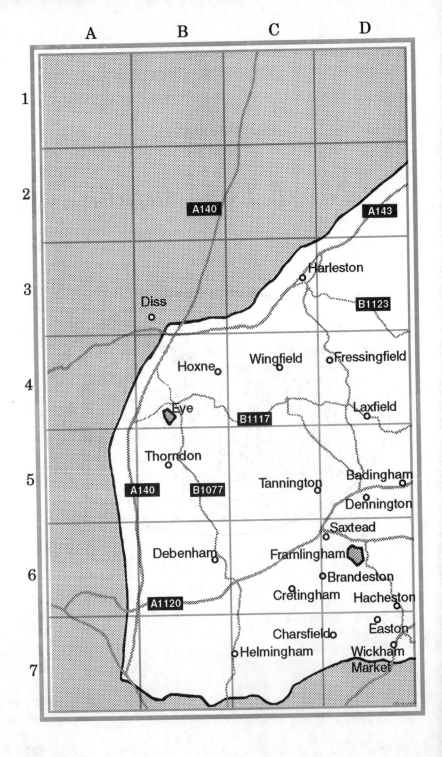

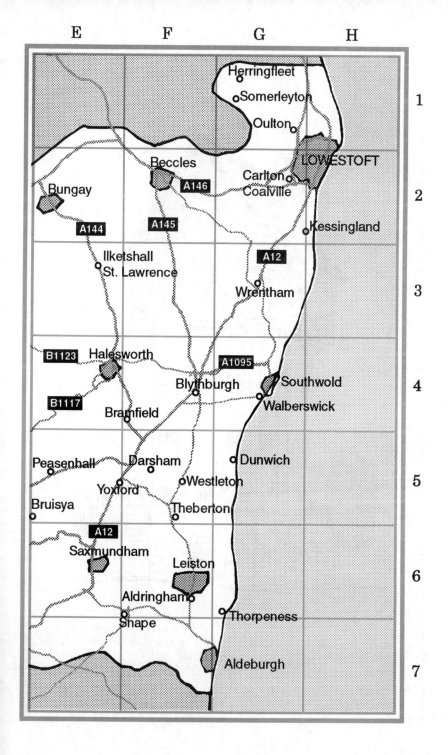

House in the Clouds, Thorpeness

CHAPTER ELEVEN

North-East Suffolk

Picking up from where we left off in the last chapter, we head east on the A1120 Stowmarket to Yoxford road and make our way slowly towards the Suffolk coast - 'slowly' for we found plenty of distractions on the way to tempt you from our chosen route.

Our first stop was to the south of the main road in the winding country lanes four miles south-west of Framlingham, where we came to the delightful village of **Cretingham**.

Here, we called in at the **Cretingham Bell**, a fine country freehouse and informal restaurant run by Jackie and Terry Bywater. Located in an idyllic village setting, this handsome Tudor building retains much of its original character. Inside, there are wooden floorboards, oak-beamed ceilings and half-timbered walls. Jackie, Terry and their staff serve an excellent range of freshly cooked meals including grills, fish dishes, vegetarian main courses and 'old favourites' such as Cretingham Papple (pork in apple sauce topped with suet pastry). Children have a special menu and are welcome in the family room and gardens.

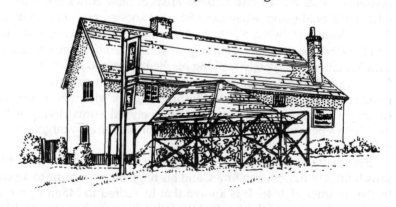

*The Cretingham Bell, The Street, Cretingham, Nr Otley,
Woodbridge 01728 685419*

A mile and a half to the east is **Brandeston**, where in 1645 the villagers took the unusual step of declaring the local vicar, John Lowes, to be guilty of witchcraft. This was during the height of the Civil War, and it is likely that their actions were prompted by the fact that Lowes was known to

327

have Royalist sympathies. He was interrogated by the infamous 'Witchfinder General', Matthew Hopkins, who put such intense pressure on the 80-year-old clergyman that he eventually broke down and admitted his 'guilt'. One of the trumped-up charges that poor Lowes had to answer to was the sinking of a ship off the coast at Harwich - despite the fact that there was no evidence to suggest that any such vessel had gone missing at that time. He was hauled off to Bury St Edmunds to be executed, and as no priest was allowed to conduct the burial service of a condemned witch, he was forced to read it to himself before his sentence was carried out.

A failed lawyer from Manningtree in Essex, Matthew Hopkins preyed upon the superstitions of those unsettled times to carve himself a new career at which he truly excelled. Between the years 1645 to 1646, his new-found profession as Witchfinder General enabled him to fully utilise his talent for bullying old women into confessing to the most ludicrous of crimes. A profitable business it proved to be too - Stowmarket, for example, paid him the then handsome sum of £23 for his services. Although the precise number is unknown, it is thought that Hopkins was responsible for the sentencing and execution of around 400 unfortunate souls.

His methods of detecting witches ranged from identifying household pets as 'familiars' to seizing upon physical blemishes such as warts or moles and declaring them to be the marks of the Devil. One of his favourite tricks was to stab at these areas of his victim's body with a retractable blade, and when astonished witnesses saw that no blood flowed from the 'wound', they could do little but agree with the witchfinder's prognosis! Obtaining the desired confession was then a simple matter of endlessly walking his victims up and down their cells for days and nights on end, starving them half to death, or employing any number of other equally dreadful tortures that fell within the bounds of the law at that time. Needless to say, any lonely old woman living on her own with a pet moggy as her sole companion was an easy target for this evil man.

Eventually, Hopkins' methods proved too much for even the hardened sensibilities of those harsh times, and his reign of terror came to an end in the summer of 1646. It is known that he retired to Manningtree in relative affluence and that he died the following year, but reports differ as to how he met his end. Some say that he died of tuberculosis, but those with a keen sense of poetic justice may prefer to believe the other story. This states that he was accused of being a witch himself, and after failing one of his own favourite tests by floating in the water into which he was thrown, he was found guilty and hanged.

Four miles to the south-west is **Helmingham** on the B1077.

Helmingham Hall is a lovely moated Tudor Hall with a working drawbridge that is still drawn up every night. It stands within a 400-acre park where you can take a safari ride and see the herds of 600 red and fallow deer, Highland cattle and wild Soay sheep to good advantage. Although the Hall itself is not open to the public, the park and gardens can be seen every Sunday between 2.00pm and 6.00pm from 28th April to 15th September. There is a superb walled kitchen garden and wild flower garden, and a more recent attraction is the traditional Knot garden with its glorious collection of old-fashioned roses - the combination of scents here can only be described as heavenly!

Traditional cream teas are served in the Old Coach House, and the Stable Shop and farm shop stock a varied range of gifts and produce from the gardens. Helmingham Hall has been the family seat of the Tollemache family since the late 15th century, and they have been in almost unbroken occupation ever since. In 1886, one of the family established a local brewery, which later merged with another to become the famous Tolly Cobbold of Ipswich - a name which every visitor to this part of England will quickly become acquainted with.

Another moated house can be found just two miles to the south-east at **Otley**. Far smaller than Helmingham, but dating from the same period, the fine timber and brick Otley Hall is open to visitors at weekends throughout the summer months. During the 16th century it was the home of Bartholomew Gosnold, the founder of Jamestown in Virginia and the discoverer of Cape Cod.

Over to the east, just off the B1078 at **Charsfield,** we discovered another garden that is open to the public during the summer. Its setting can claim neither the heritage nor the grandeur of the gardens at Helmingham Hall, for this is the quarter-acre cottage garden of a semi-detached house in Park Lane known as 'Akenfield' - so called by its owners as a tribute to Ronald Blythe's thought-provoking book of the same name. Blythe partly based his book on the village of Charsfield, which he describes as 'a little arable kingdom where flints are the jewels and where existence is sharp-edged'. This description is probably just as apt today as in 1967 when the book was first published, offering a unique insight into the harsher realities of living and working in these idyllic rural areas. The garden of its namesake is open daily between 24th May to 28th September, from 10.30am till dusk.

The lovely village of **Easton** can be found two miles north-east of here near the River Deben, and is without doubt one of the most colourful places you may encounter on this part of our tour. To say that the locals enjoy a spot of gardening would be an obvious understatement, for during the summer months the entire village seemed bedecked with flowers of every conceivable colour. Easton Park lies to the west of the village, protected by a two-mile long crinkle-crankle wall that completely surrounds it.

Easton Farm Park is a delight to visit, and will give you and your family a wonderful day out. It was opened to the public in April 1974, and has given enjoyment to thousands of people ever since.

Set in one of the most picturesque parts of the Deben valley, the farm buildings were built by the Duke of Hamilton as a model farm in 1870. Buildings on the site were either cleared or refaced to fit in with the new design. No farmhouse existed on the site. The Duke lived at Easton Park, which was demolished in 1929, but surrounded by the serpentine wall still visible in the village today. However, there are two cottages, one for the farm foreman and the other for the laundry and dairymaids. At that time there were also two small cowsheds for the milking of the Red Poll dairy herd, stables for the Suffolk Punches which worked on the farm, poultry units, a laundry, an unusual octagonal dairy, as well as the usual barns and cart sheds.

The estate was split up and sold in 1919, following the death of the Duke, who had no male successor. Since then the estate has been sold on more than one occasion, and improved farming methods and changes of lifestyle have rendered most of the buildings unsuitable for modern agriculture. However as listed buildings they lend themselves very well to be used as the centre for the Farm Park.

On the low-lying water meadows you can see the farm animals. Some are commercial, and some have become quite rare due to their unsuitability for modern requirements. The same meadows, along with the wooded areas, some natural and some cultivated, make up the Nature Trail which, along with the rest of the Farm Park, won the Farming and Wildlife Advisory Group - Bayer Farm Trails Award.

Cattle at Easton Farm Park

It is interesting to note some of the facts about Easton Park because, as well as providing a pleasant day out for all the family, it is capable of producing 1.5 million litres of milk, 1,500 tonnes of wheat, 750 tonnes of barley, 300 tonnes of sugar, 150 tonnes of oilseed rape, 300 tonnes of freezing peas and 300 tonnes of freezing beans. Impressive isn't it?

The Dairy Centre was built specifically for the use of the public, with walkways over the top of the cow cubicles and a viewing gallery over the milking parlour. It gives the public a better insight into where their daily pint of milk really comes from; not a bottle as some people think!

The Victorian Dairy

In total contrast to the very modern Dairy Centre is the Victorian Dairy, an ornate building with marble shelves and painted doors, with a fountain in the middle which was used to keep the air moist for the butter and cheese etc. It is a unique building, and is especially interesting because of its octagonal shape.

Easton Farm Park, Easton, Woodbridge   01728 746475

Do not miss seeing the 'Suffolk Trinity', the three breeds of Suffolk in their home county: Red Poll cattle, Suffolk Punch horses and Suffolk sheep; it is a rare combination. Today Red Poll cattle are a rare breed, and in today's world the Suffolk Punch horse is becoming almost as rare. It is the Suffolk sheep that are still used commercially in modern agriculture.

The farm also has a forge. You could be forgiven for thinking of a forge being a building solely for the shoeing of horses, which primarily it is, but with the mechanism of farming it became the forerunner of the modern workshop, and the blacksmith was a mechanic, mending and making machinery. The difference between the farrier and the blacksmith is distinguished here, with the latter not being qualified to shoe horses.

Old steam engines are always good to see. At Easton there is a splendid steam engine called 'Little Ben', which was built in 1878 by Ransome Sims and Jefferies. He can often be seen at work about the Farm Park.

In between seeing all these things, do find time to enjoy the tearoom which has a wide range of refreshments, including dairy cream teas and home-made cakes. There is also a gift shop, which is full of nice things, most of them at affordable prices.

There is something very special about Easton Farm Park; the ambience is right. You do not feel overpowered by commercialism, as so often happens. Visitors are free to wander about at their leisure and take in the beautiful countryside with walks down the farm trails and along the banks of the Deben.

We watched children enjoying themselves, because they can really get close to the animals. Even toddlers can get friendly with the smaller animals, such as rabbits and chickens etc. Grandparents will enjoy the sense of the past; the beautiful Victorian buildings and the vintage machinery will remind them of the 'Good Old Days'. A place wholeheartedly recommend it for all the family, no matter what the age.

Taking a lane to the east of Easton, we soon arrive at the small village of **Hacheston**, which lies midway between Wickam Market and Framlingham on the B1116.

Those looking for top quality bed and breakfast accommodation in this delightful part of rural Suffolk should look out for **Cherry Tree House** on the south-eastern side of the village. This splendid oak-beamed house dates from 1641 and inside it retains many of its original 17th century features. The well-appointed guest rooms are very spacious and are equipped with hot and cold washbasins. They also have magnificent views over the large landscaped garden and surrounding countryside. Owners Joan and Graeme Hall have a flair for English and Continental cooking and, given prior notice, can provide their guests with first-class evening meals.

Cherry Tree House, Hacheston, Woodbridge 01728 746371

Parham , whose moated grange is now a farmhouse, lies one mile further north on the B1116. Those of you who are interested in the role played by Allied fighter pilots should take time to visit the Air Museum here, which is devoted to the history of East Anglian aviation during the Second World War. A detailed exhibition of engines, photographs and other memorabilia from the RAF, the US 8th Air Force, and indeed the German Air Force too, is housed here in the control tower of the former base of the USAAF 390th Bomber Group. In addition to the excellent collection of material in the Museum itself, a library and archives centre has also been established in one of the base's old Nissen huts. The Museum is open every Sunday from 12.00am - 6.00pm, March to October, and admission is free.

Continue northwards on this road until you come to its junction with the B1119, and you will get a good view of Framlingham Castle. Sitting atop its hill, brooding over the little town of **Framlingham** below, its 13 towers and linking walls are so well-preserved that you can readily imagine the bustling scenes of medieval life it would have witnessed at the time of its construction in the 12th century. The reed-fringed mere which lies alongside adds its own special charm to the picture. One amusing aspect of the castle is that the battlements of many of the towers and parts of the walls are surmounted by somewhat incongruous looking red-brick twisted chimneys, added during the 16th century. You might assumed that these would at least serve a practical purpose, but in fact most of them are false!

The second Earl of Norfolk, Roger Bigod, built the structure that we see today on the site of his grandfather's original wooden dwelling, which was surrounded by a ditch and palisade. After the Bigods, the

Framlington Castle

Herringfleet Drainage Windmill

castle changed hands many times. The Howards, Dukes of Norfolk, were here until 1635 when they sold the estate to the Hitchams, and perhaps its most famous occupant was Mary Tudor, who was given the castle by her brother, Edward VI. It was here that she organised her campaign against Lady Jane Grey, and here that she proclaimed herself Queen.

The castle's near immaculate condition is attributable to the fact that in all its history, it was only once under seige - by King John in 1215. Apart from its defensive role, it was also used as a prison for priests who dared to defy Elizabeth I, and in the 17th century, after Sir Robert Hitcham bequeathed the castle to Pembroke College, Cambridge, it became a home and school for local paupers. The 18th century poor house was built against the inside of the west wall in place of the castle living quarters, and is now the home of the castle's custodian. Those of you with a head for heights can climb the spiral staircase and walk right around the top of the walls as far as the ninth tower, and from here you can enjoy the glorious views over mere, town and surrounding countryside. Framlingham Castle is now maintained by English Heritage, and in the north wing you will also find the Lanman Museum with its collection of farm and craft tools and domestic bygones.

Framlingham itself is a thriving little market town with narrow streets containing many buildings of character, some excellent antique shops and a number of fine inns. St Michael's Church contains the tombs of Sir Robert Hitcham and several of the Howards, together with a beautiful and very rare Carolean organ presented by Pembroke College in 1708.

While you are in the Framlingham area do take a look at **Shawsgate Vineyard**, managed by Rob and Penny Hemphill.

The 17 acre vineyard is only a mile from Framlingham, and is one of the largest vineyards in East Anglia. It was established in 1973, but it was not until Ian Hutcheson bought it in 1985 that major restoration was undertaken. New post and wirework has been constructed, windbreaks have been planted and gaps in the existing vineyard filled.

The majority of the grapes are Muller Thurgau and Seyval Blanc, but they have introduced Bacchus and Reichensteiner. All these varieties of grape produce white wine, and a rose wine is shortly being introduced.

In 1987 the winery was built. It has been fully equipped with stainless steel winemaking equipment, including a press, grape trailer, bottling line and vats used for the fermentation and storage of the wine. The grapes are picked in October and the wine is then bottled in April. Great care is taken during wine making to ensure that the highest standards are maintained, so the best quality wine is produced.

A walk round the vineyard is available to those who choose a guided tour; a very worthwhile choice. The tour comprises of a half hour tour of the winery, a walk round the vineyard and a wine tasting.

Shawsgate Vineyard, Badingham Road, Framlingham
01728 724060

The shop sells not only the vineyard wines but many wine related items. There were some beautiful dried flowers grown on the property, and vines. From time to time they cater for Wine Societies, other associations and clubs (frequently there are evening visits, by prior appointment of course, although normally their opening hours are 10.30 am to 5.00 pm) who come to learn more and enjoy the experience. It is a excellent outing for someone who is disabled, because the area is completely level. There is a children's play area, and a picnic site which you are welcome to use. We spent a very contented and informative three hours there.

It is also worth noting that Shawsgate have another outlet known as Shawsgate English Wines at Walberswick on the Coast.

From here we headed north-west on the B1119 and rejoined the A1120 at **Saxtead Green**. The main attraction here is undoubtedly the charming 18th century mill that stands on the marshy green from which the village takes its name. This is a wonderful example of a traditional Suffolk post mill, so-called because it was built on a single pivot post around which the entire body of the mill rotates when the wind changes direction. This particular mill is known to date back to at least 1796, although there has been a mill on the site since 1309. Its working life came to an end in 1947, and although it no longer grinds corn professionally, it is still maintained in perfect working order today by English Heritage. Visitors can climb the steep wooden ladder into the body (or 'buck') of the mill, which is built of elegant white weatherboarding and stands upon a brick roundhouse. Once inside, you can explore the various floors and get a close look at how the intricate mill machinery works. The mill is open from the beginning of April to the end of September, every day except Sundays.

Following a major refurbishment to restore this beautiful Suffolk inn back to its former glory with open fires, flagstone floors, timber beams, a range of fine cask ales, an excellent menu both lunchtime and evening, with a special lunchtime buffet, **The Old Mill House** is now one of the leading village freehouses in the county. Children are welcome in the restaurant.

It has wonderful gardens with a large fishpond and is situated on the village green at Saxtead, opposite the famous windmill. This house is a must for connoisseurs of good food, ales and wines.

Full of character in very warm and friendly surroundings.

The Old Mill House, The Green, Saxtead Green 0728 685064

Five miles to the west on the B1077, we discovered that the art of rush weaving still flourishes in **Debenham**, an attractive village where little streams trickle merrily along the back streets then meet to form the River Deben. The river flows beside and under the main street, and in a building beside the bridge in Water Lane you can watch the weavers practising their craft and purchase samples of their work, including baskets, mats and carpets.

On a ridge above the village stands St Mary's Church, which is known to date back in parts to Saxon times and boasts a splendid roof of alternating hammerbeams and crested tie beams on arched bases. A number of the older village houses were destroyed by fire in 1744, but there are still many interesting buildings left to see. The best of these include the fine row of Tudor houses opposite the church; the 16th century Red Lion Hotel with its original decorated plaster ceiling; the old market hall with its overhanging upper storey, which dates back to 1666 and was later used as Hitchams School; and opposite this, the 15th century timber-framed Guildhall which now houses the Debenham Gallery.

About four miles north of Debenham, and just to the west of the B1077, we made a point of stopping in the peaceful village of **Thorndon**. Here we called in at **Dowlands Restaurant**, a first-rate establishment owned and run by Jose-Luis Jaen-Galan. Parts of the building date back to Elizabethan times and inside, the atmosphere is spacious and elegant. The restaurant is renowned for the quality of its cuisine. Each dish is personally prepared by the owner and the menu is changed every day. Dowlands Restaurant is open on Thursday, Friday and Saturday evenings, and at lunchtime on Sundays. Pre-booking is essential.

Dowlands Restaurant, Thorndon, Eye 01379 71262

Two and a half miles further on, the B1077 meets the B1117 at the handsome little market town of **Eye**. It takes its name from the old Saxon word for island, and was at one time completely surrounded by water. It was founded in the 11th century by a supporter of William the Conqueror, one William Malet, who built his Norman castle on high ground above the marshes on the eastern side of the town. This was demolished by Cromwell's army in 1655, and all that now remains is the mound itself - serving no other purpose than to give you a superb vantage point over the town and the watermeadows of the River Waveney. The castellated folly that stands on top of the mound was built in 1845, using stones from the ruins of the castle. Alongside, the superb flushwork tower of the 15th century church of St Peter and St Paul soars to a height of 101ft, and inside you will find the magnificent rood screen, restored in 1925, with its exquisite painted panels depicting St Edmund, St Ursula, St Edward the Confessor and Henry VI.

Hoxne - somewhat confusingly pronounced 'Hoxen' as opposed to 'Hoxney' - can be found three miles north-east of Eye on the B1118. Its curious name is thought to mean a 'hock-shaped spur of land'. This is a lovely little village, full of charm and character, with thatched cottages around the green and houses of timber, brick and plaster on the outskirts. It was here in 870 AD that King Edmund was defeated by the Danes, and captured - according to a local legend - after attempting to hide under nearby Goldbrook Bridge. The story goes that a newly married couple spotted the glint of his spurs reflecting in the River Dove, and hoping for a reward, they denounced him to his enemies. Not surprisingly, Edmund uttered a dreadful curse on all newly-weds who might cross the bridge from that day on, and they say that bridal couples since that time have heeded his words by steadfastly avoiding this particular route.

A Benedictine priory was founded here to commemorate Edmund's martyrdom, and his body lay buried in the chapel for many years before it was transferred to Bury St Edmunds. Nothing remains of the priory today, but the 16th century timber-framed Abbey Farmhouse now stands on the site. In the church of St Peter and St Paul is an oak screen depicting scenes from the life of the saint, which was carved from the wood of a tree that collapsed in 1848 - said, in fact, to be the self-same oak to which the king was tied and shot full of arrows by the Danes centuries before. Legend has it that when the tree fell down, an arrowhead was discovered embedded in the trunk.

If you continue heading east on the B1118 then follow the signs to the little hamlet of **Wingfield**, you will find one of the most historic seats of education in this country, Wingfield College. It was founded in 1362 as a college of priests, following a generous bequest from Sir John Wingfield, Chief of Council to the Black Prince. Surrendered to Henry VIII at the time of the Dissolution, it then became a farmhouse in the 18th century and is now a private house; but behind the Georgian facade lies the original medieval building with its splendid Gothic timber-framed great hall. The College is open to the public at weekends during the summer, and is also used as a venue for a superb range of music concerts and arts events throughout the year - telephone (01379) 384505 for details.

On a hill to the north-west of the village are the remains of a castle built in 1382 by the first Earl of Suffolk, Michael de la Pole. In the church of St Peter and St Paul at **Fressingfield**, two miles to the east on the B1116, you can still see the bench where Alice de la Pole, wife of William, the first Duke of Suffolk, carved her initials in an idle moment. Perhaps the sermon failed to hold her attention that day, or maybe she was contemplating the possibilities of carrying on the literary traditions of her family - for her grand-father was none other than that great English poet, Geoffrey Chaucer. Another high-born lady associated with Fressingfield is 'Fair Margaret' of Willingham Hall, whose great beauty is said to have captured the heart of the future Edward I, here on a hunting expedition. Answering a summons from his father, Henry III, Edward left his new-found love in the care of the Earl of Lincoln - an unwise move as it transpired, for the Earl then married her himself!

South-west of here on the B1117 is **Laxfield**, where All Saints Church is distinguished by the most glorious flushwork to its Perpendicular tower, roof and nave. The village is widely held to be the birthplace of that notorious iconoclast, William Dowsing, who we met earlier in these pages. He was chosen by Cromwell to wreak havoc in Suffolk's churches and to destroy just about everything that was glorious in them. Stained glass, crucifixes, screens; in fact, anything of beauty that was deemed to be 'superstitious', carved or painted, was smashed or burned. It is said that at the height of his campaign of licensed desecration, Dowsing was destroying as many as 1,000 church ornaments in a single day! We can only assume that the memorial to him in Laxfield's church is a classic case of Christian forgiveness.

Thankfully, plenty of interesting relics remain to be viewed at the Laxfield and District Museum, which can be found opposite the church in the timber-framed, brick-nogged Tudor Guildhall. In addition to the various displays of local natural history and geology, the other exhibits include a costume room, a mock-up of a Victorian kitchen and village shop, and a beehive which gives the viewer an insight into the industrious lifestyle of these busy creatures and their fascinating hexagonal abodes.

A far more unusual creature can be found carved on one of the bench-ends in the centre aisle at St Mary's Church in **Dennington**, some four miles south-west of Laxfield on the A1120. One of many glorious carvings in the church that escaped the depredations of Dowsing, this is the only carving in England of the sciapod; a mythical creature of the African desert, humanoid in appearance but sporting an enormous boat-shaped foot which he appears to be using as a sunshade. Either that, or he is indulging in some sort of esoteric meditation - which leads us neatly on to **Badingham**, just off the A1120 to the north-east of Dennington, where Badingham House is now the home of the Academy of Transcendental Meditation. During the summer months, it is possible to visit the grounds to enjoy the woodland walks and contemplate the walled garden and tranquil lake - but those who wish to contemplate further should make their own enquiries,

Bruisyard Vineyard and Herb Centre, Church Road, Bruisyard, Saxmundham 0728 75281

South-east of here, on a minor country road four miles west of the Saxmundham Bypass, we came to the famous church of St Peter at **Bruisyard**. A short distance to the west, we discovered the **Bruisyard**

Vineyard and Herb Centre, a splendid winery producing a award-winning Bruisyard St Peter English wine. In 1974/75, 10 acres were planted with over 13,000 Müller Thurgau grapevines and in late October each year, bunches of ripe grapes are harvested and transported to the winery for pressing, fermentation and bottling. Visitors can see this process in action before trying the final product in the winery courtyard. In the grounds, there is also a large ornamental herb garden, a wooded picnic area, water gardens and a delightful restaurant and tea shop.

Back on the A1120 at **Peasenhall,** another most peculiar creature can be seen climbing up one side of the arch of the porch at St Michael's Church, all set to encounter the dragon ascending the other side. This is the 'woodwose' or wildman of the woods, covered in hair from head to toe and holding what looks like a shield, or possibly a lyre of some kind, in his left hand.

If you carry on to the end of the main road you will come to **Yoxford,** a former 18th century coaching town set in the valley of the River Yox. The Three Tuns Hotel was then the destination of coaches that would turn off the London to Yarmouth road for rest and refreshment before the last stretch of their journey into Yarmouth; but sadly the hotel is no more, having burnt down in 1926. What you will find, however, is a wealth of interesting shops displaying all manner of arts and crafts and antiques.

Those with a yen for pottery should pop into the **Milestone House Pottery** in the High Street, where they will find a wide range of pottery items for domestic use, as well as pots of all sizes for the garden in both plain and decorated stoneware. All this is housed in a wonderfully ornate 18th century building, which derives its name from a 150-year-old milestone outside. Another sign of distinction is the 1830 cast-iron signpost outside St Peter's Church, which is reputed to be one of only two of a kind in the country. Its hands, pointing to London, Yarmouth and Framlingham, are set unusually high so as to be on the level of the driver's seat on a stagecoach.

Among the varied styles of architecture to be found in Yoxford's long High Street are a number of traditional colour-washed cottages, some of them in the distinctive 'Suffolk Pink'. Visitors who have come to know and love this pretty colour in their travels around the county may be somewhat put off to learn that at one time it was achieved by mixing copious dollops of pig's blood into the plaster. However, the same effect was also arrived at with sloe juice.

A mile north of Yoxford, we turned east off the A12 to reach the pleasant village of **Darsham.** On the edge of the village, we found **Priory Farm,** a 200-acre working farm run by Hugh and Suzanne Bloomfield. Here, they provide bed and breakfast, self-catering accommodation and an excellent cycle hire service. The Granary self-catering apartment sleeps four to six people and is located on the first floor of a tastefully converted 17th century granary. It is fully equipped and has its own garden. Hugh and Suzanne also run Byways Bicycles, a hire service with a fleet of over 100 mountain, touring and childrens bikes. Priory Farm is an ideal base for exploring Suffolk's Heritage Coast and the heathlands of Minsmere and Dunwich.

Priory Farm, Darsham, Saxmundham 01728 77459

Further north on the A144 between Halesworth and Bungay and not too far from Beccles, there is a village called **Ilketshall St Lawrence**, where you will find Cherry Tree Farm, the home of **The Cider Place**. It is a small family concern run by the Coules. They produce a unique range of two- year -old cider, apple juices and country wines, which are all home products grown at Cherry Tree Farm. They use old crushing mills and a press, which are over 120 years old. These can be seen in working order, together with some 60 stillage and storage barrels.

The press can be seen working on some days from Mid-September to December but do ring to make sure, the telephone number is Ilketshall 353.

Mr Coules showed us their range of 16 or so varieties of country wines, made from English hedgerow and soft fruits grown on the farm, and mead made from local honey. In fact, when we looked around there were bottles of cider vinegar, some 25 locally made jams, jelly-preserves and several varieties of marmalade. There is also a wide collection of pickles, chutneys pickled eggs and onions, as well as Norfolk and Suffolk honey and hand-made chocolates and fudges.

We were told that the farm attracts a large number of people of all ages and all walks of life, who are pleased to discover that the produce is natural and free from preservatives. If you are lucky you will be invited to taste some of the ciders and wines, you will get individual attention, and one of the Coules family will be delighted to explain the history and process of cider making. Cherry Tree Farm is open seven days a week all the year round from 9.00 am to 1.00 pm and 2.00 pm to 6.00 pm, but is closed Wednesday and Friday mornings.

By appointment visitors may try their luck at fishing for trout or carp in either of the waters. Fees and times are upon application, and you will need to provide your own baits and tackle.

The Cider Place at Cherry Tree Farm, Ilketshall St Lawrence, Nr Beccles 01986 81353

A little further up the A12 we turned onto the A144 and headed north-west to **Bramfield**. The massive Norman round tower of St Andrew's Church is separate from the main building, and was built originally as a defensive structure with walls over three feet thick. This, however, did not deter William Dowsing from making his way here in April 1643 and destroying '24 superstitious pictures: one crucifix and picture of Christ: and twelve angels on the roof'. The church itself dates back to the 14th century and is thatched, and has two particularly interesting features inside.

The first is the magnificent monument to Sir Arthur Coke and his wife, with Arthur kneeling, resplendent in full armour, and Elizabeth lying on her bed with a baby in her arms. On a more light-hearted note is the long-winded and highly amusing epitaph to Bridget Applethwaite, who succumbed when: 'the Fatigues of a Married Life, Borne by Her with Incredible Patience', finally did for her! After enjoying the 'Glorious Freedom Of an Early and Unblemisht Widowhood' for several years, 'She Resolved to run the Risk of a Second Marriage-Bed, But DEATH forbad the Banns'. It appears that she was unwilling to give in gracefully to 'that Grand Enemy of Life', for she suffered 'terrible Convulsions,

Plaintive Groans or Stupefying Sleep, Without recovery of Speech, or Senses', before finally throwing in the towel on 12th September 1737.

The A144 then led us to the attractive little market town of **Halesworth**. Although there is nothing of outstanding architectural interest here, the Market Place has a fine (if rather shabby) example of an Elizabethan timber-framed house, and the picturesque group of buildings round a courtyard known as The Maltings are worth seeing too. We also paid a visit to the Halesworth and District Museum in Steeple End, which has been converted from a row of 17th century almshouses and contains a good collection of fossils, prehistoric flints and medieval finds from local excavations. Above this is Halesworth Art Gallery with its various exhibitions of paintings and sculptures, and entrance to both the museum and the gallery is free. While we were here, we were interested to discover that Sir William Jackson Hooker and his son Joseph lived at Brewery House to the north of the town, not far from The Maltings. Both were renowned botanists, and were, respectively, the first and second directors of the Royal Botanic Gardens at Kew.

The ancient fortress town of **Bungay** lies halfway between Diss and Lowestoft, at the point where the A143 and several other important roads meet to bridge the River Waveney. The river skirts the town on three sides and forms the natural border between Suffolk and Norfolk. It played a vital part in Bungay's fortunes for hundreds of years, with coal, corn, malt and timber being the principal cargoes of the lighters and sailing wherries that plied between here and the coast until well into the 18th century. Although it is now no longer navigable above Geldeston, the Waveney continues to be a favourite haunt of anglers and the boating fraternity.

Bungay has a great deal going for it as far as sight-seeing is concerned. To the west of the Market Place with its fine lead-covered 17th century Butter Cross are the impressive remains of Bungay Castle, built by the last Earl Bigod in 1165. To the north are Bungay's two surviving churches (the Domesday Book recorded five), the oldest and smallest being Holy Trinity; its north wall dating back to around 1000 and its Saxon round tower being added some 40 years later. St Mary's Church had to be rebuilt after it was largely gutted by a fire that swept through the town in 1688 - even the bells were melted by the flames. This no doubt accounts for the rather sparse state of the church interior today, although thankfully its magnificent 90ft Perpendicular tower survived.

Most of the town's buildings were not so lucky: above a modern supermarket opposite the west end of the church, you can still make out the carved sills in the upper windows of a 16th century merchant's house - one of the very few original properties to escape the conflagration. As a consequence, Bungay is now mainly 18th century in character, and the fine Georgian buildings with their red-brick facades still lend an air of prosperity to the town. It has also benefited immeasurably since being by-passed, making it a very pleasant place to wander around on foot as you explore the narrow streets leading out from the Market Place.

Brownes Restaurant, 20 Earsham Street, Bungay 01986 892545

Those looking for an excellent meal here should try **Brownes Restaurant**, an intimate restaurant in the centre of town, run for the past six years by Diana Moore. The lovely old restaurant building dates from 1690 and looks out over a beautiful mature garden. The menu is changed each week and offers a choice of five starter, main and dessert courses; wherever possible locally-sourced ingredients, especially fresh fish, are used. The restaurant is open on Tuesday to Saturday evenings, and at lunchtimes on Tuesday to Friday.

If you keep your eyes peeled, you may spot a rather unusual weather-vane atop a lamp-post near the Butter Cross, which, rather than the familiar friendly cockerel, is surmounted by a particularly savage looking dog straddling a bolt of lightning. This is a reference to Black Shuck (sometimes called Old Shuck), a demon dog who crops up all over East Anglia in many different guises and with varying degrees of temperament!

It is generally agreed that he takes the form of a calf-sized, shaggy hell-hound with either one or two huge eyes of fiery red or green. Around the coast, his terrifying howls are said to warn of impending disaster at sea; in Norfolk he is particularly sinister, and locals say that no one who sets eyes on him will live to tell the tale. In Cambridgeshire his appearance also presages imminent death; but if you spot him in Essex you can thank your lucky stars, for in that county he has often been known to protect those who are travelling off the beaten track.

If you cross his path in Suffolk and treat him with respect, you will find him relatively harmless - but woe betide those who do anything to upset him! Black Shuk's demeanour was far from benevolent at Bungay in 1577, when he is said to have made an unexpected and dramatic appearance at St Mary's Church during a terrible storm. According to a contemporary record, he created even more havoc than William Dowsing was to accomplish in Suffolk churches just 66 years later, by flying down the aisle in a ball of fire and tearing out the throats of at least two startled parishioners.

If you want to watch the antics of a decidedly more lovable creature, you should head for the Otter Trust on the banks of the River Waveney at **Earsham**, a mile to the west of Bungay and just over the border into Norfolk. The Trust has one of the largest colonies of otters in the world, and during the summer visitors can watch these fascinating mammals going about their daily business in their natural habitat. Those of you who have been on the aviation trail may like to add **Flixton** to your itinerary, for this is the home of the Norfolk and Suffolk Aviation Museum. The museum can be found south-west of Bungay on the B1062 between Flixton and Homersfield, and includes material on the USAAF Liberator base which was located here during the Second World War.

Take the same road heading east from Bungay and you will soon arrive at the handsome old market town of **Beccles**. Before you arrive there you will pass Roos Hall, a distinguished 16th century red-brick manor built by Sir John Suckling, an ancestor of Lord Nelson. It is still owned by his descendants today, and is open to the public by appointment. This is said to be one of England's most haunted houses: one ghost haunts a guest room, another loiters in the garden, and on Christmas Eve, a coach pulled by phantom horses and driven by a headless coachman turns into the drive and pulls up at the front door. To top it all, one of Old Nick's footprints (or should that be hoofprints?) can be seen on one of the walls!

The most scenic approach into Beccles is by water, for here the River Waveney is at its very best. This was once a busy port with wherries transporting their goods from the sea ports to the inland towns, but today it is the pleasure boats that dominate the scene, and many readers will be familiar with Beccles as the starting point for their holiday on the Broads.

The 97ft-high stone-faced bell tower of St Michael's rises above the town, detached from the 14th century church. It was here in 1749 that Catherine Suckling married the Reverend Edward Nelson, to give birth nine years later to one of the greatest seamen England has ever known. A series of fires that raged through Beccles in the 16th and 17th centuries did much damage to the church and completely destroyed most of the town's old buildings; but the church was sympathetically restored by the Victorians, and Beccles itself was virtually reborn from the ashes as a handsome red-brick Georgian town.

As you explore Beccles on foot, some of the buildings worth seeing include the flint-faced Waveney House Hotel, the 18th century octagonal Town Hall, and that marvellous old 17th century coaching inn, the King's Head. We also recommend that you make your way to Newgate, where you will find two worthwhile museums. The first is the Beccles and District Museum, whose exhibits on local history include 19th century costume, farm implements and memorabilia from the old sailing wherries; and the second is the William Clowes Print Museum. This is very informative on the history of printing since the 1800s, with woodcuts, books and printing machinery showing just how far the industry has progressed since that time. All this seems a far cry from the desk top publishing systems and laser printing available to us all today. The museum is open from June to August, Monday to Friday from 2.00pm - 4.00pm, and admission free. Guided tours around the factory can be arranged.

Joining the A146 Lowestoft road to the east of Beccles, we passed through **North Cove** where the five-acre gardens of the Hall are open to the public under the National Gardens Scheme, then turned off the main road onto the B1384 and came to **Carlton Colville.** Here in Chapel Road we found the East Anglia Transport Museum, where trams and trolley buses, all in full working order, are shown to good advantage in an authentically re-constructed 1930s street setting. Together with other interesting modes of transport such as motor cars, a narrow gauge railway, steam rollers and various battery powered vehicles, you will find plenty here to interest and amuse you for several hours. There is a reasonable admission fee (with all rides included in the price) and you should check opening times by picking up a leaflet from any local Tourist Information Centre.

Lowestoft, which has the distinction of being the most easterly town in Britain, saw its heyday as a major fishing port during the late-19th and early-20th centuries, when the rivalry between its herring fishermen and those of its sister port of Great Yarmouth was legendary. After the First World War, the herring grounds suffered from overfishing and the numbers of the fleet declined dramatically, but the fishing industry continues to be an important part of life in Lowestoft today. It is well worth wandering down to the harbour to watch the trawlers chugging in with their catch after a long night spent far out at sea. You will have to get up early to see this, but it is rewarding. Guided tours of the fishmarket and of the fishing harbour in a trawler are also available during the summer.

The town is divided into two by Lake Lothing, dug originally for peat extraction, and the old harbour that was built at the mouth of the lake in 1827-31 is now the home of the Royal Lowestoft Yacht Club and the lifeboat station. The commercial part of the port, with its dry dock and shipyard, can be found further upriver and is used mainly by ships carrying grain and timber. The main holiday resort lies south of the harbour, and was developed in the mid-19th century by the building company of Sir Samuel Morton Peto, which was also responsible for Nelson's Column and the Houses of Parliament. It is here that you will find South Beach, with its golden sands, safe swimming, two piers, and all the ubiquitous seaside amusements.

To the north of the harbour - over the bascule bridge that links the two halves of Lowestoft - the main shopping area leads you uphill to the old part of town. Here in the High Street you will still find some good Georgian houses, and leading off to the east are the steep cobbled alleyways known as The Scores. In the old days, these were lined with fishermen's cottages and curing houses and led down the cliffs to the original village on the beach; but the bombing raids of the Luftwaffe destroyed most of the older buildings, and the village site is now a sprawling industrial estate, dominated by the immense Birds Eye factory.

Things get distinctly better farther north, once you reach North Beach below Gunton Cliffs, and the northern esplanade. Built at the turn of the century, this never really had much hope of seriously rivalling the southern resort, but its failure to do so makes it a pleasant alternative for those visitors who prefer things a bit quieter.

One place that you must make a point of visiting in the northern part of town is the Maritime Museum in Whapload Road, which offers one of the finest exhibitions of maritime history we have seen so far. This includes models and displays of fishing and commercial boats, lifeboats, fishing gear, shipwrights' tools and paintings, and is open daily during the summer from 10.00am - 5.00pm. Another similarly appropriate museum that is well worth a visit is the Royal Navy Patrol Service Museum at the park called Sparrow's Nest, where you will find displays of naval uniforms, documents, photographs and models, and entry here is free.

The history of the town is not exclusively concerned with the fishing industry, however, for in 1664 a witchcraft trial took place at Bury St Edmunds involving two Lowestoft women - one that was to become so notorious that it actually set a precedent for the famous Salem trials in Massachusetts in 1692. Rose Cullender and Amy Duny were charged with the crime of practising sorcery and bewitching several local children over a number of years.

Following a series of ludicrous testimonies from 'reliable' witnesses and the children themselves - 'evidence' to rival that of Matthew Hopkins' fertile imagination 20 years earlier - the presiding judge pronounced both women guilty, and they were hanged on 16th March that year.

America may have had its troubles with witches, but at the Pleasurewood Hills American Theme Park in Corton Road, nothing unearthly (apart from some of the fun rides, perhaps) will bother you! There are over 50 rides in all, together with shows and attractions to please all members of the family, and if you would like details of charges and opening times you should ring Lowestoft 513626.

Before we leave Lowestoft behind us and head on to the neighbouring villages, we should perhaps mention that it has more than its fair share of connections with the arts. Benjamin Britten was born here in 1913, and several of his compositions were premiered in the village of Aldeburgh to the south - which we will come to at the end of this chapter. Another son of Lowestoft was the Elizabethan playwright and poet, Thomas Nashe, born here in 1567. One of his plays, 'The Isle of Dogs', was so strong in its condemnation of the abuses of state power that Nashe was able to test the phrase 'suffering for one's art' by being thrown into the Fleet prison! His final work, written in 1599 in praise of the red herring trade at Yarmouth, was 'Lenten Stuffe'. Finally, you may be surprised to learn that this was the first place in England visited by Joseph Conrad - not as a writer, but as a deckhand on a Lowestoft trawler. His experiences as such were to greatly influence his later works.

To the west of the town, easily reached from the A146 and A1117, **Lowestoft Museum** is situated in Broad House, a handsome building in Nicholas Everitt Park in the centre of **Oulton Broad**. The many exhibits on show combine to form a vivid picture of the town's archaeological, industrial and social past. There are artifacts from the stone age, examples of early industrial development including a mechanically driven corn mill, and displays of historic toys, costumes and regalia. The museum also houses a fine collection of Lowestoft Porcelain which was manufactured in the town's small factory between 1757 and 1799.

Lowestoft Museum, Broad House, Nicholas Everitt Park, Oulton Broad, Lowestoft 01502 565371

Fed by the River Waveney and connected to Lowestoft by Lake Lothing and its lock, Oulton Broad is one of the most attractive stretches of inland water in England. It is linked to the Norfolk Broads by the Waveney, and you can explore the river by taking a boat trip from the Boulevard, just to the south of the Broad. In summer this vast lake becomes a hugely popular holiday resort, with sailing regattas, motor-boat races, coarse angling, an August water carnival, and all types of boat for hire.

It is also the setting for a tangled web of ghostly intrigue, all centred on a 16th century house in the locality called Oulton High House. The spirits said to haunt the house are a phantom horseman accompanied by a pack of hounds, and a lady in white carrying a goblet of poison. The simplest version of their story is that they were a married couple, and the husband poisoned the wife after discovering that she was having an affair. The more complicated (if not totally incomprehensible) version is that the wife's lover murdered the husband, then fled with her abroad, taking the family jewels with them. Years later, the daughter of the original couple was kidnapped from the house on the eve of her own wedding - her intended husband being killed when he tried to intervene - and was taken to her mother, who for reasons best known to herself, ended up poisoning her!

Four miles north-west of Lowestoft, between the River Waveney and the B1074, you will come to the attractive estate village of **Somerleyton** . The neo-Tudor, thatched red-brick cottages grouped around the green, together with the present Hall to the east of the village, were all the work of Sir Samuel Morton Peto, the Victorian civil engineer and later Member of Parliament for Norwich who was responsible for the development of Lowestoft.

Somerleyton Hall and gardens, with its famous maze, is a beautiful family home, and one in the true sense of the word, for Lord and Lady Somerleyton living here. They have five children. They are very proud of their heritage, and their ambition is to conserve it, not just for themselves and their children, but also for the many visitors who come each year to enjoy the house and particularly the garden, which is ever changing.

The story of the house and family is recorded in an excellent guide, available when you visit the house. Each room has its own particular attraction. For example, the Oak Room is representative of the 17th century, here the panelling is from the original Jacobean house, and was made from oaks grown within Somerleyton's extensive parklands. The carvings on the chimney breasts are partly by the hand of Grinling Gibbons.

Between the windows of the northern wall of the Oak Parlour hangs an exquisite silver and gilt moulded mirror, which was originally made for the private apartments of the Doge's palace in Venice, and was once owned by Queen Anne. That is a brief description of just one room! Each room has paintings, silver Meissen and superb antiques. It is a delightful way to spend an afternoon, and that is simply talking about the house!

The gardens and grounds have long been considered of first rate importance. Twelve acres of garden surround the Hall. One of the most popular features has always been the Maze, one of the finest in Britain. There is a profusion of colour from the plants and shrubs and as you wander through the gardens you constantly come to arches and statues and a very special pergola which is 300 ft long. A miniature railway was opened in 1972, and gives hours of pleasure to children and adults alike.

Those taking a ride are able to have a different view of the house and park, also various breeds of cattle, and horses.

Three miles from Somerleyton is Fritton Lake and Country Park. It is another part of the Estate activity which is open to the public. The two mile long lake is one of the most beautiful expanses of water in East Anglia, and attracts many visitors each year, who enjoy fishing, boating, playing pitch and putt, windsurfing, viewing wildfowl, or simply relaxing in this beautiful setting. Children spend much of their time in the adventure play area. Somerleyton Hall is open to the public from Easter to the end of September. Please telephone (01502) 730224 for details.

Somerleyton Hall, Nr Lowestoft 01502 730224

Back on the B1074 at **Herringfleet**, the charming parish church of St Margaret stands above the River Waveney with its Saxon round tower, thatched roof and beautiful glass. Here too is Herringfleet Drainage Windmill, a 19th century smock mill in full working order. Access to the mill is on foot only, and if you want to time your visit to coincide with one of their pumping days, you should telephone Ipswich 265162 for details. While we were in the vicinity, we also pay a little pilgrimage to the church at **Blundeston**, a village that lies to the east of Somerleyton Hall, midway between the B1074 and the A12. Passing by on a walk from Yarmouth to Lowestoft, Charles Dickens misread the signpost, and 'Blunderstone' was later immortalised as the birthplace of David Copperfield. The morning light shining on the sundial of the church porch was the first thing to meet the gaze of young Copperfield each day, as he looked out of his bedroom window in the nearby 'Rookery'. As for the churchyard: 'There is nothing half so green that I know anywhere, as the grass of that churchyard; nothing half so shady as its trees; nothing half so quiet as its tombstones.'

Just to the south of Lowestoft on the A12 is **Kessingland**, a small resort with a wide beach of sand and shingle that extends for some two and a half miles, and a popular place for swimmers and sailors.

This was once the richest village in England and although not in possession of this title today, it still contains some impressive examples of architecture. One such example is a Georgian house built in 1834 now called **The Old Rectory** offering a very high standard of bed and breakfast accommodation. The house is set well back from the road in two acres of well maintained gardens, with a sweeping drive to the forefront.

The Old Rectory, 157 Church Road, Kessingland 01502 740020

The bedrooms are delightfully furnished with either en-suite or private bathrooms. There are colour T.V's in all rooms and tea and coffee making facilities are available. The dining room is spacious and an attractive guest lounge overlooks the gardens. All rooms feature exquisite antique furniture creating an atmosphere reminiscent of bygone times.

Turning coastwards off the main A12 once again, we made a point of visiting the impressive seaside town of **Southwold**. Southwold certainly has a lot to offer the visitor. There is an excellent sandy beach, sailing, bird watching, plenty of good walks and an attractive little theatre. Much of the town's charm is due to the variety of its old buildings which come in many shapes, sizes and styles of architecture.

One of the most elegant of these is **Buckenham House** in the High Street. With its redbrick facade and small-paned sash windows, this house looks like a classic Georgian town house, but in fact its roots go back much further. The house is named after Richard Buckenham, a prosperous Tudor merchant with business interests in brewing and fishing who owned a number of other properties in Southwold. It is likely that he had it built in the mid-1500s, and that he and his wife, Christian, were the original occupants. At that period the house would have been timber-framed and the scale of this original building can be judged by the dimensions of the present cellar. Then, as now, this spacious basement room was approached by steps from the street. In Tudor times, the cellar would have been used in connection with the family's brewing activities. Today, it houses the delightful **Buckenham Coffee House** where visitors can enjoy a fine cup of coffee, pastry or light meal in authentic Tudor surroundings. Many of the original heavy load-bearing timbers can still be seen in the ceiling, and the walls still have much of their 16th century brickwork lining.

Buckenham Coffee House, 81 High Street, Southwold
01502 722002

In the first half of the 18th century, Buckenham House was given its Georgian facade, then in 1752 it became the vicarage of Southwold. One of the last of the vicars to reside there was a keen photographer who took a wonderful series of photographs of the building's interior.

The most recent phase in the history of Buckenham House began in 1971 when it was purchased by its current owners. They began a process of careful restoration, and today the house is actively used for a variety of purposes. Apart from the coffee shop in the cellar, there are offices, an art gallery, a doctors' surgery and, on the top floor, a spacious modernised **holiday flat** with two twin bedrooms and spectacular views over the town.

It was on the outskirts of Kessingland that we discovered the **Suffolk Wildlife and Rare Breeds Park**, which has an extensive collection of all our favourite zoo animals, such as lions and bears, wolves and beavers, and reptiles and birds. Many rare breeds of cattle, pigs, sheep and poultry are accommodated here too; and among the most unusual of these are the miniature South American horses, the tail-less Manx Rumpie chickens, and the miniature Dexter cattle - standing less than three feet high!

Situated in 100 acres of idyllic Suffolk countryside, the Park provides an interesting and educational attraction for all members of the family. There is a large cafeteria and a children's play area too, so you can quite easily make a day of it here. The Park is open daily from 10.00am, from Easter to October.

Further down the coast we discovered **Wrentham Basketware**, situated in London Road, **Wrentham**. The traditional willow baskets made in the workshop here would make an unusual gift to take home with you, and with an amazing 320 alternative styles on offer, you have plenty of choice! Particularly impressive are the large food hampers, which can be made to order to suit all 'al fresco' occasions. The workshop and shop are open all year round, from 8.00am - 5.00pm Monday to Friday, and from 8.00am - 4.00pm on Saturday.

Much of this part of the Suffolk coastline is under attack from the remorseless pounding of the waves, and in the past entire villages have been completely lost to the encroaching sea. Taking a lane leading south-east from Wrentham, we carried on to the end of the road until we came to **Covehithe**, a tiny coastal village with the most remarkable church. Not especially remarkable in itself - though attractive enough - but eminently memorable because of its dramatic setting. The original 15th century church of St Andrew's was really always too large for the size of the community it served, and after it was ruined during the Civil War it became a victim of economics. The dwindling parish was simply unable to justify rebuilding the church to its former size and glory, and so in 1672, a tiny thatched church was built within the confines of the former nave, using materials from the ruins of the original church. Above this 'church-within-a-church' looms the massive tower of the old St Andrew's; one of the most effective navigational aids along this stretch of the coast, and left standing by Cromwell's men for that very purpose.

It is well worth parking the car and stretching your legs by taking a stroll along the top of the crumbling cliffs, with there view of the beautiful, seemingly endless sandy beach, backed by grey shingle and low, windswept hillocks. It is said that this sparsely inhabited part of Suffolk boasts one of England's remotest and loveliest coastlines, and given favourable weather conditions most would readily concur. Beware the east wind, however, for when it blows the sand in your eyes and chills you to the bone, even the sight and sound of wild seabirds loses its charm.

What makes Southwold so special is that it simply does not conform to most people's idea of a typical seaside town. If you come here expecting to find scores of souvenir shops, amusement arcades and burger bars, you will be sorely disappointed; the fact is that Southwold has somehow managed to remain virtually unchanged for the past hundred years and is now one of the most popular resorts on the east coast - with none of the trappings of rampant commercialism. The town is practically an island, bounded by creeks and marshes, the River Blyth and the North Sea, and its attractive mixture of period houses and colour-washed cottages are built around a series of delightful greens. These mark the sites of many of the buildings that were lost in a great fire in 1659, never to be rebuilt.

Dutch Barn Restaurant, Ferry Road, Southwold 01502 723172

There is a wide choice of places to eat and drink in Southwold, and a little to the south of the town centre on Ferry Road, we discovered the **Dutch Barn Restaurant**. This lovely old building is located near the beach and close to the mouth of the River Blyth. Inside, the atmosphere is warm and welcoming. Customers dine by candlelight, and on Saturday evenings their meal is accompanied by live music from a pianist on the baby grand. The wine list is excellent and the menu both extensive and adventurous. On the evening we visited, starters included the celebrated 'Dutch Barn Baked Avocado', and among the main courses was 'Brill Poached with a Champagne Sauce'. The Dutch Barn Restaurant is open for lunch and dinner throughout the year, every day except Mondays.

There are two particularly memorable buildings in the town, the first being the splendid Perpendicular church of St Edmund, home of a well-known character called 'Southwold Jack'. This is a 15th century mechanical figure made of painted oak and dressed in the regalia of an armoured foot soldier, who strikes the bell of the church clock with his battle-axe. The other great landmark, and one that can be seen from practically every part of the town, is the 100ft high, gleaming white inshore lighthouse, built in 1890 with a beam that can be seen some 17 miles out at sea. In the shadow of this, and much photographed as a result, is the little Victorian pub called the Sole Bay Inn; this is named after the Battle of Sole Bay in

1672 when the combined French and British fleets beat off the Dutch in a bitter sea battle off the coast here.

If you take a stroll across the common to the harbour at the mouth of the River Blyth, you can watch the fishermen landing their catch or purchase fresh fish from the black tarred sheds that line the beach. The Sailors' Reading Room in East Street is a favourite haunt of the old 'salts', who no doubt yearn for the days when fish brought in a profit and boats and skills could be safely handed down from father to son. Today's fishermen face an uphill task as EC regulations make a farce of the old traditions, with quotas and regulations being the final nail in the coffin of what currently looks to be a doomed national industry. Farther round the seafront, you can get a good view of both sea and town from Gun Hill, so called from the six 18-pounder guns that stand there. It is said that they were presented to the town by the Duke of Cumberland in 1745, who landed here on his way to Scotland to take on Bonnie Prince Charlie. The guns had to be hidden away during both world wars, after the Germans used their presence to claim that the town was fortified and bombarded it from the sea.

Those looking for outstanding accommodation in Southwold will find none better than the famous **Swan Hotel**. The Swan was rebuilt following the disastrous fire which destroyed most of the town in 1659, and two major renovations have taken place since. Today, it is a classic example of an English seaside hotel. There are 45 luxurious bedrooms (27 in the main hotel, 18 in the gardens), and all but three have en suite bath/shower. The public rooms are comfortable and elegant, and in the bar guests can savour a pint of famous locally-brewed Adnams Ale. The hotel bakes its own bread, cakes and pastries, and uses only the best local ingredients in the preparation of its delicious and lavish menu.

The Swan Hotel, Market Place, Southwold 01502 722186

If well above average bed and breakfast accommodation is your priority, then we can also recommend **No. 3 Cautley Road**. No. 3 is an elegant Edwardian terraced house, centrally located near the hospital and only four minutes walk from the shops and the safe bathing on Southwold's blue flag beaches. Mrs Julie Cleave, an experienced hotelier, has decorated the property in tasteful period style. Bedrooms are either twin or double, and are provided with en suite shower, toilet and washbasin, colour television, radio alarm clock, telephone, hair dryer and tea/coffee making facilities. In the morning, guests can choose between a full English breakfast in the dining room or a Continental breakfast in the bedroom.

No. 3 Cautley Road, Southwold   01502 723611

Exploring the coastal villages to the south of Southwold is not a simple matter of pressing on relentlessly down a convenient coast road, because there isn't one - constant erosion by the sea has never allowed for such a luxury. Instead, you must zig-zag your way down the coast via a series of minor roads and twisting lanes branching off from the A12, to reach any of the villages or towns between here and the Essex border. The positive side of this is that although it may take a little longer to get from one place to the next, you do get to see many worthwhile inland villages on the way.

We come to the first of these by heading west from Southwold on the A1095 around the estuary of the River Blyth, then travelling south on the A12 for just under a mile to **Blythburgh**. In the 15th century this was an extremely prosperous port, with a busy quayside full of ships engaged in the wool trade. Unfortunately, ships got bigger and the river silted up, and when a bad fire compounded the problems of declining trade, Blythburgh dwindled in size to become the little village it is today.

A legacy of those affluent times is the beautiful church of the Holy

Trinity, whose sheer size and splendour has earned it the inevitable nickname of the 'Cathedral of the Marshes'. Visible for miles as it rises up above the surrounding reed beds, the church is a surprising and spectacular sight at any time - but especially so at night, when it is floodlit.

During a terrible storm in 1577, lightning struck the church while a service was in progress and the steeple crashed down into the nave, shattering the font and killing two members of the congregation. The scorch marks that can still be seen today on the north door were said to be clawmarks left by the Devil in the guise of Black Shuck, as he sped from the church towards Bungay - for this was the same day that he paid his equally unwelcome visit to St Mary's there. Further trouble came in 1644, when William Dowsing and his colleagues arrived to indulge in an orgy of desecration. Windows, ornaments and statues were smashed, the wooden angels in the roof were blasted with hundreds of bullets, and the church was turned into a stable for the Roundhead's horses, with tethering rings screwed into the pillars of the nave.

Thankfully - not being classified by Dowsing as 'superstitious' or 'idolatrous' - the marvellous bench-ends at Holy Trinity have survived intact. They depict the Labours of the Months and the Seven Deadly Sins, and two favourites are Gluttony and Slander. South of the altar is a kinsman of 'Southwold Jack' (they are known collectively as 'Jacks-o'-the Clock'), a charming little fellow who strikes the bell with his hammer and nods his head if you give him a little help by pulling his cord. Another unusual feature here is the priest's chamber over the south porch; an ancient little room which has been carefully restored, complete with an altar made of wood from HMS Victory.

If the weather is fine and you are looking for a good spot to have lunch out of doors, there is a very pleasant picnic site just off the A12 to the south of the village. This is Toby's Walk Picnic Site, a 25-acre former gravel quarry which has been given a new lease of life thanks to the extensive planting of trees and the reintroduction of natural gorse.

From here, the B1387 led us back towards the coast and the pretty village of **Walberswick**; a tantalising mile south-west of Southwold across the mouth of the River Blyth, but some eight miles by road. A busy port until around the 16th century, it is now a quiet and graceful residential community with large, neat houses and well-tended gardens. At the end of the village, the little riverside harbour is packed with fishing boats and small sailing craft in the summer, and from here you can take the unmade road down to the sandy beach. When you arrive at the village, the first thing to catch your eye is the tall medieval church of St Andrew. Dwindling parish finances forced it to be partly dismantled at the end of the 17th century, and the present church was built within the ruins of its predecessor in much the same way as its namesake at Covehithe. Nevertheless, the fine tower and south aisle remain, and the interior is full of character.

Not only does Walberswick have a lovely church, but we discovered **Marys of Walberswick**, a charming and unusual restaurant with covers for 45 people. It was originally tearooms, and still has a flourishing trade for morning coffee and afternoon tea. We are told that people travel for miles to sit in the garden and enjoy a cream tea.

It was for dinner that we came to Marys of Walberswick. The interior is lovely and so informal. There are many nautical pictures on the walls, of local scenes and old fishing smacks. There are some splendid portraits of local fisherfolk, with their weatherbeaten faces. Here and there fishing nets are draped, and overall it gives a theme that is totally right for a restaurant in Walberswick, where fishing has been a major industry for generations.

The menu was a mixture of English and French, specialising in local produce, particularly fish and game. Fish is caught locally, and the game comes from the excellent shooting to be found in Norfolk and Suffolk.

The a la carte menu, which also has vegetarian dishes, is supplemented with the day's specials. There are always dishes like home-smoked cod roes or the very unusual baked banana with stilton and cream, mouth watering! The restaurant is licensed, and has a small but very well-chosen wine list, something appealing to everyone's palate and pocket.

In Winter and Spring, Marys of Walberswick has theme evenings on the third and fourth Friday in every month, they are very popular. Just before we were there, they had run a very successful Russian evening, and it was to be followed the next month by a Medieval one. On New Year's morning they had a Victorian breakfast, which was a sell out! We want to go back there.

Marys of Walberswick, Manor House, Walberswick 01502 723243

359

Heading back the way we had come we then turned south onto the B1125, and after a mile left the road again to make our way across the Walberswick National Nature Reserve in search of the dramatic seaside village of **Dunwich**.

Dunwich was once East Anglia's capital city and one of the most important ports on the east coast of England. It was founded by the missionary St Felix, who sailed here from Burgundy in 632 AD to bring his message of Christianity to the natives. Experts believe that the main part of Dunwich once extended for some seven miles beyond its present boundaries, but in a great storm in January 1326 the town was engulfed by the sea. Some 400 houses and three of its nine churches were swept out to sea, and this was just the beginning of the town's inevitable decline. The huge bank of sand and shingle that the storm threw up across the mouth of the harbour diverted the course of the River Blyth and cut it off from the sea, virtually killing the town's trade overnight.

For the next 700 years, the relentless erosion of wind and tide continued to take its toll, and all that remains of the village today are a few Victorian terraced cottages and a church. The only reminders of old Dunwich itself are the ruins of a Norman leper's chapel next to the church, the archways of a medieval friary that was built on the spot where St Felix was supposed to have landed, and a solitary tombstone from the graveyard of the medieval All Saints Church, which fell into the sea around 1920. One of the cottages houses the Dunwich Museum, which chronicles the history of this fascinating place from Roman times to the present day.

The locals say that when a storm is threatening, you can still hear the sound of submerged church bells tolling deep under the waves as they shift in the current. The more fanciful among them may speak of strange lights appearing in the ruined Greyfriars Priory, and of the eerie sound of long-dead monks chanting over the sound of the wind. Add to these stories the fact that bones from ancient graveyards are still sometimes washed up on the beach, and you have an atmosphere of undeniable drama and mystery.

Dunwich Heath (or Common) and Westleton Heath combine to form a large area of sandy heathland once grazed by sheep, but now taken over by gorse and heather and their respective nature reserves. Take a stroll over Dunwich Common - which will be familiar to all readers of the ghost stories of M.R. James - and you will be rewarded with stunning views over Dunwich Forest, the marshes and the sea. Strangest of all is the view to the south beyond the wetlands of Minsmere, where the endless vista is suddenly broken by the futuristic vision of the mighty nuclear power station of Sizewell - more of which later.

Taking the road that leads south-west from Dunwich across Westleton

Heath, we soon came to **Westleton** itself. Situated on the B1125 about two and a half miles from the coast, this delightful village is far enough away from the crumbling cliffs to be secure in the knowledge that it has nothing to fear from the cruel sea. In contrast to its neighbour, its history is not one of diminished prosperity and a dwindling population; Westleton today is presumably much as it has always been - an archetypal English village with a village green and pond, some pleasant houses and an unpretentious thatched church.

While you are here, do drop in at **Westleton Cottage Crafts**, a charming craft shop, tea room and pine furniture showroom run by Lynne Venn. The interior has been beautifully fitted out with country pine furniture which provides the perfect setting for Lynne's display of arts and crafts. Items on show include ceramics and a unique range of miniatures of local Suffolk villages. The tea shop has a truly rural atmosphere and serves delicious teas, light meals and wonderful homemade cakes.

Westleton Cottage Crafts, Westleton, Wear, Saxmundham
01728 73227

Minsmere Reserve is centred around the mouth of the River Minsmere, and covers more than 1,500 acres of reedbeds, heath and woodland, together with a series of man-made islands and lagoons. It is without doubt one of the best bird reserves in Britain, and this mixed habitat supports an astonishingly varied number of species that come here to breed. The seemingly endless list includes everything from nightjars, nightingales and marsh harriers, to bitterns and the rare avocet with its curious 'letter-opener' bill. Even those who profess to not being expert birdwatchers by any means agree a few hours spent in the hides observing native and migratory birds in their natural habitat is enough to make even those with a casual interest eager for more. You will need a permit to gain access to the main reserve, but anyone can use the large public hide to be found along the shore from the car park on Dunwich Common. Further details, opening times and permits can be obtained from the reserve's reception centre.

Those looking for excellent farmhouse bed and breakfast accommodation within easy reach of the Minsmere bird reserve and Suffolk Heritage Coast should make a point of finding **The Alders**, near **Theberton**. This former working farm is set within five acres of picturesque grounds and is situated approximately half-a-mile from the B1122 Leiston to Yoxford road. (It may be advisable to telephone the owner, Mrs Janet Baxter (0728) 831790, for directions.) Formerly two farm cottages, the Alders retains much of its original character and charm, with many of the rooms having superb views over the surrounding countryside. The three

361

spacious letting rooms are all comfortable and well-appointed, and Mrs Baxter's renowned English breakfasts include homemade marmalade and free range eggs.

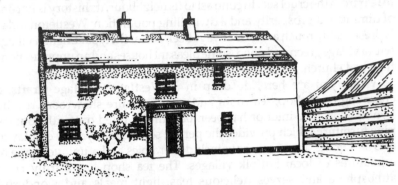

The Alders, Potters Street, Theberton, Leiston 01728 831790

From Theberton we made our way some three miles further inland to **Kelsale**, wedged between the B1121 and the A12, where we admired both the handsome 15th century Guildhall and the splendid lychgate at the church of St Mary and St Peter.

Either the A12 or the B1121 will take you directly to **Saxmundham,** which we have to admit left us feeling more than a little disappointed. There is something hauntingly beautiful about its name, and indeed this is an ancient market town which was once an important stopping place on the London to Yarmouth road. The reality, however, does not live up to expectations: the coming of the railway in the 19th century brought with it both industry and the less inspiring side of Victorian architecture, and there is little here today to encourage the visitor to linger.

Instead, we headed east on the B1119 back towards the coast, and four miles down the road we came to the decidedly more interesting town of **Leiston.** For an understanding of the character of the town, the first thing you should do on arrival is make your way to the award-winning **Long Shop Museum** in Main Street. This is housed in the restored Grade II listed factory of the engineering works that was originally founded here in 1778 by Richard Garrett. In the early days, the firm specialised in manufacturing ploughs, threshers, seed drills and other types of agricultural machinery, and then progressed to steam powered units for use in factories, farms and mills. The museum now displays many of the original Garrett products, including traction engines, a trolley bus and an 1846 fire engine. Open daily from the end of March to the end of October, this really is a fascinating place to visit.

In Station Road, we came across an impressive 18th-century building, the **White Horse Hotel**, which is owned by John and Jean Doyle. At one time, the White Horse was a centre for local smuggling; today, it is a centre for more conventional pursuits such as visits to Aldeburgh, Snape Maltings or the bird sanctuary at Minsmere. The hotel has 13 well-appointed bedrooms, most with en suite facilities, and a restaurant with an excellent á la carte menu which includes flambée dishes cooked at the table. There are also two attractive bars serving fine ales and a selection of first-rate bar meals.

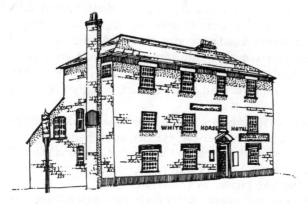

The White Horse Hotel & Restaurant, Station Road, Leiston
01728 830694

To the north of the town is the well-known Summerhill, the experimental school founded here in 1927 by the radical Scottish educationalist and author, Alexander Sutherland Neill. This is the school which 'began as an experiment and became a demonstration', and the philosophy by which it was run influenced many teachers both here and abroad. Further north are the impressive remains of Leiston Abbey, founded in 1182. The Premonstratensian order settled here in the 14th century after abandoning their increasingly uncomfortable site in the Minsmere marshes, and those parts of the Abbey where the fabric is still intact are now used as a summer school for budding young musicians who are unusually gifted.

We found it ironic that Leiston, whose former major employer once benefited so much from the coming of the steam age, has now had little alternative than to embrace the nuclear age, firmly represented by Sizewell, just two miles to the east of the town. Its presence certainly solved a potentially disastrous local employment problem when the Richard Garrett works finally closed down in 1980. Whatever your thoughts may be on this emotive subject, it is definitely worth visiting the station to get a first-hand look at this awesome monument to modern technology. There is an excellent exhibition here which should answer all your questions on energy, nuclear power and its relationship with the environment. Admission is free, and for details of opening times and guided tours you should telephone the Sizewell Visitor Centre on (01728) 642139.

Just to the south of Leiston, on the crossroads of the B1122 and B1353, is the quiet village of **Aldringham**. Here, we discovered the little church of St Mary with its quite exceptional 15th century font; the delightfully named Parrot and Punchbowl Inn, a well-known centre for smuggling activities in the 17th century and now a popular local pub with an excellent restaurant and a friendly, old world atmosphere; and, opposite the pub, the renowned Aldringham Craft Market. Founded in 1958, the Craft Market is open daily all year round, and its three galleries contain an extensive range of craft work, fine art, imaginative gifts and ladies' clothes.

Heading east from here on the B1353, we then arrived at the unique holiday village of **Thorpeness**, planned at the beginning of the century by the playwright, barrister and architect, Glencairn Stuart Ogilvie. Its half-timbered, mock-Tudor style houses stand between the sea and a 65-acre boating lake known as The Meare,

The two most unusual buildings in this decidedly eccentric village can be found facing each other on a ridge to the north of The Meare, along a track called Uplands Road. People who wander around wool-gathering are usually referred to as having their 'head in the clouds' - which made us wonder what must be said of the inhabitants of the famous 'House in the Clouds' at Thorpeness! This memorable structure, an 85ft high five-storied affair with a clapboard cottage perched on top, is not quite what it seems. In was in fact originally a water tower, and the 'cottage', complete with fake windows, pitched roof and chimney, housed the tank. Water was pumped into this by the early-19th century postmill standing opposite, which was itself moved from Aldringham for this purpose, and this provided the domestic water for the village.

The five-storied house below the tank is, however, quite genuine; and its early tenants presumably had no qualms about the 30,000 gallons of water just above their ceiling. Such fears are quite groundless today, as the water tower ceased to function as such in 1929, when Thorpeness had become so popular that a larger tank was required to cope with demand. Its replacement, incidentally, was disguised by the imaginative Mr Ogilvie as a sort of medieval keep, and became redundant itself when mains water came to the village.

Some five miles to the south-west of Thorpeness as the crow flies is the village of **Friston**. If you enjoy good food, wine and real ales, then you must visit **The Old Chequers** here; it has a reputation for good quality food within the county. David & Sally Grimwood will be there to welcome you. David is a first class chef and his lunchtime buffets must not be missed.

The evening menu is very creative and varied, with locally caught fish, fresh local vegetables, all produced in these beautiful, pleasant, friendly surroundings. You can see why The Old Chequers is always so busy. Families are welcome.

You can dine under the new canopy on the patio. Reservations at weekends are recommended, but you will be guaranteed a warm welcome and very enjoyable meal at The Old Chequers. A visit to this house is a must.

The Old Chequers, Aldeburgh Road, Friston 0728 688270

Closeby is the village of **Snape**. The village has an interesting 12th century church of flint and brick, and just to the east of this, excavations in 1862 unearthed a 48ft ship dating back to around 625 AD. We will come across contemporaries of this exciting find when we visit Sutton Hoo in the next chapter.

A mile to the south of the village, at the lowest bridging point of the River Alde, stands the famous **Snape Maltings Riverside Centre**. A hundred years of industrial development on this site has left a fascinating collection of mellow red brick granaries, workshops and malthouses which are steadily being converted for modern use.

The internationally renowned **Snape Maltings Concert Hall**, brainchild of Benjamin Britten and Sir Peter Pears, was converted from one of the malthouses in 1967. Today, it is recognised as one of the finest auditoriums in Europe. Also within this unique collection of Victorian industrial buildings are a number of specialist shops, an art gallery, tea shop, restaurant and freehouse, all of which are open daily throughout the year. There are also three self-catering units in the Centre's converted main arch.

Snape Maltings stands on the edge of the Suffolk Heritage Coast at the tidal limit of the River Alde. At this point the sea is five miles away as the crow flies but twenty miles away by river, and trips from the quay provide an attractive way to see the river and its wildlife. Enquire about the programme of activity holidays which the Centre organises in the summer.

Snape Maltings Riverside Centre, Snape, Nr Saxmundham
01728 88303

Moot Hall is a handsome manor on the seafront built with imposing chimneys. When you have finished admiring them go inside the hall and enjoy the many interesting relics including those from an Anglo-Saxon ship burial excavated at Snape.

Our final stop in this chapter was at the delightful old town of **Aldeburgh** and here is one of the many strange Martello Towers erected as a defence against the French invaders led by Napoleon. Today if it is possible to hire it for holiday let through the Landmark Trust which would be great fun. The building is said to contain a million bricks, which no one should dispute for a moment, unless you would like to count them. However if you stay there and the weathers is awful you will have your entertainment laid out for you, to prove the Trust right or wrong! Details of the let can be had from The Landmark Trust, Shottebrooke, Maidenhead, Berkshire, SL6 3SW.

We ended up on the beach gazing out to sea watching the fishermen hauling their nets over their gunwales and inspecting the catch. The town has resisted commercial ventures and benefited from this as it presents a gentle and timeless air that must have convinced Britten to live here.

His house is next to Jubilee Hall, and it struck us that the horizon has little changed, the sea still ebbs and flows, the fishermen still ply their wares much as they did in his days in the village - long may they continue to do so.

Moot Hall, Snape

Southwold

CHAPTER TWELVE

Ipswich & South-East Suffolk

Otley Hall

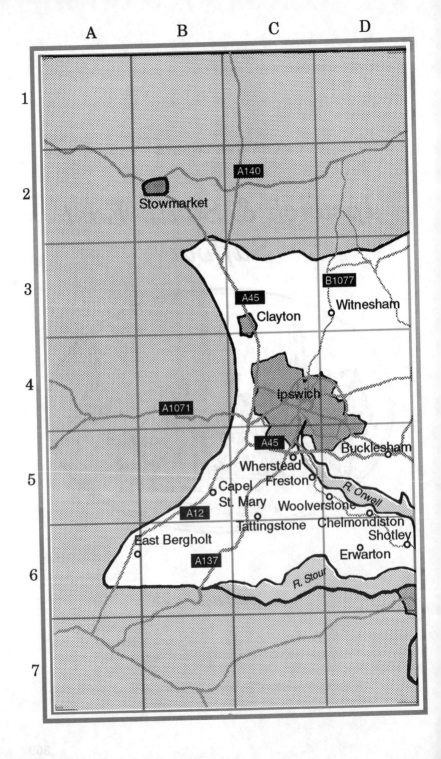

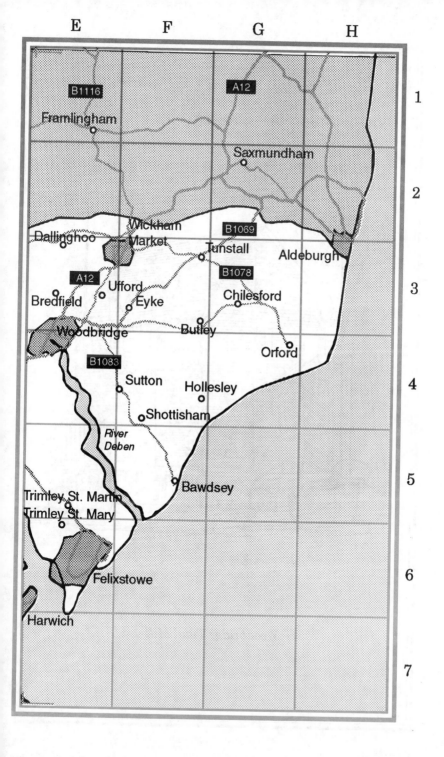

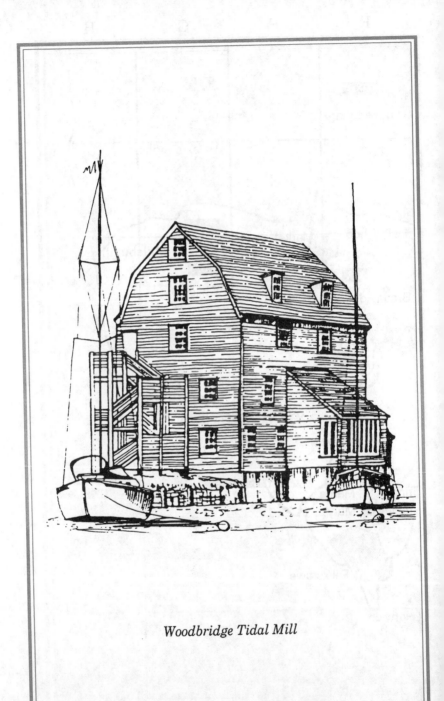

Woodbridge Tidal Mill

Ipswich & South-East Suffolk

We start the final leg of our Suffolk tour at Snape Maltings, where a lane to the west of the B1069 leads us to the village of **Blaxhall** and Stone Farm. The farm takes its name from a five ton slab of rock in the yard, known somewhat unimaginatively as 'The Blaxhall Stone'. When this innocent-looking boulder first came to public attention about 100 years ago, it was reported to be about the size of a loaf of bread. Since then, the locals claim that it has grown over the years to reach its present dimensions - and who are we to argue? Apparently, it was once a widely held belief that pebbles could grow to immense size in the potent East Anglian soil. The Blaxhall Stone it may be, but there is more than a touch of the 'Blarney Stone' about it.

Two miles to the north-west, midway between Wickham Market and Saxmundham, the main A12 passes through the attractive village of **Little Glemham**. Here, we stopped at the delightful roadside pub and eating house, **The Lion Inn**, which is owned and personally run by Peter and Pauline Fry.

The Lion Inn, Main Road, Little Glemham, Woodbridge
01728 746505

The inn dates from the 17th-century and was formerly a halt on the old

Ipswich to Lowestoft coaching route. The interior retains much of its original character with low-beamed ceilings, timbered walls and a really cosy and intimate atmosphere. There are two menus, one offering an extensive range of freshly-cooked meat and fish dishes, and the other a choice of ten vegetarian dishes. In the pleasant rear garden there is a children's play area and a splendid aviary.

The Elizabethan mansion Little Glemham Hall stands in its own parkland with delightful gardens to the south of the village. It was the 18th century home of Dudley North, son-in-law of the founder of Yale University, and is sometimes open to the public during the summer.

Follow the A12 south of here then branch off onto the B1078, and you will come to the little town of **Wickham Market**; a market no longer, as it happens, for that went to nearby Woodbridge many years ago. One of the nicest ways of appreciating the glorious countryside hereabouts would be to take a leisurely ride along the quiet backroads on horseback, and half a mile west of here on the Needham Market road, we followed the sign to **Valley Farm Riding and Driving Centre**. This truly is a fascinating establishment for those interested in equestrian activities of all kinds. Owners Sarah and Stephen Ling organise escorted hacks along the surrounding woodland bridleways, leisurely horse-drawn carriage rides through the local Suffolk lanes, and lessons in everything from ordinary riding to jumping, side-saddle, western, and carriage driving. Valley Farm is famous for *voltige*, vaulting and gymnastics on horseback, and *horseball*, a type of netball on horseback using a special six-handled ball. Look out for Britain's only herd of white Camargue horses and Gobi the camel who is being trained to accept riders.

Did You Know...

The Hidden Places Series

Covers most of Britain?

For our full list see back of book

Valley Farm Riding and Driving Centre, Wickham Market,
Woodbridge 01728 746916

If you carry on a little farther along the B1078 then take the minor road to the left just before the Charsfield turn-off, you will reach the charmingly-named village of **Dallinghoo**. On the edge of the village, we discovered the first-rate bed and breakfast establishment, **The Old Rectory**, which is owned and run by Jeremy and Bridgett Quinlan. Built in 1937, this handsome two-storey residence stands within two acres of beautiful gardens. Inside, an impressive staircase leads to the guest rooms (one double, one twin) which are spacious, comfortable and tastefully decorated. Evening meals are available by arrangement which are prepared using seasonal fruit and vegetables from the garden. Jeremy is also a keen beekeeper, so look out for his delicious home-produced honey on the breakfast table.

The Old Rectory, Dallinghoo, Woodbridge 01473 37700

Just over a mile to the south is the sleepy village of **Bredfield**, whose character is summed up perfectly by an eccentric plaque on the wall of the lovely old thatched village pub, The Crown. It states: 'On this spot 1742 absolutely nothing happened'. Nothing is still happening in Bredfield today, and long may it continue not to happen: one of the joys of exploring the back roads of England in search of hidden places is to unexpectedly stumble across a quiet little village where nothing has really changed for the past hundred years or so. Actually, something did happen in Bredfield, just 67 years after the 'nothing' that happened in 1742; for in 1809 the poet Edward FitzGerald was born here. More of him later in this chapter when we get to Woodbridge. The vicar of Bredfield in the mid-1800s, incidentally, was one of FitzGerald's 'set' - George Crabbe, son of the Aldeburgh poet who we met earlier.

Further excellent quality bed and breakfast accommodation in this pleasant part of rural Suffolk can be found at **Moat Farmhouse** on the outskirts of the village. This 16th century farmhouse is set in an acre of

375

beautiful gardens and is situated one-and-a-half miles northwest of the A12 and three miles north of the lovely old market town of Woodbridge. The accommodation is located in a completely renovated, self-contained farm building which is attached to the main farmhouse. There is one twin and one double room, bathroom and shower and a breakfast/TV room. The atmosphere is comfortable and relaxed, and the proprietor, Mrs Gillian Downing, serves an excellent breakfast. The accommodation is not suitable for pets.

Moat Farmhouse, Bredfield, Woodbridge 01473 37475

Two miles to the east of Bredfield, and the same distance from Wickham Market if you head south on the B1116, we came to the pretty little village of **Ufford** on the River Deben. This village of charming thatched cottages and farmhouses takes its name from Uffa, the founder of the Uffinga dynasty of East Anglian kings, one of whom we will meet a little later at Sutton Hoo. Beside the gate of St Mary's Church we spotted the ancient village stocks, a relic of the past not often found in this county. In addition to its beautiful Victorian stained glass, the pride of the church is its superb 15th century telescopic font cover, a great towering spire of sumptuously carved woodwork whose pinnacles soar towards the ceiling to a height of 18ft, crowned by a pelican.

A lane leading east from Ufford took us over the Deben and the railway line to the A1152 Woodbridge to Tunstall road. Some would say that the name of the historic town of **Woodbridge** means simply 'wooden bridge', or perhaps 'bridge by the wood'; while others claim that it is derived from an Anglo-Saxon phrase meaning 'Woden's Town' - which would indicate that this has been an important community since earliest times. Whatever the truth may be, this splendid old market town, which stands at the head of the tidal Deben estuary, has a distinctive charm of its own and offers visitors the chance to admire a wealth of old buildings, ranging from the merely interesting to the authentically historic.

This opportunity is greatly enhanced by the fact that traffic is restricted here during the day; the result of this excellent piece of town planning being that the humble pedestrian can enjoy the town to the full, with none of the usual problems of noise and fumes and the fear of being mown down as you cross the street. Woodbridge is a renowned centre of the antiques trade, and inveterate browsers can spent several happy hours here searching for bargains, lapping up the atmosphere and exploring the narrow cobbled alleyways.

The town's greatest benefactor was Thomas Seckford, a prosperous 16th century merchant, MP and barrister, who was also Master of the Rolls during the reign of Elizabeth I. There is a perhaps apocryphal story concerning him which claims that the Queen allowed him to attain great power and wealth, despite the fact that she objected strongly to the stench which arose from his boots! Be that as it may all seekers of hidden places owe him a great personal debt, as he was the patron of Christopher Saxton, 'the father of English cartography', whose atlas of England and Wales (published in 1579) was the first national atlas of any country in the world and provided us with England's first ever accurately surveyed road maps. What Seckford and Saxton would make of the vast network of roads and computer generated Ordnance Survey maps today is anybody's guess.

Seckford founded the original Seckford Almshouses in Seckford Street (the present buildings are a Victorian replacement) and in 1575 built the great Shire Hall which dominates Market Hill, a jewel among the many timber-framed buildings that lend the town such an air of distinction. Its Dutch gables and inner staircase were added in the 18th century, when the open ground floor - originally used as a corn exchange - was also enclosed. Opposite the Shire Hall is Woodbridge Museum, a treasure trove of information on the history of the town and its more notable residents, and from here you can stroll down the cobbled alleyway to the magnificent parish church of St Mary, where Seckford was buried in 1587. Also commemorated here with a splendid three-tiered monument is Jeffrey Pitman, a local tanner and haberdasher who exceeded his humble beginnings by becoming High Sheriff of Suffolk.

As we explored the area around Market Hill, we decided to call in at the 16th century coaching inn, **The Bull Hotel**, which overlooks the Shire Hall. The present building was a posting house for the union coaches which ran between Ipswich and Norwich, and in the entrance we spotted a list of proprietors dating back to 1734. The modern establishment has retained much of its original character and charm. The gallery restaurant serves excellent food and there are 23 well-appointed guest rooms, all with en- suite facilities.

The Bull Hotel & Restaurant, Market Hill, Woodbridge
01394 382089

Lord Alfred Tennyson was a past contented patron of the Bull, and stayed here when visiting the town. His friend and fellow poet, the eccentric Edward FitzGerald (born, you will remember, in nearby Bredfield) had lodgings over a gunsmith's shop on Market Hill, and is best remembered as the translator of that famous lyrical epic, 'The Rubaiyat of Omar Khayyam' - disrespectfully referred to by schoolboys as 'The Rubber Boat of Hymie Cohen'.

A country gentleman by birth, 'Old Fitz' (as he was known to his friends) was a man of many contradictions, for although he led a generally reclusive life ('Every year and every day I am creeping out of the world in my own way') he was also known to dress flamboyantly and had a knack of surrounding himself with renowned eccentrics. In his quieter moments, there was nothing he enjoyed more than sailing his small yacht on the River Deben. FitzGerald died in 1883 and was buried in the churchyard at Boulge (his family lived at Boulge Hall, demolished in 1956), two and a half miles north-west of the town. It is believed that the rose bush which marks last resting place is a descendant of the one on Omar Khayyam's grave in Iran.

Church Street leads into Woodbridge's main street, The Thoroughfare, with its handsome red-brick and half-timbered houses and numerous original shop fronts; and to the east of this lies the Quayside and the River Deben. The Deben is a most impressive waterway, very popular with the sailing fraternity, and the Quayside seems a different world altogether to the rest of the town. Boatbuilding, sailmaking and associated industries have been a part of life in Woodbridge since at least the 14th century, and work in these skilled professions still goes on today, albeit now with pleasure craft as opposed to sea-going vessels and warships.

It is perhaps appropriate therefore that the Woodbridge Tide Mill, an 18th century clapboard mill which dominates the waterfront, should have a roof shaped like the hull of a boat. As its name suggests, it draws its power from the tidal waters of the Deben, and we were amazed to learn that a tide mill has stood on this site since 1170. The present mill has been carefully restored to full working order and is open to the public from May to the end of September every day except Mondays, and on Saturdays and Sundays in October. Its grinding machinery operates at specific times subject to tides. Woodbridge also has a more conventional four-sailed windmill, which again is fully operational. This is Buttrum's Mill, a 19th century tower mill which can be found to the west of the town, open at weekends during the summer.

Given its close associations with shipbuilding and maritime pursuits, it seems appropriate that just a mile to the east of Woodbridge on the opposite bank of the river, one of this country's most famous ships was discovered at the **Sutton Hoo burial site**. A dozen barrows stand on this elevated site in a windswept area of sandy heath, and when the fourth of them was excavated in 1939, a 90ft long clinker-built Saxon ship was found beneath the mound. Even more exciting, it contained one of the greatest hoards of treasure to be discovered in this country, which is now housed in the British Museum. Although it is not known whether the burial was intended as a cenotaph or a tomb - for no human remains were found - it is widely believed that the treasure belonged to King Raedwald of the Uffinga (or Wuffinga) dynasty, who was King of East Anglia from around 610 to 625 AD.

The hoard itself is priceless, and includes a purse containing 40 gold coins, a bronze and iron helmet, a gilded shield and a magnificent sword decorated with gold and jewels. Further excavations and surveys were begun in the 1980s to provide a better understanding of the Anglo-Saxon period, and if you would like more information regarding recent excavation news and discoveries, you can write to: The Sutton Hoo Society, c/o National Westminster Bank, Cumberland Street, Woodbridge, Suffolk. The Sutton Hoo site can be reached from Woodbridge by ferry, or you can drive the long way round by taking the A1152 from Woodbridge then turning south onto the B1083, from which the site is signposted. There is also an exhibition concerning this exciting discovery at the Woodbridge Museum.

Those looking for excellent quality bed and breakfast accommodation in this delightful part of Suffolk should make a point of finding **Nutwood** in Fen Walk, a couple of minutes walk from the centre of Woodbridge. Situated just off the old Ipswich road, it may be advisable to telephone the owner, Mrs Anne Garrett (0394) 383078, for directions. This extended modern bungalow is situated in a secluded residential area and is surrounded by its own attractive landscaped gardens. There are four comfortable guest rooms available (two en suite twins and two singles) which are all very spacious and well-appointed. Mrs Garrett provides excellent hospitality and a first-rate Smorgasbord style breakfast with an emphasis on healthy eating. Evening meals are available in Woodbridge.

Nutwood, Fen Walk, Woodbridge 01394 383078

To begin the next stage of our journey, we made our way back to the A1152 then headed east on the B1084 Orford road through Rendlesham Forest. This is the oldest and largest of the several areas of woodland that make up the Forest of Aldewood, which covers around 14 square miles between Woodbridge and Southwold. This part of the forest is close-set with lofty pines, and its dark interior has a rather foreboding atmosphere. **Rendlesham** itself is said to have been the site of a royal village of the Wuffinga dynasty, although there is not much to support this apart from the close proximity of the Sutton Hoo burial site.

At the north-eastern edge of the forest is the village of **Butley** , where you can see the splendid 14th century gatehouse of ruined Butley Priory, an Augustinian priory founded by Ranulf de Glanville in 1171.

A more recent establishment here is **Butley Pottery**, which started 12 years ago, in a garage, and moved to the collection of barns in Mill Lane in 1982. These old thatched farm buildings have gradually been restored and now consist of the Tea Bar, the Thatched Showroom and the Workshop. Work is currently underway converting the front barn into a Gallery, Bed & Breakfast accommodation and facilities for meetings.

Butley Pottery, Mill Lane, Butley 01394 450785

Just over a mile further along the B1084, three miles from Orford and the coast, we came to the lovely old village of **Chillesford**, or 'gravel ford'.

On the main road through the village, we called in at the **Froize Inn**, a pleasant Suffolk inn named after the pancake, or *froize*, which was served by monks to travellers. Formerly a monks rest, this handsome 15th-century building has lost none of its original character. Inside there are timber beams, a feature fireplace and a magnificent wooden bar top. John and Carolyn Jones offer their customers a warm welcome and an excellent choice of bar meals. They also have three spacious letting rooms, one with a four-poster bed. Set in two acres, they have a mini farm park with goats and sheep etc., plus a tent and caravan site.

Chillesford is known to geologists for the *Coralline Crag* in which more than 400 species of mollusc have been preserved, over a quarter of them now extinct. Also, the backbone of a 30 ft prehistoric whale was discovered here in the village brickworks. There is an interesting walk across open fields from Chillesford to Orford known as Friars Walk (old maps show this as *Froize* Walk, as in the name of the village pub).

The Froize Inn, Orford Road, Chillesford 01394 450282

To the north is Tunstall Forest, another part of Aldewood. It extends up to the River Alde, and is airier by far than neighbouring Rendlesham. Its larches and Corsican and Scots pines are spaced well apart, with fern and bracken underneath, making it an altogether more comfortable place to boldly go! The rare red squirrel makes its home here, and if you are lucky you may even spot the occasional red or fallow deer.

From Chillesford, we continued on to the end of the B1084 and came to the impressive coastal village of **Orford**. Or perhaps we should call it a nearly-coastal village, for it is well protected from the North Sea by the six-mile long shingle bank of Orford Ness, and actually stands on the west bank of the river which is called the Alde to the north of the village, and the Ore to the south.

You might hesitate to call it either a town or a village, for although it boasts a market place and a castle and may therefore justifiably lay claim to the former title, the sheer peacefulness of the place and the fact that it is somewhat off the beaten track may make you lean towards the latter. The truth of the matter is that Orford was certainly an important town at one time - the sheer size of the castle keep and the obvious former splendour of the partly ruined church of St Bartholomew are ample evidence of that. It was also a thriving port, but the steadily encroaching Orford Ness (said to grow at the rate of some 15 yards each year) put paid to that as it gradually cut the town off from the sea.

Today, Orford has dwindled to the size of a small brick and timber village, surrounded by a vast area of lonely marshland to the north and south. It is certainly the place to visit if you crave peace and quiet, though in summer it presents a much livelier face when colourful pleasure craft make their way up the Ore to moor alongside the quay. From here you can take a boat down-river to the 300-acre Havergate Island, now an RSPB reserve which boasts Britain's oldest and largest breeding colony of avocets. Tours of the reserve are escorted by the warden, and permits and visiting times must be obtained in advance by writing to: The Warden (Havergate Island), 30 Mundays Lane, Orford, IP12 2LX.

The Butley Orford Oysterage, Market Hill, Orford, Woodbridge
01394 450277

Making up way up Market Hill to the broad market place in the heart of the village, we called in at the famous **Butley-Orford Oysterage**, a truly exceptional restaurant and mecca for those wishing to enjoy the very best in local fish and shellfish cuisine. The restaurant is owned and run by Mathilde Pinney and her son William, and has a menu which changes daily. What makes the restaurant so special is that it has its own fishing boats which go to sea to catch the daily ingredients for the table. The restaurant also has its own oyster beds from which the famous Butley Oysters are taken, and a smokehouse which produces salmon and trout for sale in the restaurant, over the counter and by mail order.

The sign outside this establishment commemorates Orford's very own twisted interpretation of 'The Little Mermaid'; this one decidedly less cute and lovable than the Disney version! The 'Wild Man of Orford' was apparently caught in the nets of local fishermen sometime in the 13th century. Ralph of Coggleshall chronicled the event, and relates how this naked and hairy 'merman' was taken to the castle where he lived for several months on a diet of raw fish, refusing to utter a word even under torture, before making his escape back to the sea.

Standing opposite the castle and alongside the unspoilt market square, we found the Crown and Castle Hotel, a first-rate hotel and restaurant run by Denise Bantoft and her staff. The hotel is situated a short distance from Orford Quay and has fine views of Orford Ness and the bird sanctuary on Havergate Island. The hotel building was constructed in 1879 and has an attractive timbered façade. Inside, it is decorated in traditional style and has a lovely restaurant overlooking the gardens. There are 21 bedrooms, most with en-suite facilities, 11 within the main building and the rest studio rooms within the grounds.

Crown & Castle Hotel, Orford, Nr Woodbridge 01394 450205

Orford Castle stands to the west of the market square, and is now maintained by English Heritage. It was built as part of Henry II's coastal defences in 1165, using the then revolutionary polygonal design - said to give it greater stability and to confuse its attackers. The design has certainly stood the test of time, for the superbly restored 90ft keep with its three huge rectangular turrets looks as if it could stand for at least another 800 years. If you are feeling energetic, you can climb up to the top for splendid views over the village and the coast. Seawards, the most prominent landmark is the red and white striped lighthouse on Orford Ness, and it was on the Ness, incidentally, that pre-war radar research was carried out under the supervision of Sir Robert Watson-Watt.

Finally, if you were as intrigued as we were by the history of the disappearing village of Dunwich, do take the time to pop into the Dunwich Underwater Exploration Exhibition held in The Craft Shop, Front Street. It is open daily all year round from 11.00am - 5.00pm, and provides a superb insight into the fascinating world of marine archaeology. Here you will learn all about the devastating effects of coastal erosion, and discover exactly what has been found so far during the exploration of submerged Dunwich.

To carry on round the coast from Orford we have to backtrack somewhat by making our way back to Butley, then headed south on the lanes through Capel Green, Capel St Andrew and Hollesley until we came to the aptly-named Shingle Street. Here, a row of white cottages stands above a vast stretch of shingle which has been thrown up by storms into a high bank, and runs up the coast to the mouth of the River Ore and Orford Ness. Parts of it were used for target practice during the war, but it has now been designated a Site of Special Scientific Interest due to its rare coastal plants.

To the south of the hamlet, against this backdrop of shingle beach and rolling seas, a series of five Martello towers rears up along the coast between here and Felixstowe; not the most attractive of buildings, but a memorable part of our heritage and a reminder that once, we were obsessed by the fear of invasion from France.

From here, it was back again to Hollesley, then south-west to join the B1083, where we head south to the end of the road and **Bawdsey**. If you make your way along the road to the south of the village towards the mouth of the River Deben, you will come to the late-Victorian Bawdsey Manor. Radar research was transferred here from Orford Ness in 1936, when the manor was converted into a coastal warning station, its equipment ever vigilant for German bombers. Bearing in mind that radar was still pretty much in its infancy at the beginning of the war, there must have been some fascinating blips on the screen with all those migratory birds coming in to land on Havergate Island.

It is possible to take the foot passenger ferry across to Felixstowe Ferry from here and thence make your way into Felixstowe itself. We make our way northwards back up the B1083, then turned west at Alderton and followed the road to **Ramsholt** on the banks of the River Deben. At the end we came to the **Ramsholt Arms**, a splendid pub and eating house standing on a small sandy bay with magnificent views of the surrounding shoreline. Inside, there are many fine examples of nautical memorabilia in display cabinets and around the walls. The pub is renowned for its food and has an extensive menu which includes sandwiches, ploughman's lunches, burgers, fish dishes and grills. Look out for the selection of home-made pies and daily specials on the blackboard. Owner Michael Lomas also runs the recently refurbished pub, the Wilford Bridge in Melton, just to the north of Woodbridge.

The Ramsholt Arms, Dock Road, Ramsholt, Woodbridge
01394 411229

Ramsholt is a popular haven with all those in need of sustenance who have sailed down-river from Woodbridge or up-river from Bawdsey; and it is pleasant to loiter here with your favourite tipple in hand, watching the yachts, dinghies and cruisers going about their business. In this lovely setting, and reached by a half-mile walk along a footpath from Ramsholt's disused ferry quay, stands the solitary Church of All Saints with its Norman round tower.

From here we made our way back to the B1083 and headed north once more, and midway between Bawdsey and Woodbridge, We made a point of calling in at the **Wood Hall Hotel and Country Club** near the village of **Shottisham**. This magnificent listed Elizabethan manor house is set within 10 acres of splendid landscaped grounds which contain a natural lake and a walled garden. Originally constructed in 1566, Wood Hall was enlarged and refurbished for the Dowager Lady Quilter in 1906. The present owners, Carole and Harvey Storch, have subsequently carried out a complete renovation to bring the historic manor up to its present-day luxury standard as a country house hotel and country club. Each of the superb en-suite bedrooms has been individually decorated and appointed to the highest modern standards. Most also have spectacular views over the grounds and surrounding heritage countryside.

There are no less than three intimate candlelit restaurants: the Bishop's Room with its decorative ceiling and impressive panelling, the Tapestry Room and the Nelson Room. Here, guests and non-residents can enjoy the finest English and continental cuisine in the most elegant of surroundings. In addition, there is a magnificent banqueting suite which can accommodate up to 150 guests for weddings, social gatherings or business conferences. Wood Hall also has its own exclusive country club with first-rate facilities including squash and tennis courts, sauna, solarium and heated swimming pool. Residents have complementary membership for the duration of their stay. Enquire about the special value get away breaks.

Wood Hall Hotel and Country Club, Shottisham

While we are in the area, it may be of interest to some of you to learn that there are a number of historians who claim that King Edmund was not captured and martyred at Hoxne at all, but met his end somewhere to the east of Shottisham and Sutton. Those in the 'anti-Hoxne' camp suggest that he found himself here after fleeing from a final battle with the Danes either at Orford, or possibly in Staverton Forest to the west of Butley. This, incidentally, is one of the oldest forests in England, and is known to date back to pre-Druidic times. The ferry that once took passengers from Ramsholt to the opposite bank of the Deben has long since gone.

About a mile further up the road, we stopped at **Sutton** to call in at **The Plough**, a first-rate pub and restaurant run by Marion Brain and Mike Colman. The pub is set in attractive gardens which have magnificent views over the surrounding countryside. The pub building dates from the 18th-century and inside a huge exposed beam spans the bar area. The atmosphere is relaxed and welcoming, and the food renowned throughout the area, especially the fish dishes which on the day we visited included lemon sole, red bream, mackerel, skate and monkfish. Customers can either choose from the menu in the bar or from the more extensive menu offered in the tastefully decorated restaurant area.

The Plough Inn & Restaurant, Woodbridge Road, Sutton, Nr Woodbridge 01394 411785

Having come full circle, we found ourselves back in Woodbridge once more. One mile south-west of the town lies the beautiful Elizabethan Seckford Hall, ancestral home of the Seckfords for 520 years, and said by some to be haunted by the ghost of the most distinguished member of the family, Thomas Seckford himself. When Sir Ralph Harwood purchased the Hall in 1940, it was derelict; after the war he restored it and transformed it into a hotel, and 10 years later it came into the hands of the Bunn family who it has been with ever since. Today, it is a superbly run hotel and restaurant with an international reputation, and although the atmosphere is eminently friendly and hospitable, the Hall is every bit as regal as when Elizabeth I is said to have held a Court here.

One fascinating aspect of its history is that the Hall is said to contain a secret tunnel which once ran from the hotel kitchen to the cellars of Woodbridge Abbey. The Abbey, located just below St Mary's Church in Woodbridge, was the town house of Thomas Seckford, and its earliest parts (now the preparatory department of Woodbridge School) were built on the site of an old Augustinian priory. If the tunnel does indeed exist, it has now been blocked at both ends, and it is likely that it would have been used in the days of 'the Master' for smuggling activities.

Ipswich, the county town of Suffolk, is one of the oldest towns in England. It has been a port since the time of the Roman occupation, and the Anglo-Saxons developed it into the largest port in the country in the 7th century. In 1200, Ipswich was granted a charter by King John, and it prospered throughout the Middle Ages both as a centre of shipbuilding

387

and as an important merchant community, its wealth based mainly on the Suffolk cloth trade. Periods of uncertainty were to come, however, particularly when the market for Suffolk cloth fell into decline in the mid-17th century. This particular problem was alleviated in the following century, when the town enjoyed a revival as a food distribution port during the Napoleonic Wars.

A potentially more serious problem which Ipswich has always had to live with is the fact that it is an inland port, 12 miles from the open sea, and the risk from silting is ever present. This came to a head at the beginning of the 19th century, when a vigorous programme of dredging and dockbuilding had to be introduced to stop the harbour from becoming completely choked. Trade recovered and a period of industrial growth was to follow; the Wet Dock was constructed in 1842, the handsome red and yellow brick Custom House (now the headquarters of the Ipswich Port Authority) was built three years later, and with the construction of important new rail links, the future of Ipswich was assured.

The town's most famous son was undoubtedly Cardinal Wolsey, born here sometime around 1475. The son of a prosperous butcher and grazier, he attended Magdalen College, Oxford, and through skilful manoeuvring went on to become Archbishop of York and then a Cardinal and Lord Chancellor under Henry VIII. His plan to make himself indispensable to the monarch had succeeded beyond all bounds, for he found himself deep in Henry's confidence, with full control of England's foreign policy and with more power than any minister of the Crown had enjoyed since Becket. His estates and personal wealth were considerable, and he established both a grammar school at Ipswich and what would later become Christ Church College at Oxford.

Wolsey's catastrophic fall from grace was of course precipitated by his dithering over Henry's longed-for divorce from Catherine of Aragon. This prevarication, coupled with his inherent arrogance, not only angered the king but made him many enemies both at home and abroad. Eventually he was forced to give up the Great Seal, his lands were seized by the Crown, and when arrested for high treason, he died en route to London from York.

Notables from the world of the arts with Ipswich connections include Thomas Gainsborough, who settled here for many years as a portrait painter before moving to Bath; David Garrick, the renowned actor and manager, who made his debut here in 1741 as Aboan in Thomas Southerne's 'Oroonoko'; and Charles Dickens, who stayed at the Great White Horse in Tavern Street while still a young reporter from the Morning Chronicle, hot on the local election trail. Soon after, he was to immortalise it in 'The Pickwick Papers' as the place where Mr Pickwick wanders inadvertently into a lady's bedroom, and his none too flattering description of the establishment brought threats of a libel action from the landlord. Applications in the 1960s to demolish the hotel in favour of an office block were thankfully denied, and it still stands today as one of England's great former coaching inns.

If there is one slight pall over the town, it is that many of its oldest buildings were effectively destroyed by the Victorians in their haste to bring 'modernity' to Ipswich, and we shudder to think what was lost in their fervent efforts. Of those that survived, perhaps the best loved is the Ancient House or Sparrowe's House in the Butter Market, home for 200 years to the Sparrowes who were merchants by trade. The house itself dates back to the 15th century, but its most outstanding feature was added later, sometime around 1670. This is the exquisite pargeting that embellishes the building above the ground floor, including the coat of arms of Charles II and symbolic representations of the known continents at that time. The building is now used as a bookshop, by the way - and a very good one at that.

Historic architecture of the ecclesiastical kind has proved more resilient, for Ipswich has no less than 12 medieval churches still standing. St Margaret's with its ornate flushwork and splendid double hammerbeam roof is undoubtedly the finest, while tucked away behind St Mary at the Elms you will find the town's oldest cottages, dating from 1467.

The dock area to the south of the town is a fascinating place. It stretches for over a mile along both banks of the River Orwell, and in addition to the great cargo vessels laden with everything from timber and grain to raw materials, you will also see more graceful yachts and sailing barges moored in the harbour basin.

Kwok's Rendezvous, 23 St Nicholas Street, Ipswich 01473 256833

You will also find a number of good restaurants in this part of the town, but lovers of Peking cuisine should look out for **Kwok's Rendezvous** in St. Nicholas Street in central Ipswich. (There is ample local street parking after 6.00 pm and at the nearby Greyfriars car park at other times.) For the last 10 years, the restaurant has been owned and personally run by Thomas and Lucia Kwok. Thomas is the chef and he specialises in Peking cooking, 'the haute cuisine of China', said to have originated in the Imperial Kitchens of the Forbidden City using the wealth of produce from the area of Northern China which lay within easy reach of the capital. The menu also includes a number of spicier dishes from the Szechuen region to the south-west. The restaurant is fully licensed, and is closed on Sundays.

The people of Ipswich are lucky to have a beautiful green space to the north of the town, just a few minutes walk from the main shopping area. This is Christchurch Park, 65 acres of wooded parkland, graced by the distinguished Tudor country house called Christchurch Mansion where Elizabeth I once stayed in 1561. The house contains a splendid domestic museum with furnishings from Tudor to Victorian times, as well as the Wolsey Art Gallery and the newly-opened Suffolk Artists Gallery, with a wonderful collection of paintings by Constable and Gainsborough and that ever-popular equestrian painter, Sir Alfred Munnings. The other museum in town is the Ipswich Museum in the High Street, whose galleries cover a wide range of subjects including British birds, ethnography, geology and archaeology. Replicas of both the Mildenhall and Sutton Hoo Treasures can be seen here, and we were particularly impressed by the excellent reconstruction of a Roman villa and potter's workshop. The Museum is open all year round, Tuesday to Saturday from 10.00am - 5.00pm, but closed on Bank Holidays.

We were pleased to discover that there is a good choice of guided walks and tours on offer in the town, ranging from visits to the docks and merchants' houses, a tour of Christchurch Mansion, and a 'travel through history in the footsteps of Henry VIII and Catherine of Aragon'. For dates and times of these and more, call into the Tourist Information Centre at the Town Hall in Princes Street.

Heading south from Ipswich, the A137 led us to the small village of **Wherstead** on the west bank of the River Orwell, where Edward FitzGerald's family made their home at Wherstead Lodge before moving to Boulge. In a county that is generally thought of as being flat, you probably never imagined that you would be able to indulge in anything resembling Alpine activities - but you were wrong, for the main attraction here is Wherstead's dry ski slope! If you prefer more gentle pursuits, there is a charming woodland walk just off the road through Spring Wood, renowned for its profusion of beautiful flowers throughout that particular season. The village also offers fine views of the mile-long

Orwell Bridge, which carries the A45 over the Orwell estuary and speeds heavy lorries on their way to the harbour at Felixstowe.

About three miles further down the A137, a lane leads east to the pleasant village of **Tattingstone**. On the road between here and Stutton, look out for the Tattingstone Wonder, a marvellous 18th century folly built by local landowner Thomas White in 1790. Faced with the knotty problem of having to provide accommodation for his estate workers, but not wanting to spoil the view from his newly built mansion, Tattingstone Place, he hit upon the novel idea of building their cottages in the guise of a church. Very convincing it is too, with its mock medieval tower and high 'nave' - though the brick chimney does tend to give it away!

Tattingstone lies on the western edge of Alton Water, a large reservoir neatly 'sandwiched' between the A137 and the B1080. Here you can take a pleasant country walk around the perimeter and enjoy a picnic by the water's edge, in the company of a wide variety of waterfowl and wildlife. Alternatively, you can indulge in a host of watersports and leisure activities including fishing, sailing, windsurfing and even sub-aqua diving.

The A137 led us ever nearer the Essex border, and at its junction with the B1070 we came to the strangely named village of **Cattawade**, where the railway line crosses Cattawade Creek over a low bridge. The somewhat mystifying definition of its name is 'a ford frequented by wild-cats', conjuring up a bizarre vision of ferocious moggies attempting the crossing.

We now turn onto the B1070 to make our way to **East Bergholt**. John Constable was born in this pretty, scattered village in 1776, and if it has now geared itself ever so slightly to cater for Constable-mania, who can blame it? The actual house in which the painter was born no longer stands, but its site is marked by a plaque on the fence of its successor, now a private house called 'Constables'. A little further along Church Street is the tiny Moss Cottage, which Constable once used as a studio.

It was at the Old Rectory that he first met his future wife, Maria Bicknell. There is a memorial to her at St Mary's Church, together with a somewhat garish stained-glass memorial window to Constable himself, and his parents and his old friend Willy Lott are buried in the churchyard. The unusual timber-framed structure in the churchyard is a bell-cage, built in 1531 and a 'memorial' of sorts to Cardinal Wolsey. He had apparently pledged money to the church for a bell tower, and the cage was intended as a temporary resting place for the bells until its completion. When Wolsey fell from grace and the funds were not forthcoming, the tower was left unfinished and the bells have been in their cage ever since. They hang upside-down and are rung by hand by pulling on the wooden shoulder stocks; no mean feat, as these five bells are said to be the heaviest in England.

Flatford Mill

The Gatehouse at Erwarton Hall

A leafy lane leads south of the village to the River Stour, where two of Constable's best known subjects still stand today, looking just as they did when he first painted them. The first is Flatford Mill, the brick watermill owned by Constable's father, built in 1733 and now owned by the National Trust and run as a residential field study centre. A little way downstream is the charming Willy Lott's Cottage, subject of Constable's most famous work, 'The Haywain', and also maintained by the National Trust. Neither is open to the casual visitor, but you can take the way-marked trail laid out by the Trust along the banks of the river for memorable views of cottage, mill, lock and weir. Under Flatford Bridge, a replacement for the bridge that Constable painted many times, you will find Bridge Cottage, with a National Trust shop, a tea garden and a permanent exhibition of the painter's life and works. There are also facilities for boating and fishing.

As you explore this delightful area around the banks of the willow-lined river, it is in the knowledge that here, too, Constable walked, sketchbook in hand, drawing constant inspiration from the idyllic riverside scenery. He would return here many times after heading for London to become a student at the Royal Academy, and much of his greatest work was done within a 10-mile radius of his beloved home.

Also at East Bergholt are Stour Gardens, where sweeping lawns, colourful flower beds and small ponds are laid out neatly below Stour House, former home of the journalist and author Randolph Churchill, son of Sir Winston. The gardens are open daily.

From here, we make our way back along the B1070 and A137 to Brantham, then joined the B1080 and pressed on to **Stutton** on the southern edge of Alton Water. At the Alton Water Sports Centre on Holbrook Road, you can hire windsurfers and sailing dinghies. Day membership is available, and the Centre also provides training courses in the summer. South-east of the village, St Peter's Church stands in quiet isolation overlooking Holbrook Bay, and a footpath from the church will lead you down to the water's edge, around the eastern side of the bay, and all the way along the northern bank of the Stour estuary to Shotley Gate.

As you head north-east from Stutton towards **Holbrook** on the B1080, you pass the massive neo-Georgian Royal Hospital School on your right. This is the descendant of the school for the sons of officers and men in the Royal Navy and Royal Marines which was founded in 1712, originally attached to Greenwich Hospital in London, but transferred to Holbrook in 1933. Its central tower, topped by a white stone pinnacle, is a landmark for miles around and can be seen from both sides of the Stour estuary. Half a mile further north, standing by a tributary of the Stour at the entrance to Holbrook itself, is Alton Mill. This weather-boarded mill has stood here for more than 200 years, on a site occupied by a succession of watermills since before the Domesday Survey of 1086.

Taking the lane leading south-east from the mill, we press on into the heart of the Shotley Peninsula, the marshy promontory set between the estuaries of the Orwell and the Stour. This attractive area is rich in birdlife, and is especially renowned for its breeding waders, redstart, lapwing and snipe.

Passing through Harkstead, we continued east for another two miles and came to the delightful hamlet of Erwarton. Just beyond the village the road bends sharply to the right, and here you will see an impressive red-brick Jacobean gatehouse with a rounded arch, buttresses and pinnacles. This belongs to Erwarton Hall, the family home of the Calthorpes. Anne Boleyn was the niece of Philip Calthorpe and visited the house on numerous occasions, and legend has it that her heart was buried in the family vault at St Mary's Church. Credibility was lent to the story when a heart-shaped casket was discovered there in 1836.

If you don't come to Erwarton in search of the queen's heart, then you can at least pay your respects to another part of her anatomy, for it was here that we discovered the first-rate inn and restaurant, the **Queen's Head**.

The Queen's Head Inn & Restaurant, Erwarton, Ipswich
01473 787550

This handsome red-tiled building dates from the middle of the 17th-century and is constructed in traditional Suffolk style. Inside, much of its original character and charm have been retained with low beamed ceilings, exposed timbers and historic memorabilia on the walls. The recently constructed restaurant extension blends in perfectly with the character of the inn and successfully enhances its relaxed and intimate atmosphere. In addition to charming surroundings, the restaurant also

394

serves a selection of first-class meals. An excellent value set menu is available, as well as a number of adventurous daily specials which, on the day we visited, included pigeon casserole, sweet and sour pork with brown rice, and mussels in mushroom and cream sauce. The Queens Head is also a renowned freehouse, and along with its comprehensive wine list, offers an excellent choice of traditional hand-pulled regional beers. The inn enjoys magnificent views over the surrounding coast and countryside, and across the estuary to the cross-channel ferryport at Harwich. Look out also for the fascinating display of navigational maps in the loos!

Just past the gatehouse, our road linked up with the B1456 at **Shotley**, and from here we made our way to the tip of the peninsula at **Shotley Gate**. This was once the home of HMS Ganges, training base for the Royal Navy, but now there is a busy marina where an entirely different breed of seafarer holds sway. Across the bay are Harwich and Parkeston in Essex, and on the water you will see every imaginable kind of craft, from little fishing boats to the massive car ferries that make their way across the North Sea to the Hook of Holland.

Here, on Main Road, we came across a real find, the **Old Boot House Restaurant**, which has been owned and personally run since 1990 by Ian and Pamela Chamberlain. Constructed in the early-19th century as three cottages, the building later became the Shotley Boot public house before being converted into a superb first-class restaurant. Inside, the surroundings are relaxed and stylish and the food is of outstanding quality. Both Ian and Pamela have worked all over the world and their knowledge of foreign cuisine is reflected in the restaurant's broad and adventurous á la carte menu. Booking is advisable.

The Old Boot House Restaurant, Shotley, Ipswich 01473 787755

Heading north on the B1456 from Shotley, we began to make our way up the eastern side of the peninsula back towards Ipswich. The first village we came to was **Chelmondiston** (variously pronounced 'Chelmundiston', and even 'Chempton'), where we turned down a narrow lane which took us to the tiny riverside community of **Pin Mill** on the west bank of the Orwell estuary. This is a favourite haunt of sailing and watersports enthusiasts, who flock to the idyllically situated 17th century fisherman's pub, the Butt and Oyster, with its strong associations with smuggling and the books of Arthur Ransome. Here you may catch your first glimpse of the graceful, red-sailed Thames sailing barges, a familiar sight further down the coast as far as Kent. They were once built here at Pin Mill, and if you are in the area in July, you can watch these beautifully restored vessels take part in the annual barge race which takes place from Buttermans Bay.

The origin of Pin Mill's name is unsure; some say it is a reference to the wooden 'pins' or pegs once made here that were so vital to the boat-building trade, while a more charming explanation is the story of the local landowner who gave his daughter the profits from windmills on his land as 'pin' money. To the east of the quay is Cliff Plantation, an ancient 17-acre coppice of alder and oak owned by the National Trust. From here, you can take a pleasant walk along the banks of the Orwell up to **Woolverstone**, whose large marina is used by the Royal Harwich Yacht Club. Overlooking the Orwell here is Cat House, where it is said that a stuffed white cat placed in the window of this dwelling would once have given local smugglers the 'all clear'.

Also on the water's edge, about a mile further north at **Freston**, is an odd six-storey tower built of red-diapered brickwork sometime around 1550. Some say that Freston Tower is a pure folly - and the oldest one in England, if so - while others of a more practical persuasion claim that it was used as a look-out tower to warn of enemies approaching up the river. A favourite explanation, however, is that it served as a 'day-school' for Lord Freston's daughter. And we mean a day school quite literally, for on Mondays it is said that she started off on the ground floor learning charitable works, then progressed floor by floor up the spiral staircase to tapestry on Tuesdays, musical studies on Wednesdays, classics on Thursdays, English on Fridays and painting on Saturdays, then, having reached the top floor, she was given a day off for thoughtful contemplation and worship on Sundays. Who knows if the story is true or whether she benefited or not from these dizzy 'heights' of learning, but it certainly makes a great tall story!

The final stage of our journey would take us over the Orwell Bridge on the busy A45, then south-east onto the Felixstowe Peninsula. Bounded on one side by the River Orwell and on the other by the River Deben, this is one of the prettiest areas in Suffolk; its winding lanes leading you through a delightful collection of quiet rural villages and lively riverside communities.

Our first stop was one mile north of the main A45, approximately halfway between Felixstowe and Ipswich, where we came to the picturesque village of **Bucklesham**. In the heart of the village we called in at the pretty pub and restaurant, the **Shannon Public House** which has been run since 1987 by Steve and Diane Convery. Inside, they have been successful at creating a welcoming atmosphere for both visitors and locals alike. They offer their customers a good range of ales and service which is first-class. Those wishing to eat can choose from the selection of wholesome bar snacks, or from a more extensive menu in the charming dining area. Dishes on offer include steaks, grills, daily specials and a choice of interesting vegetarian dishes.

Shannon Public House, Main Road, Bucklesham 01473 659275

Those looking for excellent quality bed and breakfast or self-catering accommodation in this lovely part of south-east Suffolk should look out here for **The White House** in the main street. Formerly a farmhouse, this handsome country residence enjoys lovely views over the surrounding fields and countryside. The letting rooms are comfortable and spacious, and are equipped with hot and cold washbasins and tea/coffee making facilities. There is also a separate guest lounge and television room. Mrs Biddy Blundell has been providing a warm welcome for her guests for the past 15 years. Her hospitality is renowned and she also provides a first-rate Suffolk breakfast.

Attached to the White House is a self-contained ground floor annexe which has been refurbished for use as a self-catering holiday cottage. Here, there is a large double bedroom, bathroom, a pleasantly furnished sitting room and a fully equipped kitchen with washing machine. An extra folding bed can be set up in the sitting room if required. Guests are welcome to use the large attractive garden and there is even space for a small boat nearby. The surrounding area offers many interesting walks, two fine golf courses and access to the local rivers which are ideal for sailing and boating. The White House is open all year round but is unsuitable for smokers and pets.

The White House, Bucklesham, Ipswich 01473 659325

Two miles to the south-west, on the other side of the A45 and the railway, **Levington** is perhaps best known for lending its name to a brand of potting compost, developed here at the Fisons plant. To the south of all this activity is a picturesque farming community overlooking the River Orwell, and those looking for first-rate farmhouse bed and breakfast accommodation should look here for the **Redhouse**.

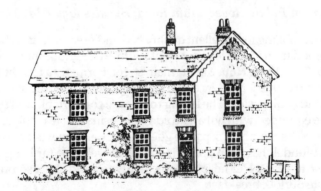

Redhouse, Levington, Ipswich 01473 659670

A delightful tree-lined drive leads to this early-Victorian farmhouse which until 1982 was part of a working farm. Today, it is surrounded by three-and-a-half acres of landscaped gardens with magnificent views over the Orwell estuary. Inside, a large sweeping staircase leads to the three spacious letting rooms which are all equipped with hot/cold washbasins and tea/coffee making facilities. Guest share a separate shower/bathroom. Mrs Nancy Matthews provides a warm welcome and evening meals by arrangement. The Redhouse is open from March to November. Children are welcome, but no pets please.

On the foreshore below the village is an extensive marina with all the normal bustle associated with boating activities, and if you want to stretch your legs you can follow the coastal footpath downstream, across the Trimley Marshes and on to Felixstowe. An alternative walk leads you north of the village, along the low wooded cliff above the Orwell to **Nacton.** Here, close to the medieval church at the southern end of Nacton village, you will find Orwell Park, now a school but in the 18th century the home of Admiral Sir Edward Vernon. The Admiral was known to his men as 'Old Grog', because of his fond attachment to a cloak of coarse grogram cloth. This nickname was then transferred to his none too welcome gift to naval life - a daily ration of rum diluted with water, to replace the tot of neat rum which sailors had previously been accustomed to.

The Hand in Hand, High Road, Trimley St Martin, Ipswich
01394 275249

Further south, we turned west off the A45 once more to reach the village of **Trimley St. Martin.** On the old High Road, we dropped in at the first-class pub and eating house, the **Hand in Hand,** run since 1979 by Vic and Pearl Ellis. Originally three cottages dating from the early 18th-century, the buildings were combined and established as an inn just over a hundred years ago. Inside, much of the original character has been retained with low beamed ceilings and traditional decoration. Vic and Pearl have successfully created an atmosphere which is friendly and welcoming, and offer their customers fine ales and an extensive menu of delicious home-cooked bar meals.

If you make your way a little further south to **Trimley St Mary**, you can leave the car in Station Road and head off on foot to explore the grazing marsh, reedbeds and wetlands of the Trimley Marshes. Created from former farmland, it is a strangely haunting area, and is renowned among nature lovers for its abundance of interesting plant life and the many different species of wildfowl, waders and migrant birds to be found here.

Of a different character altogether is the town of **Felixstowe**, our final destination on this Suffolk tour. It presents two distinctly different faces to the world, neither one intruding upon the other. To the west of the town is the busy cargo and container port, which has steadily developed to become one of the largest in Europe; while to the east is the attractive Edwardian seaside town, developed into a full-blown holiday resort by the Victorians.

In striking contrast to Lowestoft, 50 miles from here at the other end of the Suffolk Coast Path, seaside Felixstowe is unashamedly commercialised. The resort is strung out round a wide, gently curving bay, where the two-mile long seafront road is separated from the promenade by beautiful seafront gardens of well-kept flower beds and trim lawns.

Jutting out into the North Sea is the pier, once long enough to carry an electric tramway, but foreshortened during the Second World War for security reasons. The Spa Pavilion offers every entertainment from cabaret and brass bands to symphony concerts and amateur dramatics, while facilities at the Leisure Centre include swimming pools, sauna and sunbeds, indoor bowls, an entertainment hall, a restaurant and bars. There is safe swimming from the sand and shingle beach, but be warned - although Felixstowe enjoys a sheltered position and has an enviable sunshine quota, the sea breezes can be fairly bracing!

At the quieter end of this popular seafront, we called in at the **Fludyer Arms Hotel**, a first-rate establishment owned and personally run by John and Sue Nash. The building was formerly the residence of Sir Samuel Fludyer before becoming a hostelry known for 'brewing the best ale in the county of Suffolk'.

The hotel is situated 10 yards from the beach and its well-appointed guest rooms have spectacular views of the sea. These are comfortably furnished and have colour televisions, hot and cold washbasins and tea / coffee making facilities. The Fludyer Arms' two bars also overlook the shore and offer an excellent range of home-cooked bar food, including vegetarian dishes and children's meals. The kitchens are closed on Sunday evenings.

Fludyer Arms Hotel, Undercliff Road East, Felixstowe
01394 283279

Other facilities and entertainments to be found here include everything from putting greens and crazy golf to tennis, roller skating, regattas and raft races. The emphasis is very much on all-round family entertainment, and the town is also served with a good variety of shops, restaurants and pubs.

We discovered one of these on the outskirts of town in Church Road, where we called in at the **White Horse Inn**, a popular public house which has been run for the last 23 years by Paul and Vera Keeble.

The White Horse Inn, Church Road, Felixstowe

The inn was constructed in the 18th century and still retains much of its original character. Inside, Paul and Vera have been successful at creating an atmosphere which is friendly and welcoming. They offer

401

their customers fine ales and an excellent range of bar meals. They also have three comfortable letting rooms available which are spacious and appointed to a good standard. The White Horse is popular with visitors and local alike and provides a good base for exploring this lovely part of the country.

The original fishing hamlet from which the Victorian resort of Old Felixstowe developed can be found beyond the golf course at the north-eastern side of the town. This is Felixstowe Ferry, a collection of holiday bungalows, boatyards and ramshackle fishermen's sheds where you can purchase freshly caught fish or sample a tub of local cockles. From here, the little ferry will take you across the mouth of the River Deben to Bawdsey Quay, under the expert guidance of the Brinkley family who have operated the ferry for generations. Looming overhead are two Martello towers on the shingle.

At the southernmost tip of the Felixstowe Peninsula is Landguard Point, where a nature reserve of shingle beach and grassland supports a variety of coastal plants and migratory birds. Just to the north of the Point is Landguard Fort, built here to guard the entrance to Harwich Harbour in 1718, predating the Martello towers by nearly 100 years. It replaces a previous fort built in the 1540s, and today houses a collection of documents, maps, photographs and artifacts relating to its proud history. It is open on Wednesday and Sunday afternoons during the summer, and guided tours are available.

Beyond the fort you will find an excellent vantage point from which to look out across the harbour to see the ships departing from Felixstowe docks, passing perilously close to the small public viewing area. Perhaps you may be tempted to take a cruise on the Orwell and Stour estuaries, or hop across the harbour to Harwich on the ferry and from there make your way across the North Sea to Europe.

We hope for the moment, though, that you will forsake the temptations of foreign climes and keep your feet and wheels firmly on English soil. Our exploration of Suffolk ends here, but we hope that this brief account of its well-known attractions and more hidden treasures will encourage you to set off on your own journey of discovery.

CHAPTER THIRTEEN

Northern Essex

Colchester Castle

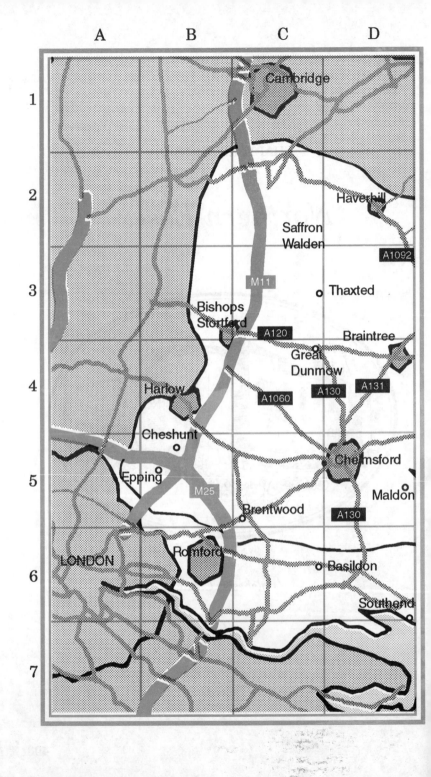

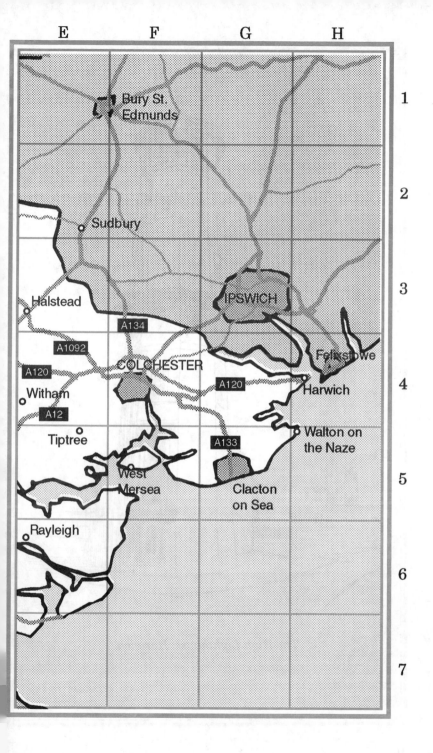

The High Lighthouse, Harwich

CHAPTER THIRTEEN

Northern Essex

The county of Essex is much maligned, the butt of many a joke but though as with every county in the land it has its sprawling suburbs and its industrial areas there is much Essex has to offer those of us seeking hidden places of interest. We start our travels in **Harwich**, the ferry port familiar to many continental travellers.

The towns name probably originates from the time of King Alfred, when 'Here' meant army and 'Wic' a camp. The attractive old town we see today was built in the 13th century by the Earls of Norfolk to exploit its strategic position on the Stour/Orwell estuary and the town has an important seafaring history which continues today. During the 14th and 15th century French campaigns it was an important naval base.

The ship which carried the Pilgrim Fathers to America in 1620, The Mayflower, was a frequent visitor and its Captain Christopher Jones lived in Kings Head Street. The famous diarist Samuel Pepys was MP for the town in the 1660's. With all this rich history its perhaps no surprise that the town has a fascinating maritime heritage trail which takes visitors around the old town. Highlights of the trail include the High and Low lighthouses dating from 1818 - when in line they indicated the safe shipping channel into the harbour. They replaced wooden structures and in 1862 were themselves replaced when the shifting sandbanks altered the channel. Both are rather unusual designs; the Low lighthouse is now the towns Maritime Museum, and the 90ft and nine sided High lighthouse is now a private residence. These two were replaced by iron structures, one of which still stands on the front at Dovercourt just along the coast. Shipping now relies on light buoys to find its way.

The Treadwheel Crane today stands on Harwich Green but for over 250 years it was sited in the Naval Shipyard. It is worked by two men walking in two 16ft diameter wheels and is the only known example. Amazingly it only fell into disuse in the 1920's. Another fascinating piece of the towns history is the Electric Palace Cinema, built in 1911, now the oldest unaltered purpose built cinema in Britain. It was restored by a trust and re-opened in 1981.

The importance of the port during the 19th century is confirmed by **The Redoubt**, a huge grey fort that was built between 1808 and 1810. Its design is an enlarged version of the Martello towers which dot the

King's Quay Street, Harwich

Electric Palace Cinema, Harwich

English coast awaited a Napoleonic invasion which never came. Today the Harwich Society has largely restored it and it is open as a museum.

The old town also contains many ancient buildings, including the Guildhall which was rebuilt in 1769 and has graffiti probably carved by prisoners of was in gaol, and is well worth putting an afternoon aside to explore.

We head inland from Harwich following the southern bank of the Stour, passing the modern freight and passenger ferry port at Parkeston heading for Mistley and its close neighbour Manningtree. If you would like accomodation in the area then just off the main A120 on the edge of the village of **Wix** you will find a haven of peace and tranquility at **Dairy House Farm**, the home of Bridget and Alan Whitworth.This working arable and fruit farm of over 700 acres has 2 lovely rooms in a very impressive Victorian building which was extended in 1876 from a small farmers cottage. There are views of the countryside in every direction and you are welcome to sit out on the patio overlooking the lawn with a cup of tea and a piece of homemade cake which we can vouch for as delicious!

This would be an ideal stopping off place if you are on the way to the ferry at Harwich and want a break in the journey with very hospitable hosts and very comfortable reasonably priced accommodation.

Dairy House Farm, Bradfield Rd. Wix Nr. Manningtree.
01255 870322.

Mistley and Manningtree are attractive ports that stand at the head of the River Stour and are a gateway into the Constable country of Suffolk.

In the 18th century local landowner and MP Richard Rigby had grand designs to develop **Mistley** into a fashionable spa to rival Harrogate and Bath, adopting the Swan as its symbol. All that remains of Rigby's ambitions is the Swan Fountain, a small number of attractive Georgian houses and **Mistley Towers**, the remains of a church, otherwise demolished in 1870, which had been designed by the flamboyant architect Robert Adams.

The Walls on the approach to **Manningtree** along the B1352 offers unrivalled views of the Stour estuary the Suffolk coast and the swans for which the area is famous. Back in Tudor times Manningtree itself was the centre of the cloth trade and later a port full of barges, carrying their various cargos along the coast to London. Water still dominates today, the town a centre of leisure sailing. The towns most notorious inhabitant though stayed firmly on dry land. Matthew Hopkins, the reviled and self-styled Witchfinder General, live here in the 17th century. Witchcraft was supposedly rife across East Anglia and many innocents were put to death in any number of barbaric ways as a result of the Witchfinders trails.

We now forsake the coast and head into the heart of the Tendring District along the B1035 and to **Tendring Hundred** itself. The 'hundred' in the name comes from the county divisions of Saxon times of which Tendring was a centre. To this day it is still called the Tendring District, although the centre has moved to the Town Hall at Clacton.

In 1582 thirteen local women accused of being witches were sent for trial at Chelmsford. One, Ursula Kemp, faced hearing her illegitimate eight-year-old son stand witness against her before she was hanged. The Witchfinder General arrived here in 1645 and more local 'witches' were executed on his evidence. Tendring's church with its magnificent hammerbeam roof provides an ideal place to ponder such unjust cruelty.

From Tendring we head east back to the sea and **Walton-on-the-Naze**. The towns seafront was developed in the 1800's and provides a fine illustration of the character of an early Victorian seaside resort. The shape of the Naze is constantly changing, eroded by wind, water and tide. 1796 saw the demise of the medieval church and somewhere beyond the 800-foot pier lies medieval Walton and much of the naze or headland. Inhabitants have been enjoying the bracing sea air at Walton since before Neolithic times, flint-shaping instruments have been found here, and fossil teeth and ears of sharks and whales have been discovered in the red crag cliffs. During the 19th century Walton was a source of seaholly for making love potions, but today offers donkeys, deckchairs and amusements on the pier. The large, windowless and rather grim looking edifice on the highest point of the Naze is Trinity House Tower, built in 1720 to warn shipping of the treacherous off-shore West Rocks.

Just along the coast from Walton is the gentile resort of **Frinton-on-Sea**. The area south of Frinton Gates has a unique local character, being laid out with detached houses set along broad tree lined avenues. The

410

Church of Old St Mary in the town contains some panels of William Morris stained glass, well worth seeking out by admirers of his work.

We return a little inland for our next destination to the village of **Little Clacton**. Though it shares it name with the nearby seaside Little Clacton couldn't be more different. It has won Best Kept Village Awards and features a lovely Jubilee Oak, planted to celebrate Queen Victoria's Jubilee. **Clacton-on-Sea** is in itself a great family holiday destination, with a beach and pier that offers a wide variety of traditional holiday amusements. It is also a major leisure centre with plenty of indoor and outdoor sporting facilities, as well as many familiar high street names for those who enjoy shopping as a sport. However the charms of candy floss and one-armed bandits can hardly be considered hidden and so we leave the bright lights and golden sands to head west to the quieter environs of the village of **St Osyth.**

This pretty little village has a fascinating history and centres around the Norman church and the ancient ruins of St Osyth Priory. The priory was founded in the 12th century by Augustinian Canons, who named their new priory after the martyred daughter of Frithenwald, first Christian king of the East Angles. Little of the original building remains, but they do include an impressive late-15th century flint gatehouse, complete with battlements. The Priory ruins stand in extensive and beautiful grounds, deer roam free in the deer park and peacocks patrol the shady lawns. In the gatehouse building is an interesting collection of ceramics and jade.

A short distance across the river estuary from St Osyth is **Brightlingsea,** though the drive is somewhat further. The town is a haven for the yachting fraternity and is the home of national and international sailing championships. The town is also the only arm of the Cinque Ports outside Kent and Sussex. The town can also lay claim to have one of the oldest occupied buildings in Essex, the 13th Century Jacobes Hall today being a restaurant. All Saints Church stands on a hill about a mile out of the town, its 97ft tower visible over 17 miles out to sea. A light was once placed in the tower to guide the towns fishermen home. There are plenty superb walks along Brightlingsea Creek and the River Colne, which offer a chance to watch the bird-life and the plethora of boats on the water.

We now travel upstream long the Colne to **Wivenhoe**, a riverside town that was once renowned as a smugglers haunt and has a very pretty quayside rich in history. There are still strong connections with the sea with boat building replacing fishing as the main industry. In nearby in Wivenhoe Park stands the University of Essex Campus.

And so to **Colchester** the garrison and market town which stands in the midst of rolling East Anglian countryside. Colchester is England's oldest recorded town a settlement being established as far back as the 7th

Colchester Castle

century BC. To the west of the town are the remains of the massive earthworks which protected pre-Roman Colchester. During the 1st century Colchester was the capital of the south-east and an obvious target for the invading Romans. In AD60 Queen Boudica carved her name in the annals of history by sacking the town and destroying its glorious temple before her uprising was crushed, an attack that led to the building of the town walls. The oldest part of the town is still surrounded by those Roman walls, which include the huge Balkerne Gate - the West gate of the Roman town - still magnificent to this day.

When the Normans arrived, Colchester (a name coined by the Saxons) was a important borough and they built their tremendous castle on the foundations of the Roman temple of Claudius.

Later occupations are marked by the houses of the Flemish weavers in the 'Dutch Quarter' to the west of the castle and the Civil War scars visible on the walls of Siege House on East Street. Today the town is presided over by its lofty town hall and an enormous Victorian water tower nicknamed 'Jumbo'. Jumbo was the name of London Zoo's first African elephant elephant, controversially sold to Phineas Barnum in 1882. The tower, its four massive pillars made of one and a quarter million bricks, 369 tons of stone and 142 tons of iron supporting a 230.000-gallon tank, was named in this honour.

Colchester was once famed for its oysters and roses. There is still an annual Oyster Feast - a civic banquet worthy of Royal patronage - and the annual Colchester Rose Show. The famous Colchester Oysters are still cultivated on beds in the lower reaches of the River Colne, which skirts the northern edge of the town

There is plenty to see and explore in the town and there can be no better place to start than the **Castle** and its museum. The Normans built the castle on the site of the temple of the Emperor Claudius using many Roman bricks in its construction. The keep, the largest ever built in Europe, is the only part still standing and now houses the Castle Museum, which contains an interesting collection of Iron Age, Roman and medieval relics. The castle is open all year round from Monday to Saturday, except Christmas and Good Friday and open Sundays from April to September.

Behind the High Street, to the west of the castle is the Dutch Quarter, a charming and quiet corner of this bustling town. Dutch Protestants arrived here in the 16th century, forced to flee the Spanish rule in the Netherlands, and revitalised the local cloth industry and creating their own prosperous corner of the town.

Close to the castle, on East Hill, is **Hollytrees Museum**, which is a fine Georgian House that houses a wonderful collection of costumes and antiquities. It opened as a museum after it was purchased for the town by Viscount Cowdray in 1920. Hollytrees is open all year; Monday to Saturday, except Christmas and Good Friday. Almost across the road from Hollytrees is the **Natural History Museum**, who's exhibits illustrate the natural history of Essex and which is situated in the former All Saints Church. Housing the museum here saved the church with its fine flint tower from demolition in 1958.

Another former church houses the **Museum of Social History**. This interesting museum contains historical displays of rural crafts and country life. Its home the historic church of Holy Trinity in Trinity Street is the only Saxon building left in the town. An arch opposite the church leads to **Tymperleys**, once the home of William Gilberd, who entertained Elizabeth I with experiments in electricity, and today houses a magnificent collection of antique clocks; nearby in West Stockwell Street lived the Taylor sisters, writers of 'Twinkle, Twinkle, Little Star'.

Close to Colchester Town railway station are the ruins of **St Botolph's Priory**. The priory was a victim of the long siege of Colchester during the Civil War, when the Royalist held out for eleven weeks finally starved into submission. On Bourne Road to the south of the town centre is Bourne Mill. This rather striking stepped and curved gabled building is constructed of stone taken from the nearby St John's Abbeygate and was built in 1591. Originally a fishing lodge, it was converted into a mill in the nineteenth century and is still in working order.

There is so much to take in that it might be best to join one of the guided town walks or even hop aboard one of the open-topped bus tours. Details from the Tourist Information Office on Queen Street.

Those with a hankering for the arts there is plenty to see; the Charter Hall features a regular programme of concerts and dance and there is live theatre at the Mercury Theatre.

For live theatre of a rather different kind you may like to head for **Colchester Zoo**, just of the A12. The zoo stands in the 40 acre park of Stanway Hall, with its sixteenth century mansion and church dating from the fourteenth century. Founded in 1963, it has a wide and exciting variety of attractions including an aquarium, birdland, all the breeds of big cat and a model railway, as well as the opportunity to meet the penguins and, for the brave, the chance to wear a snake!

Close to the zoo, in the village of **Easthorpe** is the oddly named **House Without a Name**, a building with a very chequered history dating back to the early 15th century. These former farmworkers cottages have also served time as a shop and a gentlemens drinking club before becoming licensed premises. The then owners attended court for a licence and had not chosen a name for the pub. The building was therefore listed as The House Without a Name and the name has stayed with the pub to this day.

The new owners Mr & Mrs Pitt took over a very sorry looking

building two years ago, and with a lot of hard work, have converted the site into a charming free house which retains the charm of the old, yet with all the amenities and furnishings of a newly restored building.

A good place for both food and drink there is a first class specials board, and you may eat in the bar or in the 26 seat restaurant . To complement your meal there is a wide variety of well kept ales and guest beers are changed frequently. A picture both inside and out the house can be found in the heart of the village just off the main A 12. Worth the detour.

The House Without a Name, Easthorpe, Nr. Colchester.
01206 213070.

We leave Colchester behind now and following the A12 head for the small village of **Marks Tey**. Normans from Marck, near Calais, gave the village its name when they came over. The church is certainly distinctive with its oakboarded tower, but its chief treasure is its 15th century font. Also made of oak it has eight intricately carved panelled sides which are a delight to behold.

In the village is a delight for anyone with green fingers, **Poplar Nurseries**. Run by the Cowan family, the nursery not only has everything the gardener could want but also plenty to see and do. Not only is there a specialist pond centre, nursery and garden machine centre but also beautiful display gardens, a Japanese garden, and a play area for children. There is also a tearoom, the Poplar Pavilion, where there is a wide choice of home-made sweets and savouries, a dish of the day, sandwiches and jacket potatoes, just right for taking a break.

Always growers as well as retailers the nursery has a fascinating history. Martin Cowan's father began the nursery in 1938 and since then it has, with careful nurturing, gone from strength to strength. Originally Martin's father produced tomatoes and flower seeds. During the war he grew food for the troops, including sweetcorn for the U.S. troops. Since the war many things have changed at Poplar but not the love of flowers, for many years the business was almost exclusively commercial, initially going back to flower seed growing. A new site was purchased in 1946 and large carpets of alyssum, lobelia, antirrhinum, dahlia and nemesia grew, as well as seven miles of sweet peas! In the late fifties the nursery began growing chrysanthemums, tomatoes and bulbs, moving away from producing seed. Today the company now specialises in supplying many business' with hanging baskets and has recently branched out into interior landscaping, hiring green plants to offices and showrooms. All of this wealth of commercial expertise is available to every customer at Poplar. Easy to find the nursery is just off the A12 on the A120 and well worth finding for yourselves.

Poplar Nurseries, Coggleshall Road, Marks Tey 01206 210374

To the north of the village is **Aldham**, a small village 5 miles out of Colchester, and for a time home to the famous Essex historian Philip Morant, who held the post of vicar here. He was buried in the local churchyard. Down in Ford Street you will find a wonderful old house called not surprisingly **Old House** which provides B & B in a property dating from the 14th century.

There is within the walls of this Grade II* building, a wealth of atmosphere but ,we are told, no unfriendly ghosts!

A very handy spot as the Old house is opposite The Queen's Head and there are two other pubs within 100 yards. The 3 rooms, a family, a double, and a single, all have colour T.V. and tea and coffee making facilities. Breakfast is served in the lounge/dining room which has a log fire in the cooler weather. Conveniently situated on the A604 Cambridge road and only 1 hour away from London by train, it is also just 50yds off the 'Essex Way' long distance footpath from Ongar to Harwich. This is a chance to enjoy a comfortable home full of oak beams and character . Tourist board Listed and Commended.

Incidentally Mrs Mitchell also runs a swop shop called **The Pig-in-the-Middle** which deals in an array of good second hand clothing for ladies and children, and both businesses can be contacted on the same number below.

The Old House B & B , Fordstreet, Aldham Nr Colchester.
01206 240456

Also in Fordstreet you will find Old Bourchiers Hall, home of **Bourchiers Country Furniture Store.**

Bourchiers Country Furniture Store, Old Bourchiers Hall, New Road, Aldham 01206 210724/210782

Historically the site of the home of the Earls of Essex, stables belonging to the present house have recently been converted into a beautiful showroom offering a fine range of hand painted decorative furniture and unusual giftware.

The range of finishes is very diverse and for a more unusual and personalised finish furniture can be decorated using freehand techniques following a theme of your choice, such as flowers, birds and ribbons etc. The choice of furniture is equally as wide and includes Welch dressers, armoires, bookcases, tables, and chairs, to name a few. In addition blackboards, buckets, trays and many other items are painted on the premises for sale in the showroom.

Examples of the furniture are available in raw pine for self-decoration. Weekend stencilling courses are held throughout the summer to learn how. Details from Sarah or Jane on 01206 210724. The showroom is open Monday to Saturday 9.30 am to 5.00 pm.

Just off the A604 which passes by Aldham village is **Mill Race Nursery**, just the place to stop if you want to break your journey or are looking for somewhere for an outing. Here there is an extensive plant centre with an affordable range of literally hundreds of varieties of shrubs, herbaceous, climbers, and trees.

At first glance as you drive by you may not appreciate the size of this nursery, but the site extends over 12 acres and has a large outside area which is sure to have something to suit your garden. Dried flower displays are very popular and there is a specialist shop at the nursery full of exotic dried flowers along with foliage baskets etc.for you to make a display or alternatively there is a variety of ready made arrangements.

The Mill Race Nursery, New Rd. Aldham. 01206 242324.

These include some beautifully made garlands and swags all made on the premises, and this part of the nursery really comes into its own at Christmas when they produce these wonderful decorative pieces using natural foliage.The nursery then has a Scandinavian air about it with table centres and blue pine garlands all being prepared by the skilled staff. In the Summer there is also much to enjoy here with boating and a

418

riverside picnic area being a particular feature. At any time of the year you can find light refreshments in the spacious lounge. A vast array of plants at competitive prices in a pretty riverside setting. Worth a visit.

Our next destination is **Chappel** and its close neighbour **Wakes Colne**. Here, on a 4-acre site beside Chappel and Wakes Colne Station is the **East Anglian Railway Museum**. For every train fan young or old this is the place to try your hand at being a signalman and get a whiff of steam, as well as admire the beautiful restored locos and items of rolling stock. As the British Rail line runs north it crosses the dramatic 32 arch viaduct across the Colne Valley, built 1849 and quite a sight.

To the west along the A604 is **Earls Colne**. The de Veres, Earls of Oxford, and the River Colne bestowed the village with its name. Aubery de Vere founded a Benedictine priory here in the 12th century and both he and his wife - William the Conqueror's sister - were buried there. Today the site is marked by a redbrick Gothic mansion. Though the commuter culture has spread modern housing around the village a cluster of timbered cottages helps to preserve a village atmosphere.

Further along the A604 is **Halstead**. Rather unimaginably Halstead's most famous product was mechanical elephants. Life-sized and weighing half a ton they were built by W. Hunwicks. Each one consisted of 9000 parts and could carry a load of eight adults and four children at up to 12mph. Rather less unusual but certainly better remembered are the products Tortoise Foundry Company famous for their warm but somewhat smelly 'tortoise stoves'. Certainly the most picturesque reminder of Halstead's industrial heritage is George Courtauld's white, weatherboarded, three-storey mill across the River Colne at the Causeway. Built in the 1700's it is still the most handsome building in town.

The next village on our journey is **Sible Hedingham**, birthplace of Sir John Hawkwood one of the 14th centuries most famous soldiers of fortune. He led a band of mercenaries to Italy, there he was paid to defend Florence, and died doing so. There is a monument to him in the village church, decorated with hawks and various other beasts.

There is a fascinating rarity in **Little Maplestead**, which can be reached by the tiny lanes from Sible and Castle Hedingham. Here is one of the very few round churches in the country. Built more than 600 years ago by the military order of the Knights Hospitallers, their 'Preceptory' at Little Maplestead was suppressed more than 400 years ago by Henry VIII.

Castle Hedingham takes its name form the Norman castle that stands over village. It was one of England's strongest fortresses in the 11th century and even now visitors can still get a feel for its power and strength. The impressive stone keep rises over 100ft and has 12ft thick walls. It was owned by the Earls of Oxford, the powerful de Veres family, one of whom was among the barons who forced King John to accept the Magna Carta. Amongst those entertained at the castle were Henry VII and Elizabeth I. The village is a maze of narrow streets radiating form Falcon Square, named after the half-timbered Falcon Inn. Georgian and 15th century houses comfortably jostle for space and the Church of St Nicholas, built by the de Veres, avoided Victorian 'restoration' and is virtually completely Norman.

In the centre of Castle Hedingham with views of the castle stands the **Bell Inn** run by Sandra Ferguson. The building is mostly 15th century with no less than 4 bars and a function room called the Disraeli room after the Victorian Prime Minister which is 18th century. Once a month the pub hosts a very popular Jazz night as well as serving the local community as a venue for weddings, meetings etc.

The Bell Inn, St James St. Castle Hedingham, Nr Halstead
01787 460350

To the rear of the premises there is a garden with picnic tables where you may enjoy a pint straight from the barrel as the beer is gravity fed, a very rare sight nowadays. Inside there is a bar for non smokers , which is very thoughtful, and children are welcomed. There is a range of competitively priced food available at all times except Monday evenings. For something different try the New Zealand green lipped mussels. They do taste better than they sound!

You can soak up heritage from a different age on the **Colne Valley Railway**. A mile of the Colne Valley and Halstead line between Castle Hedingham and Great Yeldham has been restored and now runs steam trains operated by enthusiasts.

Those of you who like a mystery might like to head north-east from Great Yeldham. Close to the Suffolk border lies the unassuming village of **Borley** which has the rather sinister reputation of having once had the most haunted house in Britain. Borley rectory was destroyed in a fire in 1939 but before then both house and grounds were supposedly the scene for frantic psychic activity with mysterious lights and noises and handwritten messages appearing on the rectory walls. The church not to be outdone has also been the scene of several visitations and footsteps, chanting and organ music have been heard behind its locked doors!

Not far from Borley, **Belchamp St. Paul** is a small village right on the Essex/Suffolk border set in the heart of peaceful countryside. In the village you will discover **The Cherry Tree Inn**, which has been an alehouse since the 1500's, and is today still run as a traditional pub with good inexpensive food by Sylvia & Harold Oliver.

The Cherry Tree Inn and B&B, Knowl Green, Belchamp St. Paul, Sudbury 01787-237263

A Grade II listed building, the pub contains a wealth of beams and an atmosphere only the passage of time can create. The bar with its low ceiling and open fire in the winter, is cosy and welcoming. There are completely separate rooms for pool and darts.

Outside, the extensive grounds include car park and a large beer garden with play equipment for children of all ages. On a warm day enjoy a snack down by the stream under the weeping willow.

Freshly cooked bar snacks and meals are available six days a week (closed Tuesdays), with home-made dishes a speciality. The constantly changing menu includes a very popular Steak and Kidney Pie steeped in strong ale, curries made to authentic recipes and a range of fresh fish. They are also famous for their delicious homemade puddings.

The Cherry Tree also offers B&B, with two delightful rooms in self-contained accommodation for £30 per couple per night including a huge breakfast. The accommodation is very quiet with a lovely outlook.

Stebbing Church

Ideally situated for touring historic and beautiful East Anglia, the Cherry Tree Inn is less than 60 miles from London.

Following the Suffolk border westwards brings out journey to **Steeple Bumpstead**. Edith Cavell, the Great War heroine, worked as a governess here and worshipped at the church. At the crossroads stands the lovely old **Moots Hall**, with oversailing upper storey and arched and timbered ground floor. Moots were originally Saxon meetings to settle disputes, though by 1592 this one was being used as a school, and was most probably used as a guildhall or market house at sometime.

Folkmoots were more often held in the open-air; usually at conspicuous landmarks, especially as much of Britain was then heavily wooded. These were frequently ancient barrows such as at Mobberley in Cheshire. Particular trees or stones were also chosen as at Appletree, Derbyshire, Staine in Cambridgeshire and Maidstone in Kent, and at Stone in Somerset the meeting stone still stands.

Just along the B1054 is **Hempstead** whose most notorious son, Highwayman Dick Turpin, was born here in 1705. His parent kept the Bell Inn, later renamed the Rose and Crown and more recently 'sub-titled' Turpin's Tavern. Gilt letters announce 'It is the Landlord's great desire that no-one stands before the fire' over the wide hearth where logs still burn, and pictures all around celebrate the infamy of the innkeeper's son.

Inside the village church, an impressively and life-like bust on his tomb recalls the town's rather worthier son, William Harvey (1578-1657), chief physician to Charles I and discoverer of the circulation of the blood, as recorded in his 'De Motu Cordis" of 1628.

Like many others Hempstead once boasted a village cockpit and its faint outline can still be traced, though the steep banks are now crowned with trees.

From Hempstead we follow the B1053 to the well known **Saffron Walden**. The town was named after the Saffron crocus, which was grown in the area to make dyestuffs in the Middle Ages. A great deal of the street plan of the town from those times survives as do hundreds of fine buildings, many timbered with overhanging upper floors and decorative plastering (pargeting). Gog and Magog (or perhaps folk hero Tom Hickathrift and the Wisbech Giant) battle in plaster forever on the gable of the **Old Sun Inn**, where, legend has it, the Oliver Cromwell and General Fairfax both lodged during the Civil War.

On the local Common, once Castle Green, is the largest surviving turf maze in England. Only eight ancient turf mazes survive in England: though there were many more in the Middle Ages, if not looked after they soon become overgrown and lost.

Though many miles from the sea Henry Winstanley, born here in 1644, is said to have held trials with a wooden lantern in the lavishly

Thaxted Town

decorated 15th-16th century church, before building the first Eddystone Lighthouse - which was lost with him in a fierce storm in 1703. At the Town Museum, as well as the gloves worn by Mary Queen of Scots on the day she died, is piece of human skin which once coated the church door at Hadstock.

The town was also famous for its resident Cockatrice, which was hatched from a cock's egg by a toad or serpent and could kill its victims with a glance. The Cockatrice was blamed for any inexplicable disasters in the town. Like Perseus and Medusa the Gorgon a Cockatrice could be destroyed by making it see its own reflection and turn to stone. The Saffron Walden Cockatrice's slayer was said to be a knight in a coat of 'cristal glass'.

To the north of the town **Bridge End Gardens**, a wonderfully preserved example of an early Victorian garden and includes a hedge maze - which is open only by appointment. (Appointments can be made at the Tourist Information Centre). Next to the gardens is the Fry Art Gallery which exhibits work by many notable 20th century artists who lived and worked in the area before and after the Second World War, as well as contemporary artists working in Essex today. Close to Bridge End is the Anglo-American War Memorial dedicated by Field Marshal the Viscount Montgomery of Alamein in 1953 to the memory of all the American flyers of the 65th Fighter Wing who lost their lives in WWII.

Continuing north on the B1052 is the village of **Hadstock**, and its macabre church door. The north door was once covered with a piece of human skin, now in Saffron Walden Museum. Local legend says it is a 'Daneskin' - from a Viking flayed alive. Lining doors with animal leather was common in the Middle Ages and many so called 'Daneskins' are just that. However the skins at Hadstock and at Copford also in Essex are almost certainly human, the poor wretch at Hadstock undoubtedly having his hide nailed there as a warning The door itself is Saxon, as are the 11th century carvings, windows and arches, rare survivors that pre-date the Norman Conquest.

We must pass once more through Saffron Walden on our way to **Audley End House**. The house was at one time home of the first Earl of Suffolk and the original house, with its two large courtyards, had a magnificence claimed to match Hampton Court. Unfortunately the subsequent earls lacked his financial acumen and much of the house was demolished as it fell into disrepair, though it still remains one of England's most impressive Jacobean mansions, its distinguished stone facade set off perfectly by Capability Brown's lake. The state rooms which remain still retain their palatial magnificence, and the exquisite state bed to be found in the Neville Room is still hung with the original embroidered drapes. In the rolling parkland grounds are several elegant outbuildings, some of which were designed by Robert Adam. Amongst these are an icehouse, a circular temple and a Springwood Column. A popular miniature steam railway runs in the grounds and certainly anyone visiting this corner of Essex should make time to stop and take in this wonderful house which reflects the rise and fall of the aristocratic country mansion perfectly.

We now travel the short distance to another of this corner of Essex's gems, **Thaxted**. This small country town has a recorded history which dates back to before the Domesday book, originally a Saxon settlement which developed around a Roman road. Yet though the town is full of beautiful old buildings its special character is as much an attraction as they are. To its credit Thaxted has no need of artificial tourist attractions and is today what it has been for the last ten centuries, a thriving town.

Thaxted has numerous attractively pargeted and timber-framed houses, and a magnificent **Guildhall**, built as a meeting place for cutlers around 1390. The demise of the cutlery industry in 1500s led it to becoming the administrative centre of the town. Restored in Georgian times it became the town's Grammar School, as well as remaining a centre of administration. Once more restored in 1975 today the Parish council still meet here. The towns famous windmill was built in 1804 by John Webb and last ground wheat in 1907 though it has now been returned to full working order. Close to the windmill are the towns Almshouses, which still provided homes for the elderly over 250 years after they were built for that very purpose.

Thaxted Church stands on a hill and soars cathedral like over the towns streets. It has been described as the finest Parish church in the country and though many towns may protest long and loud at this it certainly is magnificent. It was also the somewhat unlikely setting for a pitched battle in 1921. The rather colourful vicar and secretary of the Church Socialist League, Conrad Noel, hoisted the red flag of communism and the Sinn Fein flag in the church. Incensed Cambridge students tore them down and put up the Union Jack; Noel in turn ripping that down and, with his friends, slashing the tyres of the students' cars and motorcycles. A fine bronze in the church celebrates this adventurous man of the cloth. Planet Suite composer Gustav Holst lived in the village from 1914-25 and often played the church organ. To celebrate his connection with the town there is a month long festival in late June/early July which attracts performers of international repute.

Conrad Noel's wife is remembered for encouraging Morris dancing in the town, today the famous Morris Ring is held on the Spring Bank Holiday and attracts over 300 dancers from all over the country who dance through the streets. Dancing can also be seen around the town on most Bank Holiday Mondays, usually in the vicinity of a pub.

Thirsty travellers might like to head for **The Star Inn** which is unmistakable with its pink exterior beneath a red tiled roof. Nigel Gunn is the host of this 15th century pub, and the wall lights outside proclaim that Adnams beer is sold within. Excellent it is too, and the wood panelling inside gives the place a warm feel. Weather permitting, there is a beer garden where you can sit outside to enjoy a drink accompanied by something from the bar menu. Conveniently located, the Star is a good example of a pub which welcomes both locals and tourists alike.

The Star, Thaxted, 01371 830368

On the edge of Thaxted, heading out on the B184 towards Dunmow, you will find **Thaxted Pottery & Crafts** in a converted barn set back a little off the road .There is ample parking to the front of the building which is deceptively spacious inside, and here you will find an array of all sorts of crafts, pottery, terracotta, wall hangings etc .along with a tea room at the rear of the premises which is non smoking.

Thaxted Pottery & Crafts, Totman's Farm, Dunmow Rd. Thaxted.
01371 830700

427

Yolanda de Bono has made this a great place to browse at your leisure and enjoy a cup of tea and a snack which may be taken outside in the warm weather .From here there are wonderful views across open countryside towards both the church and the windmill, two local landmarks.

This is an ideal place to stop for a while , enjoy the surroundings , and pick up a gift or two.Open Weekends and Bank Holidays all year round, and Wednesday to Friday from May to October. Hours are 10.30 to 5.30.

North east of Thaxted, along the B1051, is **Great Sampford**. This pretty village has attractive gabled houses, and opposite the Bull Inn is an Elizabethan manor house. A large pond and three cornered green complete the picture. South from here is **Finchingfield**, which holds the dubious distinction of probably being the most photographed village in Essex. The village certainly has everything to complete the perfect picture postcard, with a fine guildhall, a church on a hill, a post mill, quaint cottages, a river, a charming green enlivened by the noisy occupants of the duckpond and a 'causeway' giving open views of the whole village. As you can imagine on sunny summer weekends the village can get a little fraught but on clear off-season days the village is a delight well worth a detour to see. The gardens of the nearby Elizabethan mansion, **Spain's Hall**, are open on Sunday afternoons in the summer.

Following the B1057 south brings us to **Great Bardfield**. The old market towns pleasant mixture of old cottages and shops is nicely complemented by the 14th century church and is surveyed by a timber-framed 16th and 17th century hall from its hill above the River Pant. Perhaps the town's most notable feature is however a restored windmill that goes by the strange name of 'Gibraltar'. Leaving Great Bardfield we head once again west using the country lanes to get to **Stansted Mountfitchet**. Though rather close to London's third airport, Stansted there are plenty of reasons to visit the village. Certainly pilots approaching the airport may be surprised at the sight of a **Norman Village**, complete with domestic animals and reconstructed motte-and-bailey castle, standing just two miles from the end of the runway. The original castle was built after 1066 by the Duke of Boulogne, a cousin of the Conqueror.

Next door to the new-old castle is **The House on the Hill Toy Museum** where children of every age are treated to a unique and nostalgic trip back to their childhood. There is every toy you could imagine here, many of them now highly prized collectors items. There is a shop selling new toys and a collectors' shop with many old toys and books to chose from.

Along the A120 from Stansted is the village of **Takeley**, built on the line of the old Roman Stane Street. There are plenty of pretty 17th century timbered houses and barns can be seen in the village. The church still has much of it original Norman feature and features Roman masonry. Rather unusually it has a modern font that is surmounted by a 6ft high medieval cover. If you alternatively head south from Stansted the road brings you to **Sawbridgeworth**. Quite a number of fine old buildings survive in this small town, many Georgian and to the south is Pishiobury - a fine house built by James Wyatt in 1782 and now a school. In St. Mary's Church are fifteen wonderful ancient and beautifully preserved brasses, worth the drive here in themselves. On the other side of the New Town of Harlow is **Roydon**. Around a mile south-west of the village are the ruins of Tudor Nether Hall, a manor house that belonged to the Coltes family. Here Thomas More came to woo and win the elder daughter of John Coates. Preserved in the village itself are the old parish cage, stocks, and a whipping post. Our journey now heads east from Sawbridgeworth towards **Hatfield Broad Oak**. This very pretty village has many notable buildings for the visitor to enjoy include a church dating from Norman times, some delightful 18th century almshouses, and several distinctive Georgian houses. Nearby **Hatfield Forest** which leant its name to the village, was once part of the ancient Royal Forests of Essex, the remaining 1049 acres are now protected by the National Trust and offer splendid woodland walks along its chases and rides.

South of the forest are the five Rodings, our journey takes us to **Beauchamp Roding** where local farm labourer Isaac Mead worked and saved enough to become a farmer himself in 1882. To show his gratitude to the land that made his fortune he had a corner of a field consecrated as an eternal resting place for himself and family. Their graves can still be seen in the undergrowth, besides the present drive to Rochets house. Beauchamp's church stands alone in the fields, marked by tall 15th century tower and reached by a track off the B184. Inside the raised pews at west end have clever space-saving wooden steps, pulled out of slots by means of iron rings. From the Rodings, all well worth exploring in their right, we head along B184 to **Great Dunmow** famous for the 'Flitch of Bacon' ceremony, which still takes place. In the village of **Little Dunmow** there is a pub named **The Flitch of Bacon,** which takes its name from an ancient ceremony which dates back as far as the 11th century. A prize of a flitch or side of bacon was awarded to a local couple who had been married harmoniously for a year. Amidst great ceremony the couple would be chaired and presented with their prize, although we are not sure what happened if they subsequently divorced!

This old custom is still carried on every leap year, and The Flitch has the key to the Priory where the original chair is kept.

The pub itself is over 300 years old, and is adjacent to the old Braintree to Bishop Stortford railway line. Like a lot of former railway lines the track is now popular with walkers, cyclists, and horse riders, who often stop at the pub. There is a friendly atmosphere here with 3 en-suite rooms available, ideal if you are using the railway line and need a rest! Look out for the sign in the form of a flitch at the roadside.

The Flitch of Bacon. Pub with Accommodation. Lt Dunmow.
01371 820323

To the north west of Great Dunmow is the small village of **Little Easton** and its charming 12th century church which is rich in historic features. Its Maynard Chapel features some outstanding marble monuments of the family as well as some famous brasses. The church's oldest treasures are, however, a well-preserved and priceless 12th century wall painting and several 15th century frescoes. The most recent additions, two stained glass windows, were unveiled in 1990. The Window of the Crusaders and the Window of Friendship and Peace are a lasting memorial to the American 386th Bomb Group, Known as 'The Crusaders', who were stationed nearby for 13 months and lost over 200 of their number in that short time.

Driving down the B184 you may notice a sign at the side of the road pointing you in the direction of **Crown Pictures Art Gallery** in the tiny village of **Lindsell**. It is well worth making the effort to find this hidden place which can also be reached from the B1057 . John and Judy Garrett will be there to welcome you to the gallery which has a permanent display of work by local artists including Eleanor Tanner who provided the lovely illustration of Thaxted for the front cover of this book, and Judy herself whose paintings of flowers we noticed in one of the tea rooms in Thaxted.

Throughout the year, there are exhibitions at the gallery, and this enterprising and talented couple also run a picture framing business which stocks a wide range of mouldings and mount boards.

The gallery is all on one level and there is easy wheelchair access. In

Layer Marney Tower

addition to the prints and paintings which are very reasonably priced there is also a selection of greetings cards and small gift items.

The gallery is becoming increasingly popular, and if you have enjoyed touring this lovely part of the world, what better memento to take home with you than a picture to remind you of your stay in the area.

Crown Pictures. Lindsell, Nr Dunmow. 01371 870777.

It is only a short drive along the A120 from Great Dunmow to **Braintree** and **Bocking**. These two small towns, sited at the crossing of two Roman roads, were brought together by the cloth industry in the 16th century. Flemish weavers settled here, followed by many Huguenots. One, Samuel Courtauld, set up a silk mill in 1816 and by 1886 employed over three thousand Essex folk. Samuel Courtaulds mill still survives in Braintree, whose rather magnificent former Town Hall is one of the many Courtauld legacies. It was built in 1928 with oak-panelled walls, murals by Grieffenhagen showing stirring scenes in local history, and a grand central tower with a five-belled striking clock. A smaller but none the less fascinating reminder of Courtauld's generosity is the 1930s bronze fountain, with bay, shell and fish, at the centre of Braintree. In Bocking there is an impressive parish church and a walk down Church Street repays the curious with the sight of a fine postmill. Famous naturalist John Ray born in nearby Black Notley. There is a statue of him in Bank Street, unveiled by botanist David Bellamy in 1985

Huguenot names such as Courtaulds are connected to international enterprises to this day and their reason for coming to Britain is a fascinating if poignant tale. The Huguenots formed in France in 1559 as an organised Protestant group taking direction from Calvin and the Calvinistic Reformation in Geneva. To begin with they were able to live and worship freely, but as political and religious rivalries grew the Catholic majority started persecuting them, a century of war, massacres

432

and bloodshed followed. Finally in 1685 all their rights were taken away. In the ensuing chaos many died, and thousands fled. It was to turn out France's loss, for the Huguenots were amongst the most industrious and economically advanced elements in French society. Others gained at France's expense; Huguenots poured into England, and especially East Anglia, where their skills soon made them welcome and valued members of the community.

Still following the A120 our travels bring us to the pleasant town of **Coggeshall**. The town has some very fine timbered buildings. **Paycockes**, owned by The National Trust, is a merchant's house of about 1500 and has some unusually rich panelling and wood carving. The National Trust also own the recently restored **Grange Barn**, which date from around 1140 and is a magnificent example of an estate store barn built for the monks of the nearby Cistercian Abbey. From Coggleshall we cross the A12 and head south to the Blackwater Estuary and Maldon.

Before we arrive there though ewe must take a diversion to see the magnificent **Layer Marney Towers**, these make up the highest Tudor gate house in the land and are resplendant in their red brick covered in 16th century Italianate designs. There are formal gardens to enjoy, as well as a rare breeds farm, always great fun for the children.

At the top of the waterside town of **Maldon**, a narrow staircase in a church tower leads to the wonderful **Plume Library** (open mid-week afternoons and Saturday Mornings), which is still much as it was when the founder, Dr Plume, died in 1704. He built a home for the 6000 books he collected and then gave to the town, and today the Public Library is below. The steep winding streets are full of intriguing shops and welcoming inns, one is the town's High Street, of which the Moot hall is a distinctive feature and which runs right down to the estuary - a scene filled with craft of all shapes and sizes - and the quayside Queen's Head pub, which organises an annual mud-race across the river at low tide, to the hilarity of onlookers and benefit of local charities.

Above the town stand the ruins of **St Giles the Leper Hospital**, founded by King Henry II in the 12th century, and as with all monastic buildings fell into disuse after Henry the Eighths dissolusion of the monastries, though it retained its roof and was used as a barn until the turn of the century.

Just outside the town lies the site of one of the great decisive battles of England's early history. At the Battle of Maldon in 991 the English leader, Byrthnoth, was killed by the invading Danes after a fierce three day battle. As a result of this defeat the English King, Ethelred the Unready, was obliged to pay an annual tribute to his conquerors; though the Danes soon tired of this arrangement and overthrew Ethelred putting

St Giles the Leper Hospital

Cnut on the throne. Maldon is also famous for its sea salt, produced for generations by evaporating sea water.

From Maldon we wander inland a little to **Danbury**, said to take its name from the Danes who invaded this part of this country in the Dark Ages. In the fine church under a rare 13th century carved oak effigy, a crusader knight was found perfectly preserved in the pickle which filled his coffin when it was opened in 1779. Fine carving is also a feature of the bench ends, and the oldest have inspired modern craftsmen to continue the same style of carving on all the pews. In 1402, 'the devil appeared in the likeness of Friar Minor, who entered the church, raged insolently to the great terror of the parishoners...the top of the steeple was broken down and half the chancel scattered abroad'. In 1941 another devil, a 500lb German bomb, reduced the east end to ruin. To the south is Danbury Common, where acres of gorse flower in a blaze golden colour for much of the year, to the west, Danbury Country Park offers another pleasant stretch of open country.

Roman workmen cutting their great road linking London with Colchester built a fort at what is today called **Chelmsford**. Then called Caesaromagus, it stands at the confluence of the Rivers Chelmer and Cann. The town has always been an important market centre and is now the bustling county town of Essex. The Marconi Company, pioneers in the manufacture of wireless equipment, set up the first radio company in the world here in 1899. Exhibits of those pioneering days of wireless can be seen in the Chelmsford and Essex Museum in Oaklands Park, as can interesting displays of Roman remains and local history. In nearby **Writtle**, from a tucked-away corner of St John's Green, came Britain's first regular broadcasting service - experimental 15 minute programmes beamed out nightly by Marconi's engineers. Opposite the green, the Cock and Bell is reputed to be haunted by a young woman who committed suicide on the railway, and along the street is the Wheatsheaf, one of the smallest pubs in the country. The church features a cross of charred timbers, a reminder of the fire which gutted the chancel in 1974. Ducks swim on the pond of the larger and quite idyllic main village green, which is surrounded by lovely Tudor and Georgian houses and all just two miles from the centre of Chelmsford.

Another nearby village is **Sandon**, the village green has produced a notable oak tree, remarkable not so much for its height as for its tremendous horizontal spread of its branches. Around the green are a fine church and a number of attractive old houses, some dating back to the 16th century when Henry VIII's Lord Chancellor, Cardinal Wolsey, was Lord of the Manor of Sandon.

To the east of Chelmsford is **Chipping Ongar**. Today firmly gripped in the commuter belt of London it began as a market town protected beneath the walls of a Norman castle. Only the mound and moat of the castle remain, but the contemporary Church of St Martin of Tours still stands. Explorer David Livingstone was a pupil pastor of the town's 19th century Congregational Church. Just outside the town is **Greensted** and its church. St Andrew's is famous as the only surviving example of a Saxon log church extant. The body of King Edmund is known to have been rested here in 1013, but the building is probably much older than that.

Back across the A12 is **Billericay**. There was a settlement here as far back as the Bronze Age seemingly no conclusive explanation of Billericay's name. There is no question about the attraction of the High Street though, with its timber weather-boarding and Georgian brick. The 1510 Chantry House was the home of Christopher Martin, treasurer to the Pilgrim Fathers.

The Peasants Revolt of 1381 saw the massacre of hundreds of rebels just north-east of the town at Norsey Wood; today this area of ancient woodland is a country park, managed by coppicing (the traditional way of ensuring the timber supply) which encourages plant and bird life.

North now to **Stock**, a fine old tower windmill and a delightful church with a traditional Essex style wooden belfry and spire lending character to this pleasant village of well-kept houses. Some of the timbers in the belfry are said to have come from Spanish galleons, wrecked in the aftermath of Sir Francis Drake's defeat of the Armada. The placid waters of **Hanningfield Reservoir** were created by damming Sandford Brook and transformed the scattered rural settlement of Hanningfield into a lakeside village. Now Stood on the shores of the lake the 12th century village church's belfry has been a local landmark in the flat Essex countryside for centuries.

South Woodham Ferrers stands on the banks of the Crouch, the empty marshland of the Crouch estuary, a yachtsman's paradise, chosen by Essex County Council as the site for one of its most attractive new towns schemes. At the centre is a traditional market square surrounded by pleasant arcades and terraces built in the old Essex style with brick, tile and weatherboard. Though no hidden place Woodham certainly make a pleasant change from most new town developments.

Along the Crouch lies **Althorne**. The church of St Andrew's is over five hundred years older than the profusion of local caravans. It has a fine flint and stone tower, built in the Perpendicular style and inside the church is an octagonal font of about 1400, which still has its carving of saints and angels intact. Purists have found them rough, but the less critical will enjoy the sheer vigour the capture. A brass plate dated 1508 records that William Hyklott "Paide for the werkemanship of the wall";

an inscription over the west door remembers John Wilson and John Hill, who probably paid for the tower.

To the south, where Station Road meets Burnham Road, stands the villagers' own War Memorial, the solid structure of beams and tiles affording shelter for the sad list of names. To the north, take a turn right off the B1010 as it leaves the village, for Green lane and discover the golden-thatched, white-walled Huntsman and Hounds, which is partly 14th century. A wicket gate leads through the garden to the saloon and a dark and timbered interior, with deal tables, high bacled benches and the tiniest of bar counters, where the barrels are on view behind, a fine place to reflect and enjoy a refreshing drink.

The village of **Steeple** lies to the north of Althorne, this small community of thatched and weather-board cottages standing on the south bank of the Blackwater estuary, where the dazzling white yachts with multi-coloured sails and the occasional stately sailing barge can be see. The countryside around the village is a rich green land of fertile meadows, patterned by lanes bordered with banks of trees.

At the head of the Dengie Peninsula is **Bradwell-on-Sea**. The first regular inhabitants were the Romans, who built a huge fort here. Little remains today as around AD650 the Saxons used its bricks, stones and tiles to build the tiny chapel of St Peter-at-the-Wall in the 7th century. In the 14th century the chapel was abandoned and forgotten for 600 years, except by farmers who used it as a barn. Now restored and re-consecrated it is well worth the half mile walk from the car park to reach it. In the village itself Erskine Childers, who fought for the Irish Republican Army and was shot by the Irish Free State in the 1920s, wrote the wartime thriller 'The Riddle of the Sands' at Bradwell Lodge, an attractive and part-Tudor former rectory. To the north, Bradwell's vast nuclear power station looms over a nature reserve.

To the south lies the vast and remote marches of the **Dengie Peninsula**. You can never be far from the salty tang of sea air here, brought inland by the east-coast winds, which gives an exhilarating flavour to the marshlands. Like the Cambridge and Lincolnshire fens, this once waterlogged corner of Essex was reclaimed from the sea by 17th century Dutch engineers. The views across the marshes take in great sweeps of countryside, inhabited only by wildfowl, seabirds and cattle grazing on the saltings. The old market town of Southminster and the marshland villages of Asheldham and Tillingham dramatically rise from this flat and often desolate expanse of the landscape.

We return very much to civilisation for our last destination, **Burnham-on-Crouch**. From the gaily coloured cottages along the quay, the town climbs away from the seashore, its streets lined with an delightful assortment of old cottages, Georgian and Victorian houses and shops.

This is the yachting centre of Essex. In Tudor times sailing barges thronged the estuary where now yachts tack to and fro. Seafarers still come ashore to buy provisions, following a tradition that goes right back to the medieval times when Burnham was the market centre for the isolated inhabitants of Wallasea and Foulness Islands, out in the estuary, who travelled in by ferry. The whole area was, and still is, famous for its oyster beds. With thoughts of those gastronomic delights we leave Essex. Hopefully our meander has help dispel some of the reputation that the county has unfairly gained and encouraged you to explore not just this county but all those featured in this edition of the Hidden Places. Travel Safely.

Clock Tower, Halstead

Tourist Information Centres

ALDEBURGH, The Cinema, High Street 01728 453637
BECCLES, The Quay, Fen Lane 01502 713196
BRAINTREE, Town Hall Centre, Market Square 01376 550066
BRENTWOOD, Old House, 5 Shenfield Road 01277 200300
BURY ST EDMUNDS, 6 Angel Hill 01284 764667
CAMBRIDGE, Wheeler Street 01223 322640
CHELMSFORD, E Block, County Hall, Market Road 01245 283400
CLACTON-ON-SEA, 23 Pier Avenue01255 423400
COLCHESTER, 1 Queen Street 01206 712920
CROMER, Bus Station, Prince of Wales Road 01263 512497
DISS, Meres Mouth, Mere Street 01379 650523
ELY, Oliver Cromwells House, St Mary's Street 01353 662062
FAKENHAM, Red Lion House, Market Place 01328 851981
FELIXSTOWE, Harbour Street. Leisure Centre, Undercliff Road West 01394 276770
GREAT YARMOUTH, Town Hall, Hall Quay 01493 846345
GREAT YARMOUTH, Marine Parade 01493 842195
HADLEIGH, Toppesfield Hall 01473 822922
HARWICH, Essex Conty Council, Parkeston Quay 01255 506139
HOVETON, Station Road 01603 782281
HUNSTANTON, The Green 01485 523610
HUNTINGDON, The Library, Princes Street 01480 425831
IPSWICH, Town Hall, Princes Street 01473 258070
KING'S LYNN, The Old Gaol House, Saturday Market Place 01553 763044
LAVENHAM, Lady Street 01787 248207
LOWESTOFT, The Esplanade 01502 01502 523000
MALDON, The Hythe 01621 856503
MUNDERSLEY, 2a Station Road 01263 721070
NEWMARKET, 63 The Rookery 01638 667200
NORWICH, The Guildhall, Gaol Hill 01603 666071
RANWORTH, The Staithe 01605 49453
SAFFRON WALDEN, 1 Market Place, Market Square 01799 524282
SHERINGHAM, Station Approach 01263 824329
SOUTHEND-ON-SEA, Civic Centre, Victoria Avenue 01702 355122
SOUTHEND-ON-SEA, High Street Precinct 01702 355120
SOUTHWOLD, Town Hall, Market Place 01502 724729

Index

THE HIDDEN PLACES

If you would like to have any of the titles currently available in
this series, please complete this coupon and send to:

M & M Publishing Ltd
Tryfan House, Warwick Drive,
Hale, Altrincham, Cheshire, WA15 9EA

	Each	Qty
Scotland	£ 5.90	......
Northumberland & Durham	£ 5.90	......
The Lake District & Cumbria	£ 5.90	......
Yorkshire and Humberside	£ 5.90	......
Lancashire & Cheshire	£ 5.90	......
North Wales	£ 5.90	......
South Wales	£ 5.90	......
The Welsh Borders	£ 5.90	......
The Cotswolds (Gloucestershire & Wiltshire)	£ 5.90	......
Thames and Chilterns	£ 5.90	......
East Anglia (Norfolk & Suffolk)	£ 5.90	......
The South East (Surrey, Sussex and Kent)	£ 5.90	......
Dorest, Hampshire and the Isle of Wight	£ 5.90	......
Somerset, Avon and Dorset	£ 5.90	......
Heart of England	£ 5.90	......
Devon and Cornwall	£ 5.90	......
Set of any Five	£20.00	
Total	£	

Price includes Postage and Packing

NAME..

ADDRESS...

....

................................POST CODE....................................

Please make cheques payable to: M & M Publishing Ltd